Stephen Crane Remembered

Stephen Crane Remembered

Edited by PAUL SORRENTINO

THE UNIVERSITY OF ALABAMA PRESS
Tuscaloosa

Copyright © 2006
The University of Alabama Press
Tuscaloosa, Alabama 35487-0380
All rights reserved
Manufactured in the United States of America

Typeface: AGaramond

∞
The paper on which this book is printed meets the minimum requirements of American National Standard for Information Sciences-Permanence of Paper for Printed Library Materials, ANSI Z39.48-1984.

Library of Congress Cataloging-in-Publication Data

Stephen Crane remembered / edited by Paul Sorrentino.
    p. cm. — (Studies in American literary realism and naturalism)
  Includes bibliographical references and index.
  ISBN-13: 978-0-8173-1503-0 (alk. paper)
  ISBN-10: 0-8173-1503-9
  1. Crane, Stephen, 1871–1900. 2. Authors, American—19th century—Biography. 3. Crane, Stephen, 1871–1900—Friends and associates. I. Sorrentino, Paul. II. Series.
  PS1449.C85Z934 2006
  813'.4—dc22

                                                                        2005027012

#61657774

For Stanley Wertheim

Contents

Acknowledgments

The preparation of this volume was made possible in part by a fellowship from the National Endowment for the Humanities and by grants of research time and travel money from Virginia Tech.

I thank the staff of the Interlibrary Loan Office at Newman Library at Virginia Tech and my colleagues in the American Literature Association, who have helped me better understand Crane and the 1890s through ongoing conversations. I also thank John Clendenning and George Monteiro, who read an early draft of the manuscript and made excellent suggestions for improving it; Anne R. Gibbons, who did a meticulous job as copy editor; and the staff at the University of Alabama Press for their professional help at various stages of production.

Finally, I thank my wife, who has enthusiastically supported my ongoing research projects, and Stanley Wertheim, who has contributed a lifetime of scholarship to the study of Stephen Crane. Twenty-five years ago, Stanley and I discussed the need for an edition of the reminiscences about Crane. Though only my name is on the cover of the book, Stan's guiding spirit is present throughout. In appreciation of what he has contributed to my career and to the study of American literature, I have dedicated this book to him.

Permissions

For permission to quote unpublished reminiscences of the Crane family, I am grateful to Robert K. Crane, who has contributed much to our understanding of Crane family history and genealogy.

For permission to quote from other unpublished reminiscences of Stephen Crane, I thank the libraries of Lafayette College, Yale University, Columbia University, Syracuse University, the University of Connecticut, the University of Virginia, and the New York Public Library.

Excerpts from Colonel Ernest G. Smith's comments in the *Lafayette Alumnus,* vol. 2, are published courtesy of the Lafayette College Archives.

Quotations from the Beer Family Papers are published courtesy of the Beer Family Papers, Manuscripts and Archives, Yale University.

Quotations from George F. Chandler's "I Knew Stephen Crane at Syracuse" from *The Courier* no. 1 (1963) are published courtesy of Syracuse University Library Associates.

Quotations from materials in the Stephen Crane Collection at Columbia University are courtesy of Columbia University.

Quotations from materials in the Melvin H. Schoberlin Collection at Syracuse University are courtesy of Syracuse University.

Quotations from the manuscript of Mark Barr's "The Haunted House of Brede" are published courtesy of the Berg Collection of English and American Literature, New York Public Library, Astor, Lenox and Tilden Foundations.

Quotations from the typescript of Walter Parker's "Re: Stephen Crane" are published courtesy of the H. L. Mencken Papers, Manuscripts and Archives Division, New York Public Library, Astor, Lenox and Tilden Foundations.

Quotations from Jessie Conrad's *Joseph Conrad and His Circle* (New York: E. P. Dutton, 1935) are published courtesy of Weidenfeld & Nicholson, the Orion Publishing Group.

Quotations from Madox Ford's *Return to Yesterday: Reminiscences 1894–1916* (London: Victor Gollancz, 1931) and *Portraits from Life: Memories and Criticisms* (Boston: Houghton Mifflin, 1937) courtesy of the Estate of Ford Madox Ford, David Higham Associates.

Quotations from Hamlin Garland's "Roadside Meetings of a Literary Nomad" in *Bookman* 70 (January 1930) and *Roadside Meetings* (New York: Macmillan, 1930) are courtesy of the Estate of Hamlin Garland/Victoria Doyle-Jones.

Excerpts from Willis Brooks Hawkins's "The Genius of Stephen Crane," "Stephen Crane's Struggles," and "Stephen Crane Flinches" from his manuscript "All in a Lifetime" are published courtesy of the Willis Brooks Hawkins Collection (#7835), Clifton Waller Barrett Library, Special Collections, University of Virginia Library.

Excerpts from Corwin Knapp Linson's *My Stephen Crane* (Syracuse University Press, 1958) are published courtesy of Syracuse University Press.

Excerpts from Henry McBride's "Stephen Crane's Artist Friends" are published courtesy of *ARTnews* Magazine, © 1950 ARTnews, LLC.

Excerpts from William McMahon's "Syracuse in the Gay '90s: Steve Crane Told to 'Stick to Poems' after 'Bangup' Piano Recital at Party" (20 February 1955), 13, are published courtesy of the *Syracuse Post-Standard.*

Excerpts from Arthur Oliver's "Jersey Memories—Stephen Crane" (*Proceedings of the New Jersey Historical Society* 16 [1931]: 454–63) are published courtesy of the New Jersey Historical Society.

Excerpts from Ralph D. Paine's *Roads of Adventure* (Boston: Houghton Mifflin, 1922) are published courtesy of Houghton Mifflin.

Excerpts from W. Pett Ridge's *I Like to Remember* (London: Hodder and Stoughton, 1925) are reproduced by permission of Hodder and Stoughton.

Excerpts from Don Carlos Seitz's *Joseph Pulitzer: His Life and Letters* (New York: Simon and Schuster, 1924) are published by permission of Simon and Schuster © 1924.

Excerpts from H. G. Wells's *Experiment in Autobiography* (London: New York: Macmillan, 1934) are published courtesy of A. P. Watt on behalf of the Literary Executors of H. G. Wells.

Excerpts from Post Wheeler and Hallie E. Rives's *Dome of Many-Coloured Glass* (Garden City, N.Y.: Doubleday, 1955) are reprinted courtesy of Doubleday, a division of Random House.

Introduction

I will sing of facts, but some will say that I invented them.

—Ovid, *Fasti,* Book 6:1–3

No one will ever be able to work casually at Crane and be certain of
anything.

—John Berryman, *Stephen Crane,* xvi

Although Stephen Crane is widely regarded as a major American author, he
remains largely unexplained, the relationship between his life and art still obscure. A flamboyant personality and close friend of important writers such as
William Dean Howells, Henry James, and Joseph Conrad, he was anomalously
reclusive and mercurial, retaining his inner identity while projecting opposed
images to others. Since the revived interest in his writings in the early 1950s, he
has been variously categorized as a romantic, a realist, a naturalist, an impressionist, a symbolist, and a visionist. Indeed, he employed all these perspectives
in different works and at times in the same work. Crane's elusiveness, intriguing
critics and biographers, has made him the most controversial American author
of the late nineteenth century.

This elusiveness has been exacerbated by the revelation that Crane's first
biographer, Thomas Beer, fabricated many important letters and incidents that
have been the foundation of what have passed for the facts of Crane's life, literary career, and critical stances and that have been used by every biographer since
Beer. From the beginning, scholars suspected that in essence Beer's biography was a work of fiction. Mark Van Doren reviewed it as "a realistic novel"
(Van Doren 66), and Wilson Follett questioned Beer's veracity by noting that
the biographer "could quote pages from authors who never wrote any such
pages; sometimes from authors who never lived" (Follett 1962). Yet Crane scholars, though acknowledging Beer's unreliability, have accepted letters and incidents in his biography as factual because no concrete evidence existed to suggest
otherwise. During the past decade, however, this situation has changed with the
discovery that Beer had altered the chronology of Crane's life, invented anecdotes, and composed many of Crane's letters himself.[1] Letters "by Crane" are
quoted in an early draft, then substantially revised in a later draft to fit scenarios
involving other people, some of whom, it turns out, are themselves fictional.
Beer, for example, is the only source for Crane's letters to Helen Trent, ostensibly

his first serious romantic attachment. Though frequently identified as a pivotal figure in Crane's relationship with women, Trent is Beer's fictional creation. Beer's papers also reveal that he suppressed information about Crane's love affairs with Lily Brandon Munroe, Amy Leslie, and Cora Crane and invented such incidents as the Crane-Trent affair to support his thesis that "the mistress of this boy's mind was fear" (117). Biographers have thus unknowingly relied on falsified evidence.

Because of Beer's fabrications and deceptions, such letters, accounts of incidents and persons, and chronology unverifiable from sources outside of Beer's writings must be ignored in Crane biography and criticism. The implications of this conclusion are enormous, for every biography of Crane and scores of articles have relied on Beer's work since the biography appeared in 1923. Previous interpretations of Crane's personality, his literary career, and the relationships between his life and art will be considerably challenged by these exclusions. The proverbially elusive Stephen Crane will seem more elusive than ever. Beer sought to exorcise the myth of Crane's debaucheries, that he was a drunkard and an opium addict who consorted obsessively with prostitutes and who, like Poe or Baudelaire, wrote his best works in rare periods of lucidity. But in destroying one myth, Beer created another, that of a latter-day Chatterton struggling to survive, whose tragic genius as an artist was victimized by a philistine society—a stereotyped conception of the situation of the writer in America widely promulgated by iconoclastic critics such as H. L. Mencken and Van Wyck Brooks in the 1920s. Trite and sentimental as this depiction may be, it had for Beer the powerful resonance of self-projection. Crane, the artist manqué, served Beer as alter ego. In Follett's words, Beer's book is finally "a devotional elegiac poem in prose" (Follett 1962).

Given the damage done by the reliance on Beer, the most pressing need in Crane biography has recently been the sorting out of fact from fiction. With the publication of *The Correspondence of Stephen Crane* and *The Crane Log: A Documentary Life of Stephen Crane, 1871–1900,* Stanley Wertheim and I began to address this need. The availability of Crane's letters and a factual account of his daily activities are certainly essential for understanding his life, but the more than ninety reminiscences about him by his relatives, friends, and professional colleagues offer additional sources of information,[2] as well as what Doris Kearns calls "angles of vision" for understanding an author's personality.

As valuable as an eyewitness account is for reconstructing an author's life, the genre of the reminiscence is fraught with potential problems. The most obvious is the question of accuracy. How reliable is someone's recollection of an event written decades after its occurrence? Hamlin Garland, writing in 1930, confused his 1891 and 1892 trips to the New Jersey coast and his meetings with

Crane; Abram Lincoln Travis, also writing in 1930, mistakenly believed that Crane grew up in New York City; and Post Wheeler, writing in 1955, confused the chronology of the writing of *The Black Riders* and *The Red Badge of Courage*. The problem with accuracy is compounded when unverifiable assertions in one account are contradicted in another account. For example, was Crane fired from the *New York Tribune* after writing a satirical article about the Junior Order of United American Mechanics? John D. Barry, Hamlin Garland, and Arthur Oliver claimed he was, though Willis Fletcher Johnson, day editor of the newspaper, denied it. Similarly, did Crane write a draft of *Maggie* in the spring of 1891, as Frank Noxon and Clarence Loomis Peaslee recalled, or did he compose it in autumn of 1892, as claimed by Frederic M. Lawrence and Clarence N. Goodwin?

Besides dealing with the question of memory, a writer of a reminiscence must often struggle with its narrative form. The better a reminiscence does in telling a good story, the more it relies on elements of fiction—notably plot and characterization. In shaping character and scene into a narrative, writers are giving meaning to those details they recall as significant, but in valuing one set of details over another set, they have begun to interpret events that, looked at from another angle of vision, might assume a different meaning. Among the more unreliable reminiscences are those by Willa Cather and Ford Madox Ford, both masters of the novel. Cather's obituary reminiscence is a partly fictionalized account of her historic encounter with Crane. Publishing the account under a pseudonym, she dramatized and romanticized their meeting by changing details such as the time of year in which they met and by depicting Crane, supposedly carrying a volume of Poe's work in his pocket, as despondent over the vagaries of a literary marketplace. Despite problems with its reliability, however, Cather's reminiscence cannot be totally ignored because it is the only one of Crane during his trip to the West and Mexico in 1895. Equally as problematic are Ford Madox Ford's accounts of his time with Crane. Unlike Cather, Ford clearly stated that in all his reminiscences about his contemporaries—not just those about Crane—he invented details for narrative effect: "Where it has seemed expedient to me," as he explained in *Return to Yesterday*, "I have altered episodes that I have witnessed. . . . The accuracies I deal in are the accuracies of my own impressions" (viii). As a result, an often-cited image of Crane is Ford's depiction of an American cowboy in England sitting around "in breeches, leggings, and shirt-sleeves, with a huge Colt strapped to his belt," swatting flies with his pistol. As appealing as the image has been for biographers, it is in all likelihood an example of Ford's striving for "narrative effect."

Even when writers assiduously strive for accuracy over narrative effect, they are faced with another difficulty inherent in the nature of a reminiscence. In telling of their relationship with Crane, writers are also recalling their own lives. In the act of re-creating his personality, they are creating their own seen through the lens of hindsight. Biography thus becomes autobiography as authors inscribe themselves into the literary history of the 1890s. Edwin Pugh, for example, believed that he and Crane had been extremely close friends, that they were emotionally similar, and that his own "little light of talent had something in common with the pure white blaze of [Crane's] genius" (Stallman 1973, 457). Viewing himself as an important young writer in the 1890s, Pugh concluded that he had played a central part in Crane's years in England. Despite Pugh's prolific output as an author and literary critic, however, he was largely forgotten by the time Thomas Beer's biography appeared in 1923. When Pugh reviewed the biography for the *Bookman,* he used the occasion to reminisce on his perceived closeness to Crane and to criticize Joseph Conrad's introduction to the biography for what he considered its patronizing depiction of Crane "as something of a simpleton." From Pugh's point of view, Conrad had characterized himself as Crane's closest and most important friend in England, a position that Pugh seemingly wanted to claim for himself. Given Pugh's apparent dislike of Conrad, whose literary reputation in 1923 was certainly larger than his own, one wonders whether Pugh's reminiscence of Crane was at least partly motivated by jealousy.

Issues dealing with accuracy, narrative form, and autobiography thus make reminiscences problematic by nature. Reminiscences about Crane, however, are subject to an even more damaging problem: whether a reminiscence written after 1923 was influenced by Thomas Beer. A noteworthy example is the book-length reminiscence of Corwin Knapp Linson. Spurred on by the renewed interest in Crane in the 1920s, Linson expanded upon his 1903 recollection of Crane published in the *Saturday Evening Post.* In doing so, he was clearly influenced by Beer.[3] In some cases the influence is obvious, as when he cites Beer as his source for the burning of copies of *Maggie* by a chambermaid named Jennie Cregan[4] (Linson 1958, 27), but at other times it is less certain. For example, in all the biographical accounts available, only Beer (1923, 105) and Linson (1958, 31) state that Crane liked just one of Mark Twain's books—*Life on the Mississippi.* Is Linson's recollection accurate, or is the conversation that he re-creates having with Crane about Twain based solely on Beer's assertion? Similarly, when Linson (1958, 33) says in passing that Crane disliked Dickens, he is echoing the only other source for this criticism—Beer (1923, 45, 48, 231).

Linson's extended reminiscence contains additional problems. After completing a draft of his manuscript, Linson failed to find a publisher because the manuscript lacked focus and a clear narrative form. Only after its editor, Edwin H. Cady, assiduously shaped the reminiscence into a story was it published in 1958. He deleted material pertaining to Linson's career, added "essential connective phrases," and revised dialogue spoken by Crane. For example, instead of having Crane say, "'The hair-oil he does!'"—which is the text in Linson's unedited reminiscence—Cady changed it to "The hell he does!'" because he felt that the extremely religious Linson was probably being euphemistic, though Cady acknowledged that Linson "could have been right and I wrong" (19). The accuracy of the reminiscence, however, became more problematic when Cady discovered that Linson had retouched a photo of Crane that accompanied the reminiscence. Instead of supposedly showing Crane after having written his short story "The Pace of Youth," the photo, when cleaned up, revealed that Crane was at a party smoking a hookah (Cady 20–21). "Could," Cady worried, "one trust anything Linson said, now?" (21) The matter of Linson's reliability as an accurate recorder of events raised for Cady an even larger issue: Given "the problem of the elusive Stephen Crane. . . . [t]here is ample reason to suspect that not one of the so-called eye-witness testimonies about [him] will withstand strict historiographical criticism" (Cady 21). Though Cady's caveat is still worth considering, I have attempted to separate fact from fiction in this edition of "eye-witness testimonies."

This edition includes the major eyewitness accounts of Crane's life and career, ranging from Willa Cather's brief one-night encounter with Crane in Lincoln, Nebraska, to detailed, several-year accounts of friends like Corwin Knapp Linson. For Hamlin Garland and Ford Madox Ford, who wrote several reminiscences, I have reprinted the most complete one and have included passages from the other reminiscences when appropriate. I have chosen not to reprint Linson's book-length reminiscence for three reasons: (1) its size would increase the length of this edition inordinately; (2) the Cady edition is generally available in library collections of Crane; and (3) Linson's 1903 reminiscence is more reliable because it is not influenced by Beer, and it was written when the events of Crane's life were still fresh in Linson's memory. Similarly, I have reprinted Conrad's less-known 1921 reminiscence rather than his 1923 introduction to Thomas Beer's biography because that book is also available in libraries.

Also excluded are numerous passing references to Crane in letters, magazines, and newspaper articles such as John Bass's stylized report "How Novelist Crane Acts on the Battlefield" (*New York Journal,* 23 May 1897). These references, as well as Ames W. Williams's notes recording Lily Brandon Munroe's recollection of Crane, are included in *The Correspondence of Stephen Crane* and *The Crane Log: A Documentary Life of Stephen Crane, 1871–1900.*

Some previously printed reminiscences contain problems that until now were unknown. Ford Madox Ford sometimes silently revised what were supposedly reprintings of his reminiscences. The 1932 American "reprinting" of *Return to*

Yesterday, for example, is not the same text as the 1931 British *Return to Yesterday,* ostensibly the same book. No note in the text alerts the reader to the revisions, and only a collation of both texts reveals them.

This edition of reminiscences about Crane is divided into seven parts that roughly characterize major periods in his life: Port Jervis, Hartwood, Asbury Park; school and college; New York City; the West and Mexico; Florida and the *Commodore;* Cuba, Haiti, Puerto Rico; and England. Within each part the reminiscences are arranged roughly chronologically; however, they occasionally overlap, and some reminiscences cover events in Crane's life that span two or more parts. For example, the reminiscences by McCready and Paine appear in the Florida part, because they first present details surrounding the *Commodore* incident, but they also discuss Crane in Cuba. Accompanying each reminiscence is a biographical headnote that recounts the author's life as it pertains to Crane and explanatory notes that clarify references and alert a reader to connections between and among reminiscences. When appropriate, an editorial note accompanies the headnote in order to clarify editorial problems with a particular reminiscence. Although this edition is, I hope, readable on its own, at times I direct readers to standard reference works in Crane scholarship, notably Stallman and Gilkes's *Letters,* Stallman's *Stephen Crane: A Critical Bibliography,* and Wertheim and Sorrentino's *Correspondence* and *Crane Log;* this edition of reminiscences complements them.

Because my goal is to present a scholarly, though readable, text, I have made the following alterations to the originals:

1. Punctuation is regularized so that commas and end punctuation are put inside a final quotation mark.

2. Obvious misspellings and typographical errors have been corrected. Reminiscences that exist as a manuscript—for example, that of Frederic M. Lawrence—or as letters—for example, those from Ernest W. McCready to Benjamin R. Stolper—were often written hastily and not for publication. As such, they contain errors that, if the reminiscence had been prepared for publication, would most certainly have been corrected, as in the typing of "Stevei" for "Stevie" in Edmund B. Crane's reminiscence. Similarly, previously published reminiscences occasionally contain typographical errors that a typesetter missed, as in the misprinting of "Willis W. Hawkins" for "Willis B. Hawkins" in Frank Noxon's account.

3. In newspaper titles a city name has been treated as part of the title, as in the *New York Tribune.*

4. Titles of books, magazines, and newspapers in unpublished reminiscences have been italicized.

5. Titles of short stories that were printed in italics in reminiscences are in quotation marks.

6. When a reminiscence contains unrelated material or standard biographical information about Crane—for example, a list of Crane's publications—that material has been deleted and marked with ellipses or with leaders for extended passages. When appropriate, I have included a bracketed comment to summarize a deleted passage.

1
Port Jervis, Hartwood, Asbury Park

1 / Edmund B. Crane

Edmund Bryan Crane (1857–1922) attended Centenary Collegiate Institute, as did several of his brothers and his sister Agnes. He worked as a teacher in Sussex County, New Jersey, then in the early 1890s worked in business in New York City. In 1894 he moved to Hartwood. Of all his brothers Stephen Crane was closest to Edmund. Stephen chose him as his guardian after their mother died, often lived with Edmund's family in Lake View and Hartwood, and wrote much of *The Red Badge of Courage* and *The Third Violet* in the family's homes.

Source: Edmund B. Crane, "Notes on the Life of Stephen Crane by His Brother, Edmund B. Crane," typed copy, Thomas Beer Papers, Beer Family Papers, Yale University Archives.[1]

When Stephen was born there were already two sisters and six brothers to whom he became a pet and entertainer. He was bright and very teachable. After he learned to talk I amused myself by having him pronounce five and six syllable words. After a few laughable failures, he would accomplish a correct pronunciation by spelling the word after me syllable by syllable, resolving them into their sound elements. This was great fun for us children. Stevie also enjoyed it.

When he was about three years old, an older brother, Townley, was a cub reporter on one of the Newark dailies, either the *Courier*, or the *Advertiser*, and when writing his stories at home would often call on his mother for the correct spelling of a word. Stevie was making weird marks on a paper with a lead pencil one day and in the exact tone of one, absorbed in composition, and coming to the surface only for a moment of needed information, called to his mother, "Ma, how do you spell 'O'?" this happening to be a letter he had just become acquainted with.

We removed from Newark in the spring of 1874 to Bloomington across the Raritan river from Bound Brook, where we lived for two years. We often took Stevie bathing with us in the Raritan river about half a mile above the bridge. There was a smooth, sandy bar extending from the south bank across the river, very shallow near shore and growing deeper toward the middle of the river. Stevie would wade around in the shallows watched by one of us. Wading breast deep in water he would stretch out his arms and waving his hands, would achieve what he called "fimming." He started to "fim" to Wee-wee, (Willie), my next older brother, who was farther out in the river. As the depth gradually increased the water came up to his chin, then to his mouth, and then his eyes, but he kept steadily on, and, I plucked him out, gasping but unscared, just as his yellow hair was going under. We boys were naturally delighted with his grit.[2]

After two years at Pennington we removed to Paterson and two years later to Port Jervis, where Stephen's school life began. He had always been delicate, and was not sent to school until the fall before his eighth birthday.[3] No effort had been made to teach him anything at home, from books, but every effort was made to quicken and develop a naturally good brain, without study, confinement, or effort of memory. He was naturally below children of his age when he entered school, and feeling ashamed of it, and having an older, stronger brain, he passed through class after class, and was soon even with children older than himself. Of his playtime here, there are playmates of his who yet tell of the games he originated, and how busy he kept them playacting different rolls. Killing Indians, and so forth.

In 1880, my father died, and family affairs were unsettled for several months. After a short residence in Roseville in 1880, my mother returned to Port Jervis for a couple of years and then removed to Asbury Park, where my brother Townley was operating a news bureau for the *Tribune* and *Sun* of New York City and the *Philadelphia Press*. Stephen attended school there but of the small things that make up life, I know very little as I was living in the northern part of the state. He made a creditable record in the Asbury Park schools, I know. As to his play, he had a trick pony, that he loved devotedly, and whose tricks, learned in some past circus experience, were constantly coming to the surface to Stevie's wonder and delight. The pony had a large B branded upon his shoulder, and we credited the late P. T. Barnum with having been his owner. He was probably discarded by the circus because of failing eyesight from cataract. Indoors he had a military game he played alone with buttons of different colors which to him were soldiers of opposing armies.[4] These he marshalled about the floor operating some system that I, for one, did not understand. This game would occupy him for hours at a time, especially on rainy days. In the fall of 1888, when nearing the age of seventeen, he was reporting shore news as an aid to my brother Townley in operating the news bureau. My mother covered the religious news of Ocean Grove.

A workingman's fraternity[5] held a national convention at Asbury Park, and the procedures included a parade through the principal streets. Stevie, in Townley's absence, wrote up the story and described the marchers as they appeared to him—wrote the story of what he saw. If he had described them marching with military precision, files in exact alignment and so forth, events would have turned out differently. As it was, as he saw it, so he wrote and painted a word picture of a procession of working men, with years of toil shown in their faces, and steady but weary stride. This, by some mischance, escaped the eyes of the news editor of the *Tribune* and appeared in that paper as written. There was a howl from coast to coast. The owner of the *Tribune,* Whitelaw Reid, a candidate for vice president on the Republican ticket, ordered the immediate discharge of the reporter responsible for the row, and Townley lost the *Tribune* connection.[6] Can you imagine it? A seventeen-year-old kid,[7] in an accidental position of responsibility, throwing a monkey wench into the smooth running machinery of a political party, during a national campaign, innocent of any motive but a desire to develop the faculty of vivid and accurate description that he was beginning to discover in himself.

After leaving the schools of Asbury Park, he attended Syracuse and Lafayette Universities. Though before then I think he attended a military school on the Hudson.[8] While at Lafayette, he wrote me asking that I persuade Mother to allow him to change the course of study he was then pursuing to that of belles lettres as he had decided on a literary career. She agreed to this to Stevie's delight. When at college, he was the captain of the baseball team, and told me he was the youngest captain of a college team in the United States. Of this he was proud.

Mother died before Stevie was twenty,[9] and he chose me as guardian. He was in New York much of the time making the study of life in the slums, that produced *Maggie.* After that he came to my home at Lake View and lived there while he wrote the *Red Badge of Courage.* His day began at noon when he arose and ate breakfast when my wife and the little girls ate lunch. The afternoons he spent coaching the boys of the neighborhood in football tactics. From this he gained exercise in the open air, and much amusement. The evenings were spent around the piano singing, or socially at some friend's house. When the family retired, Stephen went to the garret, where he worked and slept, and wrote far into the night, if composition was going smoothly. As soon as the story began to take shape he read it to me as the finished parts grew. He told me he did not want my literary opinion, only to know if I liked the story. That was pretty good from a kid fourteen years my junior. I liked the story. When, listening to the reading of the story, I ventured to suggest the substitution of a word that would give the meaning intended better than the word he used, he would consider the matter and then decide, oftener against than for the suggestion. He had the confidence of genius.

In 1894, I moved my family to Hartwood, New York, and took charge of a 3600 acre tract of land known as the Clapham property.[10] Stephen soon made us a visit and came often afterward. When with us he wore a disreputable looking cap, sweater, corduroy trousers and heavy shoes. His two favorite occupations when with us were riding and sailing a tiny centerboard sailboat I had built. Writing near the front window of the living room, office, and post office combined, he would keep a casual watch of the pond in front of the house. If a breeze sprang up he was out and in the sailboat to stay as long as the breeze lasted. He went from Hartwood to the dinner given him by the Philistines at East Aurora or Buffalo.[11] He remained at East Aurora several days after the dinner as guest of Hubbard. While there Hubbard procured a pony for Stevie's use and they rode together. After Stevie returned home, he spoke often of the engaging qualities of the pony he had ridden and wrote Hubbard to buy it at once if he could.[12] The pony was bought and shipped at once to Hartwood. After that Stevie and I spent much time in the saddle, as I found it more convenient to ride, than hitch a horse to a buggy.

It was around a box stove, with a crackling hard wood fire in it, that he told us the story that afterward appeared as "The Open Boat" and of his adventure with Mexican bandits.[13] I think he in that way developed the story in his mind, and gave us a great treat at the same time.

He had a strenuous game he played with the girls, his nieces. Armed with newspapers rolled into clubs, the three girls would attack Stephen fiercely and he would defend himself with such determination as sometimes to rout all three. Sturdy blows were given and taken in good part. Stevie was not a natural sportsman in regard to hunting and fishing. One day he complained of having nothing to do and I suggested that he take the setter, Judge Noble, and go after birds. He was disinclined to do so, fearing to spoil my dog. I told him to call the dog and go up the swale on Buck Mountain across the pond, to give the dog no orders, or signals, but when he pointed to move up past him until the bird flushed. He came back with two grouse and a rabbit. He was never able to repeat this success.

I went to New York to see him off when he went to Greece. And he visited us several times between that campaign and the war with Spain. I remember his freely expressed criticism of the leadership of the Greek forces, who withdrew from naturally strong, defensive positions before the advancing Turks, without a fight.

He dearly loved a good horse.[14] He would tell stories of the different horses he had ridden from the white pony with the branded shoulder to the last one ridden in Florida by the hour. Each story a complete incident. The pony that Hubbard sent him was as wide awake as a hawk and as gentle as a kitten. He had evidently come from the plains, because he feared every stone and stump in sight. When loping he was apt to see a suspicious looking stone under his nose and stop short with front feet braced. Then for the stumps he shied from side to side of the road, and his rider had his hands full. All this pleased Stephen immensely, and he had many enjoyable trips on which the interest never lagged. I never knew him to punish the pony for this, or anything else. I rode a brown mare of trotting stock that had all the courage of her race, but no trotting speed. So as to accompany Stevie I broke her to saddle. Many a race we had over the roads that back in 1896 and 1897 were anything but good, risking our necks with very little thought of the danger. We always came into Hartwood as fast as our horses could run, striking the bridge over the Green brook once each, through the straight of the "lane" and then taking reverse curves first right around the corner of the Tannery meadow and left around a stone wall corner. We talked this habit of ours over and decided that sometime we would race around that last corner and mix up with some rig coming from the other direction. The accident happened but not as we anticipated. In the middle of the last turn my horse a little ahead, and Stephen's making desperate efforts to catch her, his pony over reached and caught his left hind foot in his right front, and they went down in a heap. I, on the right, had pulled over wide to give him all the room he needed saw the accident, but could not stop my mount before reaching the crossing seventy-five yards beyond. I did see the pony struggle to his feet and come on passing me on his way to the barn. Scared cold, I rode back to meet Stephen coming, limping a little, and, brushing dirt from his clothing. The pony had fallen on his leg but as the sand was about four inches deep on the turn no bones were broken. Aside from a headache from the jolt and a few slight bruises, no harm was done. That was our last race around the reverse curves.

During Stephen's absence in New York, the personal representative of the owner of one of New York City's biggest papers came to Hartwood to see him. He arrived at 1:17 and could not return to Port Jervis before 4:53 so he and I had quite a visit. He was very entertaining being fresh from a European trip. I remember a remark of his about Kipling, whom he had met, which was that Kipling in writing of a character not only knew how he thought and talked, but he *was* that character. Stephen, when I mentioned the visit, was much interested. It seems that he came to offer Stephen almost any price for articles for use in the Sunday edition, Stephen to be allowed to write on any subject that pleased him. He wrote one, the work of a little over an hour on Jas. A Bradley, founder of Asbury Park, for which he was paid fifty dollars.[15] He refused to write any more, claiming that it was not literature and added nothing to his reputation. He cared little for money but was ready to endure privation to the extent of poor clothing and insufficient food, if he was producing what he knew to be good stuff. He has been described as a poorly dressed, half starved youth, when if he had sacrificed his ideals and descended to potboilers or reporting, for he would have considered either a descent, he could have made a good living. If he appeared poorly dressed and ill fed, it was because he stripped for the race. He held his career above his comfort, or any other personal consideration.

∽

2 / Elizabeth (Archer) Crane

Elizabeth (Archer) Crane (?–?) was the wife of Stephen's brother George.

Source: Mrs. George Crane, "Stephen Crane's Boyhood," *New York World,* 10 June 1900, sec. E, 3.

The early boyhood of Stephen Crane was spent in Newark at his father's home. No. 14 Mulberry Place. When he was about eight years old his father, who was a Methodist clergyman and presiding elder of the Newark district, was sent to take charge of a Paterson church.[16] The family afterward went to Port Jervis to live, and when Stephen was about ten years old his father died,[17] leaving a large family.

The greater part of Stephen's boyhood was spent in Asbury Park. He was a vigorous lad and was passionately fond of outdoor sports, as well as of everything pertaining to military affairs.

He loved to play at soldiers from his early childhood. Most of his playthings were in the form of toy soldiers, guns and the like.[18]

When the boy grew older he learned to play baseball and football. He was a member of a uniformed baseball team in Asbury Park, and proved one of the mainstays of the club, although he was the lightest and youngest member.

His fondness for everything military induced his mother to send him to the Claverack Military Academy.[19] While a student there he kept up his interest in athletics and became fond of horses. He had a pony of his own and spent much time riding it.

Stephen did not display any particular preference for literary work in his childhood. He was more inclined to pass his leisure hours at healthy exercises and games. But he inherited his literary talent from both parents. His father was a noted writer and his mother wrote much for newspapers and magazines. His mother's father was the Rev. Dr. George Peck, editor of the *Quarterly Review* and of the *Christian Advocate.*[20] Her uncle was Bishop Peck, a noted Methodist divine.[21]

We had not seen Stephen in seven years and so we remember him more as a boy than as a man. He was a lovable boy, full of life and animal spirits. He possessed many manly characteristics, which he displayed when scarcely more than a child.

3 / Wilbur F. Crane

Stephen's brother Wilbur Fiske Crane (1859–1918) was born in Jersey City and attended Centenary Collegiate Institute in Hackettstown, New Jersey, along with his brothers Edmund and Luther and his sister Agnes. From 1881 to 1886 he attended the College of Physicians and Surgeons (Columbia University) but did not graduate. In a prefatory note to the reminiscence, the editor of the *Binghamton Chronicle* mentioned that during this time Wilbur "wrote a good many stories for the *New York Sun,* founded on incidents in the college." Like Stephen, he worked in his brother Townley's news agency in Asbury Park, reporting shore news for the *New York Tribune.* His marriage in 1888 to Martha Kellogg, a servant in the Port Jervis home of his brother William, estranged some members of the Crane family from him. Wilbur's first child, Helen R. Crane (No. 8), published a reminiscence of Stephen's family life that further infuriated her relatives. In 1897 or 1898 Wilbur and Martha Crane moved to Binghamton, New York. Wilbur's eccentric brother Townley, then an invalid, lived with them during the last few years of his life. Some time after Wilbur's wife left him for another man in 1907, taking their four children with her, he left Binghamton. In 1915 he settled in a small town in Georgia, where he lived until his death.

Source: Wilbur F. Crane, "Reminiscences of Stephen Crane," *Binghamton Chronicle,* 15 December 1900, 3, typed copy in Box 20 (Folder "Gen. Bio."), Melvin H. Schoberlin Research Files, Stephen Crane Collection, Special Collections Research Center, Syracuse University Library.

Stephen's childhood and boyhood were comparatively uneventful. He was the youngest of mother's children, and with his blue eyes and light curls with just a glint of gold in them, he was a beautiful baby. I was eight years his senior and as he grew into boyhood we older boys made a pet and companion of him, taking him with us on our boating, swimming and other trips. He was always fearless and brave and when he was a youngster of five years I remember how he walked out into the Raritan river at the bidding of my elder brother Will, without swerving from his course, until only a patch of his hair about as large as a saucer showed above the water. When Will picked him up Stephen shook the water from his hair and laughed and climbed around onto Will's back to be carried across the river.[22]

The family watchdog was a large Newfoundland named Solomon, and it was a common thing for Solomon to swim the Raritan river when we were bathing, with Stephen lying along his back, holding onto his collar.

One fight of Stephen's is historic in the family, when as a boy of nine he thrashed the bully of Brooklyn street, Port Jervis, a boy twelve years of age.[23] Mother had recently moved into the neighborhood, and as Stephen was younger and smaller, the bully proceeded to bulldoze him as he bulldozed the other small boys of the neighborhood. Stephen stood it for a while but at some added insult to his boyhood he turned on the bully, and after some preliminary sparring, he tackled him and threw him to the ground, and sat on him until he heard a voice saying, "Let him up Stevie." Stephen then ran home and threw himself on the lounge and cried for several minutes, while the bully's mother, who had been watching the scrap, took her hopeful son home and finished the thrashing that Stephen had begun.

Stephen's most marked characteristic was his absolute truthfulness. He was in many minor scrapes but no consideration of consequences would induce him to lie out of them, and the imputation that he was a liar, made the imputer *persona non grata* with Stephen forever thereafter.

While at Pennington seminary some hazing was done which one of the professors charged to Stephen. He denied any knowledge of it, and when the professor told him he lied, Stephen went to his room, packed his trunk and went home to Asbury Park where he told his story, adding that "as the Professor called me a liar there was not room in Pennington for us both, so I came home." Nothing would induce him to return to the seminary.[24]

Stephen's love for his mother was very great, and the most absolute confidence and trust existed between them. "Mom," as he called her, or anything for "Mom" took precedence of anyone or anything else, while after father's death in 1880, mother lived almost wholly in and for Stephen.

Stephen was always fond of athletics and while at Syracuse university, he was captain of the baseball nine. Though not rugged enough for the football team he was very much interested in the game. While writing *The Red Badge of Courage* at the house of my brother, Edmund, at Lake View, near Paterson, N.J., he spent nearly every afternoon in training a football team of schoolboys, which, I believe, is still in existence. He wrote usually from what was other people's bedtime, until he finished that which he had worked out. Then he would sleep until along toward noon, and his afternoons were given to what was almost his sole recreation, the training of the football team.

In an article which Stephen sent to the *New York Tribune,* for his brother Townley, who was the regular correspondent, he described the parade of the Junior American Mechanics on "American Day," 1892, at Asbury Park as "the most awkward, ungainly, uncut and uncarved procession that ever raised clouds of dust on sun-beaten streets," and called the paraders "an assemblage of the spraddle-legged men of the middle class." This occurring shortly after Whitelaw Reid's nomination for the vice-presidency placed before the *Tribune* a first-class dish of crow, and it was served up by deputations and written protests from the various lodges of the Jr. O.U.A.M., hashed and rehashed until Reid in utter exasperation ordered by cable from London the discharge of every man connected with the story.[25]

⌒

4 / Carl F. Price

Carl F. Price (?–?) apparently did not know Crane personally but interviewed people who did. He published the reminiscence in the *Christian Advocate,* which had published articles by Crane's father and had once been edited by the Reverend George Peck, Crane's maternal grandfather.

Source: Carl F. Price, "Stephen Crane: A Genius Born in a Methodist Parsonage," *Christian Advocate* (New York) 98 (13 July 1922): 866–67.

[Price began the article with a brief introduction about Crane.]
    . . . His father, the Rev. Jonathan Townley Crane, D.D. (Dickinson),[26] one-time president of Pennington Seminary, was pastor of the Central Methodist Episcopal Church in Newark when Stephen was born, the youngest of fourteen children. He afterward served in the Newark Conference as pastor at Morristown and Hackettstown, as presiding elder for four years each of the Newark and Elizabeth Districts, then again as pastor in Paterson and Port Jervis; all of which consequently became in succession the homes of the boy Stephen.

Sound Stock

Jonathan Crane was a forceful speaker as well as a ready writer, most tenacious of the opinions which he espoused. Although not all of his readers could accept the views which he expressed in his books on *Holiness, the Birthright of All God's Children, An Essay on Dancing, The Right Way; or Practical Lectures on the Decalogue, Popular Amusements, The Arts of Intoxication* and *Methodism and Its Meth-*

ods, nevertheless the books were admittedly forceful statements of his thought on these themes.[27] One of his fellow members in the Newark Conference, Dr. F. Bloom, has told us of a typical experience of Dr. Crane's, while presiding elder,[28] in preaching for the Rev. Louis Burgess at Kingwood, N.J. When Crane rose in the pulpit and announced his text, Burgess pulled his coat-tails and said: "Brother Crane, you preached from this text here once before." The elder replied: "Well, we have another barrel load along with us, and we'll see what we can do with another text." Whereupon he launched into quite a different sermon and held his audience spell-bound as he delivered his message with tenderness and with real eloquence.

Dr. Crane, left an orphan, at the age of thirteen, began his career by working in a trunk factory until he was twenty-one; worked his way through Princeton University where he graduated; and in 1845 entered the Newark Conference, which he represented in five successive General Conferences from 1856 to 1872. His sudden death at Port Jervis on February 16, 1880, at the age of sixty, was a shock to the Church. He had preached twice the day before from his pulpit and even on that fatal Monday had conducted family worship, as was his invariable custom, using the home readings from the Berean Leaflet. His funeral service at Port Jervis was attended by fifteen hundred; and the next day his body was borne to Elizabeth, where in Saint James Church over a hundred ministers attended, and Bishops Simpson, Hurst and Spellmeyer (the last two not yet elected bishops) paid high tribute to his character. Such was the father of Stephen Crane.

Stephen's mother, Mary Helen Peck, was the daughter of Dr. George Peck, once editor of the *Christian Advocate,* and was the niece of Bishop Peck. A woman of particular gifts, she was a writer on many subjects, was much in demand as a public speaker, especially by the Methodist women's societies of the Church, to which she gave a very active leadership; and in her hobby, the making of wax figures, she displayed her artistic talents. The cares of raising a family of fourteen children seemed to weigh lightly upon her shoulders. In fact, so unconventional were her housekeeping habits that when she came under that scrutiny which the ladies of the congregation sometimes delight in lavishing upon a minister's wife, she suffered much open criticism and was finally informed that she ought to stay at home and take care of her large family, instead of making so many speeches.

A Methodist Home

Of those fourteen children, the one, besides Stephen, giving by far the most promise was Agnes Crane, who with one of her brothers attended the Centenary Collegiate Institute at Hackettstown, N.J. She was an artist of skill (we have seen some of her drawings), could sing well and write poetry or prose, serious or comic. Once she wrote a pseudo-oratorio, "Jonah," that added much to the mirth of her friends. She used to say of herself: "Mother has hope that her ugly duckling may turn out a swan." Her face was as solemn as that of anyone who ever lived; but her alert mind, her spirit of fun, and her radiant personality made her most companionable. And she was Stephen Crane's good angel, brightening his boyhood as an older sister can sometimes do.

Her most intimate friend in school days at C.C.I. was Miss Josephine Baldwin, now on the editorial staff of the Methodist Sunday school publications. Miss Baldwin cherishes many memories of the boy Stephen and his family, and especially of their camping days in the woods of Mongaup Valley, near Port Jervis, N.Y. Here Stephen's career was nearly terminated at the age of ten when he was bitten by a snake. Only the promptest medical aid pulled him through, when all thought he must surely die.

The shack which the Cranes built was whimsically called "Saint's Rest,"[29] and was usually overcrowded by so large a family. Agnes slept directly under the hammock that nightly held the slumbering Stephen. One night the hammock broke and Stephen landed in full length on top of his sister. Luckily for her, he was slight in weight, but still she bemoaned the misfortune that "his bones were not sufficiently upholstered to make it anything but an unpleasant experience."

Into the fatherless home, whence other brothers and sisters had been called away by death, came the heavy sorrow of Agnes' death in 1884, and Stephen, then a lad of thirteen, lost from his life another sustaining, guiding hand. When he entered Pennington Seminary, over which his father had once presided, the reduction in tuition, allowed him as a minister's son, was not sufficient to make both ends meet financially, so that he was obliged to work during his vacations. His mother, discerning his talent for writing, secured him a commission as correspondent of the *New York Tribune* from Asbury Park and Ocean Grove, which she had held herself in former summers. This newspaper reporting won for him his first great literary friend, Hamlin Garland,[30] and helped toward his college preparation which finally admitted him to Lafayette College. From there after a short stay he migrated to Syracuse University. At Syracuse he continued to write for the *New York Tribune*, adding also the *Detroit Free Press*[31] and the Syracuse dailies to his correspondence.

Syracuse Days

W. H. Van Benschoten, Dr. Bertrand M. Tipple and the Rev. E. H. Carr were students at Syracuse when Crane was an undergraduate there and remember his personality distinctly. Selecting his own course from the subjects he felt he needed most, he was classed as a special student. His fellows, however, regarded him as a freshman. At Lafayette he had been initiated into the Delta Upsilon fraternity, and accordingly at Syracuse made D.U. his home. One day the steward of the club-house, a senior, shouted forth: "I want a freshie to turn grindstone for the kitchen knives. Come on, Crane." Whereupon he retorted, quite red in the face, that he never had and never would turn grindstone for anybody.

His room in the D.U. house, adorned with many college banners, was the scene of animated conversations and great discussions. Dr. Bertrand M. Tipple also lived in the same "frat." house. He confesses that none of them at that time ever guessed Crane's genius. He was different, to be sure; always more or less revolutionary in his attitude toward college life, in his methods of study, in his somewhat heterodox ideas on most questions. And neither students nor faculty understood him. But whatever unpopularity this might have produced was greatly mitigated by the fact that he had a generous capacity for friendship among those whom he chose as his friends, and also that he was catcher on the Varsity baseball nine, on which team "Bert" Tipple played first base. Crane back of the bat always "froze on to the ball," as baseballese hath it, even though it came with such force as to make his slight figure seem to rebound with the impact. In the preface to posthumous editions of *The Red Badge of Courage* he is quoted as having said that in college he was more interested in baseball than in the work of the class-room.[32] Perhaps that partly explains the brevity of his career at Syracuse.

[Price summarized Crane's career after leaving Syracuse.]

5 / Post Wheeler

Known as America's first career diplomat, (George) Post Wheeler (1869–1956) was educated at Princeton, the University of Pennsylvania, and the Sorbonne. In 1895 he became editor of the *New York Press*. He began his diplomatic career in 1906 as second secretary of the American embassy in Tokyo; held diplomatic posts in the embassies at St. Petersburg, Rome, Stockholm, London, Madrid, and Rio de Janeiro; and served as minister to Albania until his retirement in 1934. Wheeler published Russian folk tales, biblical stories, and Japanese legends, and with his wife, Hallie Erminie Rives, wrote a joint autobiography, *Dome of Many-Coloured Glass*. Wheeler's religious background was similar to that of Crane: his father was a Methodist minister, and his mother was active in the Women's Christian Temperance Union.

Wheeler and Crane knew each other as children through their mothers, who were active in the WCTU, and later as fellow journalists in New York City.

Source: Post Wheeler and Hallie E. Rives, *Dome of Many-Coloured Glass* (Garden City, N.Y.: Doubleday, 1955), 20–22, 98–101, 106–7.

[The reminiscence began in the Wyoming Valley of Pennsylvania, near Wilkes-Barre and Scranton, where Post and his mother had gone to hear Francis E. Willard, then secretary of the WCTU, speak. Stephen and his mother came from New Jersey for the event and most likely stayed with family in Scranton.]

We stayed overnight at a hotel, where [my mother] was to meet another W.C.T.U. lady speaker of note, who had come from as far away as New Jersey to the "rally." Her name was Mrs. Jonathan Crane and she had brought her youngest son with her. This was my first meeting with Stevie Crane. He was a pale-faced, blond-headed, hungry-looking boy a bit younger than I, and we struck up an intimacy that was to be renewed when we were in our twenties, in New York.

Next day Mrs. Crane and Stevie accompanied us to our town to spend two days as my parents' guests. The day coach was full and we boys were allowed to ride in the "smoker," where Stevie blandly (though with some covert backward glances toward the car which held his mother) lighted a Sweet Caporal cigarette and offered me one. . . . I accepted Stevie's weed and to my surprise was not sick.

The day following was marked by a celebration in the near village of Wyoming. It was the centenary of the historic "Massacre of Wyoming," when in 1778 four hundred British and seven hundred Indians had stormed the fort into which the villagers had refuged and the Indians had tomahawked men, women, and children without mercy.[33] For the occasion the stockade had been re-erected, citizens of the town were to play the part of the unhappy settlers, and a hundred men, dressed as redskins, were to re-enact the massacre. The spectacle had been widely advertised, and a mammoth crowd was expected. My father and mother took Mrs. Crane with them in the family "buggy" and Stevie and I went by streetcar, each of us with a whole quarter to spend as we liked on the spot.

It was a red-letter day for us, with popcorn, toy balloons, rattan canes, and stick candy, and hawkers selling every conceivable gewgaw. There was even a Highlander, in kilt and sporran, playing his bagpipe for stray coppers, the first we had ever seen, except in pictures. When, in the middle of the afternoon, the horde of yelling savages, in their war paint and feathers, stormed the palisade amid the shrieks of the butchered victims, I felt that the day was complete.

Yet the peak was to come. Beside the exit gate a fat Pennsylvania Dutchman had set up a keg of beer on an upturned box on which stood a row of glass mugs, with a sign which said: *Beer 10 cents.* When Stevie took a dime from his pocket and approached it with an air of purpose, my blood chilled. "What you going to do?" I asked in a hollow undertone. Stevie did not answer. He set down the dime on the box and said, "Gimme one."

I can still see the man's rotund face as he bent down over his keg and surveyed Stevie's diminutive figure. "Hey?" he said.

"I said gimme a beer," said Stevie.

The man's fingers had closed on the eloquent coin. "You gimme a beer or gimme back my dime!" said Stevie in a shrill falsetto.

The man held a mug with a dab of foam in it toward him, but Stevie regarded it with fine scorn. "That ain't half full!" he said indignantly. "You fill it up."

The tap was turned then and Stevie drank it slowly, while I watched in stupefaction. We walked through the gate. "How does it taste?" I asked.

"'Tain't any better'n ginger ale," he said. "I been saving that dime for it all afternoon."

I was still in a daze when we came to the streetcar. Beer! Right in the crowd, too. I seemed to see Stevie, sometime later of course, hurtling along a broad descending path toward an Avernus[34] from which ascended cries of despair. "Stevie," I whispered as the driver whipped up the horses and the bells clanged, "how'd you dast do it?"

"Pshaw!" said Stevie. "Beer ain't nothing at all." Then he added, defensively but emphatically, "How was I going to know what it tasted like less'n I tasted it? How you going to know about things at all less'n you *do* 'em?" . . .

[Wheeler reminisced about the Lantern Club.]

To a small group of us newspapermen (we eschewed the word "journalist") the Press Club had no appeal, its chief qualification for membership appearing to be a capacity for entertaining liquor which we lacked ambition to develop. We made our ideal rendezvous a club of sorts which we christened Sign o' the Lanthorn. It was a decrepit penthouse on William Street, in the section called "Monkey Hill," on the roof of a building built of flat tilelike Dutch bricks brought in one of the old clipper ships from Amsterdam, which we fondly claimed was the oldest house in New York.[35]

We began with seven members and the late Irving Bacheller, of *Eben Holden* fame, was our perpetual president. Once, when in financial difficulties, a group of us issued the club's sole publication, *The Lanthorn Book,* containing a contribution from each.[36] It is rare now—the last quotation I saw in a rare-book advertisement was eighty-two dollars.

Our numbers soon grew. Tom Masson, editor of the old *Life,* Stephen Crane, Edward Townsend of the "Chimmie Fadden" stories, Gustave Verbeek, the illustrator, Charles B. Lewis ("M. Quad" of *Quad's Odds*) were among our earliest additions. Before long we were maintaining a Virginia Negro as chef, lunching at the Sign o' the Lanthorn daily, and on Tuesday nights meeting for a dinner on beefsteak that had been frozen six months and was tender as a baby, French-fried potatoes, beer, and churchwarden pipes. Over the coffee we read our most ambitious effusions aloud for general criticism, and every other week we entertained celebrities, who were invited to write their autographs, with original "sentiments," with brushes on the burlap-covered walls. For these occasions we had only two rules, but they were adamantine: no dress suits worn and the title of "Mr." not to be employed.

It would be difficult, perhaps, to name a person famous in the nineties for literature and the arts whose name was not recorded there. The Old Guard of the magazine world—William Dean Howells, Richard Watson Gilder, Edmund Clarence Stedman, Richard Henry Stoddard—were frequent visitors. Kipling, Amelia E. Barr, Charles Dana Gibson, Ethel Barrymore, Richard Harding Davis, Tarkington, Francis Wilson the comedian, then at his heyday, Stanford White, Madison Square Garden's architect whom love-crazy Harry Thaw was to shoot down on its roof over Evelyn Nesbit the chorus girl—we enjoyed them all. Mark Twain loved to come.

It was a red-letter day for me when the Stevie Crane of my boyhood days and I renewed our ancient friendship. He was, I learned, living on the Jersey shore with his older brother Townley, who was correspondent of the *New York Tribune* for north Jersey, and I journeyed there to talk of old times.

Townley needed only a crossbow and a dead albatross slung about his neck to be Doré's ideal model for the Ancient Mariner.[37] His habitual costume was a long overcoat with turned-up collar, a bandanna handkerchief knotted around his neck, and an incredibly dirty slouch hat. I do not believe he ever wore a shirt. A single visit to the *Tribune's* office in New York *in propria persona* must have cooked his goose, but he was one of the best correspondents the paper ever had. One suspected that Stevie, who had the cleanly grooming of a wild animal, was not too proud of his brother, and that this had to do with their diminishing intimacy during Townley's last years. My liveliest recollection of Townley connects itself with a bottle which he kept "for emergencies," an emergency being an hour when his wife had gone to prayer meeting and he could emerge into the freer life.

Stevie was "reporting" for him on north Jersey social activities. The phrase was technical, he was a reporter only in the sense that Pierre Loti or Lafcadio Hearn[38] was one, and his contributions were for the most part short stories, inimitable for color and overtones, which appeared in the *Tribune*'s weekly edition.

Our old association renewed, my epistolary efforts to entice him to New York, where I felt he belonged, for a time were checkmated by vacuity of the exchequer, for the *Tribune*'s space rate was niggardly. "You appall me," he wrote, "by mentioning a couple of bottles. If I were sure you meant beer no one would reply with more fervent and fraternal joy. But I have a damnable suspicion that you mean wine. Know then, my old companion, that I am living upon the glory of literature and not upon its emoluments. Nevertheless we have gone too many leagues together to let the matter of beer or wine separate us."[39]

Later unfriendly fate conspired to close the *Tribune*'s doors to him (an incident made overmuch of by the biographers and too long to recount here) and he came to New York to sink or swim.[40] I had my quarters in an enormous loft in Twenty-third Street,[41] a few doors west of Sixth Avenue. There Stevie had his divan in the front room, and there he wrote *The Black Riders* and much of his *Red Badge of Courage*.[42] In the rear room of evenings a poker game was apt to be in progress at stakes that were not allowed to become embarrassing to any of us. He was by nature too reckless and impatient to be any kind of a star at the Great American Game. We all commonly adjourned in the tail of the evening for the Black Cat, or Maria's, or for a bite at the uptown Mouquin's or grilled bones at the Sixth Avenue Shanley's.

Stevie was a great acquisition to the Lanthorn crowd. He was a little shy at reading his sketches aloud to the rest of us, but occasionally did his bit, and took our criticism seriously, as we did his. I soon learned that he had a subtle mind, and when it came my turn I listened for his comment with some trepidation. I recall a short story I thus read which I had titled "The Lapse of Fifine." It was the tale of a Paris grisette who, deserted by her lover, becomes converted and joins the French Salvation Army. Her Hypolite returns to her, and she ties up her Salvation cloak and tambourine in a neat bundle to be left on the Armée doorstep, and goes off with him. I had not thought of the tale as "daring" or as any sneer at religion, only as a bit of human nature. But Gilder, to whom I sent it, found it quite offensive on both counts. He wrote me that he feared the *Century*'s readers "would not be edified by this story of a young girl's lapse from a life of rectitude to one of sin."

His point of view properly enraged me and I wrote inquiring if a slight alteration in the plot would make it acceptable to his readers. If, for example, Fifine should convert Hypolite, and the close show him with the bass drum, leading the Salut procession to the chapel, where the smiling priest waits to marry them. Naturally I received no answer. I wished later I had written him *au grand sérieux*. I might have had a reply that would now be a landmark in America's literary history. Of course Fifine's real "lapse" was her lapse into the Salvation Army, and in the Lanthorn Club discussion that followed my reading of the story Stevie was the only one of the crowd who got the point. This is what I mean when I say he had a subtle mind.[43]

Stevie had written his much-discussed *Maggie* before those Lanthorn days. The *nom de plume* he used ("Johnson Smith") I had suggested to him only as a joke.[44] It was a foregone conclusion that Gilder would get only nausea from the story. I could see him being seasick when Stevie told me Hamlin Garland had sent him the manuscript.[45] And I should have expected Howells to react similarly, if not to the same degree, but he was unmeasured in his praise and was to be Stevie's friend as long as he lived. Garland understood that Stevie was blazing a new path through the mawkish and hypocritical jungle of goody-good American letters, though he had not a mind to adopt that trail himself. I used to talk with him often about Stevie in those early days, and we discussed *Maggie* together in Hollywood the year he (Garland) died.

Our evenings at the Lanthorn and our poker séances in Twenty-third Street were now and then enlivened by *The Black Riders,* with whose exotic fantasies Stevie regaled us when he was in the mood, and which we used to applaud vociferously, with no thought whatever of their appearing in covers. When they did and the critics' fusillade began, it occurred to me that they would make a good build-up for Stevie, and I began to satirize them in "The Last Column"[46]:

Stephencranelets
MDCCCXLIII
I saw a man brushing furiously
At his bald head.
Round and round he brushed.
I accosted the man.
"Why brush?" I asked. "There is no—"
"You lie!" he shrieked,
And brushed on.

The exchange editors fell upon them with unholy glee. It was all grist for Stevie's mill. The Lanthorn crowd (and he no less) got some fun out of them, he understanding with the rest the purity of my blurbal intentions.

I treasured my copy of the Copeland and Day volume for many years, with his indited flyleaf and with the longest and most characteristic letter I ever got from him pasted in the back. It was stolen out of my study at Rayleigh House in London, when I was American Chargé d'Affaires there in 1925. I hope the thief burns in hell for it.

What stands out most boldly in all my memories of him is the fact that from the start he knew with profound certainty where he was going. His letters to me hold many a fling at the "literary darks" who congregated at the old Authors Club at Carnegie Hall. For them he had only gibes to the end. One, dictated to his wife, Cora, reminded me that he had once been callow enough to second my nomination to membership,[47] and one of the last he wrote from Brede in England, with his own hand, says, "What the hell your reasons were for joining the club I can't see!"

That letter was some years in reaching me: when it was written I was some thousands of miles away, in the upper Yukon, and with a man strangely like him in genius and history. That was Jack London. Both had the undying thirst to taste all experiences. London's South Sea episode, in motive and meaning, paralleled Stevie's Mexican and Cuban adventure. London's last year at Valley of the Moon, in his attitude toward his publishers, his baronial love of open-house entertainment, the role played by his wife—in a hundred smaller things— mirrored Stevie's closing year at Brede.

Shy, sensitive, quick-tempered, restive, reckless, and generous to a fault, that was the Stephen Crane I knew. I never knew him to do a mean thing. I never saw him drunk. The aloof manner he showed to strangers was the protective coloration which one sees so often in the British. The dope stories which clung about his name after his passing were incredible to all who knew him best. . . .

[Hallie Erminie Rives reminisced about the Lantern Club and *Maggie*.]
. . . [O]nce or twice, on a ladies' night, [Post Wheeler] took me to an odd little club of writers he belonged to away downtown. It was called the Sign o' the Lanthorn. It had a rubbishy little back yard with nothing but a big cactus tree growing in it, and the building, he told me, had been the resort of Kidd the pirate and his cronies, when they anchored in the port of New Amsterdam, as New York was then named. . . . I met Stephen Crane. . . .

Crane was apparently the only one of the younger writers whom Wheeler had much use for. For the average run of the popular novels he had a kind of contempt. Crane he recognized as the leader of a new era which was bound to come. Most of the Lanthorn Club members seemed to be of the same persuasion, to some degree committed to what they called "realism." Crane had just published his first novel, *Maggie: A Girl of the Streets,* and it had fallen flat. He had had to print it at his own expense, and it had met with such a fusillade of abuse that the booksellers, even, would not handle it.

Wheeler was furious about it. One of the few times I ever saw him really angry was at a tea where someone damned the book in his hearing, and he exploded. It was high time, he declared, that more writers had the courage to rebel against the unco guid[48] obstinacy of the magazine trust, which was bent on reducing American letters to the status of Sunday school goody-goody, and decreed that no hint of the existence in real life of unconventional human relations must stain the pages of our literature. In real life men swore, yes, even in the hearing of delicate virgins, but it must not be mentioned in print. Never! The other day, in an installment of one of his novels running in the *Ladies' Home Journal*, Kipling had introduced a brandy and soda. Bok, its editor, had cabled him that it must come out, and Kipling had wired back, "Make it Mellinsfood." Why, he said, it had got so bad that if you wrote for the printed page you mustn't even use a good honest "Damn!" You must write it "D dash." What hypocritical mumbo-jumbo! For his part he thanked God that New York at last had one author who dared to write of things as they were, and that was the author of *Maggie*.

The outburst blanketed the conversation of the whole room, to Wheeler's embarrassment, as one could see, for he stopped abruptly. But I liked him the more for it. I read *Maggie* the next day. The dialogue at first appalled me, but its impact was terrific. Though I could never gain such experiences or require such a vocabulary, it taught me the value of realistic treatment.

〜

6 / Arthur Oliver

Arthur Oliver (?–?) was a classmate of Crane at Lafayette and operated a news agency, along with Post Wheeler, at Asbury Park, New Jersey. His reminiscence offers a firsthand account of a seminal event in Crane's professional development: the publication of his satirical article covering the annual American Day parade of the Junior Order of United American Mechanics (*New York Tribune*, 21 August 1892). Offended, the Order demanded an apology, which the *Tribune* printed (Wertheim and Sorrentino, *Crane Log* 780). Garland (No. 20) and Barry (No. 28) agreed with Oliver that Stephen was fired, though Johnson (No. 7) denied it. Following the incident, the *Tribune* never printed another piece by Crane and vilified his books, though toward the end of his career the newspaper's reviews of his books were less critical. It is uncertain whether Oliver is correct in suggesting that the incident helped to defeat Whitelaw Reid, publisher of the *Tribune,* in his Republican bid for the vice presidency of the United States in 1892.

Source: Arthur Oliver, "Jersey Memories—Stephen Crane," *Proceedings of the New Jersey Historical Society* 16 (1931): 454–63.

In recalling some things that have to do with persons and events in New Jersey in the last fifty years or so, I shall try to follow the advice of a friend and fellow-Jerseyman who set a bright example for all who write of life's experiences. As this advice of his had a rather odd significance in his own case, I shall start out with a little incident that leads into the story.

He and I had strolled down to the beach at Asbury Park and were sitting on the sand watching the long rollers come in. We were young then and our thoughts were as vagrant as sea birds. But there was one pet subject we usually drifted to sooner or later, and that was our ambition to write something out of the ordinary. On this particular occasion I was much upset because I had been wasting a lot of paper in an attempt to describe a "tingling" experience I had had in rounding the storm that is still described by old-timers along the coast as "the big blow of '89." I told my troubles to my friend "Stevie," because I knew it was just the kind of an experience he reveled in when it came to drawing word pictures with a pencil.

"Somehow I can't get down to the real thing," I said. "I know I have something unusual to tell, but I get all tangled up with different notions of how it ought to be told."

"Stevie" scooped up a handful of sand and tossed it to the brisk sea breeze.

"Treat your notions like that," he said. "Forget what you think about it and tell how you feel about it. Make the other fellow realize you are just as human as he is. That's the big secret of story-telling. Away with literary cads and canons. Be yourself!"

We all agree that Stephen Crane knew how to tell a story. In telling mine I shall remember what he said to me then and try to go to the heart of things, forgetting frills and notions. I have not lived a romance like this world-author whose life was an "Open Boat" on the sea of adventure, but in my long experience as a writer for newspapers and other publications I have been brought into contact with many well-remembered characters and happenings. If I can throw a new light on some of these and bring an occasional thrill of inspiration out of the past, I shall accomplish all I have set out to do. As a Jerseyman writing mostly for Jerseymen who know their State, I realize I may touch upon certain things they are more familiar with than I am.

In this loosely woven texture of reminiscences I shall take the liberty that makers of tapestry do, and weave in a colorful personality, scene or incident here and there, without any serious attempt at narrative form or chronological sequence. I have taken "Stevie" Crane as a sort of keynote at the outset and shall go along with him for awhile, for I do not know of a more delightful companion one could have for a stroll down the lane of memory through the light and shade of unforgotten days. The little incident I have recalled was in the Summer of 1892. "Stevie" and I were "budding journalists," whatever that may mean, and, as we sat there on the gray sands and watched the waves rush in and spend themselves with the froth and fury of passionate, youthful ambitions, life was all before us like the great ocean that sparkled in the sunshine of a perfect Summer day. "Stevie" was a boy of twenty. To hear him talk you would say his passionate ambition was baseball. At this he was something of a hero among his fellow collegians. As to literary fame—well, he had his eye on that, too, but as yet he was not highly distinguished above any other boy of twenty who had gained a reputation for saying and writing bright things. Neither he nor I could know of the glory that would come to him in a few short years. Nor could we know as we sat there talking about my adventure with a tempest that in only a few days he would be the storm center of a tempest quite as wrathful and spectacular as the one that tried to wreck my little whaleboat up in Casco Bay. Nor yet could we know that the obviously excellent advice he had just given me would so soon bring disaster to himself when he applied it in his own original way.

Now that it is all over and done, I think of the dramatic episode I am about to tell of as just a characteristic incident in his adventurous career. As I chanced to be with him at the time the whole affair originated, I can plead privilege in re-opening an old discussion by presenting first-hand testimony which a number of my friends, including Max J. Herzberg, President of the Stephen Crane Association and Literary Editor of the "Newark Evening News" have frequently requested me, in view of the interest anything new about Stephen Crane always arouses, to set down what I know. I say "the case" advisedly, because poor "Stevie" committed a terrible journalistic *faux pas* by letting his feelings get away with him, thus following overzealously the advice he gave to me, and was pilloried therefore in the most approvedly-drastic journalistic fashion.

"Stevie" and I were beachcombers along the Jersey shore. We picked up all kinds of flotsam and jetsam that furnished material for news or special stories and sent it by mail or wire to the big city papers. "Stevie" and his brother, J. Townley Crane, were correspondents for New York and Philadelphia newspapers, with headquarters at Asbury Park. Their mother sent out religious happenings from Ocean Grove. J. Townley was the older of the two brothers. The "New York Tribune" claimed his special pride and devotion. Residenters along the shore looked upon him as the veritable incarnation of that great newspaper. He existed for the "Tribune," and at times, when you were admitted to the *sanctum sanctorum* of his confidence, he almost made you feel that the "Tribune" existed for him. "Stevie," as we liked to call him, because it seemed a little more affectionate than "Steve," was looked upon as just a "bright kid," a sort of field office boy for his brother, for the "office" of J. Townley took in an indefinite stretch of coast line, making him quite at home in his official capacity, whether he wrote a religious item on a faro table in Phil Daly's gambling emporium in Long Branch or a faro episode on some convenient table or chair bottom in the quiet seclusion of the Tabernacle in Ocean Grove. To divorce J. Townley from the "New York Tribune" or from his dignity as dean of the shore correspondents was as inconceivable as to divorce Asbury Park from James A. Bradley or Ocean Grove from the Methodist Church.[49] All this is apropos, because it sets the stage for the highly original and unconventional dramatic thriller which "Stevie" produced for an astonished public and a shocked and outraged group of citizens *sans reproche*.

Two or three days after our little talk on the beach, "Stevie" and I met on the street in Asbury Park. It was in the morning, and we swapped notes on the prospective news of the day. J. Townley was away for a few days and "Stevie" was left to his own devices. I invited him into a billiard and pool parlor to have a cigar. As we came out we caught our first glimpse of "the parade that made Stevie Crane famous," as the shore correspondents used to say.

Down from the railroad station came the marchers. Flags and banners dispelled the drab sobriety of the street with the flash and flutter of gay and variegated color. Badges bedizened each manly breast. If the marchers did not know just how to keep step or alignment, it was probably because they had done most or all of their soldiering in the plodding ranks of the great army of Labor. If they were not so dapper as a squad of West Pointers, it was because they never had been taught to know the graces of dress and carriage, or the beauty of *esprit de corps*. It may be that they did not march at all, that each just ambled along in his own way, serenely innocent of any suspicion of cavil or criticism. They were not prize beauties in face, or form, or fashion. If they did not all hold their bodies erect and straight, it was perhaps because they carried the torturous legacy of years of humble and heavy and honest toil. But it was their annual field day, the one day of all the year when they cast their cares and troubles to the winds and came down to take a fall out of Old Neptune and be just as reckless and rollicking and independent as anybody. It was their day, and they had earned it. They were proud and happy, and perhaps a bit egotistical because of this golden opportunity to exhibit themselves in such impressive numbers and in gala array.

I took a look at "Stevie." He was leaning against the frame of a street door. His keen eyes were glued on the procession with the half-amused, half-quizzical expression of one who looks into a kaleidoscope. His cigar had gone out and was clenched tightly in his teeth. He stayed just that way until the last rank had passed. While he had been watching the parade I had been watching him. He was a puzzle. Some inscrutable, internal influence was at work.

"Well, Stevie," I said, "how about it?"

He took the cigar from his mouth and delivered himself of a few strong words. At this he was an artist, in the finer sense. Then he put back the unlighted cigar, clamped his teeth on it rather savagely, as I thought, and set off post haste for his headquarters in the Lake Avenue Hotel to write his story before he lost the inspiration. Naturally, I wondered what the story would be. I was not prepared for what I read in the "Tribune" the next morning. It was just one sizzling roast. Not only at the parade did he hurl his glittering javelins of invective, but also at Asbury Park.

Before I saw "Stevie" again I made a stop-over trip to Newark and New York, leaving a handsome, young "budding journalist" named George P. Wheeler, now better known as Post Wheeler, author and diplomat, to look out for me while I was away. When I came back I found him at the "Asbury Park Journal" office talking to the editor, Mr. Wallace.

"Have you heard the news?" they queried in the same breath.

"What news?"

"Townley Crane was fired by mail and Stevie by wire! Stevie's out now and Townley goes at the end of the season."

They did not need to tell me the parade story did it. I was not surprised. I was sorry. There was just as much chance for the Crane combination to stay intact after that madcap prank of "Stevie's" as if he had dropped a match into a magazine. It was not so much that he had held up to public ridicule an exemplary community and a great organization of honest and self-respecting American citizens. The crowning atrocity was that his diatribe had put in jeopardy the election of the boss of his own newspaper to the office of Vice-President of the United States! Knowing what I do about the whole matter, I often wish I could have seen the expression on the face of Whitelaw Reid when he read "Stevie's" description of that perfectly innocent parade down there by the sea and realized what it might mean to himself and to the Republican Party. Each word must have sawed into his brain like a very coarse rasp. And the joyous artistry of the diction must have imparted its own peculiar thrill.

There are those who think it cost the Republican Party the defeat of its national ticket in 1892. Reid himself is said to have thought so.[50] What Benjamin Harrison thought about most things he had a profound way of keeping to himself. I really did not have to find out what J. Townley and "Stevie" thought about it. As nearly all of the species of ephemera aptly named journalists are in the class of the turkey at Thanksgiving time, I could feel with them as well as for them. I paid a visit of condolence. Townley was glum as a king who had lost his crown. "Stevie" greeted me with a saintly smile he always had ready for every disaster. He asked me if I had read the story, and I thought there was just a bit of pride in the look he gave me. I said I had. He asked me what I thought of it. I opined that it was clever, and good for almost any purpose except publication.

"Especially publication in the 'New York Tribune,'" he said with a grin. Continuing he said: "You see, I seemed to have forgotten for the moment that my boss on the 'Tribune' was running for Vice-President. Those jolly paraders read my story and annoyed him with a telegram, informing him that his newspaper had better eat its words or he had better retire as a candidate, or something to that effect. So it was decided that the 'Tribune' should eat its words; or so I understand. You'd hardly think a little innocent chap like me could have stirred up such a row in American politics. It shows what innocence can do if it has the opportunity!"

It may or may not be that "Stevie's" article aided to defeat Harrison and Reid and elect Cleveland and Stevenson. As for the article per se, there are not two ways of thinking. It was good reading but bad journalism, and the Editor who passed it was more to blame that the green young correspondent who was practising a literary style. As a bright boy collegian "Stevie" ran true to form, but as a "budding journalist" he got away to a false start. It was probably a good thing that he did, for it threw him on his own responsibility and out of competition with the penny-a-liners into the class where he belonged. Furthermore, it gave him salutary experience.

When things had simmered down a bit and the woeful incident could be discussed calmly, I asked "Stevie" about the advice he had given me that day on the beach. I wanted to know if under the circumstances he would revise it any.

"No!" he said emphatically. "You've got to feel the things you write if you want to make an impact on the world."

I reminded him that he had made such an impact.

"Well," he replied in his mild, kindly way, as he put his hand on my shoulder, "that bears out just what I said."

It is nearly forty years since it all happened and the time since "Stevie" left us is thirty years and more. Strange it is that the newspaper article which produced such a sensation and marked such a high spot in the history of a popular world author should come to light only a short time ago. Buried in the archives as a journalistic freak, it was exhumed as a literary curiosity. Exhibited in the press to the public, it claimed its due wonder and amusement, so why pull out the skeleton and rattle it now? It is in the closet, properly labeled and catalogued, and if any one desires to see it and examine its capricious anatomy I shall be pleased to tell him how it can most easily be found. The original article was in one edition of the "New York Tribune" of Sunday, August 21, 1892. It was reproduced, without the name of the organization it refers to, in the "Newark Sunday Call" of January 14, 1931. The exhumation from the "Tribune" files was effected by Dr. B. J. R. Stolper, formerly a high school instructor in Newark and now a research worker in Columbia University. It was hailed by lovers of literary curiosities as a real "find." As the "Sunday Call" was courteous enough not to name the organization it refers to, it is just as well to follow its example here. Suffice it to say that it was an organization much cultivated by politicians because of its strong voting power and that it might easily have turned the national election either way in the nip-and-tuck race for Presidential and Vice-Presidential honors in the memorable campaign of '92.

As an intellectual personality "Stevie" Crane always impressed me as very old for his years when we were young chaps together down on the Jersey shore. Beneath a somewhat diffident exterior, he had a keen sense of the real meaning of things. He saw and felt deeply. Even as a boy, he had a richly developed vein of satire. At times this led him into moods that seemed vindictive, as in the story of the parade. But it wasn't vindictiveness. It was the urge of a wonderful literary gift which made him produce something startling now and then, even bizarre. There are those who do not credit him with a heart, who say that his characters are marionettes motivated to strikingly original actions and attitudes by his masterful manipulation of the strings. Having known the real "Stevie" as well as I did, having shared confidences with him in those little things of great importance which enter into the life of us all, I cannot fully agree with this view. If his characters were actors of a sort, with a penchant for doing "something different" on the stage of mimic life, it was, I believe, because he put a heart into them, as the Almighty Master of the Great Show has put a heart into each one of us, and permitted them to act in a way that was natural to them, just as all of us do. "Stevie" was an insurrectionist. He liked battles, with guns or words. His cannon enfiladed the line of literary canons which had made literature a thing apart from life. When he set the stage so realistically and made his players talk and act like human beings in the grasp of circumstances and subject to the immutable laws of nature, he was not exactly understood by all. Like Rodin's statues, it was artistic in its realism, but to some it seemed fantastical because it was so different from anything they had known. So, without going deeply into it, it was easy for them to suppose that "Stevie" had been amusing himself with marionettes.

"Stevie and his Parade story" continued to be a subject of gossip all the rest of the season down Asbury Park way. I talked it over then or later with Ralph D. Paine,[51] now famed as an author and in those days star reporter on the "Asbury Park Journal"; with Post Wheeler,[52] who was associated with me in the Wheeler-Oliver Correspondence Bureau with offices in the Monmouth building, Asbury Park; with William K. Devereux, Editor of the pink sheet known as the "Asbury Park Daily Spray," on which I had served my journalistic apprenticeship, and with "Founder" Bradley, around whom the affairs of Asbury Park gravitated as life gravitates around a spring of water in a sunny clime. All were fond of "Stevie" and were very sorry he had "toyed with a boomerang," as Devereux expressed it. Yet all agreed it might be the making of him, for it had given him some marvellous advertising and had jolted him into the conviction that he must "cut loose on something on his own hook," as Post Wheeler said. Big Ralph Paine, who afterwards drew a colorful picture of "Stevie," *con amore,* in his delightful autobiography, "Roads of Adventure," seemed to think his young friend had struck an inspiration, though not just the kind Ralph himself would have turned to such account. Ralph's brilliant mind was well qualified to appraise "Stevie" at his true worth. "Founder" Bradley was nettled by what "Stevie" said about Asbury Park, but when I talked to him he was generous enough to pass it off with a smile and with the remark that "boys will be boys."

Stephen Crane's birthplace at 14 Mulberry Place, Newark, is preserved as a literary memorial. But I think New Jersey remembers him best as a struggling young newspaper writer at Asbury Park. Whenever I go there and sit on the beach there comes to me a vivid memory picture of his clean-cut, aggressive profile, as he sat bareheaded looking at the ocean and snapped out defiance to the whole breed of literary oracles, his hair streaming backward like the pennant of a trim little fighting craft in the stiff sea breeze.

〜

7 / Willis Fletcher Johnson

Willis Fletcher Johnson (1857–1931) worked for the *New York Tribune* between 1880 and 1920, serving as day editor during the time of publication of Crane's controversial article covering the parade of the Junior Order of United American Mechanics (*New York Tribune*, 21 August 1892). A friend of the Crane family, he was also a contributing editor to the *North American Review* and a lecturer on foreign relations at schools and colleges.

Source: Willis F. Johnson, letter to the editor, *New York Evening Post Literary Review* 14 (2 April 1921): 14.

Sir: Pray let me correct a few strange errors in the very interesting article about Stephen Crane, by Ford Madox Hueffer, which you published Saturday, March 19,[53] which I feel authorized to do because I knew Crane so very well. His father was one of my early friends and I knew Stephen intimately from his boyhood up. Indeed, I can claim to have accepted for (newspaper) publication his earliest efforts at fiction, which he brought to me, shyly and apologetically, and asked me to read and to see if they were any good and if I thought it worth while for him to try to write. They were capital sketches of romance and adventure among the hills of Sullivan County, N.Y.,[54] and I was so pleased with them that I urged him to devote himself to authorship. (That was while he was yet in school or college.)

But as to Mr. Hueffer's errors:

He speaks of Crane as "newly come from the Bowery," "dragged up in the Bowery," "his defiant Bowery surface," and "this Bowery boy of New York."

But Crane was not a "Bowery boy." He never was in the Bowery until he had attained manhood, become a writer, and gone thither in quest of "material" and "local color." He was born in Newark, N.J., when that now great city was an overgrown village in tone and aspect, and until his twentieth year lived chiefly in the country. Much of his time was spent at and near Port Jervis, N.Y., and amid the hills of Sullivan County, N.Y., and Sussex County, N.J., and his early writings had to do with such surroundings. He also lived much at Asbury Park, N.J. He was a student at Lafayette College, Easton, Pa., and at Syracuse, N.Y., University. It was not until he had left college and become a professional writer that he visited the Bowery. In his "Maggie"—of which he showed me the first rough draft in MS—he employed Bowery scenes and Bowery dialect, but I never knew him to use Bowery slang in his own conversation.

Again, Mr. Hueffer speaks of him as "the prodigal son of an Episcopalian Bishop." Crane's father, whom I knew very well, was not an Episcopalian, and was not a bishop. He was a minister of the Methodist Episcopal Church, who never rose above the rank of elder.

Mr. Hueffer's article is so interesting and generally authoritative that it would be a pity to have it give permanent currency to these errors.

Very truly yours,

Willis Fletcher Johnson

Source: Willis Fletcher Johnson, "The Launching of Stephen Crane," *Literary Digest International Book Review* 4 (1926): 288–90.

A fate resembling that of Edgar Allan Poe seems to be threatening Stephen Crane. During his life he was strangely misjudged and misrepresented, and since his death he has been alternately the object of aspersions and of adulation of an extravagant and unwarranted character. Some of the determining incidents of his early career, especially, have been grotesquely falsified. In these circumstances it is not surprising that people are beginning to speak of the "legend" and the "myth" of Stephen Crane; particularly since the appearance of two recent publications in which injurious misrepresentations of him appear.

One of these is the somewhat elaborate critical biography by Mr. Thomas Beer, with an introduction by the late Joseph Conrad. The other is a biographical sketch by Mr. Max J. Herzberg, President of the Stephen Crane Association, prefacing a fine new edition of Crane's chief work, "The Red Badge of Courage."[55] The appearance, following these, of a complete and presumably definitive edition of Crane's writings makes it seem fitting to correct some of the errors which do grave injustice to Crane himself as well as to others who, like himself, have now passed beyond the power of self-defense.

I shall not be so fatuous as to attempt to dispel the entire fog of fiction with which Stephen Crane has been surrounded. There is a folly against which even the gods strive in vain. But at least I may put on record the facts, especially concerning that one salient incident which proved the turning-point in his work, and which has persistently been exploited in versions wantonly untrue. I refer to the publication of his first tales of fiction, the incident which turned him from news-reporting to book-writing, and the creation of his two most characteristic and most meritorious volumes. Of these things I am able to say, with Aeneas, that all of them I saw, and if not a great at least a material part of them I was, since practically all of that early work of his was done under my direction and was published under my editing. .

Crane's first writing for publication and for pay was done in the summer of 1888, in a very small and unnoticed way; when he assisted his elder brother, J. Townley Crane, Jr., in reporting the news of Long Branch, Asbury Park and the adjacent resorts on the New Jersey coast for the *New York Tribune*. His work was so unimportant that his brother, who paid him for it out of his own pocket, did not inform the office of it, but sent Stephen's news in and collected space-rate pay for it as tho it were his own. The same arrangement continued through the next two summer seasons, tho in 1890 J. Townley Crane explained to the office that his "kid brother" was assisting him. I should add that during this entire period, and for some years thereafter, I was the day editor of the *Tribune*, and had all such news-correspondence under my direct and sole charge.

The next step was in the fall of 1890, when I engaged Stephen as the *Tribune*'s correspondent at Syracuse University, whither he had gone as a student. His work at Asbury Park had convinced me that he was competent for the job; besides, I felt a warm personal interest in both of the Crane boys on account of my former friendship with their father.[56] There was, of course, no room for "fine writing" in brief college news-items; but Stephen did employ words and phrases which indicated the possession of an imaginative and impressionistic mind.

Thus far I had not seen Stephen since his early childhood. But the summer of 1891 was spent by me at Asbury Park, and as the hotel at which I lived was a chief rendezvous for newspaper correspondents, I saw him there almost daily. He was at first shy and diffident; and one day Townley told me that Stephen had some writings that he would like to have me see, but was afraid to speak to me himself about them. So I sent for the boy, reminded him of my friendship with his father and other members of the family, and told him that I should be glad to see anything he had written, to talk with him about his work at any time, and to give him the benefit of any advice which my experience might suggest.

The writings which he then wanted to show me were two stories, of about two thousand words each. They were fantastic and impressionistic fiction sketches, which he had conceived while he was visiting another of his brothers at Port Jervis, N.Y., and their scenes were set, not as some have said, in Pike County, nor as others have said, in the Wyoming Valley, but amid the picturesque hills of Sullivan County, N.Y. I was very favorably imprest by them and told him so, and at once accepted them for use in the Sunday supplement of the *Tribune*. They, and a number more, were printed in that newspaper in 1891 and 1892, and attracted much flattering attention.[57] I have always thought that "Four Men in a Cave," printed in the *Tribune* in 1892, was one of the best pieces of writing that Stephen ever did.

One day in the summer of 1891 he brought me a big bundle of manuscript, and asked me to read it and tell him what to do with it. I found it to be not a Sullivan County sketch, but a tale of the slums of New York; the first draft of "Maggie: A Girl of the Streets."[58] It was in some respects crude, but powerful and impressive. Three features were conspicuous. One was the writer's mastery of the speech and manners of the denizens of New York slums, altho he had spent little time in that city and had enjoyed little opportunity for observation of its ways.[59] The second was the throbbing vitality and dynamics of the story; every line seemed alive and active. And the third was, despite the stark brutality and astounding frankness of it, the absolute lack of prurience, of erotic suggestiveness, of the "sex-motive," which nowadays dominates so much of our fiction. Compared, let us say, with the novels of Hall Caine,[60] which I mention because they were just then in great vogue, "Maggie" seemed almost Puritanical. The notion that it was "obscene" was grotesque in its silliness. Its chief fault was in that exuberance and extravagance of adjectives which Stephen never was able wholly to outgrow.

I told him that the book, with some revision, would be worth publishing, and ought to be successful. But I warned him that it would be difficult to find a reputable publisher who would dare to bring it out; and that if it were published it would so shock the Podsnaps and Mrs. Grundys as to bring upon him a storm of condemnation.[61] At that he suggested that in order not to compromise his future it might be well to print it under an assumed name; and he discust the same point also with Mr. Post Wheeler,[62] then a leading New York journalist, and with some others. The outcome was that he put upon the title page the name of "Johnston Smith," suggested by the two names which were most numerous in the city directory—he first made it "Johnson Smith," but finally inserted the "t" in the former name, in order that, as he whimsically explained to me when he told me of it, neither Mr. Podsnap nor Mrs. Grundy might suspect him of being the guilty author!

The crux was to find a publisher. The book was quite "out of the line" of the house which had produced my books,[63] and there was no use in trying it. The man whom I knew best in the New York publishing trade was my very dear friend and former colleague, Ripley Hitchcock, then literary adviser of D. Appleton & Co.; so I sent Stephen to him.[64] He appreciated the merits of the book, but hesitated to recommend its acceptance. He told me, however, that "That boy has the real stuff in him," and a few years later eagerly accepted for publication Stephen's next work, "The Red Badge of Courage." Other publishers were no more hospitable to "Maggie." Richard Watson Gilder read it, regarded it as brutal, and would not print it in *The Century*.[65] Finally Stephen borrowed enough money to print it on his own account—and never got back half of its cost.[66] But he took the book in its printed form to Hamlin Garland,[67] and through him—I think—to William Dean Howells, who entertained him at dinner. They both praised the book and encouraged him to persevere in writing; and I shall never forget the illumination of countenance and exaltation of spirit which he displayed when he came to tell me of his interviews with them.

At this time he was also greatly engaged with "The Red Badge of Courage"; not so much on paper as in his own mind. He spoke frequently of its hero as "growing."[68] "He's getting to be quite a character now," he said one day; just as a fond parent would say "My Johnny is getting to be quite a big boy." The character was as clear and vital to him, in his mind, as a living person could have been; and it was such conception and development of him that made him, when Stephen finally got him upon paper, appear so marvelously real. And the same gift which enabled him to put into Maggie the speech and manners of a region and a people with which he was scarcely acquainted, enabled him to portray the actions of war which he had never experienced.

And now I come to the most interesting incident of all, which has never thus far, to my knowledge, been truthfully told. The summer of 1892 was a strenuous one for all of us in the *Tribune* office. Whitelaw Reid, the owner and editor of the paper, was running for the Vice-Presidency of the United States; news of all kinds was phenomenally abundant and taxed our capacity to handle and publish it; and the editorial offices were being remodeled and were in a state of physical confusion. Stephen was busy helping his brother with summer-resort news, and also writing Sullivan County sketches for the *Tribune*. In those years the resort season closed, for news purposes, with Labor Day, the first Monday of September, and on that day in 1892 there was a State-wide gathering of councils of the Junior Order of United American Mechanics at Asbury Park, marked with a great parade, in which thousands of working-men participated.[69]

Some writers have said that this was a parade of strikers, which is absolutely false. Mr. Thomas Beer in his biography of Crane says that it was a Harrison and Reid political campaign parade, which is equally inaccurate. Says Mr. Beer: "These good men lugged banners praising Harrison and Reid, and Crane, looking at the motion of this spectacle, forgot that Reid owned the *New York Tribune*. He merely saw a number of sweating persons who mostly worked with their hands, marching on behalf of capital, and the thing amused him."[70]

Practically every statement and suggestion in that passage is erroneous. The men did not carry a single banner praising or in any way referring to Harrison and Reid. They were not "marching on behalf of capital," but in behalf of their own Order. Crane did not forget that Reid owned the *Tribune*, and he was not "amused" by the spectacle. Neither did he, as Mr. Herzberg says, report it "in humorous style."[71] But what did happen was this: In impressionistic style he pointed out the contrast between the marchers, clad in plain and often ill-fitting "store clothes," and showing in gait and bearing familiarity with the work-shop and farm rather than with the ballroom and promenade, and, on the other hand, the fashionable idlers and pleasure-seekers, arrayed like Solomon in his glory, who patronizingly and often sneeringly gazed upon them from the hotel piazzas; and he trenchantly suggested, with irony and sarcasm, that the marching workmen were the really "worth-while" figures in the scene, of far more account than the spectators.

It was a clever paragraph. But unluckily it was susceptible of garbling and misrepresentation, and it was instantly seized upon and thus treated by the papers opposed to Reid's candidacy, which made it appear to be intended to make fun of and insult the workingmen. Such distortion was nothing less than a wilful and malicious lie, and was one of the most unscrupulous performances in a campaign that was characterized by entirely too much "mud-slinging." But it was probably accepted as true by many who had not seen the article itself, and for some days created a great sensation.

I have mentioned Mr. Thomas Beer's error in calling that a Harrison and Reid parade. Far worse is one of Mr. Herzberg's statements. Let me quote his exact words: "The news item, it is alleged, caused great indignation among some of the readers of the paper and turned them against the ticket. New York State, the vote of which decided the election that year, was carried by Cleveland by about a thousand votes. Hence, argue those who recite the story, Stephen Crane was responsible for making Cleveland President of the United States."[72]

Now for the facts. Cleveland carried New York that year not merely by "about a thousand votes," but by far more than forty-five thousand votes. The vote of New York did not "decide the election that year," for Cleveland received 277 electoral votes out of 444, and as only 223 were required to elect, he would have won by a margin of 18 even if New York had gone against him. Finally, that election did not for the first time "make Cleveland President," for he had been elected President eight years before.

One more error needs placing in the pillory; namely, that Stephen was "discharged" from the *Tribune* on account of that news item. He was not discharged.[73] Neither was I, tho I was as much responsible for passing the item and printing it as he was for writing it. Whitelaw Reid was, of course, much interested in the matter, especially as he did not see the original article, but only the garbled exploitation of it. He at once asked me for the facts in the case. I gave them, showing him the item as it was really published; and that was the end of the case, so far as he was concerned. Stephen was much agitated over it, and came to me to know what he should do, or what would be done to him. My reply was, nothing. The responsibility rested upon me, not upon him. But I "improved the occasion" with two suggestions. One was, that ordinary news reporting was not a good place for subtle rhetorical devices. The other was that a man who could write "Four Men in a Cave" ought not to waste his time reporting that "The Flunkey-Smiths of Squedunk are at the Gilded Pazaza Hotel for the season."

That was, as I have said, the end of the season, and there was no more resort-news wanted until next year; so Stephen stopt his reporting, as he would have done just the same if no such fuss had been raised over the item. But he continued to write occasional articles, especially his Sullivan County tales, for the *Tribune,* until he made an engagement on the staff of another paper.[74] But that episode of the garbled paragraph from Asbury Park caused him more and more to give his attention to book-writing.

Of the other elements of the "Stephen Crane Legend" I trust it is not necessary for me to speak at length. It has been said that he was a "dope-fiend," that he never could write unless under the influence of drugs or liquor, and other drivel of the same sort. Stephen was an almost incessant smoker, but in drinks I never knew him to take anything stronger than beer, and that always in moderation.[75] I knew him for a considerable time, when he was doing some of his best work, about as intimately as any of his associates, and I have no reason to think that he was ever intoxicated or under the influence of any drugs. He has suffered overmuch from blame which he did not deserve, and also from extravagant exploitation beyond his real deserts. This has doubtless been in large measure because of his own temperament. He was in an exceptional degree sensitive, and, like most sensitive persons, introspective, self-contained, reserved, even secretive. Few people ever really knew him, and many people are prone to misjudge those whom they are not permitted to know. But his place is secure as a youth of extraordinary promise and of some brilliant achievements, whose early death was a sore loss to the world of letters.

8 / Helen R. Crane

Helen R. Crane (1889–?), daughter of Wilbur Crane, used her middle initial "R." to avoid confusion with her cousin Mary Helen Crane, William Howe Crane's daughter who also went by Helen. According to a reprint of the reminiscence (*Asbury Park Press,* 7 January 1934, p. 3), Helen R. Crane was "a newspaper woman on the Pacific Coast" when she wrote the reminiscence. It angered the Crane family and was the first public statement about Cora Taylor's background as a madam in Jacksonville, Florida.[76] It also gives important information about Crane's time in Havana in fall 1898.

Source: Helen R. Crane, "My Uncle, Stephen Crane," *American Mercury* 31 (January 1934): 24–29.

A youth whom men later come to look upon as a genius may not have attracted any special attention in his family. His brothers and sisters may be the last persons in the world to note his gifts; if they happen to be many years older, married, and engrossed in their own children, he probably always remains much of an outsider to them.

It was like that with Stephen Crane. He created no furore whatever in his family, except by being born so tardily. The Reverend Jonathan Townley Crane's parsonage was for a time all agog because it had been such a long while since a baby had appeared there, but things soon quieted down, and after that Stephen brought upon himself no more interest than babies generally do.

Stories are told everywhere about how his brothers watched over the budding flower of his art (his father died in his early childhood and his mother during his first year in Syracuse University), how they guided his uncertain, faltering footsteps with encouraging words, beefsteaks, and dollars.

The truth is that they did many things for him when they thought about it, for they were all kindly men, but they had their own responsibilities and interests and did not think of it often. It never occurred to them that he was a promising boy: he was merely their younger brother, rather strange and erratic, and a person who, if he mentioned his needs, did so in such a light manner that they did not take him seriously.

Being a Crane he was born with printers' ink in his veins, and therefore it was not surprising that he should run a column of gossip in the *New York Tribune* while he was at the university.[77] Since the age of fifteen or sixteen he had been writing for newspapers, contributing to his mother's *Tribune* column, and covering certain affairs for his brother Townley who was with the Associated Press.[78] His brother Wilbur was also on the *Tribune,* and sometimes he had written stuff for him. No one thought anything about these activities; they were the same as the rest of the family's.

Thomas Beer and some others would give the impression that the dark, hungry days of the young author of "The Red Badge of Courage," before fame came to him, were ones which might have been avoided had he but gone to the ever-open doors of his solicitous brothers in Port Jervis, a few miles from New York.

My father was Wilbur, one of the brothers, and—the saints console his shade!—was as indifferent and unconcerned about Stephen as the others, Townley, Will, and Edmund. He made no pretense of understanding the queer, uncommunicative boy who used to show up at odd times, often in the middle of the night, and after staying with one or another of them for a few days, would disappear in the same wonderful manner.

Father enjoyed talking with him; he enjoyed his marvelous command of English and his sardonic humor, but he felt with the others that the boy was not going to make a success on the papers. Dad joined Will and Edmund in suggesting some other kind of work—perhaps he could fit in somewhere, if he would only make the effort, and if he would only stop fooling away his time on the East Side with that driftwood of humanity! Why did he not try to get a job? But when the conversation had developed this far Stephen turned away—with no ado he was on his way back to New York City and his driftwood on the East Side.

The casual quality of his visits was not the only thing that tried his relatives; there was also his untidiness. His clothes reeked eternally of tobacco and garlic. He did not bother to explain about the house-keeping facilities of the loft on Twenty-third Street, where he was living with a group of struggling young artists,—how they slept on the floor and cooked on a miserable old wood-stove, all in one room.[79] He slept in his clothes half the time—it was too cold to take them off—and they looked it. As for the garlic—his comrades were Bohemians and so garlic was essential to their well-being.

He never had a clean shirt—I am speaking still of those dark days, those days that eventually broke his health and caused his early death,—and most of the time his toes were coming through his shoes "most lamentably," as he expressed it. His old gray ulster would have made quite a satisfactory stable-mop, but was scarcely good for anything else. His hands were finely textured and small, but they were always stained with cigarette yellow, and his hair—that was sailing in the general direction of the last wind.

How could he go up to his brothers' home very often? Will was a respectable small-town lawyer, quite the leading light of Port Jervis, even to singing in the choir. He was painfully respectable. Edmund undoubtedly was respectable too, but he was not so affluent, except in children;[80] and then there was my father who, between children and asthma, never got anywhere in the world. Father had, by the way, temporarily deserted the city in hopes that the mountain-air of Port Jervis would enable him to throw off his asthma, and so, during all that period of Stephen's difficulties, we were in the up-State colony. Will had money, that is, he had what was a comfortable amount for a small-town lawyer in the 90's. With the rest of us it was different; we did not have much, but to compensate for this lack we sheltered ourselves in an exclusiveness which was very satisfactory.

II

It is easy to see how Stephen failed to fit in to the nicely-laundered lives of these relatives. Even discounting his unheralded popping up out of the ground and his want of grooming, there were still his unfortunate views on life, views that did not fit in very well with those held by the "best people" of the town.

For he was by this time in full rebellion against the traditions on which he had been nourished and reared. His mother's memory was dear to him, he had nothing dearer, and although he never questioned her ways when he was outside the family portals, he did marvel always that such an intellectual woman, a university graduate, and capable of being a regular contributor to magazines and newspapers, could have wrapped herself so completely in the "vacuous, futile, psalm-singing that passed for worship" in those days.

His rebellion was a not a quiet one, to be enjoyed by himself alone; he must cry it everywhere; and while he raised no clouds on Broadway with it, the gentle citizenry of Port Jervis were made of sterner stuff—they had a happy acquaintance with the tribal god which was to be unquestioned. A man who was brooding over "Black Riders" could hardly be a companionable soul.

He wilfully and painstakingly went about it to shock them. No power on earth could have dragged him into a church, but the whole social life of the community was founded upon its bulwarks, and escape from it was impossible wherever he went or whomever he saw. The bourgeois complacency of everyone, even of his brothers and their families, goaded him to act in a manner which at times was a bit disconcerting.

His sisters-in-law never knew what he was going to do.[81] There were instances when he behaved very nicely, but there were more when he did not. Sometimes, on being introduced to a socialite, he would assume an East Side accent (which he could do perfectly) and blare forth yarns he had picked up in the night-courts.

My mother and my aunts never got quite used to the idea that he might suddenly interrupt a dinner conversation which was running along smoothly on croup or hats to inquire earnestly if any of the guests had ever seen a Chinaman murdered in Mott street. Nor did they feel any happier when he called attention to his black eye and explained how he had got it in a grand fight on the Bowery.

It was impossible for him to be a social lion, because he could not understand small talk. He could spend hours with Mike Flanagan who drove a beer-truck on the East Side, for Mike's life was so foreign to his own world that all its details were colorful, and he could talk all night with Theodore Roosevelt, Hamlin Garland, or William Dean Howells about the virtues of the Single-Tax[82] or the genius of Flaubert,[83] but when it came to the inanities of ordinary gossip, he was sunk. And he did not get along with young people, the boys and girls of his own age. They thought he was cracked and he thought they were stupid.

When Dad got Stephen alone they had most interesting confabs. He would lay aside his rôle of One in Rebellion and just be himself. He could not talk unless he was walking up and down the room with his hands stuffed into his pockets and a cigarette balanced on his lips.

We never heard him laugh, and former friends of his I have met say the same thing, but he had a charming way of smiling quickly and with his eyes. He was humorously bitter and always kept his hearers laughing and urging him on to say more.

There is no doubt in my mind that my uncle courted hunger and privation. This was before he realized that one may not turn the tap and cut off these unpleasant things at will. He had never known want at home and had no idea it could hurt so much.

When his father died, he left a goodly income to his wife, and at the time of her death this was divided among the six surviving children. Much of the inheritance was in the form of coal stock in Pennsylvania mines, and Will, the lawyer, being more affluent than his brothers, bought up their shares for a very low figure. Stephen's were among these.[84] He received a little money as down payment and hied himself immediately to a poker-table, and that was that.

The period of starvation followed—a period which lasted for three years, until lifted by the phenomenal success of "The Red Badge." During this period he published "Maggie: A Girl of the Streets" at his own expense with money Will gave him—most of it the last payment on his stock and a little bit on loan.[85]

Thomas Beer says that Will kindly loaned him this money but,[86]—well, anyway, Stephen, like my father, sold shares for a meagre sum which are still, forty years later, supporting members of the family and probably will go on doing so for a long time to come.

Most of "Maggie" was written at our house in two or three nights. It did not sell very well, and I remember playing over yellow piles of copies in our attic.[87] What happened to them I do not know, but Mother, like the rest of the family, had no respect for them, and I presume she burned them sometime when a house-cleaning spell came upon her.[88]

III

I said a while back that Stephen's rebellion did not raise any clouds on Broadway: that is not wholly correct, of course. It did raise clouds but they were the kind that brought him fame; so if we must stick by our metaphor we will say that Broadway saw the light beyond and Port Jervis saw only dust.

Stephen did not change after fame came. He moved into better quarters, had more to eat, and wore decent clothes. He made plenty of money but never seemed to have much of it, for he gave it away to his East Side friends and he was always playing poker.

We never believed the story that went the rounds of the clubs in New York about the country girl he lured into the primrose path and then abandoned to the streets. He was laconic and brief but not secretive, and would not have lied about his behavior. I can't imagine him lying about anything. In fact, he was the kind of person who would have got a great thrill out of being shot at sunrise and all that sort of thing. He said there was nothing to the story and we believed him. So far as we knew he never had a real love affair. He had many romances, for he appealed much to women, but a great love eluded him.

It was when he went to Florida in 1897 for the Bacheller Syndicate to write up the filibustering expeditions into Cuba that he met Cora Taylor, who later became his wife. In Jacksonville in those days there were many luxurious houses of joy—beautifully appointed clubs they were, where all the men about town and visitors went to gossip and drink and, if it so pleased them, to pass the time of day with the fair ladies who lived there.

There was one famous house, the most exclusive of them all, and it was run by Cora Taylor. Stephen met her there and, according to all reports, she fell for him on first sight. She knew he was famous, but many famous men came to her place and so that was nothing: it was the man himself that she loved. A few days after their meeting he was in the *Commodore* adventure and nearly drowned, and while he was laid up for a time recuperating she went to see him regularly and became more and more enamoured.

Stephen wrote my father about the sinking of the *Commodore*.[89] He seldom wrote letters and probably would not have written this one if he had not been bored to desperation by having to stay in his room and nurse a cold that threatened to turn into pneumonia. Father was a champion swimmer and canoeist when he was in Columbia University, and he had helped Stephen learn to swim and paddle, so now the latter wanted to explain that doing those things for fun was one thing, and spending two nights and a day in an open boat with "barbariously abrupt waves"[90] leering at you with every breath you drew was an entirely different one.

He pointed out that he had always loved the water, but remarked that he doubted whether it would interest him in the future. When he sent that letter he apparently had no intention of writing "Open Boat," at least he did not mention it. He did not speak of Cora in this letter, nor in any subsequent one, until he announced his marriage to her later on when he was in Greece.[91]

She followed him over there. From Jacksonville he went back to New York, and then William Randolph Hearst asked him to go to Greece to cover the Balkan War. Before he sailed he spent a few days in Port Jervis,[92] and he said then that his "equatorial zone" was causing him considerable unrest. I am sure he had tuberculosis in his lungs before he went a-filibustering, and that the experience caused the infection to spread to his intestines.[93]

Poor Mr. Hearst made a bad bargain when he sent my uncle to Greece, for he became so ill that he was good for nothing, and his work as a war correspondent was quite a flop.[94] Cora Taylor learned of this further illness of his and, selling her house in Jacksonville, went to Greece.[95] She was several years older than he and was very motherly in her manner. She nursed him until he was able to leave his bed, and then he married her.

He wrote home an embarrassed, self-conscious letter telling what he had done, but he never mentioned her romantic life. Other correspondents, however, who had been in Jacksonville and knew her, were quick to spread the story. The whole truth has not been published before—only whispered with many beautiful and tasty embellishments. But no one who whispered these things bothered to tell how good she was to Stephen, or that her care unquestionably prolonged his life a couple of years.

After their marriage they went to live in England, and when the Spanish-American War broke out he left her there and rushed to Havana for the Bacheller Syndicate.[96] Then the story that he was lost flashed throughout the United States and Europe, and Cora went almost crazy. His brothers suddenly realized that he was an extraordinarily nice kid, and they started routing editors out of bed, and consuls, too. The American Ambassador cabled to Washington and Washington cabled to everybody. Finally, the British Foreign Office took it up, and its consul in Havana, Lucien Jerome, found Stephen. He was hiding away at Mary Horan's house, doing some writing.[97]

Stephen told us all about it later when he came back to New York. It seems that Bertram Marburgh of Leslie's Syndicate had never met the famous author of "The Red Badge," but he had heard he was in town. One day, when all the correspondents foregathered at the American Bar, Matthews and Nichols of the *American* told Marburgh that Crane was lost, had perhaps been done away with by the people who did not like newspaper publicity. Marburgh immediately sent the news back home.

Now, the attention of the Leslie man had been attracted for weeks before this to a mysterious slight figure in a white suit that used to slink along the street around eleven o'clock every night near the house where he was stopping. He had no idea who the man might be or why he was furtively dodging the lights about the same time every night.

The story soon appeared in print and created a good deal of excitement around Havana. Crane was found, but still Marburgh did not meet him until one evening, when he was sitting in the American Bar, this mysterious white figure came in and sat down alongside of him. They began talking and the Leslie man offered his name. "I'm Stephen Crane," said his new acquaintance. Marburgh apologized for what he had done and Stephen explained that "certain dignified and venerable Ambassadors, not to mention a few Cranes, had been sorely upset by the news."

This Mary Horan, in whose house Stephen was found, was a well-known character in Havana. She was a huge Irish-woman who ran a small boarding-house and bullied the men, and when any of them were ill, nursed them as she would her own children. My uncle shut himself up there in her place for forty days and nights to do a piece of writing. I don't know what it was, but it was something he was anxious to get done and out of the way.

Mary did not approve of his long hours of work, and she used to go in and hover over him with a great tray of food. "I don't want to eat, please go away." "Go away, me eye, you're goin' to eat this if I have to feed it to you spoon by spoon!" And Stephen ate. It was she who made him go for a walk every night about eleven. She came into his room, pulled the chair out from under him and drove him bodily into the street. This woman became quite famous for her care of the American boys, Dick Little of the *Chicago Tribune* being one of those she nursed during a serious illness. But Stephen was one of the first to live at her house and he was alone there—that was how he got "lost."

After Stephen's death in Germany in 1900 Cora was crushed for a time. She had no money, and so she went back to Jacksonville to her old trade.

Someone told us that she was doing it to support her two sons. I think that was just another rumor. Stephen Crane never had any children.

$\backsim$

9 / Edna Crane Sidbury

Edna Crane Sidbury (1886–1927) was one of five daughters of William Howe Crane. Her reminiscence is an affectionate portrayal of the relationship between Crane and his nieces, and it offers convincing evidence that Port Jervis is the setting for Crane's Whilomville stories.

Source: Edna Crane Sidbury, "My Uncle, Stephen Crane, as I Knew Him," *Literary Digest International Book Review* 4 (1926): 248–50.

I can not remember a time when I did not know my Uncle Stephen, but my memories of him begin around the year 1895. We lived at that time in the town of Port Jervis, New York, a pleasant place of less than 10,000 inhabitants.

Our grandfather, Jonathan Townley Crane, brought his family there in 1879,[98] and it was there that Stephen, a lad of eight, went to school for the first time.[99] Grandfather was the pastor of the Methodist Church, a dignified, kindly man, and the father of fourteen children. These children sometimes seriously compromised his dignity, as when two of them appeared in the church aisle one Sunday morning, waving a rat-trap and crying: "Here it is, Father. You said to bring it to you as soon as we found it." Another time, he gracefully shook out a folded handkerchief in the face of his congregation, to find, to his horror, that it was a child's undershirt. He had a great sense of humor, and was so noted for it that a movement was once made to publish a book of his witticisms.

Grandmother Crane, who was Mary Helen Peck, descendant of a long line of New Jersey ministers, herself a graduate of the College of the City of New York,[100] was a woman of great ambition, public spirited, devoted to intellectual pursuits, able to sketch well in pen and ink,[101] and the Lord showered her with children. In spite of a handicap which would have proved insurmountable to most women, she succeeded in doing really valuable work for the W.C.T.U.

My father, William Howe Crane, settled in Port Jervis with my mother and sister Helen in 1882. Four of his five daughters were born there, and two now lie in Evergreen Cemetery at the end of the town. One died as an infant, while Helen, who was with Uncle Stephen when he died, lived only a year after she assisted in the unveiling of the tablet placed to his memory upon the front of the Newark Public Library.[102]

We children would have remembered Uncle Stephen well if he had never written a word, for we never had a more charming playmate.[103] Whole mornings he spent chasing us around, we a band of lawbreakers, he a "red-headed police-man," to the scandal of the neighbors, who did not approve of a young man in his twenties so disporting himself. He was so entirely one of us, that when some one told me that he had written a book which was making him famous— "The Red Badge of Courage"—I had to laugh. Uncle Stevie famous? It was a joke.

Years later, upon reading his "Whilomville Stories," it became clear that he was studying us while we frolicked together, for Whilomville was Port Jervis, and many of the expressions we used are to be found in those stories. How well he describes the band concerts (they are still being given at the same old stand), the boys of fourteen and over standing by the sidewalks watching the girls go by in twos and threes, the smaller boys using football tactics and hurling themselves against the affectionately linked girls. Sometimes a young man, bold by nature or made bold by love, joins one of the girls. Then her companions leave them, and they walk around the square together.

Father was Dr. Trescott in the Whilomville stories (he always claimed that the characterization flattered him), and we and our friends and cousins helped to supply the material for them. We were an active, healthy band of savages, keen as briars, father says, out-of-doors all day, and receiving a boy's training. There are memories of Stephen Crane's own not-so-far-distant boyhood in those stories. We see him in little Jimmy Trescott when he shot the cow.[104] He himself tried to shoot a cow with a toy gun my father gave him.[105] From Port Jervis he also got the idea for "The Monster." A certain man there had his face eaten by cancer. He used to haul ashes, and we children often met him with his cart, as we drove around town with our pony. He was an object of horror to us, for it could truthfully be said of him, "He had no face." One day I mentioned him to my father, and he told me that there is where the idea of "The Monster" originated.[106]

But my uncle did not spend every morning capturing us after a desperate chase and locking us up in the closet under the stairs. There were times when he donned his white flannel "pants" and went out bent upon social activities. We greatly admired the "pants," which we considered the height of sartorial elegance. They started out immaculate each time, and came back badly grass-stained after his games of tennis. We were deeply jealous of the vague young ladies who were entertaining our playmate and keeping him from us.

Then there were days when he sat at the end of the front porch in a large wicker chair almost screened from sight by a syringa bush, and wrote. Such a stupid waste of time, when he could be playing with us! Our mother gave us strict injunctions to leave him alone, but I am sorry to say that I remember sneaking around by the bow-window and saying:

"Ah, Uncle Stevie, come on and play."

"Go away now, Ed, I'm busy."

Crushed, I went. He never talked to us like that excepting when he was writing, or had his white pants on. At no other time would we think of minding him. Any other time he was ready to lay down book or pipe at our invitation to play. There behind the syringa bush, he was writing "The Third Violet." Our old setter, Chester, is fully described in that book. It would seem impossible that the people of Port Jervis could call back recollections of us children without thinking of Chester. He was a pedigreed English setter, took many blue ribbons in his time, and was our constant companion and protector for ten years. I dare say that Uncle Stephen had him in mind when he insisted to Joseph Conrad that every boy should have a dog.[107] When Chester was a pup, father was teaching him to lie down at the command, "Charge!" One of his brothers began to quote:

"Charge, Chester, charge!

On, Stanley, on!"

Thereupon the dog was named Chester, and when he appears in "The Third Violet," he is called Stanley. He was a dog with a soul, and I am sure has been in heaven all these many years.

My uncle was very popular with the young people in our town. He went upon camping trips with the other young "bobcats,"[108] to use his own expression, and young ladies came frequently to play croquet upon our front lawn. We were not permitted to join in these games, although we were willing, so retired to the back porch and made "lemonade" for our beloved uncle, so that he could not quite forget our existence. We took any seasonable small fruit and crushed it in a sieve, allowing the juices to run into a silver mug—we could not break that—then added sugar, water and ice, and bore it out to refresh his spirits. I think that all the children in the neighborhood who were about my age assisted in making the concoction. We took turns presenting it. When it was my turn, I would wait until he had played, then go up to him.

"Uncle Stevie, here is some lemonade we made you."

"Thanks," he would say, tossing off the innocuous beverage.

"How was it?" I would ask hopefully, for we worked hard making it, and thought it delicious.

"Out of sight," he always answered, and I left perfectly satisfied. The rest of the children would be waiting for me around the corner of the house.

"How did he like it?"

"He said it was out of sight."

And we made him suffer in other ways. They made bread at our house, and on rainy days we would beg pieces of the dough. These we kneaded until they were streaked with grime from our unwashed hands, then baked until hard and dry, and later presented to father and Uncle Stephen as especial marks of our favor. They never had a chance to renege in the eating of it, as we always stood by and watched them enjoy it. One day when my uncle had been presented with a particularly streaked sample of our culinary art, my mother, watching him making away with it, said:

"Stephen, how can you?"

And he made answer, "Why, I wouldn't hurt their feelings for the world."

Is it any wonder we loved him and haunted his footsteps?

In the year 1921, when memorial services were held in Newark in commemoration of the fiftieth anniversary of his birth, many of the speakers touched upon the hardships he suffered in the city of New York, stating that at times he went hungry. We—my sister Helen, Cousin Agnes Post, and I—denied that there was any truth in it, and thought it but another of the romances told about him. But later in the evening, listening to the men who had known him best at that time, we had to believe. We still wonder why he went through such experiences, when he was always so very welcome at both our house and Uncle Edmund's. Perhaps he was seeking his own "Experience in Misery" (the title of one of his Bowery tales),[109] although doubtless it came also through his desire to make his own way independently.

My mother and Mrs. Edmund Crane were very fond of him. They both knew him as a lad of ten or twelve, and regarded him more as a brother than as a brother-in-law. My mother had as much faith in his literary ability as did my father, and was always glad to see him, in spite of the fact that he used to smoke in bed and burn holes in her sheets. It speaks volumes for his personality that he could still be popular with my mother in spite of such heinous habits. Many were the tales I heard him unfold to her on the porch on a summer evening, or by the sitting-room stove in cold weather. It is unfortunate that my interests were in the stories as stories, and I never questioned whether he was telling tales he had heard, recounting his own experiences, or telling us a story he had made up. I will repeat one of the stories. My impression is that the incident occurred upon one of the camping trips in Sullivan County.

Four young men were camping in a little cabin in the woods. It may be that they were two of the Senger boys, Fred Lawrence and Stephen Crane.[110] One day, one of them was shaving by the aid of a small mirror propped against a beam. Suddenly the mirror fell and disappeared down one of the wide cracks in the floor. Muttering imprecations, he took up one of the loose boards and felt around in the darkness under the cabin. Suddenly he gave a horrified yell, which startled the others greatly.

"A snake bit me on the hand!"

The others rushed to him, and sure enough, a tiny drop of blood was oozing from an abrasion on his hand. They laid the injured youth upon a cot. One cauterized the wound with a hot poker, another plied him with whiskey, that time-honored cure for "snake-bite," while the fourth ran around and knocked things over in an attempt to be useful. It was of no avail. The patient was failing rapidly, as in faltering tones he gave them the last messages to his family. His friends stood around him gloomily; then one spoke up.

"Well, as we can't do anything more for poor old—, I, for one, want a whack at that snake."

"Me too!" chorused the others, their pale faces flushing with resolution. Arming themselves with suitable weapons, they lowered a lantern under the cabin and all gazed intently down the opening, clutching their weapons. Then one gave a yell.

"B'Gosh, it's a setting hen!"

The others gave a look, and began to laugh hysterically. The pallid youth upon the couch, who had been giving a noble exhibition of how a brave man can die, suddenly became very drunk. I can still hear my uncle say:

"The funny thing about it, Cornelia,[111] was that when he thought a snake had bit him, he was as sober as a judge."

If you have heard it before, please accept my apologies. I heard him tell it many years ago.

Then Uncle Stephen went away. It was to a foreign country, either Mexico or Greece, but there is no place on this globe as far away as that place seemed to me. I wrote him a letter and he replied, but he made an unfortunate remark, and our correspondence ceased. It is strange that one who knew children so well should make such a *faux pas*. It must have been in an absent-minded moment that he wrote that I was a "poor correspondent."

"What is a correspondent?" I asked my mother.

"One who writes letters," she made answer.

"So he says I am a poor letter-writer?" I asked. And I had taken such pains with the letters, too.

My mother tried to explain, but it was no use. I wrote no more.

But I had forgiven him when he came back and paid us a short visit.[112] He had acquired a mustache, and it improved his appearance considerably, we all thought. He had more stories to tell, and we listened eagerly until we were sent off to bed.

Then another time he came to see us and brought Mr. Corwin Knapp Linson.[113] The latter delighted our hearts by drawing for the three youngest of us, paper-dolls, a smiling face on one side and a crying face on the other. It was very convenient to be able to make our children stop crying by simply turning them over. I have often wished since—but that does not belong in this article. We were very sorry to see them go away.

I believe that is the last time I ever saw him. He married, settled in England, and later wrote and asked my father to allow Helen to visit him and his wife.[114] She was the eldest, and always a great favorite with him. After a great deal of indecision, it was decided that she should go. What great preparations were made! A dressmaker came and stayed for weeks, and made her many wonderful dresses, which later she was to learn, from Cora Crane, were all wrong. At the steamer, father gave her, as a surprise, a Columbia chainless bicycle, for which he paid the fabulous sum of $100. In England, she got in much difficulty with it by riding on the right side of the road instead of the left.

Remembering Stephen Crane with the affection we do, one can imagine how the unkind gossip about him hurt us. People held that as he used "swear words" in his books, he must naturally be profane, not at all the proper companion for little children. Yet none of us ever heard him swear. I am sure that, had he done so, we would have remembered it, as we were not used to hearing strong language. It is amusing to realize that the language which so shocked his contemporaries could be used to-day in a Broadway play without causing the audience to quiver an eyelash. It takes stronger medicine to shock them to-day than any Crane ever used in his books.

My mother tells me that often he would have manuscripts returned by publishers who said: "Take the swear words out of it, and we will publish it."[115] His reply was unvarying: "I can't, as that is how such men talk." He had a passion for truth, and felt that to make such a change would not be sincere; his writings must be sincere if he nearly starved in the meantime. As he wrote to one of his publishers: "To keep close to this personal honesty is my supreme ambition."[116]

When Mrs. Edmund Crane was asked by Thomas Beer for her recollections about Stephen Crane, to be used in his biography, she, not knowing the sympathetic treatment he was to receive at the hands of Mr. Beer, gave her information reluctantly. She did this out of loyalty to his memory. She had been grieved for years because of the falsehoods told about him, his blasphemies and drunkenness, so made answer: "The Stephen Crane I knew is not the Stephen Crane you write about." Few people knew him better than she, for he spent a great deal of time at her house and wrote "The Red Badge of Courage" while under her roof.[117]

Recently the Stephen Crane Association was formed in Newark, the city where he was born. A scholarship has been planned for young and promising writers, to be called the Stephen Crane Scholarship. It would seem especially appropriate that young writers should be encouraged in his name, as he never lived to be anything but a young writer himself, as he lacked four months[118] of being twenty-nine when he died.

The more the world learns about Stephen Crane, the more clearly will it see him as we knew and loved him, and not as some of his contemporaries choose to paint him.

〜

10 / Anna E. Wells

Anna E. Wells (?–?) was an acquaintance of Crane who met him in Port Jervis through her friend Agnes Lawrence, whose brother was Frederic M. Lawrence (No. 22). Her father was one of the owners of land at Twin Lakes near Milford in Pike County, Pennsylvania, where Crane and his friends camped during the summers between 1891 and 1895 or 1896. She later became children's librarian in the Poughkeepsie Public Library in New York.

Source: Anna E. Wells, "Reminiscences of Stephen Crane," typescript, 6 pp., R. W. Stallman Collection, University of Connecticut Library, Storrs, Conn.[119]

. . . Among Fred's friends was a young man whom Agnes spoke of as "Stevie" and of whom she seemed very fond. One day we came in from school and saw a group of Fred's friends on the porch engaged in a lively discussion. Naturally we were curious as to what the big boys were talking about. We stood nearby, listening eagerly and to our astonishment found that they were talking about *Alice in Wonderland*. We looked at each other and said disdainfully, "Why they are talking about a child's book! We read that long ago!"

Agnes pointed out one boy as Stevie Crane and said he liked books as much as we did.

He was slender, pale and had the look of a student. Though quiet, he seemed to have a real following among these young people. He sometimes came over to Port Jervis from Middletown and stayed at the Lawrences or went to Hartwood where he had a brother. . . .

[Wells recalled an anecdote involving Crane at Twin Lakes one summer.]

It was necessary to walk a couple of miles each morning for the day's supply of milk, chicken, eggs and vegetables. This meant an early start so the hungry campers could have milk with their morning cereal.

One morning, two of our party passed through Camp Interlaken on their way to the farmers for milk and found Stephen Crane stretched out on the ground near the embers of the camp fire with his head in a wooden box, just in case of rain!

Fearing that an infrequent horse and wagon might be going through and might not see him in the darkness they roused him. He laughed and said he enjoyed sleeping outside the tents and assured us that the teams made such a noise on the terribly stony road that he always heard them in plenty of time to roll out of danger. . . .

2
School and College

11 / Abram Lincoln Travis

Abram Lincoln Travis (?–?) attended Claverack College and Hudson River Institute and Syracuse University with Crane. After graduating from Syracuse, he taught at Claverack for a year and later established the Travis Classical School in Syracuse.

Source: Abram Lincoln Travis, "Recollections of Stephen [*sic*] Crane," MS, 4 pp., with cover letter to Mansfield French, 20 March 1930, Alumni Folder, Special Collections Research Center, Syracuse University Library.[1]

It was back in 1887–88 that Stephen Crane and I happened to be in preparatory school together—The Hudson River Institute at Claverack, N.Y.[2] "Steve" as he was generally known by his school fellows was a friendly boy and was generally liked by all except some of his teachers from whose classes he was generally absent.

Baseball and lawn tennis were practically all the school athletic sports of those days. "Steve" was a devoted follower of baseball and frequently his presence on the diamond accounted for his absence from class. He enjoyed tennis but did not seem fascinated by it.

In the later eighties, baseball teams were not equipped as they are today with suits made to the occasion and protection of the face, chest and body from the on-coming sphere. Usually the individual player selected his own suit so the diamond frequently presented an appearance of Joseph in the Bible days with his coat of many colors. These things did not daunt Stephen however, for he played the game because he liked it.

The year he was captain of the baseball team, his boys made an excellent record winning seven out of nine games played. Crane was catcher all the season and a boy named Van Horn assisted by one named Locke pitched in all the games. In more than half the games played "Steve" caught the ball in bare hand and it was not until the season was well advanced that he secured a heavy buckskin glove which he used effectively and so saved much iodine and witch hazel which he had before used.

Our friend was an inveterate smoker of cigarettes whether in his sports or at his studies, he was always smoking as his nicotine fingers would witness.

Although Crane was not an all around student, yet he was far in advance of his fellow students in his knowledge of History and Literature.[3] He preferred these subjects and always seemed glad to enter the Regents examination in them as he was sure of passing with a fine marque. If he passed in Mathematics or Science, it would be by some power other than Crane. He was a prodigious reader of all the nineteenth-century English writers and reveled in the classics of Greece and Rome. *Plutarch's Lives* was his constant companion and even at this age he was familiar with the English and American poets. He would frequently quote from Tennyson's "In Memoriam" and Bryant's "Thanatopsis."

Crane began his literary career while at the Hudson River Institute. He spent his summer vacations along the New Jersey coast and reported regularly to the *New York Tribune* under the caption of "Avon by the Sea."

Like many boys whose early life has been spent in New York City, Crane became familiar with the police procedure of that great city. This led him while in preparatory school to write *Maggie: A Girl of the Streets.*[4] He could not get any publishers to print this manuscript. However after the phenomenal success of his *Red Badge of Courage* publishers were eager to publish the manuscript before rejected by them.

After graduating from the Hudson River Institute, Crane entered Lafayette College so we did not see each other again until we met as students in Syracuse University to which Crane had transferred from Lafayette.

⤳

12 / Harvey Wickham

Harvey Wickham (?–?), who grew up near Crane in Middletown, N.Y., was his schoolmate at Claverack College and Hudson River Institute and later became a professional musician. Though Wickham disliked Crane's bohemianism, his reminiscence contains incisive comments on Crane's rebellious and contradictory nature.

Source: Harvey Wickham, "Stephen Crane at College," *American Mercury* 7 (March 1926): 291–97.

It was at Claverack College, New York, the year that Browning died. On answering a knock at my door I discovered two youths, both blond and very amiable looking, one dressed in the height of collegiate fashion, the other in a dirty old sweater and wearing a whimsical, wistful expression.

"We're taking up a collection of tobacco," exclaimed the wistful one.

Now, tobacco was a forbidden thing in those Methodist precincts, and for that reason I naturally had some. Why I parted with it was—to me at the time a mystery; there was something about the wistful one that took me at once. Thus, all inadvertently, I made the acquaintance of Stephen Crane and, incidentally, of his chum and roommate, Earl Reeves, the richest boy in school.

Little has been written about Crane's years at Claverack, and for a very simple reason: the material has been lacking. "The school was in high repute at the time," his biographer contents himself with saying, concluding with Crane's own declaration that he was "very happy there."[5] As a matter of fact, the high reputation once enjoyed by the school was wholly in the past, and no longer survived save among the uninformed. Robert Fulton was educated at Claverack, but Fulton, in 1887, when Crane came there, was long dead. The large classes of earnest young men, all anxious to bring about the era which today has finally come to pass, had dwindled year by year until there were not more than a few, mainly would-be ministers, upon the rolls. The college, in fact, had become all absorbed in the Hudson River Institute—a mere boarding-school, quartered like an octopus in the college dormitories, taught by the college faculty and drawing much of its patronage from parents cursed with backward or semi-incorrigible offspring.

This transformation spelled an important change in the whole character of the college. The young dolts were not a new element in the school, but under a certain Dr. Flack, a worthy Solomon in the birch rod sense of the word, they were shown no mercy, and a little sense was rammed into their skulls. Life at the college then was hard. I have heard old students say that when first haled to Claverack they believed themselves to be entering a reformatory. But when Stephen Crane first set foot there—Claverack is a tiny Dutch village just across from the Catskills—Dr. Flack had already gone and Professor Flack, his son, reigned in his stead.[6] Before long the student body had lost all of its old character and the Institute itself was being eaten into by an annex, which was not up to the level of even a high school. Old Claverack was dead.

. . . There was always, under Professor Flack, a certain devilish, care-free spirit abroad. Discipline, you see, had done a nose dive. Students—we were co-educational, and the boys wore handsome military uniforms of blue and gold—roamed as in a terrestrial paradise like packs of cheerful wolves out of bounds, out of hours and very much out of hand. No wonder at all, then, that Stephen Crane was happy there.[7] Fate, playing a scurvy trick upon his well-intentioned parents, had placed him in an environment made as if expressly to his order. A good school might have forced or coaxed him into a conventional mold and we would never have had such things as, "There is nothing; save opinion—and opinion be damned." Claverack, as I have heard him say himself, was "simply pie."

The pie, for its part, was hardly conscious of its Simple Simon. It had other things to think about. Was not Robert Browning dead? Imagine the excitement. I, for my part, wrote a full page of purple rhetoric for the *Vidette*,[8] the college paper, chronicling this dire event. There was nobody in a position to protest. J. Hall Jones, our editor-in-chief, pretended to have heard of Browning before, but in my opinion General Van Petten,[9] the whitehaired professor of elocution, was the only honest-to-goodness sharer of my distinction. I know Van Petten had heard of him, for I had taught Pusey, a student come up from the annex, to recite "All the Shade and the Shine of the Sea," from "Asolando," for a meeting of the Fourth Form, and the General had suggested that the line, "In the kiss of one girl," might advantageously be altered as to the third word, "smile," he said, "being more chaste." Yes, the professor was in the know. Stephen Crane, I am almost certain, was not. Yet he, too, came in for a share of the *Vidette's* attention, though not as subject matter for a literary note. We went, I think, as far on one occasion as to speak of "the Stephen cranium"—undoubtedly the first bit of Craneana ever published—but our best effort ran something like this: "Stephen was the first martyr. He seems also to be the last. Anyway, these red sunsets must be very Harrying.[10] Why, oh why, did the S. S. T. Girlum have to be, just now when Indian Summer is coming on?"

This may sound a trifle obscure. The S. S. T. Girlum was a secret society, a misogynist association whose members—there were six—sought to wrap themselves with mystery. I did not belong, so I do not know what the S. S. T. stood for—*sic semper tyrannis,* perhaps. Vain boast, the voice of six crying in the wilderness and they among the earliest to be vanquished in that great war which led to universal suffrage! It happened one golden afternoon, when a party of twelve—half of them in uniform, the rest in fluffy ruffles—set out for a walk along a paradisiacal, not to say aphrodisiacal, stretch of highway locally known as the Great North Road. Came a fork. The girls were for going on, the boys for dallying with the by-way. There was a hot squabble, and from this excursion the doughty half dozen returned alone and defeated. They banded themselves together by an oath, and for several weeks thereafter maintained a resolute, monk-like attitude toward feminine society. Crane was one of them. And this—unless one counts his recorded predilection at the age of two for the red skirt of Miss Rutherford, of Newark[11]—was his very first love affair.

II

You will have divined from the *Vidette's* carefully chosen diction that her name was Harriet, and that her crowning glory was of the sort which made famous the contemporary Mrs. Leslie Carter.[12] Already Crane's blazonry showed gules, though it had not yet become a badge of courage. Harriet Mattison was our best pianist, the pride of that small group of us calling ourselves the Music Conservatory. I all but fell in love with her myself during the S. S. T. Girlum interlude. That malady was rather prevalent, for she was very pretty, with a clear complexion tending to freckles and an adorable Irish nose. But, alas she died the next year. And I remember Stanton Grabill—another Girlum member, and one who eventually, as Dr. S. Becker von Grabill, attained to some key-board celebrity of his own—claiming that her spirit visited him one night at Buffalo, where he had gone to study under Antoine de Kontski. It brushed across his Steinway, he wrote me, eliciting a melody which he subsequently wrote down and played in such materialistic centers as London, Paris and St. Petersburg. But I cannot vouch for the ghost. Personally, I never heard Harriet play anything more heavenly than Schumann.

It was I who broke up the misanthropic Girlum clan, though the boots of Professor Charles W. Landon had something to do with it. I was only a special music student, and Landon, the director of the Conservatory, was a giant. When he attempted to play the organ, his boots insisted on bringing down two pedals at a time—an excess of lateral reach tending to nullify whatever advantage he derived from the corresponding breadth of his hands. In consequence I became his proxy as organist and choirmaster of the village Methodist church, and Crane was my leading tenor. He had a light, pleasant voice, true in pitch, if of no very great power or compass—Mr. Beer is mistaken in saying that it was a baritone—, and though he pretended not to like to sing, the pretense was not convincing. Tenors are tenors. So I ordered a quartette rehearsal in the Music Hall, knowing very well that Stephen would be on hand. And—perhaps out of pure Christian charity, perhaps in hopes of getting rid of a rival, who shall say?—I invited nobody else but Harriet, who did not sing but thought it was an appointment to practice a four-hand arrangement of Schubert's "Rosamunde." Crane, hearing us, mistook the music for mine and came like one of those who rush where angels fear to tread. The look he received was my cue to leave, and when I saw him next the S. S. T. G. was a thing of the past.

"Damn you, Wickham!" said he by way of thanks. Damns were considered quite naughty in those days. But what would we have thought had we known that Crane was dreaming of taking his into print?

There have been many theories as to the source from which he drew the material for that culminating blasphemy against the God of War, *The Red Badge of Courage*. The English reviewers explained it by promptly calling him "Captain Crane." His American biographer tells us that he pored over the *Century's* "Battles and Leaders" and other historical records of the Civil War.[13] No doubt he did. But this is not going back far enough. The Hudson River Institute was a military academy, equipped by the Government with antique rifles in furtherance of some naïve plan of preparedness, and that touch of personal experience so essential to the birth of a great idea must have come to Crane through his connection with Claverack's student battalion. Its four straggling companies were in fact the nucleus of that "blue demonstration," the very heart of his subsequent conception of an army. And yet it has been said that he took no interest in the military drill!

The truth is that he merely pretended to take no interest in it—the tenor again. For it was his pose in those days to take little interest in anything save poker and baseball, and even in speaking of these great matters there was in his manner a suggestion of *noblesse oblige.* Undoubtedly he felt himself peculiar, an oyster beneath whose lips there was already an irritating grain of some foreign substance. Not altogether welcome, either. All his life he strove to win recognition as a regular fellow. He tried to climb Mount Popocatepetl, and exposed himself unnecessarily to gunfire in the Cuban War—fish-out-of-water stuff. And he failed. Only women and other hero worshippers ever really liked him. He wanted to be a democrat and yet a dictator. Hence that contradiction, self-depreciation coupled with arrogance, which has puzzled so many. It was no fortuitous circumstance that his chum was the richest boy in school. In the slums or among aristocrats he could breathe. With the middle class he was always a little David throwing unmannerly stones at the collective Goliath.

It was his fear of ridicule, especially of his own, which gave him his slightly sheepish air on the parade ground, for there is in all martial maneuvering an element of personal display in which it requires no great amount of intellectual detachment to detect the absurd. When I arrived at Claverack he was already a first lieutenant, with enough of the true officer in him to have a perfectly hen-like attitude toward the rank and file. Well do I remember the anguish I caused him by dropping my gun during a prize-drill!

Prize drills are instruments of torture, pure and simple. We had them to determine which company was the best, also to pick out individuals least unworthy of promotion. It was in one of these latter contests that I figured, a wretched private hoping to be endowed with corporal's stripes. And though I have since dared audiences in many audacious ways, I can truthfully say that I have never known such stage fright as was mine while one of a squad being marched up and down the Claverack Drill Hall to the nasal orders of Lieut. Stephen Crane. You never know what the next order is to be, that's the rub. No wonder that my piece escaped from my nerveless grasp and went clattering to the floor.

"Idiot! Imbecile!" stormed Crane when it was over. "You were fairly decent up to the last minute. And then to drop your gun! Such a thing was never heard of. Do you think *order arms* means to drop your gun?"

No, Stevie was not tender of other people's vanities. I even think he considered self-expression the exclusive privilege of the few. Witness, now, this little incident.

It was St. Patrick's Day, and Pusey and I—the very Pusey of Browning fame—had felt called upon to constitute ourselves a parade and to dress fantastically with our coats wrong side out on the pretense that we were Irish. Crane confronted me at the moment of demobilization, and drawlingly remarked: "So! You're a professional damn fool. That is it."

His tone was interested, curious, exasperatingly impersonal. Yet it was not for any such reason as this that we failed to become friends. The cause lay deeper, and was—for me, at least—to have a tragi-comic outcome, as will be seen.

We had with us a considerable colony of Cubans, and as they qualified very well as social outcasts, Crane was much among them, acquiring that liking for things Spanish and that smattering of their language which afterward stood him in good stead in the making of such stories as "The Four Blind Mice."[14] Among these Cubans was a certain Antonio, always called Chick after a nickname given him by Crane. He roomed with me for a time, and one night attempted to cut my throat with my own razor, alleging that I had stolen a postage stamp. And I, still half asleep but moved to see red, partly by the fact that I was guilty and partly by the vision of a sinister figure caught leaning over my bed, picked up a chair and chased him out into the corridor and down the stairs, he shouting murder at the top of his voice in the true Cuban manner. It is a commentary upon the environment, perhaps, that the faculty took no notice of the incident. Neither did Stephen. It was, after all, only one little boy being chased by another! But when Chick subsequently challenged a third little boy to a fist fight, and incidentally kicked him in the shins, Crane insisted upon a formal Queensbury affair.[15] He had, poor genius, the insane idea that the world might be regulated by justice.

III

Crane's defiance of a society which is regulated quite otherwise seems a small affair now. He did, indeed, advise his old man with the white beard to go and seek for justice in a more kindly land, but most of his thunderbolts were hurled at a God of straw blustering across the sky, which fact has caused, I think, his really profound radicalism to be overlooked. He did not believe that smug pretense was of divine origin, and he had, beside, a sneaking fondness for the under dog as such. We, his contemporaries, did not know this, but no doubt the faculty saw deeper. They may even have sensed that he would live to begin a sentence with the word *too,* and that he would defend a fallen woman in a police court.[16] But his overt acts had as yet amounted to little more than the deliberate splitting of an infinitive.

Later, when he had been expelled from Syracuse University[17] and had published *Maggie: A Girl of the Streets* and *George's Mother,* I went back to Claverack

to give an organ recital and discovered that they had all along predicted some
such bad end. They bridled at praise of their now-conspicuous alumnus, and,
when pressed for reasons, fell back upon criticisms of the "roughness of his
style." But, obviously, it was the wiry coat of a moral challenge which disturbed
them. He had by this time dared to fancy that "God lay dead in heaven,"[18] and
he had boldly announced that it was possible to disagree with St. Paul.[19]

This *George's Mother,* by the way, was a book drawn from two relatives of
mine.[20] George, whose real name was Frank, was in life a handsome youth much
given to dress and to leisure; his mother was a most estimable lady and a devout
follower of Mrs. Grundy.[21] Crane transposed them to the slums, preserving
only the characters—a plausible and worthless young man with an indulgent
and credulous parent. The vaunted Crane realism was never of the photographic sort. Thus the only incident which really happened was George's amazing lunch—a charlotte russe and a beer. Frank actually gave this order and consumed it, much to Crane's delight, in that rather lurid resort which used to be
on Fourteenth street directly opposite Tammany Hall.

But if Crane enjoyed a certain reputation for villainy even while at Claverack—
and such was certainly the case—it must have been chiefly due to that nice
instinct which the Pillars of Society have for distinguishing veritable young
Samsons from among the ordinary bad boys who merely scribble adolescent ob-
scenities upon the temple walls. True, he frequently was to be seen in Mrs. Myers' pie shop, in company with Reeves and sometimes as late as eleven at night,
consuming, if not charlotte russe and beer, at least equally insipid banana cake
and coffee. But, then, the same was true of Grabill and myself, and our essential
uprightness was never called into question. We were even allowed on one occasion to go to New York to hear Hans von Bülow play Beethoven. And although
we scandalized Professor Landon by failing to keep away from Lillian Russell,
against whose "Grand Duchess" at the Casino he had warned us,[22] we retained
the privileges of trusties to the end. Crane had to sneak out even to attend the
functions at Mrs. Myers'.

Strange to relate, he seldom went to Judd's, a rival pie shop, where the necessary supplements to college cookery were themselves supplemented by a dark
stairway whereon it was possible to sit with members of the opposite sex. Nor
was it Crane, but a theological student, who bought so many flowers for the
decoration of a sweetheart upon exhibition days that he had no money with
which to pay the Hudson florist upon the day of reckoning. Hudson, our neighboring and deliciously wicked city, where, according to rumor, initiation was to
be had into the ultimate mysteries of life, seemed to hold no charms for the
destined singer of the black ride of sin. He must as yet have been a theorist, for
he never even jumped a freight train to cover the intervening three miles. And

it was while in pursuit of quite another culprit that "Sammy," one of the professors, finding himself in a Hudson retailer's and compelled to account for his presence to the clerk, gave birth to his historic inquiry, "Have you got any of those long, round, brown, stout—shoestrings?"

Charles Knapp, afterward a successful physician, discovered the Bible and used to read it aloud to Grabill at night, edifying an entire dormitory with roars of laughter over the obscene passages. Crane would have been expelled for such a caper. Knapp, however, was promoted to the responsible post of night-watchman. Crane even avoided Schram's, notwithstanding the reprobate old shoemaker's extensive repertoire of Rabelaisian tales. Nor was his name, to the best of my recollection, ever read aloud in Saturday morning chapel among those whose bearers were to lose a half holiday for being caught mashing with co-eds in the romantic vicinity of Buttermilk Falls. Crane did not "rush" rooms—that is, he did not pick the locks of fellow students' chambers and turn the furniture upside down. He did not take his pillow case and go out into the night to fill it, according to established ritual, with stolen apples. And when Grabill and I caught Mr. Hermance asleep in his grocery store, tied his legs together, locked the door, and then hammered on the window as an experiment in behaviorism, Stevie did not even think it funny. He held aloof, too, when an indignant undergraduate mob hanged a certain unpopular student in effigy. He was rather given to holding aloof, especially if the human animal was manifesting its capacity for collective action. And when he did appear and mingle it was frequently to deliver a pronunciamento, clothed, it might be, with profanity but of a distinctly ethical purport.

"I hear you're bad—I hear you're damn bad," I once knew him to inform a youthful Don Juan.

"A damn nice girl," was his verdict upon the belle of the village.

"My God, what a lot of harm she is going to do before she dies!" he prophesied of another belle in another village—a prophecy which has long since been most accurately fulfilled. . . .

IV

A year or two must have passed. I had just finished lunching at a tiny resort bordering the Wallkill river and known as Midway Park, at the central point on the trolley line joining Middletown and Goshen.

"Hello, Harvey!" called a voice.

There stood Crane, getting ready to board a car. And immediately something perverse, absurd, took possession of me. I had never been shocked by this man's profundities, not knowing that he had them, for one thing. But I was at the time an indifferently poor musician, with all an indifferently poor musician's horror of the impolite. Steve's sweater was still unwashed, and I was in that stage of culture which judges the world by its neckties. Here, evidently, was somebody to be put in his place. So I answered stiffly: "How do you do, Mr. Crane?" Simply this, and nothing more.

. . . I have good reasons for thinking that this first voice of free verse crying in the wilderness was reduced to words in three days at Twin Lakes. Crane subsequently told me that it was the outcome of a fit of desperation. "No one would print a line of mine," he said, "and I just had to do something odd to attract attention."

When I last saw Crane it was . . . in Hagen's drug store, Middletown. He had by this time apparently forgotten the Midway Park incident, at least to the extent of permitting himself to discuss in my presence the plot of a projected novel, "better than anything yet,"—a novel to be called "A Woman Without Weapons,"[23] destined never to be written. But an ill-timed compliment soon shut him up—for he was always bashful—and, turning to Young,[24] he began planning the details of a trip which the two were hoping to make in a far country where the women were said to go about displaying a "very fetching" zone of nakedness by way of the waist-line, with other attractions beyond the ordinary. Like the masterpiece, this excursion was never achieved. . . .

⌒

13 / Ernest G. Smith

Ernest G. Smith (1873–1945) was a classmate of Crane's at Lafayette who later distinguished himself in business and in the military.

Source: Ernest G. Smith, "Comments and Queries," *Lafayette Alumnus* 2 (February 1932): 6.

In a somewhat jumbled maze of names and faces of those I first met upon entering in the fall of 1890, Crane is rather conspicuously revealed.

He was of medium height, slender, of sallow complexion and an inveterate cigarette smoker. Outside members of his own Fraternity, his acquaintance among fellow class or college mates was limited.[25] Not given much to athletics, he nevertheless appeared frequently in the motley crowd of baseball enthusiasts who occupied the old campus at convenient intervals even before March Field was acquired. As a promising player he was looked upon by many of us as a candidate for the varsity team then in process of formation for the following spring. One unusual incident in my recollections of Crane stands out. Hazing was rather generously indulged in at that time, although a somewhat tragic result had previously been widely recorded in newspapers attending the hazing in South College of two of our class, Shockley and Brice. During the course of which eventful proceedings a baseball bat had wrought painful damage to several invading Sophomores. Without a President at that time—Dr. Warfield having entered "Freshmen" in our Sophomore year—the incident had been glossed over by the leaderless faculty with a couple of firings and some Butler-arian reprimands. Whereupon the ambitious Sophs resumed their nefarious but engaging pastime at a later date that year.

In the course of which resumption the customary rites were duly performed upon the writer and other inoffensive classmates within the cloistered walls of South, after which we were permitted to follow the wrecking crew of our superiors to the lairs of other class members. Many of us did with a thought, perhaps, of getting our hand in for next year. East Hall was the next objective and in a rear room of that even then somewhat unsavory structure, Steve Crane occupied a single room. No response followed the dire commands of Sophomore gangsters seeking admission and the door was forced. An oil lamp burning in the room indicated plainly to the attacking force and to a fringe of already hazed Freshmen on the outskirts the figure of Crane backed into a corner with a revolver in hand. He was ghastly white as I recall and extremely nervous. There was no time to escape what might have proved a real tragedy until Crane unexpectedly seemed to wilt limply in place and the loaded revolver dropped harmlessly to the floor. I have often thought since, particularly while reading his "Red Badge of Courage," an autographed copy of which he long afterwards sent me, how the imagination ofttimes outruns performances of the flesh. Of the incident he never afterwards spoke, as I recall.[26]

I have talked with many of our class who knew him somewhat casually as I did, to find that their impressions usually tallied with my own. He seemed at that time just one of the average of us, somewhat more sophisticated and rather more cynical perhaps, but anyhow a normal product of his time and circumstance. As I see the picture now, I would set him down as a sort of conventional newspaper reporter in appearance and prospect. His future was to belie that estimate, although many reporters in the erratic history of letters have gained high place.

∽

14 / Frank W. Noxon

Frank W. Noxon (1872–1945) was a Delta Upsilon fraternity brother of Crane at Syracuse University; he was poet of the class of 1894 and published stories and poems in the *University Herald*. He became a reporter for the *Syracuse Herald* in 1892–93, drama critic for the *Boston Record* from 1893 to 1900, and managing editor of several other Providence and Boston newspapers until 1905. For most of his subsequent career Noxon was secretary of the Railway Business Association. Active in the Presbyterian Church, he wrote several books on religion and government. His reminiscence is especially important because of its comments on the dating of *Maggie,* Crane's interest in Goethe's discussion of color, and the Philistine Banquet.

Source: Frank W. Noxon, "The Real Stephen Crane," *Step-Ladder* [Chicago] 14 (January 1928): 4–9.[27]

One of Stephen Crane's characteristics was a haunting solicitude for the comforts and welfare of other people, especially those of narrow opportunity. He thought about it as one thinks about an art or craft, developing a style and inventing original methods.

My acquaintance with him began at Syracuse University, where we were in the Class of '94 and in the Delta Upsilon Fraternity, which Crane had joined at Lafayette earlier in the year. The earliest thing I remember concerning him was an essay which he read one night in chapter meeting on some serious political subject related to Russia.[28] I saw the manuscript and in conversation later exclaimed at its exquisite legibility. This astonished me in a daily newspaper reporter such as Crane had already been. He replied that from the outset of his writing he had kept in mind the compositor, whose earnings depended on the amount he could set, and this in turn upon the time it took to read the copy.

Among his favorite objects of solicitude were his dogs. He loved them and was beloved by them. He embraced without question the well-known theory, which I had then never heard before, that the instinctive attitude of a dog toward a new human acquaintance was an infallible test of character, and that no man who felt repugnance or even indifference toward canines, familiar or casual, could be wholly trusted for a kind heart toward those of his own species. Crane wrote of a dog named Jack; and I distinctly recall the fondness he showed for a story about this Jack, which he let me read.[29] The *St. Nicholas* magazine returned it, explaining that too many good dog stories were already in hand, but speaking in complimentary terms.[30] I got the impression that Stephen regarded this as friendly not only to him but to the dog; and his gratitude in literary defeat had a note of affectionate pride.

No doubt some of our acquaintances in those days as well as critics and readers since have ascribed Crane's interest in unfortunate women to another instinct than sympathy and compassion. Nobody can be sure. But knowing him pretty well and seeing him a good deal in the company of girls, toward whom he showed respect and deference, I have no difficulty in believing that when he wrote about scarlet sisters or vehemently defended one as later he did in a New York police court,[31] the dominant impulse was a desire to serve the helpless. *Maggie: A Girl of the Streets,* at least in its early form, was wholly or in part written at Syracuse.[32] With typical carelessness the author left the sheets lying about in the front corner room which he shared with Norton Goodwin.[33] Some of these pages were picked up and read by droppers-in. The other day a '93 man whom I had not seen for many years asked me what I thought of Crane as a man at the time, knowing that he was writing that sort of thing. Had it been my observation, as it had been his, that Crane's own conduct seemed to contrast with his choice of literary themes? In 1927 this sounds primitive. It was 1890, and it was a Syracuse much more Methodist and very much more "divinity" than now. By the way, in after years Crane told me about the publication of *Maggie.* He had vainly peddled it among the publishers, though to his delight the gentle realist, Howells, reading it for somebody (Harpers?) had written an enthusiastic memorandum.[34] Finally he paid for bringing it out himself, using the pseudonym "Johnston Smith." The cover was yellow paper with the title in large black letters. Four men were hired to sit all day one in front of another in New York elevated trains, reading intently and holding up the volume so that passengers would think the metropolis was *Maggie*-mad.

With his catholic taste in people Crane in one day combined considerable sense of social form. At the fraternity house one function was an annual party to which every co-ed on the hill was invited, the requisite number of partners being recruited from our chapters at other Central New York colleges. For the party one winter with us, Crane, after getting into his own evening dress, went about the house with a box of shirt studs and a punch, detecting local brethren whose well starched bosoms were innocent both of studs and of holes and rectifying the deficiency.

Crane was brave, physically, morally and socially. Nothing would do, therefore, but he must pity the coward and try to understand him. So we got *The Red Badge of Courage.* Incidentally, the use of the word "Red" in this title was part of a program. After the book appeared he and I had somewhere a talk about color in literature. He told me that a passage in Goethe analyzed the effect which the several colors have upon the human mind.[35] Upon Crane this had made a profound impression and he had utilized the idea to produce his effects. Do you remember the colors of the burning chemicals in "The Monster"? There you had them all at once.

Most of us were surprised, though we needn't have been, when this lover of his kind got into a war. It is well remembered how the description of Chancellorsville in *The Red Badge of Courage,* written by a youth not born until 1871, stirred the Civil War veterans and singled out the author as the one surefire war correspondent should war come. War came—with Spain, and Mr. Hearst's people annexed Crane for Cuba. The next fall, driving in a "hack" from Boston to Cambridge, where he was reporting a football game, Crane in the intervals between those harrowing coughs which got him in the end told me about Santiago. He said he was of no use whatsoever. The moment the fighting began Crane started carrying buckets of water to the wounded and paid no attention whatever to the observation necessary for writing newspaper despatches.

Not even Crane, love him as most men did, was always able to command from others that tolerance which he diffused so infinitely. At our era, security against nicotine was still a hope to which a he-man might aspire. The heating system in the chapter house carried smoke from one room to another. Whether the brethren (assaying then pretty high in divinity students) were more annoyed and alarmed at having to inhale attenuated whiffs so penetrating to their castles, or concerned for the salvation of the smokers, the iron heel descended, and an unregenerated group captained by the grinning Crane and consisting of Goodwin, Congdon, and perhaps others (I never smoked until I was 50 but often went along) were translated to the cupola, where on freezing days in ulsters, ear-laps, mittens and arctics they exhaled the fumes unsmelt to heaven. Some years ago in Northampton, Mass., I visited F. K. Congdon, who was, and I suppose is, superintendent of schools there. Congdon with a Sherlock Holmes air wanted to know whether in 1907 I was an editorial writer on the *Boston Herald.* I was, and his clue had been an article on Crane mentioning the cupola smoker, which Congdon said no other newspaper man could have known about.

If you go to East Aurora you will see on exhibition handwriting and other souvenirs of Crane, but Crane was one of the series who were driven from Elbert Hubbard by what they believed was Hubbard's abuse of them. In 1893 or thereabout, soon after I went to Boston, Hubbard ended by his and the Dean's mutual consent his short sojourn at Harvard,[36] leaving behind him among other things an unexpired rental on a Cambridge post-office box, to which subscriptions and contributions might be sent for a new magazine called *The Philistine.*[37] It seems that one Bickford and one Taber[38] (with the latter of whom I became intimate and enjoy to this day quinquennial reunions) for a brief while in Denver, where they worked on the *Times,* published a *Philistine.* When Hubbard quit the soap business for literature he did not instantly acquire either that classic appearance or that confidence in his pen which subsequently amazed all the continents, so he took on a series of editors of whom Taber was the first. Taber proposed the revival of *The Philistine*. Not knowing these worthies, but dwelling in Boston and noting the Cambridge address, which made them seem near, although they were in fact far away in East Aurora, I sent them some pieces of nonsense about a character named Clanginharp, which were published, and an acquaintance began by mail with both Taber and Hubbard. Presently Crane appeared likewise among the contributors. A by-law of the Society of the Philistines published on the magazine cover prescribed as a duty of members to attend the annual dinner. Some years went by without the first annual dinner, but about 1895 it was announced that the annual dinner was coming off with Crane as guest of honor.[39] Borrowing money and probably clothes, I made the journey to Buffalo, where the feed was held at the Genesee House. There must have been 15 or 20 there, most of us freaks or near-freaks, and on the menu were scriptures by others who couldn't come but admired the guest. Hubbard, still timid, sat at the foot of the table and Taber at the head; Crane on Taber's right; Claude Fayette Bragdon (who these days without the Fayette designs scenic and costume investiture for theatrical productions)[40] on his left, with me next; and on Crane's right Willis B. Hawkins, editor then of *Brains*. Hawkins borrowed cuff links of me which I never got back.

After dinner Taber rose and began his speech. "Probably," he said, "the most unique—" That was as far as he got. A voice somewhere down toward Hubbard called out "Can 'unique' be compared?" This was the signal. It determined the tone of the festivities. In the best clown and gridiron manner Taber and all the other speakers were guyed and ragged from start to finish. Crane, having the time of his life, was called up, and they had as much fun with him as with the others.

When Crane sat down up rose Claude Bragdon. After 31 years I can still hear the sound of his voice and see the look on his face. "I come here," he said, "to do honor to Stephen Crane, not to ridicule him. I regret to take this step, but I cannot longer remain in the room." The door was on the far side of the table. To get out, Bragdon had to walk around behind Taber and Crane. Hawkins stood and blocked him. "One moment," he said. "I am the oldest man in this room. I know Stephen Crane better than any one else here. I have slept with him, eaten with him, starved with him, ridden with him, swum with him. I know him through and through, every mood. I have taken part in all that has occurred, and he knows I love him and admire him. He knows that you all do. I have come here, like our friend, to do honor to Stephen Crane. I assure you he feels more complimented by the spirit of this meeting than he would have been by all the solemn eulogies that could be pronounced." Crane was nodding his head off. Everybody applauded.

"I am sorry," said Bragdon, "if I have made a mistake. I ask your pardon."

"Pardon is granted you," Hawkins answered, "on one condition."

Bragdon looked up inquiringly.

"That condition," said Hawkins, "is that you turn around and take your seat."

I never knew the particular circumstances under which in Crane's case the author, like so many others, fell out with Hubbard, but have always assumed that it was the Fra's democratic prejudice against royalties.[41] Whatever the reason, the inevitable assault appeared in *The Philistine,* and in Crane's case it was no less than a serious and circumstantial narrative of his having been "drowned in the Irish Sea,"[42] though Crane considerably survived this obituary.[43]

Source: Frank W. Noxon to Corwin Knapp Linson, letter, 14 April 1930, Box 11, Stephen Crane Collection, Special Collections Research Center, Syracuse University.

There was another little thing that I would have put in [my reminiscence] if I had thought of it. Crane . . . told me he thought his indifference to religion exceeded the intrinsic merits and attributed this to a re-action against too much. In Syracuse he and I used to go Sunday nights to St. Paul's where from a rear pew we sang a robust obligate to the music of the boy choir.[44] Perhaps the most significant aspect of these Sabbath evening pilgrimages was that I can remember no feminine attraction and believe that to draw us there St. Paul's first had to overcome the dominant social magnetism of what was then Central Baptist. If the keynote of Crane's harmony was that compassion for the helpless which was taught in precept and example by the Founder of the Church, we can understand that when our knight was minded to enter the courts of praise he felt drawn to the particular house of faith in which he imbibed as an infant his first spiritual sustenance.

〜

15 / Mansfield J. French

Mansfield J. French (1872–1953) was on the Syracuse baseball team with Crane. After graduating in 1894, he worked in Syracuse as a civil engineer and architect and was active in local and alumni affairs.

Source: Mansfield J. French, "Stephen Crane, Ball Player," *Syracuse University Alumni News* 15 (January 1934): 3–4.[45]

. . . [Crane] spent more time on the baseball field than in the class room. According to the records of the University he appears to have registered in only one subject, English Literature, with the Freshman class.[46] Dr. Charles N. Sims, Chancellor of the University, taught this subject to the two divisions of the class. Crane was doubtless not interested in Bede, the "Lay of Beowulf" or the "Canterbury Tales" and much less can he be imagined as lugging that huge tome, that formed the text-book, up the hill to a class at 7:45 A.M. Only one member of the class has been found to state that he remembers Steve Crane as present in the classroom and he, a veracious youth in short trousers, a worshipper of any one able to make the "varsity" ball team, and undoubtedly the impression made by Crane's presence near him in class was indelible. Crane's presence in Syracuse was undoubtedly due to a family relationship. His mother, whose maiden name was Mary Helen Peck, was a niece of Bishop Jesse Peck of the Methodist Episcopal Church, one of the founders and benefactors of Syracuse University. Bishop Peck's widow was living in the home left by him to the University and Stephen's mother undoubtedly had made arrangements with the University for his attendance and for a domicile with the Widow Peck. Stephen's great-aunt was not in sympathy with his ideas and ideals of living and his stay under her roof was of short duration. He found a more congenial and less restrained atmosphere at the Delta Upsilon Fraternity house at the top of Marshall Street hill.

When George Shepherd, manager of the baseball team for the year 1891, issued the call for candidates to report, Stephen must have been among the first to arrive as he obtained a fairly respectable and well-matched uniform. The uniforms in those days consisted of a miscellaneous lot of clothes purchased at second hand from the Syracuse Stars, the local professional ball team, and it was a case of "first come, first served" in the assignment of garments. However, the choice did not extend to hose. "Steve," like the others of us, wore what he chose. He should have worn white stockings of the heavy ribbed kind but of necessity he wore black of a fine knit that made his slender legs look like pipe stems. He was of a sallow complexion, his skin, hair and eyes appeared to be all of one dull and lifeless hue. That is, his eyeballs were of the same deep cream tint but the iris was of a cold, bluish gray color. His hair never would stay combed and parted; even after a "washup" following a game there were bound to be stray locks hanging down at the forehead and a bristly bunch at the end of the part in the back. Crane was very quick and active on his feet, his body was slender, his shoulders somewhat drooping, his chest not robust and his knees inclined somewhat to knock together. He was about five feet six inches in height and did not weigh over one hundred and twenty-five pounds. He played ball with a fiendish glee. Usually of a quiet and taciturn mien, on the ball field he was constantly in motion, was free of speech, wantonly profane at times and indulged in biting sarcasms when a teammate made a poor play,[47] but generous in praise of a good play. He was first tried out as a catcher and proved to be, in his ability to hold the ball, the best candidate for that position. His throwing arm was weak, however, and although he threw with the whole body, he was unable to line the ball down to second base in acceptable form. He would not stand on his two feet and snap the ball down to the base. It was necessary for him to throw off his mask, cap and protector, give a hop and skip and throw with a complete body swing. The strain upon the ligaments of his shoulder would, at times, cause him to double up with pain. This predicament led him to develop a simple method of catching the runner after he got on the bases that often proved effective. As a pitcher, the writer of this sketch had not cultivated the "winding up" arm action before pitching the ball, giving attention strictly to the delivery. Crane would always signal his judgment as to the particular curve that he thought would be effective but I usually shook my head and pitched the ball that I thought best suited. Crane taught me to seemingly neglect the base runner but when he saw the runner leave the base sufficiently to offer the possibility of catching him, he signalled me by a slight and seemingly natural movement of the hand. Then I whirled and threw the ball directly to the base. The baseman had seen the signal and it was up to him to meet the ball at the base and touch the runner. This piece of strategy we worked in many games. Redington, the second baseman, was the best player on the team and he could always be depended upon to meet the ball at the base and touch the runner. The large, round catcher's mitt had just come into use but Crane found it awkward and preferred a padded glove for his left hand, the right hand being bare. He had the habit of striking his bare, clenched fist three or four times into the palm of his gloved hand to express his approval of a "strike" when missed by the batter. When we succeeded in striking out our man an expression of diabolical glee would light up his face and he always expressed to me his appreciation when our opponents were retired at the end of their inning.

After four or five games as catcher the manager decided to try Crane in other positions. He was placed in center field for one game, then on first base and then at short stop. In the latter position, as he usually stopped the ball while on the run, he could get his throw off to a base more quickly and proved to be more effective in that position than did any other man in training. Crane was a good batman, although not a hard hitter. He placed his hits well and was a fast base-runner.

One of the early games of the season was scheduled with the Syracuse "Stars," the city professional team. For some reason Crane did not appear at the beginning of the game and it was necessary to borrow a catcher from our opponents. The *Syracuse Standard* said of this incident: "Quinn of the Stars caught the first inning for the University on account of the tardiness of Catcher Crain." However, the paper said: "Crain was applauded for his good work behind the bat."

Crane loved to talk baseball and took great delight in telling of his experiences on the ball field and of his acquaintance, at least by newspaper reputation, with the leading professional players of those days. When on trips to play with other college teams he proved to be sociable and companionable. I remember to have seen his fingers deeply stained with nicotine but do not recall that he smoked during the baseball season; at least in public, for the manager had issued the rule under date of February 9th: "2. From this date until the close of the season candidates shall abstain from use of tobacco in any form and of spirituous or malt liquors." Crane spent considerable time in reading and we knew that he wrote for the *New York Tribune*.

Source: Mansfield J. French to Melvin H. Schoberlin, letter, 14 October 1947, Box 11, Stephen Crane Collection, Special Collections Research Center, Syracuse University Library.[48]

. . . One of his biographers,[49] a man of a German or Jewish name, states, in his biography of Crane, that Steve said that Josh French stole his college pennant.[50] I was called "Josh" in my college days and distinctly recall buying a small college pennant for twenty-five cents, but I certainly did not come into possession of Steve's pennant by any means, fair or foul. I doubt Steve having cared enough about a pennant to buy one. I think, if he made that accusation, it was with "malice aforethought" and quite like the "harum-scarum" youngster of those days. . . .

~

16 / Clarence N. Goodwin

Clarence N. Goodwin (?–?) was Crane's roommate at Syracuse and later a lawyer in Chicago.

Source: Clarence N. Goodwin to Max J. Herzberg, letter, 3 November 1921, Stephen Crane Collection, Newark Public Library.

. . . [Stephen Crane] managed to combine perfect poise and assurance with a very gentle and diffident way of speaking. He confessed afterwards that he had some anxiety to know what I was like and to have found reassurance in learning that the somewhat over large pipe which was near at hand was in practical use and was not merely an ornament.

He soon proved himself to be unstudious, brilliant, volatile, entertaining and giftedly profane. He was at that time in years about 19 and in worldly experience about 87. He was then a correspondent for the *New York Tribune* and had had other newspaper experience.

He wrote short stories in a round beautiful hand but I think they were quite generally rejected. He had a keen sense of the dramatic and his countenance usually displayed an amused, satirical, but kindly grin. His keen mind instantly caught the absurd, bizarre or ridiculous aspect of any incident and he would draw out an account of it in his own entertaining fashion.

Once when I was going to an intercollegiate athletic meet which he was prevented from attending by complete financial destitution, I took along his silk college pennant as well as my own; the two were exactly alike. When I returned I told him very truthfully that I had loaned his pennant to Josh French.[51] He replied that I reminded him of a man, who, when he was cooking two beef-steaks, one for himself and one for his partner called out, "Jin, your beef-steak fell in the fire."

I did not see him again until two years later when I spent the Thanksgiving Holidays in New York. At that time he was living on Avenue A, opposite Black-well's Island, then a most unattractive neighborhood.[52] While at his rooms he read to me the manuscript of *Maggie: A Girl of the Streets* which was afterwards so highly commended by the late William Dean Howells. He visited us at the Delta Upsilon Chapter House in Syracuse during my junior year at the time of our annual fraternity reception, and together with Frank Wright Noxon[53] we spent most of the time in the back room of Palmer's Restaurant eating and smoking and incessantly talking. We would have our luncheon on the hill and appear at Palmer's for another luncheon about 1:30 when Frank Noxon would join us. The meal would move slowly along until about 6:00 o'clock when, of course, it was time to eat again, and this feast would continue until the last car had left for the hill.

. . . My recollection of him is that of a boyish smiling young man, slight in figure, kind in heart, keen in mind. He saw into and through the conceits, hypocrisies, weaknesses and selfishness of mankind, but continued to smile with amusement but without bitterness. . . .

~

17 / William McMahon

William McMahon (?–?) was one of Crane's friends at Syracuse University.

Source: William McMahon, "Syracuse in the Gay '90s: Steve Crane Told to 'Stick to Poems' after 'Bangup' Piano Recital at Party," *Syracuse Post-Standard,* 20 February 1955, 13.[54]

. . . There was a Music Hall on North Salina street, a door or so north of Hier's Tobacco House, where one could saunter in, sit at a table and order a glass of beer from the waiter, price five cents. Rarely did any one tip the waiter. Generous sports might give him a dime during the evening, or maybe two.

The show was the thing, however. Pretty girls sang and danced on the stage daringly clad in low neck waists and skirts just above the knees. This music hall afforded a large part of my social life, aside from Madge[55] and her friends who lived in the Florence flats located near the junction of South Salina Street and West Onondaga.

One evening, whom did I run into as I entered this amusement emporium, but Steve Crane, my old college classmate. Steve sat at a table with a tall, serious girl. He invited me to join them. The girl was an artist, so she said. We ordered beer.

Steve admitted that he, too, was an artist—that is, an artist in words—a poet.

Some weeks before, he showed me a poem he wrote, confessing that he intended to be a writer, and the poem was produced as proof that he already had the spark of genius. I forget the exact lines but I can write down a fairish copy of one verse.

Pearl, coming in Ethiope night
With straw upon her head
And gray ashes on her yellow glove
She was not buried
But dead.

I was too obtuse to see the genius in this ebolition, but not so obtuse as to fail to appreciate the genius, a few years later, in his "Red Badge of Courage."

So a happy evening was had by all at this Music Hall. Steve paid the shot, explaining to me in a whisper that he had just received an extra dollar from his father, a minister in New Jersey.[56]

Now I wanted to do some entertaining. I called on Madge at the Florence flat and proposed that she give a little party. A couple of her girl friends were students of the piano at the Fine Arts Branch of Syracuse University.

The time was set and invitations sent out, particularly to Steve and Pearl and the two piano girls. From Doolittle's Wholesale Liquor Store I bought a gallon of whisky for $3 and a gallon of sherry wine for 90 cents. Madge and I mixed up the mess, half and half, in ornate quart bottles.

I had heard the two piano students play on several occasions and never could detect any music in any of it. Of course, I must have lacked the classical ear. Pearl, Steve's friend, was an artist in painting and drawing. I was shown one or two of these drawings, but I could not understand what they were all about—a bunch of cubes and circles and grotesque feet, or an upside down tree.

It dawned on me at the very beginning of Madge's party that these artists of varied line were simply adventurers in pretense. The period was the beginning of a cult that has grown in influence over the years, the primary object of which is to make music, art and poetry perfectly unintelligible and incomprehensible.

When Steve and Pearl appeared at the party, I called Steve to one side and said:

"Steve you can't fool me. Your poetry is pretense, Pearl's drawings are pretense and these girls who pound out their own compositions on the piano are pretending even to themselves."

"Well, what then?"

"Let's forget all the pretense and have some fun tonight. I'll pass the word around in secret that you are a marvelous pianist."

"Oh, no," protested Steve. "I don't think I ever touched a piano. I don't know one note from another."

"Perfect," I whispered. "They'll invite you to play—you demur a little. Then they'll insist. Then you yield and reluctantly consent to play one of your own compositions."

This scheme gradually began to intrigue Steve. I knew he could carry on the sham in good shape. He consented to do it, with a devilish gleam in his eyes.

The party began by every one sitting stiffly alone, looking at the others, smiling a little, venturing a bromidic word now and then. Some one suggested music. This meant, of course, one of the two piano girls. She didn't need any coaxing as she eagerly but gracefully wended her way to the piano.

She showed at once that she possessed, at least, digital dexterity. The piece was a pretty long one and I was afraid the poor girl would keel over from exhaustion, but she stood it bravely and at the end arose and bowed to left and right while the audience cheered.

The first piece went so well that she volunteered to play another and still another. After she had played three or four, the other pianist took over. She seemed to have even more muscle in her slim arms and dainty fingers than the other. She regaled us with about an hour of this ultra classical stuff to the applause of the audience.

After this musical festival, Pearl announced that she had just happened to have with her a couple of her latest drawings, and so every one insisted that they have a look. So Pearl carefully unstrung the package and set up the pictures on the mantelpiece. Then there were exclamations—"Oh how beautiful! What wonderful technique! What marvelous originality!"

Quite a long time was passed in praise of Pearl's peculiar pictures but finally this died down. Then I announced:

"Now all of you listen. I have my friend Steve Crane with me and I will tell you something about Steve that few people know. Old Steve, here, is a marvelous pianist. Some of his own compositions are out of this world. Let's make Steve play us something, what say?"

There was a clamor for Steve. He bashfully hung back with about the right percentage of modesty, but went over to the piano. He sat on the bench a moment, lifted his hands in the air and brought them both down—bang on the keys. Then he ran his fingers over the keys and such a jumble of discord never was heard on land or sea.

Once some one whispered and Steve turned around slowly and glanced gloweringly at the offender. Then he turned again and began pounding the keys occasionally thumping one key a long time with his forefinger. He kept this nonsense up for quite a while.

I could hardly keep from laughing, especially when I noted that every one was listening in awe and no one seemed to suspect that it was all a fake.

As Steve ended the performance with a loud bang, there was wild applause.

I noticed one thing, however. As Mandy, the servant, appeared in and out of the room with the drinks and as the party broke up, she whispered to Steve as we were getting ready to go:

"Mistah, I think you'd better give up yo music and stick to yo poems."

⌐

18 / Clarence Loomis Peaslee

Clarence Loomis Peaslee (1871–?), a lawyer and an aspiring writer who published poetry and short stories, was one of Crane's friends at Syracuse University.

Source: Clarence Loomis Peaslee, "Stephen Crane's College Days," *Monthly Illustrator and Home and Country* 13 (August 1896): 27–30.

Stephen Crane came to Syracuse University during the college year of '90. He had previously been a student at Lafayette, and while there had been initiated into the Delta Upsilon Fraternity. Upon his arrival in Syracuse he came immediately to the D.U. House, as one of his friends says, "in a cab and a cloud of tobacco smoke."

I well remember my first knowledge of him. Calling one afternoon at the D.U. House to see a friend, I passed up the stairs and was just turning into one of the rooms on the second floor, when the appearance of the room opposite, the door of which stood right open, attracted my attention. College rooms are proverbially disorderly, but this one made the ordinary every day chaos turn to cosmos in comparison. The floor was literally covered with loose sheets of paper, books, football shoes, newspaper clippings, canvas trousers and jackets, baseball masks and bats, running trunks, chest-protectors and other athletic and literary sundries. The table was running over with books and papers and scribblings, together with pipes and tobacco cans, and the walls were hung with pictures, trophies, signs and pen-drawings. Certainly the occupant was nothing unless athletic and literary. The apartment was a large one in the northeast corner of the house, and contained a deep bay-window. It was quite elegantly furnished, some of the pictures being particularly good, for Mr. Crane has always been an ardent admirer of fine paintings. Just then some members of the fraternity coming along the passage, I asked who lived there, and was told: "A new fellow from Lafayette, 'Steve' Crane." Later in the afternoon, on the athletic field, I met the future novelist, then the new catcher of the 'Varsity nine, a wiry, slender youth, under the average height, with a complexion almost yellow, and very large and expressive eyes. I remember that he did not have one of the old gray 'Varsity suits, but wore a crimson sweater, buff-colored trousers and a pair of broken patent-leather shoes. He was very gritty, and stood up to the plate like a professional. The pitcher at that time was a rather large man, who threw a very swift ball, and Crane was so light that he seemed to bound back with every catch. Little did the motley crowd of students and onlookers that bright April afternoon think that the plucky boy behind the bat would so soon be a character of international interest; for all this happened a little more than six years ago. He was the best player of the nine, and one of the best catchers that the University ever had.

Mr. Crane was then about eighteen years old,[57] small, quiet, and unprepossessing. His face was long and sallow, eyes deep set, and hair very light, almost white. He was very quick and agile in his movements and was a good runner. He had very few intimate friends, cared little for society, and never seemed to be particularly interested in anything that transpired in college except baseball. He was somewhat careless in his dress and negligent of his lectures; was always cool, never worried about anything, smoked infinite tobacco and took life just as it came.

Of Stephen Crane's college life there is little to be said. He was not possessed of a strong individuality. He was simply unimpressive, and his student days gave no promise of the talent he has since displayed. Of the eight or nine hundred students in attendance at Syracuse University during his stay, only a few will remember him at all. From the standpoint of his professors, Mr. Crane's college course was a failure. He was but an indifferent student, not from lack of ability but from want of application. He had no natural taste for study, and never tried to cultivate one. His favorite study was history, and his reading in this branch of instruction has been considerable.[58] He left the University without a degree, and was never enrolled as a student in any regular course, but was classed as a special, taking whatever took his fancy.

Yet the college days of Stephen Crane were not wasted. He preferred to select his own course of instruction rather than follow the cut-and-dried curriculum of a university. Men have always had a greater interest for him than books. When he ought to have been in recitations he was strolling the streets, looking at the faces that passed. One of his favorite haunts was the Central Railroad station, where large numbers of people daily congregated. His course in college was highly "eclectic," and he never pretended to follow it closely. A man of less mental insight and stability would surely have been led amiss by such a general and indifferent method of action, but Stephen Crane had a purpose in view from the very first, and steadily and unswervingly worked to it. He wanted to produce something that would make men think, that would make men feel as he felt, and to do this he early realized that for him it must come through hard work. In the course of a literary correspondence he wrote me a letter, dated at Lincoln, Nebraska, February 12, 1895, in which, after citing various criticisms, he says: "As far as myself and my own meagre success are concerned, I began the war with no talent, but an ardent admiration and desire. I had to build up. I always want to be unmistakable. That to my mind is good writing. There is a great deal of labor connected with literature. I think that is the hardest thing about it. There is nothing to respect in art, save one's own opinion of it."[59]

It has been charged against Mr. Crane that he scorns scholarship, and is proud of the fact that he has had little or no schooling. Nothing is farther from the truth. He has a deep regard for true learning, but not for the rubbish that often passes under that name, and if he has not burned the midnight oil in search of "school" knowledge, he has worked as but few men have, in the field of observation and the study of mankind.

In college Crane was an omnivorous reader,[60] and sat up late at night, diligently poring over the masterpieces of literature, or trying to put upon paper his own peculiar views of men and life. It is interesting to note and is an indication of his genius that his stories are all in a new field, and that he is indebted to no "school" of letters or coterie of thinkers for the ideas that he so intensely presents. The outward acts and lives of men are to him but the evidence and outworkings of a strange and unaccountable inner life that is going on in the darkened recesses of the mind. Whether he is stronger as a scene-painter of the great panorama of human action or as a philosopher of life is difficult to determine. He is certainly remarkable for both.

While Stephen Crane was a student in Syracuse University he did a large amount of newspaper hack-work. It was his habit after lunch to repair to the cupola of the Delta Upsilon Chapter house and read, smoke his water-pipe—of which he was very fond—and write sketches which found their way to the *Detroit Free Press*[61] or the various Syracuse dailies. He also did the city correspondence for the *New York Tribune*. It was his delight to block out the plot of a story and then tell his friends about it, putting it in various lights and constructions, and then asking which was more effective. His book, "Maggie: A Girl of the Streets," was thus detailed to some of his acquaintances.

Crane never really enjoyed being treated as a freshman, and always resented any encroachments on his freshman dignity. One day the steward of the club (a senior) was going to sharpen the carving knives. He came into the library, which was crowded, and said: "I want a freshie to turn grindstone; come on, Crane!" "Steve" didn't come, but retorted, with a red face, that he "never had and never would turn grindstone for anybody," which was voted as very bad grace for a freshman. He was always a great admirer of nature, a beautiful landscape or flower appealing strongly to his artistic taste. Coupled with his love of nature was a strong poetical imagination, which was quick to seize on a passing scene. One day, going down the campus, when the fields were fairly yellow with dandelions, he said: "If I could only write poetry I'd tell about the Goddess of Money showering down the gold-pieces."

Mr. Crane was born in Newark, N.J., in 1872,[62] and is therefore only twenty-four years old. His ancestry is English. He is a son of the late Rev. Jonathan T. Crane, D.D., and is a lineal descendant of Stephen Crane, who came from England in 1635 with the company that settled at Elizabethtown, N.J., thus planting the first English colony in that province. His mother was a daughter of Rev. George Peck, D.D., an eloquent Methodist minister and at one time editor of the *Christian Advocate,* of New York, the official organ of the Methodist Episcopal Church. Stephen Crane's father was a learned divine, a man of broad scholarship and generous enthusiasm, an alumnus of Princeton, president of Pennington Seminary, Pennington, N.J., for nine years, and four times a member of the General Conference, the legislative body of the Methodist Church. He was a manuscript preacher and a writer of rare ability, adorning his discourses with a style of rich beauty. He was also a noted wit, which was particularly evident in debate and private conversation. Stephen Crane inherits much of his intensity of expression from his gifted father. The family tree has produced several clergymen and soldiers. It is an interesting study in heredity to note the influence of these two professions in Mr. Crane's literary work, the one furnishing the basis of style, the other of incident. . . . [63]

[Peaslee briefly summarized Crane's literary career after college, listed his books, and quoted from Letter 206 (or an identically worded one) in Wertheim and Sorrentino, *Correspondence.*]

He has just signed a contract to write for *McClure's Magazine* on a salary, which is a very comfortable arrangement indeed.

~

19 / George F. Chandler

George F. Chandler (?–?) was a member of the class of 1894 at Syracuse University.

Source: George F. Chandler, "I Knew Stephen Crane at Syracuse," *Courier* 3, no. 1 (1963): 12–13.

[Crane] was not popular but I liked him. He always talked about how hard life was and how unfair it all seemed to him. He certainly was unusual and all along showed me that he intended to do as he pleased with his life, and would not be bossed by any one.

I told him in 1891 that I was changing from my course in Music and was going to try to get enough points at the College to obtain a Medical Students Certificate from the Regents of New York state so that I could enter the College of Physicians and Surgeons, Columbia University, New York City. He answered, "That's interesting. I also am going to leave here very soon. College life is a waste of time." I then asked him what he was going to do. He said, "I am going to be a newspaper reporter."

3
New York City

20 / Hamlin Garland

Hamlin Garland (1860–1940), an early crusader for realistic fiction and an important mentor of Crane, grew up in Wisconsin, Iowa, and the Dakota Territory, an experience that led to his bleak depiction of farm life in *Main-Travelled Roads* (1891) and *Prairie Folks* (1893). Between 1891 and 1894 he published a series of essays that articulated a new theory of realism called "veritism," that emphasized local color and impressionism, and that greatly influenced Crane; the essays were published as *Crumbling Idols* (1894). Though the two writers drifted apart in Crane's later years, Crane remained indebted to Garland.

Following Crane's death, Garland published four accounts of their relationship— one in 1900, one in 1914, and two in 1930—that span a period of thirty years and that are the only sources for important events in Crane's time in Asbury Park and New York City. Unfortunately, the accounts are contradictory. To clarify the relationship between Crane and Garland, I have reprinted the most complete reminiscence, Garland's 1930 account in *Roadside Meetings;* the endnotes point out the major differences between it and the three other reminiscences.

Source: Hamlin Garland, *Roadside Meetings* (New York: Macmillan, 1930), 189–206.[1]

In July of 1891, I gave a series of lectures at Avon-by-the-Sea in a summer school managed by Mr. and Mrs. Alberti of New York.[2] Among other of my addresses was one upon "The Local Novel," and I remember very distinctly the young reporter for the *Tribune* who came up to me after the lecture to ask for the loan of my notes.

He was slim, boyish, with sallow complexion, and light hair. His speech was singularly laconic. "My name is Crane," he said. "Stephen Crane," and later I was told that he had been a student in a school near by, but had left before graduating to become a newspaper writer in New York. As I recall it, his presence at Avon was due to the Albertis, who knew his family—anyhow, he was reporting for the assembly.

Although not particularly impressed with him in this short interview, the correctness of his report of my lecture next day surprised me.[3] I recognized in it unusual precision of expression and set about establishing a more intimate relationship. We met occasionally thereafter to "pass ball," and to discuss the science of pitching, the various theories which accounted for "inshoots" and "outdrops," for he, like myself, had served as a pitcher and gloried in being able to confound the laws of astronomy by making a sphere alter its course in mid-air.

In the middle of my second week he turned up at my boarding house in a very dejected mood.[4] "Well, I've got the bounce" he said with a sour twist of his mouth. "The *Tribune* doesn't need me any more."

Not taking him seriously, I laughingly said, "They're making a mistake."

"That's what I told them," he answered. "But you see I made a report of a labor parade the other day, which slipped in over the managing editor's fence. When he read it in print he sent for me, made a little speech, and let me out."

"I should like to see that report," I remarked.

Thereupon he took from his pocket a clipping from the *Tribune* and handed it to me. It was very short, but it was closely studied and quite merciless in its realism. It depicted that political parade of tailors, house painters, and other indoor workers exactly as they appeared—a pale-faced, weak-kneed, splay-footed lot, the slaves of a triumphant civilization, wearing their chains submissively, working in the dark for careless masters, voting for privilege, seemingly without the slightest comprehension of their own supine cowardice; but it was Crane's ironical comment, his corrosive and bitter reflection upon their servility, and especially their habit of marching with banners at the chariot wheels of their conquerors, which made his article so offensive to the party in power.

Handing the article back to him I asked, "What did you expect from your journal—a medal?"

He smiled again in bitter reflection. "I guess I didn't stop to consider that. I was so hot at the sight of those poor, misshapen fools shouting for monopoly that I gave no thought to its effect upon my own fortunes. I don't know that it would have made much difference if I had. I wanted to say those things anyway."

He went away a few days after this, and I forgot all about him till in the winter of 1892 when I met his friends, Mr. and Mrs. Alberti, with whom he kept in touch in New York City.

My brother Franklin was playing at this time in Herne's famous New England play, "Shore Acres," and I, busied on some unimportant book, was "baching it" with him, in a small apartment,[5] when there came to us through the mail a yellow, paper-bound volume called "Maggie: A Girl of the Streets."[6] The author's name was given as "Johnstone [i.e., Johnston] Smith," and across the cover in exquisite upright script were these words: "The reader of this book must inevitably be shocked, but let him keep on till the end, for in it the writer has put something which is important."[7]

The first sentence of the story had not only singular comprehension and precision, it threw over its sordid scene a somber light in which the author's tiny actors took on grandiose significance. "A very small boy stood on a heap of gravel for the honor of Rum Alley. He was throwing stones at howling urchins who were crowding madly about the heap and pelting him. His infantile countenance was livid with fury. His small body was writhing in the delivery of great crimson oaths. His features wore the look of a tiny insane demon."[8]

In another paragraph the bully appears. "Down the avenue came boastfully sauntering a lad of sixteen years, although the chronic sneer of an ideal manhood sat already upon his lips. His hat was tipped with an air of challenge over his eyes. Between his teeth a cigar stump tilted at the angle of defiance. He walked with a certain swing of the shoulders that appalled the timid." This was Pete.

Such were the principal male characters. Maggie was the sister of one, the victim of the other, and the heroine of the book. On her fell all the tragedy, all the disgrace of a life in the East Side slums. Frail flower of the muck, she went early to her decay and death.

It was a bitter story, but it interested me keenly. I secured Crane's address from Mrs. Alberti and wrote at once to him, accusing him of being the author of the book.[9] I gave my own address and asked him to come and see me. Soon afterward he came to our little apartment and confessed his authorship of the book.

"Maggie," he said, "has been only privately half published and therefore remains entirely unsold." (A sample copy of this edition of "Maggie" sold recently for over two thousand dollars, illustrating once again the unpredictable trend of literary taste.)[10]

He was living at this time with a group of artists or art students ("Indians," he called them), in an old building on East Twenty-third Street.[11] According to his acridly humorous description of their doings, they all slept on the floor, dined off buns and sardines, and painted on towels or wrapping paper for lack of canvas. He complained of the noise and confusion of these "savages, all dreaming blood-red dreams of fame."

He was distressingly pale and thin at this time, and appeared depressed, but no sooner had he filled his "crop" with the meat and coffee which my brother served, than he gave out an entirely different expression. He chortled and sang as he strolled about the room, comically like a well-fed hen, and for an hour or two talked freely and well, always with precision and original tang.

He interested me more than he did my brother, and although his change of mood was very flattering to Franklin's skill as a cook, he never offered to assist in washing the dishes. I did not ascribe this to laziness; on the contrary, he always appeared to my brother and me as one remote from the practical business of living. We were amused rather than irritated by his helplessness. He never mentioned his kin and I assumed that he was estranged from them.

One day late in March[12] he arrived, reeking as usual with stale cigarette smoke, with a roll of manuscript in the side pocket of his long, shabby gray ulster.

"What have you there?" I asked, pointing accusingly at his conspicuous burden. "It looks like poetry."

He smiled sheepishly. "It is."

"Your own?"

"Yes."

"Let me see it!" I commanded, much amused by his guilty expression. Handing the roll to me with a boyish gesture, he turned away with pretended indifference, to my brother. Upon unrolling the manuscript, I found it to be a sheaf of poems written in blue ink upon single sheets of legal cap paper, each poem without blot or correction, almost without punctuation, all beautifully legible, exact and orderly in arrangement. They were as easy to read as print and as I rapidly ran through them, I was astounded by their power. I could not believe that they were the work of the pale, laconic youth before me. They were at once quaintly humorous and audacious, unrhymed and almost without rhythm, but the figures employed with masterly brevity were colossal. They suggested some of the French translations of Japanese verses,[13] at other times they carried the sting and compression of Emily Dickinson's verse and the savage philosophy of Olive Schreiner,[14] and yet were not imitative.

"Have you any more?" I asked after I had come to the end of the roll.

"I have four or five up here," he replied, pointing toward his temple, "all in a little row," he quaintly added. "That's the way they come—in little rows, all ready to be put down on paper. I wrote nine yesterday. I wanted to write some more last night but those 'Indians' wouldn't let me do it. They howled so loud over the other lines that they nearly cracked my ears. You see we all live in the same box," he explained with sour candor, "and I've no place to write except in the general squabble. They think my verses are funny. They make a circus of me."

I was greatly interested in his statement that the verses were composed in his mind all ready to be drawn off. "Do you mean to say that these lines are arranged in your head, complete in every detail?"

"Yes, I could do one right now."

"Very well. Take a seat at my desk and do one for me." Whereupon with my pen he wrote steadily, composedly, without a moment's hesitation, one of his most powerful poems. It flowed from his pen like oil, but when I examined it,

I found it not only without blot or erasure, but perfectly correct in punctuation. I can not be sure of the poem but I think it was the one which begins: "God fashioned the ship of the world carefully" and goes on to tell how "a wrong called," God turned His head and this ship without rudder slipped down the ways, and as a result has ever since wandered helplessly, going foolish journeys, doubling on its track, aimlessly drifting through the universe.

It appealed to me with enormous force at the moment. Coming from this hungry, seedy boy, written in my commonplace little study on a sunlit winter morning without premeditation—so he said—it wrought upon me with magical power. I understood a part of the incredulity of "Those Indians" who could not take their fellow "Indian" seriously. He declared that it had never been on paper before and that he had not consciously arranged its words in his mind. He just knew in a general way that it was there to be drawn off.[15]

After he went away I read the poems aloud to my brother pausing to exclaim over their ironic humor, their brevity their originality of phrases. "What has the fellow been reading? If they are wholly the work of this unaccountable boy, America has produced another genius as singular as Poe," I concluded.[16]

I confess that I took these lines very seriously. I hastened to show them to my most scholarly friends in order to detect the source of their inspiration. They remained original. I could not say that Crane had imitated any other writer.[17]

He continued for some weeks to "precipitate" others but in diminishing flow. I recall that he came into Herne's dressing room at the theater one night to tell me that he had drawn off the very last one. "That place in my brain is empty," he said, but the poem he showed me was not a cull—it was tremendous in its effect on Herne as well as on me.[18]

Later, much later, he wrote to say that he had gained the power to "turn the poetic spout on or off," but my interest in his verse was momentarily weakened by another and still more amazing demonstration of his subconscious endowment.

One day[19] he turned up just in time for luncheon with another roll of manuscript, a roll so large that it filled one of the capacious pockets of his ulster. "What have you there," I demanded, "more lines?"

"No, it is a tale," he said with that queer, self-derisive smile which was often on his lips at this time.

"Let me see it," I said, knowing well that he had brought it for that purpose.

He handed it over to me with seeming reluctance, and while he went out to watch my brother getting lunch I took my first glance at the manuscript of "The Red Badge of Courage," which had, however, no name at this time.[20] The first sentence fairly took me captive. It described a vast army in camp on one side of a river, confronting with its thousands of eyes a similar monster on the opposite bank. The finality which lay in every word, the epic breadth of vision, the splendor of the pictures presented—all indicated a most powerful and original imagination as well as a mature mastery of literary form.

Each page presented pictures like those of a great poem, and I experienced the thrill of the editor who has fallen unexpectedly upon a work of genius. It was as if the youth in some mysterious way had secured the cooperation of a spirit, the spirit of an officer in the Civil War. How else could one account for the boy's knowledge of war?

I spoke of this and in his succinct, self-derisive way, he candidly confessed that all his knowledge of battle had been gained on the football field! "The psychology is the same. The opposite team is an enemy tribe!"

At the table, while he applied himself with single-hearted joy to my brother's steak, I brooded over his case, and looking across at him, sallow, yellow-fingered, small, and ugly, I was unable to relate him in the slightest degree to the marvelous manuscript which he had placed in my hands. True, his talk was vivid, but it was disjointed and quaint rather than copious or composed.

Upon returning to my little study I said to him very seriously, "Crane, I daren't tell you how much I value this thing—at least not now. But wait! Here's only part of the manuscript. Where's the rest of it?"

Again he grinned, sourly, with a characteristic droop of his head. "In hock."

"To whom?"

"Typewriter."

"How much do you owe him or her?"

"Fifteen dollars."[21]

Plainly this was no joking matter to him, but my brother and I were much amused by his tragic tone. At last I said, "I'll loan you the fifteen dollars if you'll bring me the remainder of the manuscript to-morrow."

"I'll do it," he said as if he were joining me in some heroic enterprise, and away he went in high spirits.

He was as good as his word,[22] and when I had read the entire story[23] I set to work to let my editorial friends know of this youngster.[24] I mailed two of his completed sketches to B. O. Flower of the *Arena*,[25] asking him to be as generous as he could, "for the author is hungry"; and I suggested to Crane that he call upon Irving Bacheller,[26] who was then running the Bacheller Syndicate, and say to him that I had advised Crane to make certain studies of East Side life in New York City and that I hoped the Syndicate would commission the writing of them.

Crane seemed grateful for the little I was able to do, but was not at all confident of earning a living with his pen.

I remember talking with him about "the bread lines," which regularly formed each night at certain bakeries which gave away their stale bread, and at my suggestion he went down one winter's evening, joined one of these lines, and made a study which he afterwards called "The Men in the Storm," a fine sketch which syndicated, I believe, along with others of somewhat similar character.[27] And yet in spite of my aid and these promising activities, he remained almost as needy as ever. Thin and seedy, he still slept on the floor—according to his own story, smoking incessantly and writing in any possible corner.

One day when he was particularly depressed I said to him, "You'll be rich and famous in a year or two. Successful authors always look back with a smile on their hard times."

"You may be right," he replied soberly, "but it's no joke now. I'd trade my entire future for twenty-three dollars in cash."

Without claiming too much for my powers as a fortune teller, I could not believe that this boy would long remain obscure. He had too much to give the reading world. His style was too individual, his imagination too powerful, to fail of winning the applause of those who count originality among the most desired qualities of American literature. Some of his phrases were to me quite inevitable for their condensation and clarity.

He had a genius for phrases. For example: in speaking of a truck driver he said, "In him grew a majestic contempt for those strings of street cars that followed him like *intent bugs*." As for Maggie, "To her the world was composed of hardships and insults." Of the mother, "It seems that the world had treated this woman very badly and she took a deep revenge upon such portions of it as came within her reach. She broke furniture as if she were at last getting her rights."

Of course I am aware that the character of these books did not make for popularity, but I was sure that the marvelous English which this boy had somehow acquired would compensate for his street loafers, birds of the night, beggars, saloon keepers, drunken tenement dwellers, and the like.

"Your future is secure. A man who can write 'The Red Badge of Courage' can not be forever a lodger in a bare studio."

He replied, "That may be, but if I had some money to buy a new suit of clothes I'd feel my grip tighten on the future."

"You'll laugh at all this—we all go through it."

"It is ridiculous, but it doesn't make me laugh," he replied smilelessly.

In the *Arena* for June, 1893, I reviewed a novel by Bourget and "Maggie" under the caption, "An Ambitious French Novel and a Modest American Story."[28] So far as I knew this was the earliest review of Crane's first book.[29] In this notice I made use of these words: "It is a story which deals with vice and poverty and crime, but does so not out of curiosity—not out of salaciousness, but because of a distinct art impulse to utter in truthful phrase a certain rebellious cry. It is the voice of the slums. The young author, Stephen Crane, is a native of New York City and has grown up in the very scenes he has described. His book is the most truthful and the most unhackneyed story of the slums I have ever read—fragment though it is. It has no conventional phrases. It gives the dialect of the people as I have never before seen it written, crisp, direct, terse. It is another locality finding voice. Mr. Crane is but twenty-one years of age."[30]

II

Shortly before I left for the West he called to tell me that he had shown his verses to Mr. John D. Barry and that Mr. Barry had "fired them off to Copeland & Day."[31]

"I am sorry—I was on the point of interesting a New York publisher in them."

The poems appeared soon after in a form which too strongly emphasized their singularities. With the best intention in the world, Messrs. Copeland & Day gave a leading to the critics who quite generally took the "Black Riders" as a cue for laughter.

I saw nothing of him during 1894,[32] but in May of that year he wrote me from Chicago[33] a letter in which he mentions the poem he read to Herne and me:

> I have not written you because there has been little to tell of late. I am plodding along on the *Press* in a quiet and effective way. We now eat with charming regularity at least two times per day. I am content and am writing another novel[34] which is a bird. That poem, "The Reformer," which I showed you in behind Daly's theater, was lost somehow, so I don't think we can ever send it to the *Arena.* I can't remember a line of it.
>
> I saw "Hannele."[35] Its reason for being is back somewhere in the Middle Ages, but as an irresponsible, artistic achievement, it's great. I sat and glowed and shivered.
>
> When anything happens, I'll keep you informed. I'm getting lots of free advertising. Everything is coming along nicely now. I have got the poetic spout so that I can turn it on or off. I wrote a Decoration Day thing for the *Press* which aroused them to enthusiasm. They said in about a minute, though, that I was firing over the heads of the soldiers. I am going to see your brother soon. Don't forget to return to New York soon, for all the struggling talent miss you. Yours as ever.

His next letter[36] was from 143 East 23rd Street., Nov. 15:

> So much of my row with the world has to be silence and endurance that sometimes I wear the appearance of having forgotten my best friends,

those to whom I am indebted for everything. As a matter of fact, I have just crawled out of the fifty-third ditch into which I have been cast and I now feel that I can write you a letter that won't make you ill. McClure was a Beast about the war novel and that has been the thing that put me in one of the ditches. He kept it for six months until I was nearly mad. Oh, yes, he was going to use it, but finally I took it to Bachellers. They use it in January in a shortened form. I have just completed a New York book that leaves 'Maggie' at the post. It is my best thing. Since you are not here, I am going to see if Mr. Howells will not read it. I am still working for the *Press*.

Another note[37] written at 111 West 33d Street, City, Wednesday P.M., begins abruptly: "I have not been up to see you because of various strange conditions—notably, my toes are coming through one shoe and I have not been going out into society as much as I might. I hope you have heard about the 'Uncut Leaves Affair.' I tried to get tickets up to you, but I couldn't succeed. I mail you last Sunday's *Press*. I've moved now—live in a flat. People can come to see me now. They come in shoals, and say I am a great writer. Counting five that are sold, four that are unsold, and six that are mapped out, I have fifteen short stories in my head and out of it. They'll make a book. The *Press* people pied some of "Maggie," as you will note."

Another note[38] from the Lantern Club, New York City, July 17, 1895, refers to his book of poems: "I have lost your address and so for certainty's sake send this to the *Arena*. I am just returned from my wanderings in Mexico. Have you seen 'The Black Riders'? I dedicated them to you, but I am not sure that I should have done it without your permission. Do you care? I am getting along better—a little better—than when I last saw you. I work for the Bachellers."

Thus it appears that in spite of the booming of friends and the talk of critics he had not achieved even comfort. His letter was written at the old place in Twenty-third Street.

The serial publication of "The Red Badge of Courage" brought him an admirer in the person of Ripley Hitchcock of Appleton's, who made him an offer for the book at "customary royalty."[39] He accepted, glad of the chance. This helped him somewhat, but as royalties are only paid annually and as the book sold very slowly, he continued to suffer need.

At this point his affairs took a sudden turn upward. He became the figure I had hoped to see him become two years before. Some English critics wrote in highest praise of "The Red Badge,"[40] and the book became a critical bone of contention between military objectors and literary enthusiasts. Crane was accepted as a man of genius.

Some time in the summer of 1896 he called at my New York hotel and, not finding me, left the following note:[41] "Just heard you were in town. I want you to dine to-night with me at the Lantern Club, sure! Roosevelt expects to be there. He wants to meet you. Don't fail. I will call here at six, again."

He also left a book, "George's Mother," in which he had made this characteristic inscription, "To Hamlin Garland of the great honest West, from Stephen Crane of the false East."[42]

This dinner at the Lantern Club was important in several ways. I do not recall meeting Roosevelt, but Irving Bacheller was there and we had much talk about Crane and other matters. The club met in a very old building, in its loft, as I recall it, on Williams Street and the walls of the dining room were covered with the autographs of so many distinguished writers that I hesitated to add mine. It was a bit of the Colonial New York which had perilously survived, I say perilously, because it gave way soon after to a modern building, and remains but a pleasant memory to the older newspaper men of to-day.

I saw Crane several times during his troubles with the New York police,[43] and while I sympathized with him in his loyalty to a woman whom he considered had been unjustly accused of soliciting, his stubborn resolve to go on the stand in her defense was quixotic. Roosevelt discussed the case with me and said, "I tried to save Crane from press comment, but as he insisted on testifying, I could only let the law take its course."

The papers stated that Crane's rooms had been raided and that an opium layout had been discovered. Altogether it was a miserable time for him. The shady side of his bohemian life was turned to the light.

Meeting him in McClure's office one day, I said to him very earnestly, "Crane, why don't you cut loose from your associations here? Go to your brother's farm in Sullivan County and get back your tone. You don't look well. Settle down to the writing of a single big book up there, and take your time to do it."

Impulsively thrusting out his hand to me, he said, "I'll do it." Alas! He did not. He took a commission to go to Greece and report a war. On his return from Greece he went to Cuba.

Long afterward Louis Senger, one of his companions on this mission, wrote to me conveying the information that just before they went to Cuba Crane told him to write to me in case anything happened to him down there.

[Garland quoted the 9 October 1900 letter from Crane's boyhood friend Louis C. Senger (Stallman and Gilkes 318–19), though he misread the name "Linson" as "Lawson":]

There was no particular message for you, but if you do not already know it, I believe he wished me to assure you that the appreciation shown for his early work by yours and Mr. Howells was the first of that particular success which he so much craved. I read your article in the *Post* and liked it much, but Crane's force was entirely in himself, I think, and entirely natural. I'm sure I do not know why he should have showed me so much of his work, and God knows I must have hurt him. I read "Maggie" from chapter to chapter in a house over on the far East Side, where he lived with a crowd of irresponsibles. I brought Lawson who is my cousin, and Crane together and we were the first to read his "Lines." One day he told me he was going to write a war story and later he showed me some chapters of the "Red Badge." "I deliberately started in to do a pot boiler" he told me then; "something that would take the boarding-school element—you know the kind. Well, I got interested in the thing in spite of myself, and I couldn't, I couldn't! I *had* to do it my own way." This was the first and only time I ever knew Crane's courage to falter in the least, and this was after five years of it, and he was writing then on the paper the meat came home in.

I saw him only once after the Cuban affair. He was sick, and joked mirthlessly that they had not got him yet. You know that he was essentially a soldier. He would have elected to die in battle rather than wait for the slower death of which I believe he had a prophetic knowledge.

He spoke of you often, and always with a sense of blame for himself lest you should think him ungrateful. He was never that.

After the Cuban war, Crane married and went to England, where he lived till he was ordered into Germany for his health. I have only one letter from him while he was in England, and in that he told me nothing of himself. It was all about a new writer he had discovered, a certain Joseph Conrad.[44] "Get his 'Nigger of the "Narcissus,"'" he wrote. "It is a crackerjack. Conrad knows your work. You should meet him when you come to England."

It was more than twenty years later when I met Conrad in Bishopsbourne and talked of "The Nigger" and of Crane. "A wealthy admirer[45] turned over to the Cranes a great, half-ruined manor house not far from here," said Conrad, "and Stephen kept open house there. The place was so filled with his semi-bohemian associates in London that I seldom went there—I didn't enjoy his crowd, but I liked him and valued his work. I went over to see him when he was brought to Dover on his way to the Black Forest. He wore a beard and was greatly emaciated. The moment I looked into his eyes I knew that he was bound for a long voyage and that I should not see him again. He died soon after in Bavaria."

In an article written soon after Crane's death, I said:[46]

He was too brilliant, too fickle, too erratic to last. He could not go on doing stories like "The Red Badge of Courage." The weakness of such highly individual work lies in its success by surprise. The words which astonish, the phrases which excite wonder and admiration, come eventually to seem tricky. They lose force with repetition and come at last to be distasteful. "The Red Badge of Courage" was marvelous, but manifestly Crane could not go on repeating a surprise. When he wrote in conventional phrase his power diminished. If he continued to write of slum life, he repeated himself. It seems now that he was destined from the first to be a present-day Poe, a singular and daring soul, irresponsible as the wind. We called him a genius, for he had that quality which we can not easily measure or define.

His mind was more largely subconscious in its workings than that of any man of my acquaintance. He did not understand his own processes or resources. When he put pen to paper he found marvelous words, images, sentences, pictures already formed in his brain, to be drawn off and fixed on paper. His pen was "a spout," as he himself says. The farther he got from his own field, his inborn tendency, the weaker he became. Such a man can not afford to enter the dusty public thoroughfare. His genius is of the lonely wood, the solitary shadowland.

To send him to report actual warfare was a mistake. His genius lay in depicting the battles which never saw the light of day, and upon which no eyes but his own had ever gazed. He was a strange, willful, irresponsible boy, one that will not soon be forgotten out of American literature.

I see no reason to change this estimate of him.

↬

21 / Corwin Knapp Linson

Corwin Knapp Linson (1864–1959), one of the artists and illustrators that Crane lived with in New York City between 1893 and 1895, spent part of his childhood in Port Jervis and Sullivan County. His cousin Louis C. Senger introduced him to Crane in the winter of 1892–93, and they became close friends. In May 1894 they visited coal mines near Scranton, Pennsylvania, on assignment, and Linson drew the illustrations that accompanied Crane's article "In the Depths of a Coal Mine" (*McClure's,* August 1894). Crane depicted Linson as Corinson in "Stories Told by an Artist"; as Gaunt in "The Silver Pageant"; and partly as Hawker in *The Third Violet.*

Linson's 1903 reminiscence offers details about Crane's life in New York and circumstances surrounding his writings. Linson later expanded his reminiscence to a book-length manuscript that was published posthumously in 1958; passages from the extended reminiscence appear in the notes.

Source: Corwin Knapp Linson, "Little Stories of 'Steve' Crane," *Saturday Evening Post* 177 (11 April 1903): 19–20.

I was closely associated with Stephen Crane during the years just preceding his success, when we both had our feet in the same Slough of Despond.[47] We parted—for a season, I thought—when he went to Athens at the time of the Greek War, after a last evening together in New York.

My first meeting with him was in the winter of 1892–3. One Sunday afternoon, Mr. Louis C. Senger, a cousin who was one of his intimates, brought him to my studio in the old building on West Thirtieth Street and Broadway. It was a dreary day, and the gray light filtered in through the cobwebby panes of the great sidelight, finding us in a kind of half-gloom. He talked little, sitting on a divan quietly smoking cigarettes. He impressed me as an unusual individuality, at first reserved, but soon expanding in the warmth of our comradeship.[48]

It was a good beginning. His long rain-ulster became a familiar object, for those were slushy, drizzly days, and the winter air was oftener sleety with cold rain than fluffy with feathery snow. One day a pocket contained a yellow-covered book—the *Maggie,* which was left for me. It was read with enthusiasm and immediately clamored for. His vigorous English and deep human sympathy fairly took me by storm. The book was resigned with a smile. "There are heaps of them left; the public isn't crazy about having them."

And then its history came out: how no publisher would take it, so that he had had it printed at his own expense; how it had been turned down by the newsdealers,[49] icily received by prominent clergymen who did not preach that way,[50] and how two eminent literary men alone had stood by him with encouragement.[51] Afterward I saw the yellow stacks of unsold books in his rooms.

My place was a black den in those days, and my affairs harmonized, so that it was quite a congenial retreat for Crane. It was his daily habit to come and compare notes. When the news-stands declared war, he became savagely caustic; when such men as Howells and Garland, who were to him the last word in American literature, called his book a great performance,[52] he was seriously elated, happy beyond expression. I have often wondered if Mr. Howells knew the deep joy with which his good opinion filled Crane.

His facility used to astonish me. Sitting on my couch, rings of gray smoke circling about him, a pad on his knee, he would turn out a complete story in a half-hour. Sometimes it was a fragment that would be laid by for future use. Several sparkling sketches were invented and written in that atmosphere of melancholy, while I sat at my easel dabbling at a drawing and wondering how a new illustrator could get in his "wedge."

A visit to his rooms one morning[53] discovered him in undress with a wet towel turban-like about his head, feverishly writing. He waved me to a seat, and soon handed me the first pages of a story. "Been at it most of the night, and it's nearly finished."[54] It appeared long after in one of the papers. Its characters were taken from the class that furnishes cheap entertainment at the seaside resorts, and it was slight enough as a tale. But what amazed me was the vivid drawing of these people, his picturing of their life and environment, his insight into their motives and habits, months after he could have been in touch with them at all, revealing keenest observations and understanding.[55] One might say that like qualities are the common equipment of the artist, but he had them in an uncommon way.

Crane had many loyal friends then, but, unfortunately, they were as poorly situated as himself: young doctors working out their hospital apprenticeship, boyish reporters and artists for obvious reasons unspoiled by prosperity; my cousin, who was none of these but equally at home with all; a half-dozen as ardent souls as ever banded together, widely scattered as to domiciles but easily mobilized for whatever there was afoot, to whom economy was at once a bugbear and a necessity. There were joyous days, and when fortune once sent us oysters and a beefsteak the notable occasion was duly celebrated.

It was about that time that he had a story of two men who went bathing on the Jersey coast, and, in toying with a derelict raft, were carried out to sea, picked up by a little coast schooner, and taken to New York.[56] He asked me to illustrate it, "on spec," and as I had no other work to do I went through it from title to tailpiece, and never had more fun with anything.

There no editor hounding me for urgent haste, the author was delighted as things progressed, posed himself for the tall man—he was thin enough!—stuffed a pillow in the clothes of a friend for the fat man (it was funny to see that pillow swelling from beneath a tightly-fitting bathing-suit), and I grimaced in a glass for the bath-ticket seller in his box.

When finished, the whole thing was sent to a magazine, which had already printed a sketch of his. Then I went camping up in Ramapo.

When I returned, the package had also reappeared, having been "considered" for most of the summer. Crane had reported it accepted, and we were correspondingly happy, but somehow it lost its bearings.[57]

The after fate of our effort was unknown, except that it disappeared in the mazy offices of one of the magazines, and never came to the surface.[58]

In the spring of '93 Crane used to spend hours in my place rummaging through old periodicals, poring over the Civil War articles.[59] I did not then grasp his drift, nor did he explain his interest in them. But he was sounding, trying to fathom the inwardness of war through the impressions on record, as I afterward understood. He did express some impatience with the writers, I remember.

"I wonder that some of those fellows don't tell how they *felt* in those scraps. They spout enough of what they *did,* but they're as emotionless as rocks."

He was evolving *The Red Badge of Courage.*

He had, also, several short sketches in hand which he casually called the Baby Stories.[60] I had three of them in camp that summer to study for pictures, but nothing came of them. For lucid analysis of the very young human heart I never saw their like. The winter following was a hard one for Crane. It was not honey for me, exactly, but it was growing kindlier, while for him it presented a face of stone. He was now in the old League building on Twenty-third Street, rooming with several young illustrators and newspaper artists.

One morning early, after a blizzardy night, I found him in bed.[61] He looked haggard. He was alone, the others being presumably in pursuit of the art editors.

Pulling a manuscript from mysterious seclusion, he tossed it to me. It was the sketch, "The Men in the Storm," suggested by Mr. Garland. He had been all night at it, out in the storm in line with the hungry men, studying them; then inside, writing it.[62]

This was the period of his tramp studies, written for a press syndicate. He disappeared from view for days, and was suddenly dug up looking as if he had lived in a grave. All this time he had inhabited the tramp lodging-houses nights, and camped on the down-town park benches days. With grim delight he related how an old acquaintance had passed him a foot away, as he sat with a genuine hobo in front of the City Hall, and how the police had eyed his borrowed rags askance, or indicated with official hand that another bench needed dusting.

One evening he came to me, bringing several loose sheets of manuscript.[63]

"What do you think I have been doing?"

"I can imagine anything, Steve."

I've been writing—poetry!"

"Great Scott! let me see."

Well as I knew him, I was not prepared for what came. The sheets of legal-cap were handed over, and I read those marvelous short poems. I did not know how good they were. I confessed that they were something new to me, but that they made me see pictures, great pictures.

"Do they, honest?" delightedly.

I added that they moved me profoundly.

"Is that so?" seriously.

"Indeed they do, Steve, they're immense! How did you ever think of them?"

"They came."

That seemed to be the way of it, they just "came." And that was my introduction to his new character.[64] I have two of those poems now.

One, happening to be there, seeing some of them and handing them back with, "I don't know much about poetry," called forth an energetic protest after he left.

"I know every one can't like them, but I hate to give a man a chance to hit me in the neck with an ax!"

It was not very long after that that an "Authors' Reading" was given, and my cousin Louis went with me, for some things from *The Black Riders* (still unpublished) were to be read.[65] Far from reading his own work, at the idea of which he was aghast, Crane could not be induced even to go and hear—"would not be dragged by the neck"—so in dread was he of a misunderstanding of his work. He could stand up to adverse criticism like a catcher behind the bat, or retort to a gibe, giving better than he received—for his wit had a keen edge, and he was a master of repartee—but cold indifference was the "ax in the neck." The war of the newsdealers upon his *Maggie* was unjust, and he scorned them, but the slight put upon his book by the clergymen to whom he sent it chilled his blood.

So he awaited our report in his room. We made it glowing, for the audience was enthusiastic and the "Lines" had been most effectively read by Mr. Barry.

As to Crane's environment at that time, his statement of it could hardly have been greatly exaggerated. The fellows with whom he lived used to receive his verses as good material for the comic papers, for they jeered at everything. It is the attitude of youth. Once, as we sat by ourselves amid the confusion of tables laden with all the litter of writing and drawing tools, unwashed coffee-cups, newspaper drawings, tobacco, bread, pipes, while about us were crazy chairs, unkept beds, disorderly trunks and shelves, and room-long reach of quaking stove pipe—everything at war with everything else—he said to me:

"Confound their cheek; they even parody my verse!" Then he laughed and pointed to a pinned-up squib on the wall, with a caricature of himself above it. It was a parody, and clever, so like his style that he might have been its author.[66]

"They make me ill—but they don't mean it, and I get my innings! They're a husky lot."[67]

There were at least five of them, all on the war-path. More than once I was one of the roomful of "Indians" whose vision of things was distorted in the dim haze of smoke.

Something of this life of his is reflected in *The Third Violet*.

We knew all the Cheap-John restaurants together. There was one to which many congenial spirits flittered on Saturday nights; where absolute liberty of emotion was allowed, where a table could break out into song and wild gayety without annoying any one particularly, where there was much confusion of tongues, where bad wine took the place of "draw one," and where the waiters conjured the knives, forks and spoons from the depths of cavernous breeches' pockets and wiped them on their sleeves! There could be no etiquette in a place like that, except that of good humor. We Americanized its French name into the Buffalo Mode,[68] and once each week we carried our troubles to its murky atmosphere and joyous company. The life of our table—always the middle one of the room—was Crane, and the cheeriest sallies were from his lips.

I had almost forgotten the "towel painting."[69] During that camping summer in the Ramapo backwoods, I had my only two yards of painting canvas slung on a line over my hammock like a roof, to shed the rain, and the next best thing was to make more. The only form of linen up there was in the shape of coarse towels, which I used singly, or sewed together, painting over a coating of glue. They did very well until one of them got rained on, when my hardly secured study flaked off in great spots. But my picture of that year ('94) in the Society was painted on one of those towels!

That summer we were sent to do the mines at Scranton. It was Crane's first assignment from one of the magazines,[70] but he had not enough money to pay his fare from New York.[71] Luckily, I had enough just then to see us through, and we undertook it joyfully. We were expecting after that to do the sea-divers, going down in diving rigs—but it did not happen.

After this, I saw less and less of him, for in '95 he made an extended tour through the West for a press syndicate, going into Mexico, and not returning for some months. A note or two only, from the West and New Orleans, were the only signs I had of his existence.

But he grew rich in material on this trip. He suddenly appeared one evening, and held me breathless and intent with tales of adventure. One of them I saw afterward in print, but his vivid telling was so much more effective than even his strenuous pen-picture, that the written story seemed to lose color as I contrasted the two in my memory.[72] That his luminous phrasing was not a trick was never more evident than then. It was simply Crane.

His speech was free from the danger that his writing ran, of weakening with repetition. Each scintillation eclipsed the last, but left a complete impression of delight.

He brought back a half-dozen opals, some with the lambent flame of the sunset in their fiery depths. He freely gave me the choice of the lot. I took a little one that flashed at me with the gleam of a rainbow. Crane laughingly added a fine water opal to it. The next morning he said:

"It's [a] good thing you came in for a deal yesterday, for the newspaper Indians gave me a dinner last night,[73] and they got my pretty pebbles!"[74]

I frankly regretted that I had made no better use of my opportunity!

And now—'96—our meetings were less frequent. He spent much time away from New York, and I also was absent some months abroad. Finally he sent for a box of manuscript that had been some time in my care, and soon after unexpectedly showed himself at my door,[75] just before his departure for Athens and the Graeco-Turkish war. He was full of his prospective trip. It was a new phase of life, actual war, and the excitement of it was upon him.[76] It was late when we parted, and it was my final "good-by."[77] Almost his last words were references to his almost native Sullivan County (New York) which was also my own, provoked by some inane remarks of men at a nearby table at dinner.

"If they only knew it as we do, eh," he said laconically, "they couldn't make such brilliant asses of themselves before old inhabitants."

After that, only occasional reports came, of his living in England, of his presence in Cuba. From a brother with the army at Santiago,[78] I heard of him.

"I met your friend Crane at Santiago. He's going to Manila, he says. He's a hustler, isn't he?"

And then a long blank, until, living in Paris, I heard of his illness in England, and before I could realize his condition the news of his death came.

It is inevitable that there must exist a nipping regret at the cutting off of a brilliant individuality in its early development. His was a cometlike career. And undeniably erratic and irresponsible in much as he was, he was lovable to a degree, daring and chivalrous, generous as the air, compelling a genuinely warm affection from those who best knew him; and for his genius I sometimes felt not a little awe, as for a power mysterious and unaccountable.

22 / Frederic M. Lawrence

Frederic M. Lawrence (?–?) and Crane first met as Delta Upsilon fraternity brothers at Syracuse University in January 1891. That summer and for five summers afterward, they and their friends camped in Sullivan County, New York, and Pike County, Pennsylvania. In the fall of 1891 Lawrence went to New York City to attend medical school. During the autumn and winter of 1892–93, he and Crane roomed together in a boarding house on Avenue A that they shared with a number of other medical students, which they named the Pendennis Club. Here Crane made the final revision of *Maggie: A Girl of the Streets*. In fall 1893 Lawrence moved to Philadelphia to complete his medical studies. After getting his degree in May 1894, he stayed in Philadelphia to practice medicine. Crane occasionally visited him, most notably in October 1896 when he left New York City to avoid the publicity surrounding the Dora Clark incident.

Source: Frederic M. Lawrence, "The Real Stephen Crane," typescript, 25 pp., Newark Public Library, Newark, N.J.[79]

Editor's note: The dating of the reminiscence "The Real Stephen Crane" is uncertain. Following the publication of Beer's biography in 1923, Lawrence wrote Beer to say that though he liked the book, "it seems to me that it misses much of the real Stephen Crane." In all likelihood, Lawrence's letter inspired him to write his own "Real Stephen Crane," which he did not complete before 1930, a year he mentions in the reminiscence. The reminiscence exists as twenty-five typewritten leaves numbered [1]–3, 2a, 3–23. Internal evidence suggests that the twenty-five leaves are portions of three different drafts. Leaves 1–3 are part of the first draft, leaf 2a is the sole extant leaf of the second draft, and the remaining leaves, 3–23, represent the final draft. When Joseph Katz edited the reminiscence for publication as part of a November 1980 celebration commemorating Stephen Crane Month in New Jersey, he combined the drafts to create an eclectic text that deleted repetition, an appropriate decision given that his audience was primarily laypeople. I have chosen, however, to reprint the complete text for a scholarly audience. Though Lawrence retells certain incidents at Syracuse, he recounts them differently in the drafts. Because he did not cancel text, it is not certain that a detail described in the first or second draft would have been ultimately deleted from a final draft.

To prepare the drafts for publication, I have made the following editorial changes: Because Lawrence sometimes underlined book titles, sometimes used quotation marks, and at other times used both with the same title, titles are regularized with italics. Obvious typographical errors and missing punctuation have been silently corrected. In a few cases Lawrence could not complete the typing of a word at the end of a line because of a lack of space; because in each case it is clear what the word would have been, I have silently reconstructed it. Occasionally Lawrence typed additional text between lines. In some cases these revisions were to be inserted into a sentence; at other times they replaced a word or phrase. Although Lawrence did not always cancel revised passages, I have inferred that an interlined word or phrase above uncanceled text should be read as a revision. For example, Lawrence first typed "with travail," then inserted "amidst" above "with," thus implying that the final reading should be "amidst travail." In each case Lawrence's final intention seems clear, and the revisions are stylistic rather than substantive. Lawrence also left a blank space for the name of the editor of the *Philadelphia Press,* Talcott Williams. I have added the name in brackets.

[leaves (1)–3]:

It was in Syracuse; the year, 1890.[80] As I started up the long plank walk that led to the fraternity house, I saw one of the upper-classmen waiting for me, and with him was a stranger. "I want you to meet Brother Crane," he said, a formula as orthodox with fraternity men as with Methodist preachers. "He has just come to us from the Lafayette chapter."

We fell into step as we climbed the long hill and silently took stock of each other. The newcomer was a youth of about twenty, slim, wiry, potentially athletic in type, with yellowish blond hair, high cheek bones, deep-set grey eyes and a tawny complexion. He was silent for a time—I soon came to know this as his habit—but finally said: "You come from Port Jervis, don't you? Perhaps you know my brother Will Crane, the lawyer."

Of course I did. Few inhabitants of that village were unacquainted with each other. The conversation thus established then flowed on into the quick intimacy of boyhood. Soon it appeared that our respective fathers had been intimate friends in their day, and from the random recollections thus evoked I was able to piece together the structure of Crane's own family. His father had been a Methodist clergyman of the lovable type now almost extinct, and at one time was president of Pennington Seminary. His mother, of another type and one unfortunately less extinct, was a sister of Bishop Jesse T. Peck, that shining light in the Methodist hierarchy, and she herself was an early and ardent crusader for temperance, prohibition and public morals along approved Wesleyan lines. Unkind observers had been heard to remark that it might be better for her brood of fourteen if she could spare them a little more time from the great work—but even a Jeanne d'Arc could not escape criticism in this man muddled world. I judged that it was her command, predicated on a free scholarship in Syracuse, that had wrenched an unwilling Stephen from the delights of Easton[81] and brought him to this more saintly environment.

Here, at any rate, he was, and almost at once he became a reproach to the industrious, anathema to the pious and a joy to the un-Godly. The rest of us studied, some; Crane, not at all. His contempt for the canting, self-righteous group of eminent clergymen that surrounded him was little concealed. As for the college faculty, a few casual visits to the class-rooms inspired in him no respect for their characters or their attainments, and he disdained to submit himself to their exactions. He ceased even to appear in the classes, and to this day I wonder what, unless it was regard for his saintly forebears, saved him from expulsion from the university. Yet when I look back I know that a mind such as Crane's was utterly unfitted for ritualistic educations. One cannot conceive him moiling over Greek verbs or Sanskrit roots. Words meant much to him, to be sure, but they must be English words, short and curt by preference, words to depict a scene or clarify a thought. As to mathematics, his whole career gave evidence that figures, such as may be represented in money, meant nothing at all to him. His mind was as keen and incisive as his speech, quick in perception, logical in deduction, but it simply could not be cramped into the ready-made mold of any educational system. It was better so. The literary mind differs intrinsically from the scientific mind. Purely technical studies can only stultify it.

Having thus promptly and fearlessly raised the standard of revolt, Crane settled down to acquire such education as he desired in his own way. Already he was mature in mind. His intellect was indifferent to authority or tradition. It examined any new conception with complete detachment, reached conclusions with utter disregard for accepted beliefs. His room in the chapter-house, heavily curtained to keep out—and in—unwelcome light and sound, speedily became a citadel for the un-Godly. That small group of rebels which is always found even in the most unintellectual of institutions made it a headquarters. Crane, often taciturn, never by any means the most loquacious, directed the trends of thought. His own future was determined. He was to be a writer, and by no uncertain implication a great one. Already his room was littered with stray bits of manuscript, and he could talk with pride of his success as correspondent for the *Tribune* at Asbury Park, N.J., where "the ocean of the Lord adjoins the beach of James A. Bradley."[82] One of his older brothers was a newspaperman in New York, a member of the Press Club, and "Stevie" spoke of him with the reverence of an acolyte. Afternoons—he was never an early riser—were apt to find him, bull-dog pipe clenched in his teeth, turning out copy, college items or whatever came his way, for such of the metropolitan journals as specialized in such news. Already his handwriting was notable for its round legibility, its carefully accentuated punctuation. Each sentence was carefully thought out, precisely constructed, before it was committed to paper, and composition was necessarily slow. Thus toilfully he wrote his first story. It was entitled "Jack" and was the tragic story of a dog. Looking back through the years, I still regard it as a remarkable bit of sympathetic narrative. Crane loved all animals, and particularly dogs, and none could write of them with more perfect understanding. He sent the manuscript to *St. Nicholas,* then scarcely entered upon its long decline, and when it came back our disappointment was only slightly tempered by the appreciative editorial note that accompanied it.[83] So far as I know, he never submitted the story to another editor.

[leaf 2a]:

educational system. Perhaps it was better so. His mind was already mature. It was indifferent to authority or tradition, examining each new fact of conception with complete detachment and reaching conclusions without regard to accepted beliefs. It was, however, a literary rather than a scientific mind. Purely technical studies would have meant distraction. Words and their mastery, the ability to use them with simplicity and accuracy, was his one ambition. Even then, his room was littered with stray bits of manuscript; and where he went, throughout his life, his trail was marked by such odds and ends. His reading was but casual. In fact, he once confessed to me that he feared to read lest it influence his own style.

Strange to say, his scandalous indifference to prescribed studies seemed to arouse no resentment on the part of the university faculty. If they remonstrated, we never heard of it. There was about Crane, with his sombre face, his silences, his occasional ironic utterance, a *noli me tangere* that effectually rebuffed all criticism. He went his own way, and nobody ventured a protest.

His room speedily became the headquarters of that small group, always found in student communities, which rebels against the current conventions and hypocrisies. In that sanctimonious environment protest against the pet prohibitions of the pious Wesleyans seemed a duty. Since smoking was on the index, we laid in a heterogeneous supply of pipes and puffed at them all day long and half the night. Only when the supply of "Mastiff"—or was it "Jack Rose"?—ran out were the furnishings of that room more than faintly visible.

[leaves 3–23]:

this it may be divined that our finances were not always flourishing. Nevertheless, since the theater was under theological proscription, we attended it as near nightly as possible; and since strong drink was anathema, we made violent efforts to conquer our dislike for various untempting beverages. I still recall the night when each of us, firmly convinced that in its brilliant green color lay the very essence of evil, sipped eight small glasses of frappéd *crème de menthe*, and reached home around midnight more nauseated than intoxicated. Other sins eluded us. Crane could never subordinate himself to the set movements of the dance, so that prohibition escaped violence. As to women, there were romantic whispers, nothing more.[84] We played cards almost incessantly and we made the late hours cheerful with song, with a special predilection for drinking chants and more ribald ditties. We played hearts, fan-tan and even essayed poker. Once we attempted an all-night session and grey dawn found four sad-eyed youths, unsustained by the alcohol of their elders, seated around the littered table in a room reeking with stale smoke. Naturally there was nothing left but to go to bed for most of the next day, and it was a long time before we repeated the experiment. As I look back, there is something pathetic about the effort of those youngsters to be gay young dogs in that grim Methodist environment.

Most of us studied, some, Crane, not at all. For the university's faculty he had conceived such a fierce contempt that he rarely climbed "the hill."[85] For one of them, Prof. Charles J. Little,[86] then teaching ancient history, he maintained a whole-hearted admiration, but this was not enough to drag him forth to classes. Individuality such as Crane's never could be subordinated to ritualistic education. He spent the greater part of each day lounging about his room, reading in desultory fashion, writing occasionally and smoking incessantly. His build was that of a natural athlete and he played baseball so well that his indifference to a place on the team made him the despair of the coach. His tennis, too, was above the average. He played a bit almost daily, but his favorite recreation was found in long walks over town and country. Then his rather sententious habits of expression disappeared, and he talked enthusiastically of the world, of life, of himself. His early training at the old Claverack Military Institute, on the Hudson, had aroused his enthusiasm for military affairs that colored his entire life. Already he was an authority on the organization, equipment and methods of every important war force in Europe. He could mention offhand the numbers of each standing army, the tonnage of each navy and its gun-power. The place and character of the "next war" was a perpetual subject of speculation. As to himself, his future was in literature, and never for an instant did he doubt his own success. One of his older brothers was already on the staff of the *New York Tribune*[87] and Stevie regarded him almost with reverence. He himself had done newspaper work as a special correspondent from Asbury Park, and he had already taken on something of the patronizing attitude of the professional writer. He was contributing occasional bits of college news to the *Tribune,* and now for almost the first time he began to turn his hand to fiction. Many an afternoon found him, bull-dog pipe clenched in his teeth, turning out copy in that clear, legible hand of his. Each sentence was carefully thought out, precisely constructed, and then committed to paper. Naturally such composition is slow, and one or two pages might constitute a day's work. Thus toilfully he wrote his first story. It was entitled "Jack" and was the tragic story of a dog. Looking back through the years, I still think of it as a remarkable bit of sympathetic narrative. Crane loved all animals and particularly dogs, and none could write of them with better understanding. He sent the manuscript to *St. Nicholas,* then just entering upon its long decline, and when it came back his disappointment was slightly tempered by the appreciative editorial note that accompanied it. So far as I know, however, he never submitted it to another editor. For a long time it lay among the scattered papers in his room. At Syracuse there persists a tradition of lost Crane manuscripts. If any persist, this might well be one of them, but the chances are that it lay about collecting dust until some clean-minded person swept it out and away.

About this time interest in literary pursuits languished while we created for ourselves a new den. The top of the house was surmounted by an old, unfinished cupola, and we were struck by its possibilities. At vast expense we laid in a stock of thick paper and tacked it to the protruding beams, and from various odd sources we procured an ancient if not antique rug and several odd bits of furniture. Each of us managed to add a Turkish pipe to his already large equipment, and soon we were lounging around the floor in true oriental fashion, talking for long hours of science, art, literature and of course our own lives. If the set courses of the university were contributing little to our education, we were doing a lot for ourselves.

Spring came. I went home to Port Jervis, and soon Crane turned up at his brother's house. His college education might be said to have ended before it had fairly begun. His studies thenceforth were at that far greater institution that comprehended nature and life itself. With two added friends[88] who today are scarcely less distinguished than those who made up our little coterie in Syracuse we entered upon much the same kind of a life. We spent the days wandering into the nearby hills and occupied the daylight hours with pipes, books and conversation. In the evenings we played cards, still with much conversation. For August we organized a real camp, almost a *de luxe* affair for those days, and spent four weeks in the wilds of Pike County, Pa. As I recall it, our days were devoted mostly to ransacking the shores of the adjacent lakes for logs with which to maintain the night's huge camp fires. The choicest hours were those spent around its blaze, and when the light died down at last, we wrapped ourselves in blankets and slept on the ground like true savages. Crane loved this life, and his health was magnificent. As the month wore on, exposure to the sun gave his skin a copper color almost like that of an American Indian, and it formed a strange contrast to his still light hair. So great was the success of this camp that for several subsequent summers we made similar incursions into Pike County. Between times we made shorter journeys, often into Sullivan County, N.Y., and from our experiences there Crane drew inspiration for his first published stories, a series of short, droll stories of four campers in which the writer—alas—figured as "the pudgy man."[89] The first of them, I recall, was entitled "The Octopush" and appeared, as they all did, in the Sunday editions of the *Tribune*.[90] So far as

I know, they have not been reclaimed from anonymity for inclusion in Crane's works.[91] After our return from one of the greater camps, Crane was seized with a desire to chronicle its strange doings in true newspaper form. As a result there appeared one issue of the *Pike County Puzzle,* a four-page six- or seven-column journal in which everything from headline to closing period was Crane's own work.[92] Probably every copy by this time is lost, mislaid or crumpled into dust. It is a pity, for as an example of his early dry, half-humorous, half-sardonic style it can have no rival.

When Autumn came, I went to New York to study medicine and saw little of Crane for several months. In those days the medical term was short, however, and Spring found us together in Port Jervis. Much too early, in May, we attempted to go camping in Sullivan County. We had scarcely pitched our tent when rain set in, one of those cold, penetrating storms that lingers for days. We had no firewood at hand, the tent was utterly inadequate and for four days we sat about and shivered. Between times Stevie ventured out to a nearby tree and decorated its trunk with an appropriate inscription: "Allah il Allah! And it rained forty days and forty nights." As soon as the storm ceased and the roads became passable, we struck the tent, gathered up our traps, and hiked back to town. Out of that drab experience, mixed with the dreaded night noises that assailed our youthful ears, Crane fashioned a bear story that appeared later in, I think, the old *Cosmopolitan.*[93] He was writing more or less steadily, now, and all the time observing with that quiet intentness. That summer went as had its predecessors, but we had added one vice to our list: we were learning to drink beer. Crane was twenty-one now, I not far behind him, and it behooved us to acquire the habits of adults. I am sure the watery concoction never did us the slightest harm, and it added, as such beverages always have, the one touch needed to make the social evenings complete. We spent our days in the open, the month of August in Pike County, and it would have been difficult to find a hardier specimen than the lithe and muscular Crane of those days.[94]

In October, when I returned to New York, Crane went with me. Eight of us, all medical students except himself, had arranged to take over a house at 1064 Avenue A—who then could have foreseen the Sutton Place of today![95]—and the informal organization was christened "The Pendennis Club."[96] Stevie and I shared a large back room on the second floor whose windows looked directly over the East River. Feet on the window-sills, pipes in our mouths, we spent long hours watching the busy traffic of the river and the long, slow-crawling caterpillars over on Blackwell's Island which we knew to be lines of lock-stepping convicts. While I worked—more or less—during the day, Crane loafed about the room, read a little, smoked a great deal, and between times sallied forth to observe the teeming life of the tenement-lined side streets near us. During the previous year he had met Hamlin Garland,[97] then writing some notable stories of the West, and had become an admirer of the latter's rather mild realism. A more important influence, though he might later have disclaimed its strength, was our reading. At that time our library, as I recall it, consisted of Voltaire's *Candide,* a collection of short stories by de Maupassant and one of Zola's books, I think it was *Pot-Bouille.* The forceful naturalism of the French school had its profound effect. The narrow cross-streets around us were filled with squalid habitations whose denizens almost filled the roadways, and here was material hitherto little used. Crane observed it all with keen and sympathetic, if detached, vision. To a certain extent he could enter into an understanding of this submerged populace, and he made it his task to peer beneath the surface. One day he came in, his usually somber face alight, and queried abruptly. "Did you ever see a stone-fight?" And when I replied in the negative, he launched into a glowing description of one that he had just seen. A little later that same day the description had been set down on paper, and the first chapter of *Maggie* was written. As the story, a sordid tale of life in the tenements and the under-world took shape in Crane's mind, he became enthusiastic, I with him, and we sallied forth into the mean streets and dangerous neighborhoods in search of the local color that would give life to the great work.[98] Our search took us far afield. We explored the Bowery, then in the heyday of its multicolored existence. We saw life and incidentally spent many a pleasant evening in the old Atlantic Garden or at Blank's, nearer Fourteenth street, in either of which one could enjoy good music and passable variety at the cost of a few glasses of beer. In moments of affluence we bought cut-rate tickets for Koster & Bial's huge music hall in Twenty-third Street,[99] where two hours of good specialties were followed by a shortened but not inadequate rendition of one of the great opéra bouffe.[100] Frederick Solomon, brother of Lillian Russell's one-time composer husband, was producer as well as comedian, and to him we were indebted for a wide acquaintance with those classical operettas. Carmencita[101] came, too, and in memory I can see the long line of Spanish students that were her orchestra. We saw the opening of a new music hall, further uptown, that a few years later was to attain fame as Weber & Field's.[102] Sometimes we could afford theatre tickets, always at cut rates, and thus we saw Loie Fuller[103] produce her famous dance for the first time. Our crowning luxury, indulged only in some period of great opulence, was a dinner in one of the little French or Italian restaurants that were springing up in the side-streets. There for fifty cents one could have half a dozen appetizing courses and a bottle of the wine not yet known to the cognoscenti as "red ink." To us it represented luxury, and to this day the memory of those dinners is a happy one.

All the time Crane was observing details of this more or less seamy side of life and mentally grouping them. During the afternoons he wrote. His method was unchanged. For a long time he would sit wrapt in thought, devising his next sentence. Not until it had been completely formulated would he put pen to paper. Then he wrote slowly, carefully, in that legible round hand, with every punctuation mark accentuated, that always characterized his manuscripts. Rarely if ever did a word or mark require correction. That sentence completed, he would rise, re-light his pipe, ramble around the room or look fixedly out of the windows. Usually he remained silent, wrapt in deep thought, but sometimes he would break into some popular song or bacchanalian ditty and sing a single bar of it over and over again while he waited for his inspiration to come. No friend would break in upon him at such times, but occasionally an idea would occur to him and his face would light up while he broke into conversation. Then the fire would die away and the tense, glum expression would return to his face. Each sentence seemed born amidst travail. He did not seek suggestions, however, nor did he welcome them. His work was completely his own.

Naturally composition such as this was slow. Often a single page represented a day's work and rarely did the output exceed two or three pages. Sometimes he did not dip pen in ink for days at a time. Yet slowly and surely the manuscript grew, and thus *Maggie: A Girl of the Streets* came into being.[104]

I never knew whether Crane actually offered the manuscript of *Maggie* to any publisher or not. Stevie was a strangely reticent person in some respects. His friendships, for example, were kept in separate compartments of his mind, and rarely did one acquaintance even hear another mentioned. It was thus also with any disappointment or rebuff that came to him: he kept it to himself. So complete was his confidence in his own genius and its future that to even appear conscious of a slight would have seemed an unworthy concession. Yet this egotism of his was inoffensive. It was never paraded, was scarcely apparent to those who knew him best. His charm, and it was a great one, is difficult to explain. He had great capacity for friendship, though his circle was always somewhat restricted. His sympathy was felt rather than expressed. His long silences in themselves were pervaded with this elusive factor. He was intuitive, entering into the unexpressed thoughts of his associates without effort. In short, he was a keen natural psychologist, a reader of the minds of men, and to this he owed his remarkable hold on all who got to know him well. When he spoke, it was in a pleasant rather deep drawling voice with quaint idioms of his own manufacture. It was Stephen Crane the man rather than the writings of Crane that exercised such a spell over all his acquaintances.

At any rate, his first book was finished. Its depiction of slum life seemed far more startling in 1892 than it would in this year of our Lord 1930. In fact, Crane hesitated to bestow his own name on so shocking an intellectual child.[105] He had always, he explained to me, maintained that distinction could be conferred on the most commonplace of names by a bit of manipulation. For example, a very slight change would transform plain "John Smith" into aristocratic "Johnston Smith," and over that imposing *nom de plume* the book could appear without attracting any thunderbolts in the direction of its daring author. At her death his mother had left a small estate, and suddenly Crane found himself in possession of about a thousand dollars.[106] As I have said, I do not know whether any publisher had even had the opportunity to decline the book, but now that mattered not at all: the book would be printed at once. I don't suppose he ever gave a thought to what would happen after that. He did not even go to an experienced printer of books. He went to a little printing shop on lower Sixth Avenue whose sign we had often noticed, they set a price and it was agreed to without demur. I cannot even remember the name of the firm, but I do recall Crane's asking me, not long afterwards "Did you ever hear of Ferdinand Ward?—you know, of Grant & Ward?"[107] The catastrophe that overtook that Wall Street firm and brought ruin to the old general as well as his Napoleonic partner was still too recent to have been forgotten. and I replied in the affirmative. "Well, I saw him today"; and with that he stopped and never referred to him again. Whether it was in connection with the printing of the book I cannot say. Crane was undergoing the pangs and ecstacies of reading his own proof those days, and his mind was remote.

At last the work was done, and perhaps a hundred copies of the volume bound in traditional yellow paper were delivered to our room. We read and re-read them ourselves, and Crane mailed presentation copies to his few literary friends and reviewers, and copies to the leading magazines and journals. Then he waited. Nothing happened. The skies did not fall, and Earth-bound editors seemed serenely unaware of the new star in the literary firmament. So far as I know, not one review appeared.[108] The critics did not even trouble to castigate the author of so daring a bit of realism. I have never known quite what Crane did expect to happen, but whatever that was, it simply didn't. Worst of all, he had spent his entire patrimony on this profitless venture. All that he had to show for it were the packages of books stacked about the room.

Just about this time a group of young architects, among them several friends of ours, had formed the "Kit-Kat Club," and we offered them the use of our "clubhouse" for their first smoker. Of course we in turn were invited to join in the festivities, and we did. In fact, we took a very active part in brewing the huge bowl of punch which constituted the main decoration. As each guest arrived, all those already assembled drank his health; and as the company arrived by ones and twos, the results to early comers were rather disastrous. By the time the party was complete, all were in a highly cheerful state. In fact, the uproar coming from that house was so great that the entire neighborhood was soon hanging out of its windows in an effort to determine whether it was a riot or a political convention. In the midst of the uproar one of Crane's friends who knew his predicament was seized with an inspiration. With a threatening hammer in one hand and a package of the neglected volumes in the other, he circulated among the guests and demanded that each possess himself of a copy of the master-piece at the extravagant price of fifty cents each.[109] I verily believe that these were the only copies of that edition of *Maggie* ever sold. Presumably not one who bought the book that night has retained it; but if he has, it must rank as rela-tively the most profitable purchase of his entire life. As to the evening itself, it was so joyous that we rather resulted [resented?] the vulgarized account of it which Crane subsequently utilized as a scene in his second "slum" book, *George's Mother.*[110]

Naturally the profits from this sale did not go far toward solving Crane's most pressing problem, that of subsistence. He was not earning a penny, and such money as came his way then and always slipped through his fingers without leaving a trace. He was not and in fact never became a newspaper man in the usual sense of that term. He was utterly incapable of maintaining the regular hours of work necessarily demanded by a newspaper from its staff, he could not bring himself to report in routine fashion the stories that he unearthed, and his slow, meticulous method of composition was the last thing in the world for a man expected to turn in a definite number of words at a set hour each day. Crane's was not a genius that could be harnessed to routine, and this more than one editor was to find out to his sorrow. That he made more than one earnest effort to meet with journalistic requirements is undoubted, but his report of a case was apt to fix itself on some one trivial detail, such as the viewpoint of the criminal or the aberrations of a witness, in forgetfulness of the rounded story that the public demanded. In consequence he held no position whose attached salary assured a living, and these were lean days for S. Crane. Most of his time was spent in the room, smoking—he was the only man I ever knew who could impart a mahogany color to clay pipes—writing and between periods of silence breaking into rather slow, whimsical speech more or less decorated with slang of his own invention. He turned out stories, sketches of incisive if sardonic humor, but few of them were readily marketable and even when accepted the payment was delayed until publication. I recall one of them. It was a study of a young man engaged in surreptitiously reading a French novel in search of erotic cli-maxes, and was entitled "Why Did the Young Clerk Swear?" It was accepted by the old *Vanity Fair*,[111] forerunner of the present smart chart. When Crane re-ceived fifteen dollars for it, he celebrated with a champagne supper and next day was as poor as ever.

One ray of sunlight burst through the clouds. Crane had sent a copy of *Maggie* to Hamlin Garland, and the latter brought it to the attention of William Dean Howells, at that time the undisputed head of American letters. Mr. Howells, ever on the look-out for budding genius, sent the young writer an invitation to call at his apartment at 40 West 59th Street. Intense was the excitement in one house in Avenue A the night that Stevie, arrayed in his best, went forth to call on the great man, scarcely less subdued was our interest in the report of the meeting; but when he returned Crane took refuge in his customary taciturnity and told practically nothing. Only subsequently and at intervals, bit by bit, did I hear the details. Mr. Howells, himself a sincere if unexciting realist, had received the young man with friendly informality, praised the promise of his work and encouraged him to go on with his studies of East Side conditions. Thus probably was Crane induced to persist in this profitless field. He was soon at work on his second book, *George's Mother.*

. . . Once when his fortunes were at lowest ebb,[112] he slept for weeks on the couch in the studio of an artist-friend in the old National Academy of Design building in East 23rd Street, and for days his only food was the "free lunch" of the little saloon at the corner. When it happened that he sold an article and was flush with money, his opulence was magnificent but fleeting, and for long intervals the Crane fortune was at its lowest ebb. He was becoming known, however, to the powers of the literary world, and if they deplored his bohemianism, they did not doubt his genius. An optimistic publisher gave him a commission to do a series of articles on Mexico.[113] Crane passed comet-wise through Philadelphia, ran out of funds by the time he reached New Orleans,[114] and lingered on to commend the blue skies and happy life of the old city until a fresh remittance arrived. Then he slipped away into the wilds and emerged in a couple of months with a deep tan, a very practical Spanish vocabulary and a set of enthusiastic impressions; but the actual literary crop was small. He wrote a few such stories as "One Dash—Horses," but must have left some fairly large figures on the debit side of the ledger.

Then one day he descended upon me bursting with enthusiasm. He had been commissioned to go South and write a Civil War article.[115] Already I have mentioned his interest in military matters. For years he had never failed to draw out from Civil War veterans their memories, their experiences in the everyday life of an army, and he knew more of war as it appears to the private in the ranks than most of the historians. For a day or two he browsed through my library, selected the best of the Civil War books (of course I never saw them again) and then departed southward. In a few days he wrote from Fredericksburg giving a graphic account of the recollections of Confederate veterans who had seen the Union troops cut down "in winnows" as they attempted to cross the river. He was back in a week or two fairly gloating over his assembled glimpses of war as it really appeared to the common soldier, and set to work at once on a war story that was to depict the impressions of just such a man. He went to his brother's camp in Hartwood, Sullivan County, N.Y., and by Autumn *The Red Badge of Courage* was completed.[116] Though he did not find a publisher at once, Irving Bacheller,[117] then active in the Bacheller-Johnson Newspaper Syndicate, undertook to have it published serially in various journals scattered over the country. It did not attract much attention, though [Talcott Williams], then of the old *Philadelphia Press*, was quick to see and call attention to its merits. Later D. Appleton & Co. had the courage to issue it in book form. I will never forget the day Crane and I went round to Wanamakers[118] and actually purchased our first copy and tenderly carried it around the corner to the old Rathskellar, there to feast our eyes on its pages. Finally Crane, in that careful round hand of his, wrote an inscription:

> Stephen Crane
> and
> F. Mortimer Lawrence, M.D.
> Of a friendship that began when books and
> medicine alike were dreams
> and ended—
> This from one to the other.

and the date.[119] To both of us it seemed then that dreams were coming true. We little anticipated what the next few years would bring.

[Lawrence alluded to the critical praise in the British reviews of *The Red Badge of Courage*.]
. . . The next time he was in Philadelphia Crane dragged me down to Carpenter's Hall, to look at the portraits of the members of that First Continental Congress which had assembled there in 1776. The representative from New Jersey had been another Stephen Crane,[120] direct ancestor of this one, and strange to say in the profile there was a striking likeness. Stranger coincidence, the capture of this Stephen Crane by the Coldstream Guards and his refusal to betray his knowledge of the position of Washington's army was one of the incidents of the American Revolution.[121]

In the flush of his new prosperity Crane and a friend felt wealthy enough to take a flat over in the West Twenties in New York.[122] It wasn't much of a place, but it sufficed for two young men eager to sample life. For a time I saw little of Stevie, but I judged that he was leading a rather lurid existence. He had friends galore now, artists. actors and aspiring writers. Occasionally I would slip over for a week-end and dine with the crowd down at the little old French restaurant known as the "Buffalo Mode" in easy pronunciation of its more dignified title,[123] and there would be much conversation, much red wine and singing galore. Later a new literary club came into being, with many a writer, arrived or aspiring, as members, and Crane its recognized genius. These steadfast friends resolved to emphasize their admiration by giving him a complimentary dinner, and to it the great and the near-great of the literary world were invited.[124] Many came, others sent complimentary messages. Richard Harding Davis, whose "Van Bibber" stories had offered a literary promise that was never, alas, to be fulfilled, did neither. He sent regrets and casually added "I have not had time to read 'The Blue Badge of Bravery.' My regards to Mr. Crane." Though later they were to be thrown together as war correspondents rather intimately, I am sure that Crane never forgave him for that.

Crane turned his hand to poetry. He hadn't the courage to call it that. From Copeland and Day, of Boston, came a slim volume: *The Black Riders and Other Lines* by Stephen Crane.[125] Those "lines" were rhymeless, meterless, reminiscent of the succession to Whitman and the forerunner of the *vers libre* of today. Whatever the volume may have missed in sales was more than atoned for by the storm of criticism that it aroused. Reviewers exhausted their vocabularies of criticism and rhymesters devoted themselves to humorous parody. For once Crane was thoroughly peevish. Nothing could reconcile him to this misunderstanding of the thoughts to which he had given this new form of expression. "They say I am irreligious!" he exclaimed, as he read one criticism. "On the contrary, I am deeply religious," and went on to explain that his resentment was merely against a God who could inflict punishment upon the second and third generations for sins for which they could not have been responsible. I protested that this was but a statement of biologic fact. "That is just it," he broke in. "If there is such a God, I am against him."

That was just it. Crane, descendent of a line of churchly forbears, could not rid himself of a certain degree of religious superstition, but ancestral tradition could not bring him to acceptance of dogma. He had a hazy hope of future life, perhaps because his strong ego could not endure the thought of extinction. In that early article,[126] in speaking of mules deep in the coal mines, some of them born there with never a chance to see the light of day, he had added with sardonic humor that some of them, "especially the young mules," did not believe that such a light existed. Later on he was to speak of death as "the hedge we all have to cross."[127] Yet his mental attitude was closely akin to that of his friend Mark Twain. When a lady, shocked by one of the latter's utterances, exclaimed "But doesn't Mr. Clemens believe in God?" a mutual friend replied "Yes, but he hates him." Pessimism can go no further, but the modern world has come to think thus of the Jewish Jehovah.

At any rate, Crane was not concerning himself deeply about religion. He was leading at last a comparatively carefree life, was working perhaps none too seriously much, but was making great plans for the future. Though he was self-indulgent, he was also kind if sometimes a bit sardonic; and despite all experience he was persistently and unalterably romantic in his conception of women— many of whom, it need scarcely be added, did not deserve it. This brought him close to catastrophe.

[Lawrence began to summarize the Dora Clark incident. For details concerning the incident, see Wertheim and Sorrentino, *Crane Log* 205–8, 210–14.]

. . . So great was the uproar that Crane journeyed over to Philadelphia[128] in order to escape interviewers and let the noise die down; but it refused to do so, and it seemed that the only way to end the innuendos against himself was to bring charges against the offending policeman. Had Crane been wisely counselled, he would have realized the folly of such an attempt against the system that thrives on the vice of cities. He might have realized that in this case, as always, the whole force of the police power would be turned against him. But no, he explained; young Theodore Roosevelt had just been made Police Commissioner of New York, and he would see that he had a square deal. So we drafted a telegram to Mr. Roosevelt telling him that Crane was coming back to bring charges against the policeman, we sent it from the nearest office, and Mr. Galahad caught the next train.

The story of the ensuing trial was told in shrieking head lines all over the country. It was not Stephen Crane against a crooked policeman. It was the police force of New York, it was the entire civic administration, it was Tammany Hall itself against one citizen that had dared defy its minion. Everything conceivable was brought forward in an endeavor to blacken Crane's character and discredit him as a witness. In his absence his flat had been raided, and among his possessions—undoubtedly one of the souvenirs he was so fond of collecting, only to lose them again—was an opium pipe. From this it was presumed that in addition to all his other vices Crane was a dope fiend. To this and to every other slanderous implication the press gave freely of its space. If Theodore Roosevelt possessed any influence, it was never manifested. The policeman was upheld by authority, and Stephen Crane, newspaper man, looked on alas at the harm wrought by irresponsible journalism. Later he gave it voice, but in the meantime he knew and his friends knew that it would be dangerous for him to linger in New York. Hurriedly, plans were made, and almost as quickly put into effect.[129]

[Lawrence concluded his reminiscence by summarizing portions of the rest of Crane's life.]

◠

23 / Nelson Greene

Nelson Greene (1869–1956), along with R. G. Vosburgh and William W. Carroll, was one of several artists and illustrators that Crane lived with intermittently in the old Art Students League building in New York City between 1893 and 1895. Greene moved to Buffalo to work as an illustrator for the *Courier* and later the *Illustrated Buffalo Express* but returned to New York in 1898 to do freelance work for major magazines and companies and was a political cartoonist during World War I. Interested in sculpture, he designed the piece titled *Allies United for Liberty,* which remained on display at the Flatiron Building in New York from 1918 to 1921. Greene left New York City again, this time to become editor of the *Standard* in Fort Plain, New York. A state historian, he is best known for the four-volume *History of the Mohawk Valley: Gateway to the West, 1614–1925* (1925) and the five-volume *History of the Valley of the Hudson: River of Destiny, 1609–1930* (1931).

Greene wrote three reminiscences pertaining to Crane's time in New York City during 1893–95. The 1944 reminiscence, "I Knew Stephen Crane," was published in 1976 (Wertheim 1976); two other reminiscences were written in 1947 for Melvin H. Schoberlin's unfinished biography, "Flagon of Despair." Among the most vivid of the few reminiscences of Crane by friends who knew him during the crucial period when he was writing *The Red Badge of Courage* and *The Black Riders and Other Lines,* these latter two reminiscences offer much greater detail about the events alluded to in the earlier reminiscence and reveal the autobiographical relationship between Crane's art and life in *The Third Violet,* his novel partly based on the studio life he shared with Greene and other artists and illustrators. Reprinted below are excerpts from the two reminiscences written for Schoberlin, with additional material from the 1944 reminiscence in the notes.

Source: Nelson Greene, untitled reminiscence, with cover letter to Melvin H. Schoberlin, 4 September 1947, MS, 24 pp., Box 14, Melvin H. Schoberlin Research Files, Stephen Crane Collection, Special Collections Research Center, Syracuse University Library.[130]

Fort Plain NY

Sept 4/47

—The old Art Students League building at 143 East 23rd street. This was the place where I knew and met Crane in the years 1893, 1894 and 1895. . . .

I went to the Old League building about December, 1893 and went into a small room on the 2nd floor, which was rented by Frederick Vosburgh,[131] a former League student with me. We paid $14 for it monthly. It was heated by a small stove and its furniture consisted of a table, a double bed, several chairs and a long coal box—and an oil stove for cooking.[132] It was here I met Crane who hobnobbed with a number of us who were former art students, and who flocked in there and often jammed the small room. If I remember rightly, Crane came there from his home in New Jersey where I think he was living with an Uncle.[133] I am under the impression his parents were then both dead. Crane mixed easily with us artists and our easy-going ways.

Soon there were four people living in the little room—after Dec. 1893. They were Frederick Vosburgh (Vossy), William Waring Carroll (Bill),[134] Nelson Greene (Ned) and, part time, Stephen Crane (Stevey). I lived there from December, 1893, to about March, 1894, when I went upstairs to share the studio of F. C. Gordon for several months before I went to Buffalo in July, 1894. Crane came and went at the little room. Sometimes he was there for days. Very often over weekends, Friday, Saturday and Sunday. He was generally flat broke, sometimes had a little money. His pants were out at the seat and I loaned him a pair to go to see Howells and Hamlin Garland, also loaned him an overcoat, which I finally "sold" him—a gift.[135] We were about the same size—I about 5 ft. 8 and Stevey a little shorter, maybe 5 ft. 6 or 7. He was short and slender—I was short and stout. . . .

When Crane was there, it made four of us. We slept two or three in the big bed, and one on the coal box. The three others, Carroll, Vosburgh, Crane played poker and smoked constantly from the afternoon till midnight or after, while I went to bed early so I could put in 9 hours daily as a proofreader at $18 per week—for a time on the Funk and Wagnalls Standard dictionary, as, at first, I could get no work as an artist. The four of us were often so hard up that we were down to $2 on Saturday morning. This we invested in a big wad of frankfurters, rye bread, coffee and condensed milk, which took us through the two days. After a month or so Vosburgh got work on a recently established newspaper syndicate, as an artist, and then things got better.

At that time Crane had written *Maggie* and he was writing *Black Riders* and *Red Badge*. We read *Maggie* in paper covers and discussed *Black Riders*. He

showed us some of this verse in MS. Of course as young fellows we discussed
and argued literature, politics, art, religion—everything.

Stevey was an avowed Socialist—Carroll, a Florida man, and I were Demo-
crats of a very very left type and we sympathized with Crane's views.[136] Vosburgh, I think, was a weak Republican, and non-committal.

Crane's literary idols were De Maupassant first (in English) and Zola. I think
he also considerably admired Tolstoi—but De Maupassant was his favorite as a
literary technician.[137] However, he liked anyone who favored his impressionistic
new approach to fictional composition. Carroll and I (both fairly well read)
agreed with him, and we read several French works (English translations), some
of Crane's and Gordon's.

We covered the whole art business from cave men's art to the present (the
then present). It was a time of art revolutionaries. Crane was very fond of color,
and one of our favorite recreations was walking to the pier at the east end of
23rd street on spring and summer evenings and watching the colored lights of
the Brooklyn shore and their light reflections dancing on the waves of the East
River. I think Crane put this in one of his *Black Riders*.[138] Crane bemoaned the
poverty of motives of the painters of the day—the too great following of the
French modernistics. He urged more native impulses, technique and American
pictorial patterns. He had been in the Adirondacks and I remember him saying
"Why don't the American painters do some of those Adirondack trout streams
and their shores, why don't they paint some of those black pools and rocks?"[139]

Not only were we four friends of Crane but he was friends of many other
former League students and a few of their friends who packed this little room,
particularly on Sunday nights. Often then we would all chip in and have a lot
of beer in the smoke filled room. Occasionally some of the fellows got drunk
this way but not often. Vosburgh got full one time and fell and his head landed
in the coal scuttle and he and the floor were a mess of ashes—of course, laughter.
On several Sunday nights (you might as well have the whole rather sordid picture) a rather tough guy, named Eddie Mayhew, brought his "girl" there. She
was a slender, rather plain prostitute, living in a bawdy house, and Sunday was
her "night off." Nobody ever made a pass at her. However she invited us all to
come to her place and stay with her but nobody ever did—*probably* too poor
and female not particularly attractive. Mayhew was a decorator. He was a rather
bad character but he had money. He lent Crane some and they had trouble when
Crane could not pay.[140]

While there in the winter of 1893–1894, there were other former students
who had studios in the building. There were about 10 studios in the building.
In one of these, we had a painting class on several Sunday mornings with about
six fellows working. I painted a very good head of Vosburgh there.

You will probably like the names of the fellows who hobnobbed in the little room, all of whom Crane knew. As I remember them they were:

Stephen Crane (Stevey)
William W. Carroll (Bill)
Frederick Vosburgh (Vossy)
Nelson Greene (Ned)
Dave Erickson[141] (Dave) Swedish stock. He had only one leg, had a studio in building.
Dr. W. A. Dunckel (Dunck) (an old school pal of mine from Fort Plain)
Fred C. Gordon[142] (studio upstairs, very straight laced).
—— Wolfrom (he had been a cowboy, quite a character. Died crazy several years later)
Edward Mayhew (good looking but a bad actor)
—— Hamilton (Hanny) a landscape painter.[143]

There were others but I cannot remember them.
These fellows were all young men—Crane, 23; I, 24; Carroll, 25; Dunckel, 25; Vosburgh, 23; Erickson, 24; Wolfrom, 23. We considered Gordon an old man, at 35. I had shared a studio with him when I was an art student.

I want to stress the fact that those of us who read Crane's stuff in the little room and talked with him absolutely believed in him as a prophet of a new day in American literature. We were much interested in all he produced and read what he showed us with vast appreciation. We felt this way although we knew then he was unrecognized and almost unknown. We sympathized with his utter poverty—but we were all often in the same situation.

Their poker playing was a sort of dope to Steve, Bill and Vossy. I did not play—only very occasionally. I think it was generally for matches, once in a while for pennies. I sat in once in a great while. I considered both Stevey and Bill good poker players—but not brilliant. Steve had a real poker face and I think he was a natural gambler.

. . . Crane got in touch with Irving Bachellor[144] and he began to sell stuff to his syndicate. It was then that Crane and Carroll got into the oldest clothes they had and spent three days and nights in Bowery flop houses. When they came back they looked like perfect bums. Crane wrote it up for Bachellor's syndicate.[145] Is it Batchellor? I forget. Crane's returns from the occasional syndicate articles were small. Crane had an instinctive feeling for the lowest bracket human—probably the Bowery bum, before this adventure but I think it gave him thought and literary material. The gang also toured the Bowery and 14th street sectors and we visited some low down dumps, but not the whore houses (pardon my plain English)—That is we did not as a gang but individually we had a very rare encounter with a street walker or one of the 14th street dives women. I do not think Crane ever took one on then at that time. He was a fellow of remarkably clean mind and speech.[146] Please remember that during all this time he was writing *Red Badge* but he talked little of it, although I remember sometimes we discussed Civil War and its soldier life.[147] This was during the 6 or 7 months of the "little room" life, when he talked more of his *Black Riders,* than anything else.[148] He seemed very much intrigued by this mode of expression—free verse. . . .

2—Date of *Red Badge of Courage*—It was completed and typed in 1894. It was in the early summer that Crane was trying to raise the $15 to get the MS. "out of hock" at the typist's. I had lost my job and had little money. I think it was about May or June,[149] 1894, that he asked me to lend him the money. When I could not, he said he would pawn his Civil War sword—either his Father's or Uncle's.[150] A month or two after this, I received a letter from William (Bill) W. Carroll, who had gone to Buffalo to work as a newspaper artist on the (morning) *Buffalo Courier.* I left the studio at 143 E. 23rd street in July 1894, . . . Carroll's letter contained an offer of a job for me at $10 a week—as a newspaper artist and I accepted it. I made about $4 a week—additional. Crane said I was a capitalist.

3—Back at 143 E. 23rd st., in May, 1895. There I settled down to hard work, writing special stories and illustrating them for the *Express.* The gang that was left took up much of the old life. We often went out (Crane often too) to French table d'hote dinners in the 20s—from 24 to 28 st between Broadway and 6th Avenue. They ranged from 25¢ to 50¢ each. We also ranged up and down 6th Avenue and Broadway when we had money.

. . . [H]e met my model, Gertrude Selene, who was probably the "Florinda." She was reputed at 18 to have the best figure of any model in New York City.[151]

She had beautiful blond hair, gray eyes and she was not beautiful. Nevertheless she was attractive and she was distinctly a man's girl. Kindly do not use her name. She later married a doctor and became highly respectable. She and Crane got on very well. She admired his keen mind and often talked with him and discussed him with me. He never tumbled with her however. A new fellow came in—Dr. Frank B. Cross, of Cincinnati, a friend of Dr. Dunckel. He lived with me in the studio about two weeks.

Another new member also came into the group—William Schindler, a newspaper artist on the *New York Press.* He was an Englishman, not like the rest of the Americans, although he was completely accepted. He was a fairly good boxer and very strong. On one evening, in the summer, four of us—Dunckel, Cross, Crane and Greene and Gertie—put on a dinner party in the studio, with Gertie cooking. . . .

I was at the 23rd street studio from May until the latter part of October—five months. During that time, Crane was with me two weeks, living in the studio, where he wrote the first half of his story "A Gray Sleeve," with a stiff Spencerian pen on long ruled foolscap paper. I read his first half of the story and it was good and I told him so. He seemed to somewhat value my opinion[152]—but he was very decided as to his approach, method and technique and allowed no one to sway him. Together, we talked art and literature with Dunckel and Cross. Schindler and Erickson also came in. This was before "Selene" as we called Gertie came in. Crane then had the *Red Badge* running in syndicate form and I think he had book publication assured. He had returned from his Mexican trip for Batchellor syndicate.[153] I thought his articles were very poor and told him so. I think he agreed. He asked me to go to the Lantern Club, with him for lunch one day, when he was to take his Mexican expense account with him. Batchellor founded the club. He was mildly interesting but the other members seemed like rather weak sisters. Crane was very smart and I noted how he subordinated his quick, keen, flashing mind to their mediocre level. After the rapid fire chatter of the studio, even Batchellor seemed stodgy.[154]

Crane was broke as usual and he was trying to pad up his "swindle sheet" of the Mexican trip. So he took with him a big Army service type revolver, which he said he had to get for the journey. It belonged to another friend, Dr. Biggs, whom we saw very seldom. The "cost" of the revolver went into the expense account. At that time, I was not up on "swindle sheets" and so when Crane showed it to Batchellor that day, I blurted out "Why Steve that's just like Doc. Biggs' gun." Without a flurry he passed it off but on the way home on the 3rd Ave. L. he said "Greene, damn you, what was the matter with you about that gun. You nearly queered my expense account." However the storm soon blew over and, as I remember it, Stevey cashed in his expense account.

At that time, Crane and I had breakfast in my studio and he went to the Lantern Club for lunch. As far as I could make out that made up his day's feed, although he probably had evening snacks in the studio where there were always eats, coffee, tea and often beer and ice cream.

However, Crane's poverty and slackness kept him from eating properly. His teeth were bad at 23 and 24—very bad—and he would do nothing about them—largely from poverty. He smoked cigars incessantly when he could get them and drank quarts of coffee—both black and with condensed milk.[155] His teeth, his bad hours and his disregard of his health and proper food caused us much concern—among his friends. We urged better care on him but he paid no attention. I think these things helped to cause his early death.

As I said, he was about 5 ft. 6 or 7 in., light hair, almost blond, light bluish gray eyes—very direct glance. He had very good features, excellent pointed nose—face slightly narrower than medium—eyes fairly wide apart. He had a rather, kindly, tired tolerance in his eyes, face and attitude. . . .

[At this point, Greene briefly summarized his professional career up through 1918.]

. . . Selene started to pose for me, and Crane, Dunckel, Cross, Selene and I often held evening bull sessions in the studio with tobacco and beer accompaniments. Crane's talk was the high spot. He had a razor edge mind and a clearness of thought and direct exposition of truth, in plain concise quiet expression that was unrivaled. He and I were practically one in our evaluations, and Gertie close behind. Two of the men were conservatives and, on occasion, one of them would dish up the old musty decayed tripe, about amounting to "what is, is right." Crane did not hesitate to stab at such balderdash and I can remember his cutting—"Why do you persist in talking like a damn fool"—and he got away with it. Even a stuffed shirt would have been much impressed by his rapier like statements of truth, his rapid fire meaningful talk. Our night bull sessions were indeed something to remember—particularly contact with a mind like Crane's. It always seemed to me that he was even superior to his literary productions. They did not measure up to the man or his mind at its best.

Potentially, he had the urge to produce, combined with the recurrent lassitude that comes to every creative mind.

When he finished the "Gray Sleeve" first half, he stopped and said "Ned, I'm all written out, my mind's a blank. I can't write any more. I don't believe I'll ever write again. I'm through." After which, being somewhat dumb and with a fierce creative energy inherited from my practical tireless mother, I lectured him—told him it was temporary, that he hurt himself by living on cigars and coffee and that it was his personal reaction. He took it silently, but he didn't change.

[Greene continued a summary of his career and attempted to respond to Schoberlin's questions about Crane's career.]

Source: Nelson Greene, untitled reminiscence, with cover letter to Melvin H. Schoberlin, 3 October 1947, MS, 11pp., Box 14, Melvin H. Schoberlin Research Files, Stephen Crane Collection, Special Collections Research Center, Syracuse University Library.

Fort Plain NY

October 3 1947

. . . First—I want to note two or three men Steve knew at the time of my connection and living with him—November 1893 to July 1894 and the summer of 1895—men not noted before

They were
Gordon Pike—architect
Charles Pike[156]—sculptor
Dr. Biggs
three close friends of each other

The Pike brothers were giants for those days 6 ft. 1 about and heavy. They had both studied in Paris for several years and were close friends of my close friend Lucius Hitchcock, painter, illustrator and teacher of art—with whom I palled for four years of living in Buffalo—1894–1898. Gordon worked as an architect. Charles was slightly clever as a sculptor but never did anything. Their parents had made a big income from brownstone quarries in Connecticut. When that stone went out they went pretty flat—that was after they returned from Paris. They were fine fellows and gentlemen. Very seldom came to our dump but I went to theirs. Dr. Biggs was their close friend.

Crane knew the three moderately well.

Both Pike men were very artistic—Yale grads most agreeable—but not highly creative—too much rich men's sons in their early years. I was very friendly with Gordon.

That covers the Pike boys and Doc Biggs.[157]

Second—In Steve's artists' sketches and *The Third Violet*.

The Den,—as he calls it is an *exact description* of our little dump room where we lived on the third floor of the Old League building. It is also a good description of the halls and stairs.

However—Steve—as throughout in *The Third Violet*—and as any novelist does, has not stuck to exact personal and other descriptions. The big studio, he describes more curtly, was not "across the corridor." It was on the fourth floor above the den.

Now first as to this studio and *"Hawker,"* the successful painter. The fourth floor studio was occupied by Fred Gordon (also my friend, with whom I lived in another studio, while studying art at the League—under Chase and Mowbray 1890–1891). Gordon was not the type of "Hawker" at all.

So Crane is using two actual studios—or a room and a studio (in both of which I lived) but he is fictionizing as to *Hawker* or bringing in another artist type he knew and putting him in Gordon's studio—of that I am positive,—and that is the setting for the parts of The *Third Violet,* which deal with this scene and these artists—the four in the little room or "den" as Steve calls it. However the setting is absolutely the old League building and the room and studio.[158]

Now as to the Characters in "The Den"

He moderately used some of us four—taking what he needed but they are not drawings from life—rather sketches.

W. W. Carroll Wrinkles—positively *must be* Bill Carroll, who played the guitar as one picks up a cigarette to smoke. He had a fund of real southern darky tunes, he had picked up from the niggers in Monticello, Fla., where his father ran a general store.[159] Bill and all his fine family were brought up by mammies— and Bill said he had a good one. He also had fine parents—I met them—and Bill was one of the finest, most cultured men I ever knew—a graduate of a small southern college. The name *WRINKLES* is appropriate as he always looked as though he slept in his clothes.

The Other Characters—they are not so definitely marked.

Great Grief—I would take to be Vosburgh—I forget his first name. We called him "Vossy"—rather an irresponsible, lanky, negative type who had a god-awful mournful face.

Purple Sanderson—I rather think—in a mild way—that is myself—The "Purple" may be a twist of "Greene." Also he speaks of "Purple" not being there in the day and coming in at night. I was proofreading at $18 per week, while the others were out of a job—and that is a twisted turn of "proofreading" into "plumbing."[160] The others had *no "trade"* outside of being artists and the writer, Crane.

As there were only four of us there—Crane, Carroll, Vosburgh, Greene—and as Steve put in another one—"Pennoyer"—I rather think he just invented him. He didn't use himself unless he considered himself "Penny."

Steve evidently wrote the first draft—the artist's sketches while he was with us[161]—or he did it when he went home sometimes and stayed a week or so, and then came back to the den. He did this often—I think he did his writing home—Nov 1893–June 1894. . . .

Florinda—I know positively no *model* ever came to the "den." Gertrude Selene was my model in 1895 in Gordon's big studio, when Fred was abroad and I sublet it—and we all cooked and had meals there and several night parties. Crane was in 4 or 5 evenings when she was there. Dunckel says Gertie now says she only saw him 3 or 4 times but I think it was more than that. She says she only saw him in my studio—one night I remember we had a party for 6 hours with Steve, Gertie, Dunckel, Cross and myself.

It seems Gertie is still alive and around.—so my friend Dunckel writes me,— so I know you will kindly handle her with kid gloves and of course not mention her *name* for she was a pretty swell girl in many many ways and smart.

I still think Crane meant "Splutter" for Gertie. He never saw her nude but she had some marvelous nudes taken of her by a talented artist-photographer. Thoroughly artistic with nothing suggestive. Her slim figure, she was 18, corresponds to Crane's characterization and I feel positive there was no other model in NY that had such a figure and I worked in the life class with a nude woman model every other week and never saw any one that could even approach her beauty of figure—except one *about ten years after* when Crane was in England.

I bought the set of four of these Gertie's photos and had them when Crane was there in 1895 and he saw them. He must have been starting on *The Third Violet* about that time.

[Greene concluded with passing comments about Gordon, Dunckel, Crane, and the Art Students League. He also praised Schoberlin's collection of more than one hundred etchings, alluded to his own paintings and those of his wife, and continued to summarize his own life.]

༄

24 / R. G. Vosburgh

R. G. Vosburgh (?–?) and two other artist-illustrators, William W. Carroll (No. 29) and Nelson Greene (No. 23), lived with Crane at the old Art Students League building on East 23rd Street intermittently between the fall of 1893 and spring of 1895. His reminiscence supplies details about Crane's working habits while writing *The Red Badge of Courage*.

Source: R. G. Vosburgh, "The Darkest Hour in the Life of Stephen Crane," *Criterion*, n.s. 1 (February 1901): 26–27; rpt. in *Book Lover* 2 (1901): 338–39.

The months following the sinking of the money inherited from his father's estate in the unsuccessful publication of *Maggie: A Girl of the Streets*,[162] marked the lowest ebb in the fortunes of Stephen Crane.

When one firm after another had refused to publish the book, Crane finally invested his own money in the enterprise and lost it all. He then went to live in a boarding house on East Fifty-seventh street, near Avenue A,[163] and from there moved with the proprietor to West Fifteenth street. The Fifteenth street undertaking was not a success, and when the house was given up, Crane went to Lakeview, N.J., for a time. When he returned from Lakeview he was wearing rubber boots because he had no shoes, and he slept and lived at the studios of various artist friends until he was asked to become one of the proprietors of a studio at 145[164] East Twenty-third street.[165]

With Crane the studio had four occupants. He could contribute nothing to its maintenance, but he added very little to the expense, and the others were glad to have him. For seven or eight months, from one autumn until the following summer, the four men lived together. It was during that time that *The Red Badge of Courage* was written. At the time he came to live in the studio, Crane was reading over the descriptive articles on the Civil War published in the *Century*.[166] War and fighting were always deeply interesting to him. The football articles in the newspapers were an especial pleasure. "Ah!" he would say after reading one of them, "that's great. That's bully! That's like war!"[167] And whenever there was a warship coming into the harbor, if he could get the ferry fare, he would go down to Fort Wadsworth[168] and stand on the hill there to watch the vessel come in. He has stood for hours in a drenching rain to see a war vessel enter the harbor.

The articles in the *Century*, then, were full of interest and fascination for Crane, and when he moved to the studio on Twenty-third street he borrowed the magazines and took them with him to read and study. All of his knowledge of the war and of the country depicted in *The Red Badge of Courage* was gathered from those articles and from the study of maps of that region.

He always worked at night, generally beginning after twelve o'clock, and working until four or five o'clock in the morning, then going to bed and sleeping the greater part of the day. Crane and two of the others slept in a large, old-fashioned double bed, taking turns at sleeping in the middle; the fourth man occupied a cot. They pooled their resources, and the first man up was usually the best dressed for the day, unless one of them had a particular reason for wishing to present a good appearance. For men struggling as they were against poverty and privation to force themselves into recognition, there was little incentive to go out except in the search for work. On such occasions, when one of the four men had an idea for getting money, the most presentable combination of clothes that could be made was gotten together for him; and many a time one of them has gone out wearing his friends' clothes bravely over a stomach that had missed more than one meal.

Crane spent his afternoons and evenings studying the war and discussing his stories. Every incident and phase of character in *The Red Badge of Courage* was discussed and argued fully and completely before being incorporated into the story. In this he worked differently from the way in which his short stories were written.

At the time of beginning *The Red Badge of Courage* he was writing sketches of East Side children, some of which have been published since; he could not sell them when they were written.[169] These sketches were quite brief, and most of them were written in one night without previous discussion. After writing a story he would put it away for two or three weeks, and work on something else until his mind was thoroughly clear for a fresh consideration of it. When the story was taken out for revision it would be turned over to his friends for criticism, and Crane would argue with them about the objections they would make. He often accepted suggestions for changes, but it always seemed as though these changes were those he had already decided upon himself before they were mentioned by others. This was also characteristic of the discussions of *The Red Badge of Courage*. He convinced himself; others might help him, but he arrived at his own conclusions.

In his work he always tried for individuality. His daring phrases and short, intense descriptions pleased him greatly. They were studied out with much care, and after they had been trimmed and turned and changed to the final form, he would repeat them aloud and dwell on them lovingly. Impressionism was his faith. Impressionism, he said, was truth, and no man could be great who was not an impressionist, for greatness consisted in knowing truth. He said that he did not expect to be great himself, but he hoped to get near the truth. Although he did not expect to be a great man, he often declared that he would be famous, and sometimes for hours in the intervals when he was not working he would sit writing his name—Stephen Crane—Stephen Crane—Stephen Crane—on the books, magazines and loose sheets of paper about the studio. There were plenty of them.

His manuscripts were always scrupulously neat and clean, written in ink on legal cap paper without erasures and without interlineations. In revising his work he would rewrite a whole sheet when a correction was necessary rather than make an erasure, if only to change one word.

The poems published under the title *Black Riders* were also written during this period. Crane himself had a very high opinion of these poems, in which he was confirmed by Hamlin Garland, who, besides William Dean Howells, was his greatest favorite among American authors. The friendship and encouragement of these two men gave him strength and courage in his struggle, and he often spoke of them with pride and gratitude. A critical article by Hamlin Garland[170] comparing Crane and Richard Harding Davis which appeared in the *Arena* during that winter was of immense value to him. The conclusion of the article was that Crane was far superior to Davis, and this opinion Crane often quoted when, under the burden of fresh disappointments, the future seemed to offer no hope. The hard and meagre life—two poor meals a day, a bun or two for breakfast and a dinner of potato salad and sausages warmed over the little stove that heated the room, frequently eaten cold because there was no coal for the stove—could be borne if he were progressing towards his end.

Just after *The Red Badge of Courage* was completed, and two or three months before a publisher was found, Crane received the only commission that he obtained during all of this period. The Wilson Syndicate gave him a commission to write a story[171] about the New York lodging houses. Crane and one of his friends[172] in the studio spent a night and two days as tramps on the Bowery and East Side, about the lodging houses. This was the kind of work that pleased him best, for he said, it was in such places human nature was to be seen and studied. Here it was open and plain, with nothing hidden. It was unvarnished human nature, he said.

~

25 / (Axel) David Ericson

David Ericson (1869–1946) was one of the artist-illustrators that Crane lived with in the old Art Students League building on East 23rd Street at various times between 1893 and 1895. He drew the pen-and-ink sketch that accompanied the May 1895 *Bookman* article on Crane. After studying art in Europe, he developed a successful career as a painter in Minnesota. His portrait of Crane is in the Tweed Museum of Art at the University of Minnesota, Duluth. His reminiscence describes Crane's method of writing and his bohemian lifestyle.

Source: David Ericson to Ames W. Williams, letter, 4 November 1942, Tweed Museum of Art, University of Minnesota, Duluth.[173]

Provincetown
Nov 4th 1942
Dear Mr. Williams:
About the year 1893 Stephen Crane drifted into my studio in the old Needham building, East 23rd St. The Art Students League had just moved up town to the new quarters on 57th St. My studio was one of the many occupied by painters, and illustrators. We were all poor struggling

for means of existence. He was at that time writing *The Red Badge of Courage*. I remember one time when he was lying in a hammock of his saying "That is great!" It shocked me for the moment. I thought how conceited he is. But when he read me the passage, I realized at once how wonderfully real it was, and said that the writer had that advantage over us painters in that he could make his men talk, walk and think. Whereas a painter can only depict a man in one position at a time. He seemed very pleased with this compliment. That was a week or so before I painted his sweetheart's portrait.[174] After that he gave me a copy of *The Black Riders* which he promised to sign, but which he never did. We both forgot about it. About that time he went down to the slums with an artist by the name of Carroll.[175] They were gone about a week. That was when he was writing *Maggie*.[176] Steve said nothing, but Carroll told me it was a horrible experience. Crane only smiled about it for to him it was the cream of life. He got what he was after. He would drift away for days, and then come back sometimes staying with me, and sometimes with the other fellows. He went about a good deal with a young man by the name of Vosburgh, an illustrator from Chicago.[177] Vosburgh would sometimes lie a bed all day and when asked why he didn't get up? Answered that he had had nothing to eat. So of course we would go out together and have something. One time after Stephen Crane had been with me for several days he said Well! Dave let's go out to lunch. It is my treat now. I got my pay today. (Seven dollars a week, from the *New York Tribune*) So we went to one of the little cheap restaurants on East 23d St., where we sat down at a table for two. He immediately pulled out his pad and pencil, and began to write as usual. Then we ate silently or talked very little. I think I ate no more than usual but anyway when we had finished, he walked out. So it was my turn again as usual. I enjoyed it very much for I could see how completely he had forgotten his promise. (It was the real Bohemian.) He was absolutely indifferent to comfort or discomfort. I can remember so well how when he came down from the country he would come in and put his little hand bag down in the middle of the Studio floor, sit down on a little sketching stool, pull out his pad, pen, and bottle of ink, and begin to write with only a few words of greetings. I do not remember that he ever erased or changed anything.[178] His writing was clean and round with a ring around his periods.[179] He wrote slowly. It amazed me how he could keep the story in mind while he was slowly forming the letters. This I thought the most extraordinary thing I had ever seen. I do not think that any one ever noticed it. I felt an awe for him when I saw how naturally his imagination worked through his hand as though he really lived in another world. It seemed as though his concentration of ideas of what he had seen, and heard with a certain artistic perception enabled him to draw his characters so vividly. "The Beefsteak Club"[180] entertained him once and they began to query him when he got up to speak. So he told them all to go to Hell! He was sometimes sarcastic about people's thoughtlessness, and felt that life was an accident. I can not remember any of our conversation. I was very busy with my painting and classes at that time. He was slender, youthful, mild and his voice was soft. His complexion was sallow, gray eyes, and light brown hair. Howells, and Garland appreciated him more than any one else. I am afraid that this will not be very useful to you. But it is all that I can remember. With best wishes for your success. I am yours

very sincerely.

David Ericson

26 / Frederick C. Gordon

Frederick C. Gordon (1856–1924) lived in a large studio in the Art Students League building on East 23rd Street upstairs from the cramped studio that Crane, W. W. Carroll, Nelson Greene, and R. G. Vosburgh shared in 1893–94. Later Crane moved in with Gordon. Gordon drew the original design for the cover of *The Black Riders.* Copeland and Day asked Gordon to modify the design; but because he was too busy to make changes, the publisher had its own artist adapt Gordon's design for the first trade edition of the book.

Source: Frederick C. Gordon to Thomas Beer, letter, 25 May 1923, Thomas Beer Papers, Beer Family Papers, Yale University Archives.

High Orchard, Westfield, N.J.

May 25, 23

Dear Mr. Beer:

I am afraid I can be of little use to you in the matter of dates, which never interested me. The few letters I had from Crane have disappeared. I think it was the fall of '92[181] and the winter following that he lived with me. I know it was the year that Tammany was defeated after the Lexow investigation, for Steve and I pushed through the excited crowds on election night, picking up material for an article he was to write for the next morning's *World.*[182] If Edward Marshall, who was editor of the *World* at that time, is still alive he should be able to help a lot, for he believed in Crane's future, and gave him all the commissions he could. Hamlin Garland was also greatly interested in him then.

He had spent the previous summer camping in the wilds of Sullivan county, where he wrote a large part of *The Red Badge of Courage.* On his return in October he took a little room near my place, and began to hunt for a job. Toward the end of a black, cold rainy day he came in to see me, soaking wet, shivering and coughing—utterly done up. He had been down to see Marshall, who had refused to take him on the *World* staff, because he believed the hectic newspaper work would ruin his genius for imaginative writing, but offered to buy special articles from him. Steve hadn't a nickel for car fare—too proud to mention it to Marshall—so he tramped in the cold downpour from the *World* building to 23rd street— no overcoat, and literally on his uppers. He was ripe for pneumonia. I got him into an extra bed I had, and in a week he was up, nearly as good as new. My shop was so big that he might just as well stay, and so he finished *The Red Badge* there, and wrote a lot of other things.

The memory of that time is really precious to me. Crane was a delightful and stimulating companion, with no faint resemblance to the vicious portrait of him you so rightly refuse to accept. Whatever his conduct may have been at times (and I have no knowledge of anything wrong there) his ideals were fine, his sense of honor high, and his faith in mankind unshaken. He was all that we used to mean by the word *gentleman.* I never saw him even slightly intoxicated. True, I did not go out with him much on his night wanderings. Daylight was necessary for my work, and so I slept religiously at night, while night was usually his best time for the studies he wished to make. Then he associated with those of the underworld, with an intense curiosity to understand their point of view. He never could have been really drunk when he returned, or I should have known it.

I wish you could have known that old shack of a studio building. It had been the home of the Art Students League. There were three street entrances, and it had been remodeled and twisted about so much at various times, to suit the growing needs of the League, that it took an expert pilot to guide a stranger through its mysteries. The upper floors were filled with artists, musicians and writers, young men and women, decent people all, who were glad of the low rents and really congenial atmosphere. The landlord was an artist, and as considerate of our financial difficulties as he could be in reason. Our life there was free, gay, hard working—and *decent.*

I had one of the biggest studios, and naturally people gathered there a good deal. Smoking, talking, and sometimes a little cards. There was no money going—no one had any—but I remember some game that required the loser to go out and fetch a can of beer. Once he failed to come back, and a search party with lamps (the hall lights went out at 11) found him comfortable on a remote stairway, but the can was empty! He explained that he had lost himself in the labyrinth, but was not worrying so long as the beer lasted.

And there you see the sum of Crane's sins while he was with me—so far as I know.

I can recall no party I gave in a restaurant, but do remember one in my studio. . . .

As for the restaurants, those were the lean days, and we generally fed at the cheapest places we could find. On rare occasions we would blow ourselves to a real 50 center, *with wine*! They could be had then. A favorite place for that was the Hotel Griffon on West 9th Street, the original of the Casa Napoléon of Thomas Janvier's stories.[183] I suppose it is gone now. But we were not often enough at any of those "expensive" places to be known there.

As for the knife throwing incident,[184] I know nothing of that. I have a vague memory of having heard something about it, but I fancy I didn't believe it, and so the tale made little impression. . . .

Very sincerely yours
Frederick C. Gordon

27 / Curtis Brown

Curtis Brown (1866–1945) had a long career as a journalist and literary agent. From 1894 to 1898 he was on the staff of the *New York Press*. As assistant to the Sunday editor, Edward Marshall, Brown was partly responsible in 1894 for the publication of many of Crane's stories and sketches and for the Bacheller syndicate's abridged version of *The Red Badge of Courage*. Starting in 1898 he represented the *Press* and other American newspapers in London; in 1899 he established his own literary agency and later included Ernest Hemingway among his clients. Among his other notable achievements was the founding of the International Publishing Bureau.

Source: Curtis Brown, *Contacts* (London: Cassell, 1935), 222–27.[185]

Stephen Crane drifted into the editorial rooms of the old *New York Press,* from nowhere in particular, and sold occasional little articles at $5 a column. He was frail and thin, and looked as if he didn't always have enough to eat. He was so gentle and wistful that everyone liked him; but he had little interest in news, and his occasional contributions were thought "queer." One of them that came into my hands was entitled "Sixth Avenue,"[186] and there was little left of it after the crossing-out of comments and descriptions that would have caused sorry in-roads on the newspaper's Sixth Avenue advertising receipts, to say nothing of libels. Then the editor read the remainder, and threw it away, too, as not being exciting enough. So perished a manuscript for which a dealer in autograph let-ters would have given much, a few years later.

The *Sunday Press* subscribed to the Bacheller Syndicate Service, run by a jolly, blond person named Irving Bacheller,[187] who afterwards became famous as a novelist. Included in the service was usually a page novelette, and one week this feature was an American Civil War story entitled "The Red Badge of Courage," by Stephen Crane. Stephen said it was a cut-down version of a novel he had written without ever having seen a war, and was much excited when he learned that we were to run it.

On the winter Sunday morning of the appearance of "The Red Badge of Courage,"[188] pitilessly compressed into seven columns, I went to the office for the reason that many a hard-and-fast newspaper man goes to his office on his day off—because his desk and the morning mail mysteriously draw him—and on emerging, met Stephen on that bitter, wind-swept, acute corner of Park Row and Beekman Street where the Potter Building stands, and within which *The Press* was housed. He was without an overcoat, but his face, thin and white, lit up when he saw me. He threw his arms around me and said: "Oh, *do* you think it was good?" Fortunately I could guess what he meant, and said: "It's great."

"God bless you," said he, and hurried on to anywhere in the sleet.

[Brown recalled receiving an inscribed copy of *The Black Riders,* which he mis-dates as "May 16, 1895" rather than "May 29, 1895," and a letter mentioning *The Red Badge of Courage* and *The Third Violet.* As with *The Red Badge,* Crane had hoped that the *New York Press* would publish his romance serially, but Brown wrote that "[w]e couldn't." For the inscription and the letter, see Wert-heim and Sorrentino, *Correspondence* 103, 161. Brown also recalled hearing from Stephen and Cora about the three-day post-Christmas party in 1899 at Brede Place, which he could not attend because a "violent cold prevented my going."]

At the risk of giving too much space to this particular week-end, Stephen's story of sweet corn must be told.

H. G. Wells and his wife, who were then neighbours, had heard talk of the delights of American corn, and wished to grow some of their own; and were given some kernels for planting. According to Crane, he inquired, at a proper season later, how that corn had fared.

"Very well," said "H. G." "We quite enjoyed it."

"How did you cook it?"

"Cook it! We didn't cook it. We cut it when it was six inches high, and ate it for salad. Wasn't that right?"

[Brown concluded with a brief statement about a visit with Cora Crane that he and his wife made to pay their respects following Crane's death.]

28 / John D. Barry

John D. Barry (1866–1942)—author, journalist, and critic—was an early supporter of Crane's literary career. Though he recognized Crane's talent in *Maggie,* he disapproved of its harsh treatment of reality. He preferred Crane's poetry and read unpublished poems at the Uncut Leaves Society in New York on 14 April 1894 because Crane, shy about public speaking, could not do it. (For an account of the event, see Linson [No. 21] and Linson 1958, 54–56.) Barry arranged for Copeland and Day to publish *The Black Riders* and is the first critic to suggest the influence of Emily Dickinson on Crane's poetry.

Source: John D. Barry, "A Note on Stephen Crane," *Bookman* 13 (April 1901): 148.

Not long ago, the *New York Evening Post,* in an editorial discussing "The Decay of Decadence," grouped the late Stephen Crane, as a poet, with the Symbolists of France and England. I was struck by the association, for the reason that I happened to be familiar with the peculiar circumstances under which *The Black Riders and Other Lines,* from which a quotation is made in the editorial, had come to be written. As a matter of fact, at the time of writing that volume it is probable that Mr. Crane had never even heard of the Symbolists; if he had heard of them, it is pretty certain that he had never read them. He was then about twenty-one years of age, and he was woefully ignorant of books.[189] Indeed, he deliberately avoided reading from a fear of being influenced by other writers. He had already published *Maggie,* his first novel, and by sending it to Mr. Hamlin

Garland he had made an enthusiastic friend. Through Mr. Garland he met several other writers, among them Mr. W. D. Howells.

One evening[190] while receiving a visit from Mr. Crane, Mr. Howells took from his shelves a volume of Emily Dickinson's verses and read some of these aloud. Mr. Crane was deeply impressed, and a short time afterward he showed me thirty poems in manuscript, written, as he explained, in three days.[191] These furnished the bulk of the volume entitled *The Black Riders*. It was plain enough to me that they had been directly inspired by Miss Dickinson, who, so far as I am aware, has never been classed with the Symbolists. And yet, among all the critics who have discussed the book, no one, to my knowledge, at any rate, has called attention to the resemblance between the two American writers. It is curious that this boy, feeling his way toward expression as he was then doing, should have been stimulated by so simple and so sincere a writer as Miss Dickinson into unconscious cooperation with the decadent writers of Europe. Perhaps an explanation may be suggested by the association of Mr. Crane at this period with a group of young American painters, who had brought from France the impressionistic influences, which with him took literary form.

The Black Riders received comparatively little attention, though it was favourably noticed in *The Bookman*[192] and in other periodicals, and it was ridiculed in several. Its publishers apparently made no effort to take advantage of the success achieved by Mr. Crane a few months later with *The Red Badge of Courage*. Few readers are now aware of its existence. Whatever may be thought of its qualities as verse, no one can dispute its being a curiosity of literature.

While writing of Mr. Crane, it may not be amiss to give a detail or two of his life which I have not seen in print. His bent toward the writer's career probably came from his mother, who, he once told me, had been a newspaper writer. It was his mother who secured for him his first chance to write regularly for money as a New Jersey correspondent for the *New York Tribune*. I think he said that she had held the post herself. I have a distinct recollection of Crane's remarking, with a humour made grim by his poverty at the time, that he had been discharged from the position of correspondent because he had given offence to some organisation of workingmen by writing satirically of one of their parades.[193] For the *Tribune* he wrote some sketches which had all the qualities of observation, humour, and grotesque originality of expression that characterised much of his later work.[194] At the time of his death he was acquiring from the world the education he had missed in his brief experience at college. Among other things, he was learning new words, fine words, the words that most writers know and never use. He snatched at them as a child snatches at bits of flashing jewelry, and he stuck them into his stories with a splendid disregard of their fitness. *Whilomville Stories,* one of his latest books, instead of being written in the simple language suitable to the child-life described, is full of such words; they fairly stick out of the page. If Mr. Crane had lived a few years longer, he would undoubtedly have stored those words in his memory, kept them shut up there, and returned to plain speech.

⌒

29 / William Waring Carroll

William Waring Carroll (?–?), along with Nelson Greene and R. G. Vosburgh, was one of Crane's three roommates in the old Art Students League Building at 143–47 East Twenty-third Street during the autumn and spring of 1893–94. He began his career as an artist and illustrator and later became a Methodist minister. Carroll sent this account of his experience with Crane in Bowery saloons and flophouses to the *Atlantic Monthly,* but the magazine did not publish it.

Source: William Waring Carroll, untitled reminiscence, with cover letter to Thomas Beer, 20 March 1924, Thomas Beer Papers, Beer Family Papers, Yale University Archives.

Having just laid aside Thomas Beer's *Stephen Crane,* I opened the *Atlantic Monthly* at the "Bookshelf," and saw Charles R. Walker's review of Beer's book.

These two wrenches at a long-shut door swung it wide, and I have been musing over unwritten pages in the life of Stephen Crane.

We were room-mates, bedfellows, in the fall and winter of '93–'94, when Emil Fischer and Marie Ritter-Goetze[195] were trying in vain to embrace each other in *Die Walküre,* and hurdy gurdies were playing "Sweet Rosie O'Grady."[196] Thomas Beer carries Stephen Crane along to a stumbling into Gordon's studio. Then there is a vague, blurred streak,—and I claim that as my part in the life of Stephen Crane.

In the old Art Students League Building, 143–7 East 23rd Street, New York, Frederick C. Gordon was established in one of the large, well-lighted studios. Directly underneath was a less commodious room occupied by three would-be artists. Into this company came Stephen Crane in the late summer of '93, flat broke, physically weak, regarding casually the apparent interest of William Dean Howells and Hamlin Garland, waiting for some sharp voice of command that he felt sure would come to lead him out somewhere.

We were all stony broke, except for a small deposit I had in the Seaman's Bank. We eked along on this dole, eating potato salad, bread and ham from a little delicatessen shop "aus der Avenue A," cooking frankfurters on a gas spider, washing down our fare with beer or cocoa. After food there were quiet games of "hearts" and much smoking of "Long Tom" tobacco. The rubber tube from the gas jet to the cooking "spider" grew short by degrees, and to avoid buying new tubing we would pile up books, kindling blocks, anything, until it would be difficult to manage our cookery.[197]

This was a sober crowd, perhaps because we were so poor. However, Stephen Crane was no voluptuary and no drunkard, not when I knew him. He experimented without scruple with all sorts of sensations, but he did not plan in his mind to do wrong.

There was a cot and a double bed in our room. The cot belonged to Vosburgh. The bed belonged to me. Nelson Greene, Stephen Crane and I slept in the bed. While Crane was taking his turn sleeping in the middle, he had a "spell" of crawling out and writing. In the morning "The Black Riders"[198] and three other short poems were on the table, and we urged that weird diet had done its work.

I read proof on the typewriter's draught of *The Red Badge of Courage,* Stephen Crane holding copy. We read it in sections, as the typist held part of the story for the typing charges, $25.00.[199]

Thomas Beer speaks of Stephen Crane's attempts at reporting. Garland and Howells got him an assignment with the Bacheller & Johnson syndicate to cover the "bum lodging houses" of New York. At Crane's invitation, I went with him on this dreary round. We went as hoboes with about thirty cents each, endured much misery for four days and three nights, and landed finally at Corwin Knapp Linson's studio, where we dozed and rested after being served with some stout punch and some real food. In the 5, 7, or 10c beds, Stephen Crane slept like a healthy baby while I struggled with a myriad host that did murder sleep. His stories of these days and nights[200] were strings of words that made one see flaring gas jets and dark interiors, where one could smell crude disinfectants mingled with exhalations from many human bodies. He made much of a little round-headed, pot-bellied man, who cried out in nightmares with a shrill treble voice. A Bowery sign "*Delectable Coffee 1¢,*" the elaborate arrangements of the Charity Organization Society to circumvent and defeat any hungry person's efforts to eat,[201] and the directness and efficiency of the saloons in filling us up with hot soup and cold beer—these things delighted Stephen Crane. The saloon men were good to us, especially at Steve Brodie's. We saw Steve himself, acting as his own bouncer, handling "repeaters" in his daily bread and soup line.

We were posing dejectedly at a saloon entrance, when a big raw-boned

Howard Pyle type of pirate[202] panhandled us for the price of a meal. We re-proved him sadly. He looked us up and down and said, "Yous lads look like yous were in hard luck, but yous are woikin' some game." He went away—and he came back. He said, "Wot are yous lads doing? Wots yer lay? Yous have got me guessin'. Tell me, wots de game?" We told him. We knocked around with him and watched him panhandle promising passersby. He steered us into some sleep-ing places. Finally he got so friendly he became a nuisance, and we shook him.

Memories of the quiet brown lad are up since Joseph Conrad[203] and Thomas Beer have raised this ghost for me.

⤳

30 / Reginald Wright Kauffman

Reginald Wright Kauffman (?–?) was apparently a journalist who worked for the *Philadelphia Press*. His reminiscence, published within months of Crane's death, demonstrates how quickly gossip muddied the attempt to tell the "true story of Stephen Crane."

Source: Reginald Wright Kauffman, "The True Story of Stephen Crane," *Modern Culture* 12 (October 1900): 143–45.

[Kauffman began by briefly summarizing Crane's early life and noted various rumors surrounding the origins of *The Red Badge of Courage*.]

. . . [T]here were two persons of influence in their respective spheres who had interested themselves in Crane. Early in 1894 the well-known New York correspondent who writes under the name of "Holland" described, in the course of a letter to a Philadelphia paper,[204] the literary hardships of a rather remarkable boy. This lad, not yet twenty-one, had, he said, written a story called "Maggie: A Girl of the Streets," based on his observations as space-paid reporter. Un-able to find a publisher, he had gone into a job-printing office and himself set some of the type[205] for a small edition which appeared over the pseudonym of "Johnston Smith." Only a few copies were published, and these went to the author's friends. But one fell into the hands of Hamlin Garland, who introduced Crane to William Dean Howells. The latter was sufficiently impressed by the quality of the work to look further into the writings of his new acquaintance.

The result was the discovery of some unusual poetry which, at Mr. Howells's suggestion, was read before a meeting of one of those New York societies which indulge in the generally dubious luxury of what they please to call "Uncut Leaves."[206]

Meanwhile Crane was seeking a market for "The Red Badge" and shortly after, in what was for them an evil hour, this tale was bought by a large literary syndicate. They paid their usual price for it, but were able to sell it to but one large paper,[207] the very one, as it chanced, to which "Holland's" letter about Crane had been written. At the time this journal, "The Press" [Philadelphia] . . . was printing, somewhat after the French fashion, a series of novels in daily instalments. The stock had run low, but the demand had increased, and the literary editor, Mr. James O. G. Duffy, was in great need of available "copy" when the syndicate offered "The Red Badge of Courage." At first glance everything was against the story. For their own purposes the temporary owners had reduced it from 60,000 to 40,000 words, and, with the usual unerring instinct of the blue pencil, had managed to "cut" the best portion. Moreover, the book dealt with a struggle in which a fickle public was already losing interest and, above all, the narrative was, unlike its predecessors in the series, the work of a totally unknown writer. Being, however, a man of the keenest literary instinct, Mr. Duffy, although he had forgotten "Holland's" letter about its author, immediately saw that he had made a discovery of importance. He accordingly accepted the story and began its publication at once, the first instalment appearing December 3, 1894.

Unfortunately for the profession, a journalist has small opportunity of judging the effect of his work upon his public. Yet several letters of inquiry reached the office in regard to Crane's tale, and three days after the first chapters of the story appeared one of the editors of the paper, a man of more than national reputation in the literary and scientific world, came into Mr. Duffy's office where several of the staff were gathered.

"Who is this man Crane, anyhow?" he asked.

Nobody recollected the New York correspondence of some months before, and a general ignorance was expressed.

"Well," continued the inquirer, "if he keeps this up, we'll all know who he is in a few years," and he wrote an editorial which appeared the next day declaring that "Stephen Crane is a new name, but everybody will be talking about him if he goes on as he has begun."[208]

This was the first critical notice of Crane's work, and it appeared—be it remembered—in that department which a newspaper generally holds sacred to a very different sort of comment.

Upon Crane the effect was decidedly buoyant. Almost at once he took heart so far as to call at one of the largest publishing houses in New York with two new short stories. These were read over by the firm's adviser, Mr. Ripley Hitchcock, who, when the author came to learn his decision, replied:

"Mr. Crane, I like your work very much. It has strength and originality; but these stories are too short for us. Haven't you got something we can make a book of?"

Hesitatingly, Crane answered that he had a rather "long thing" which had been coming out in a Philadelphia newspaper and which "some of the boys around the office seemed to like." Mr. Hitchcock asked to see it and was sent the clippings, together with the editorial comment. The story was at once accepted, the missing 20,000 words were inserted, and as soon as Crane returned to read the proofs from a journalistic expedition into Mexico, the book was published by the Appletons.

This is the true story of Stephen Crane's literary beginnings. For some reason or other, it has never before been made public, but it is high time that it should be known in order to put an end to the mistaken gossip which is passing current as the true facts of the case. Crane never spent a night in a Mills Hotel except in search of material. The men who first accepted and praised his book were not New York but Philadelphia journalists. Chancellorsville only suggested the battle-scene, and the publication of the story in book form occurred in this country five months before it occurred in London. It was its American success that first brought the work to the attention of the English critics.

31 / Irving Bacheller

Irving Bacheller (1859–1950), a prolific author of fiction and an influential journalist, joined with James W. Johnson in 1884 to form a press syndicate that supplied articles to newspapers and magazines throughout the United States. He arranged for the serial publication of *The Red Badge of Courage* and employed Crane as a journalist. His reminiscence captures the excitement created by the appearance of Crane's war novel.

Source: Irving Bacheller, *Coming Up the Road* (Indianapolis: Bobbs-Merrill, 1928) 276–79, 292–93.[209]

One day a pale slim youth with blue-gray eyes, a rather dark skin and a cast of countenance "comely and good to look upon," as the ancients were wont to say, came to my office. His head was picturesque and beautiful in its shape and poise. He said that his name was Stephen Crane. I had heard of him. He had come to New York to try to earn a living with his pen and was finding it a difficult thing to do. There were certain editors on Park Row who because of their liking for the boy gave him an assignment now and then. He was not a trained reporter and lacked the "ironbound nerve" to be expert in that kind of service. But one editor had discovered his great and unusual gift for vivid phrasing. This editor whom I met often at Mouquin's on Fulton Street was the brilliant and now famous Ed Marshall.[210] He had begun to talk of a remarkable young chap of the name of Stephen Crane. Meanwhile, the boy was sleeping in artists' studios and eating, mostly, the bread of friendship. I knew nothing of that when he came to my office, but I had acquired some notion of his talents.

He brought with him a bundle of manuscript.[211] He spoke of it modestly. There was in his words no touch of the hopeful enthusiasm with which I presume he had once regarded it. No doubt it had come back to him from the "satraps" of the great magazines.[212] They had chilled his ardor, if he ever had any, over the immortal thing he had accomplished. This is about what he said: "Mr. Howells and Hamlin Garland have read this stuff and they think it's good. I wish you'd read it and whether you wish to use the story or not, I'd be glad to have your frank opinion of it."

The manuscript was a bit soiled from much handling. It had not been typed.[213] It was in the clearly legible and rather handsome script of the author. I took it home with me that evening. My wife and I spent more than half the night reading it aloud to each other. We got far along in the story, thrilled by its power and vividness.[214] In the morning I sent for Crane and made an arrangement with him to use about fifty thousand of his magic words as a serial. I had no place for a story of that length, but I decided to take the chance of putting it out in instalments far beyond the length of those permitted by my contracts.[215] It was an experiment based on the hope that my judgment would swing my editors into line. They agreed with me.

So it happened that the vital part of *The Red Badge of Courage* first went out to the public.[216] Its quality was immediately felt and recognized. Mr. Talcott Williams, the able editor of the *Philadelphia Press*,[217] one of the newspapers in which it had appeared, begged me to bring Crane to his office.

One afternoon[218] Stephen and I went over to Philadelphia. We presented ourselves at Mr. Williams' sanctum.[219] Word flew from cellar to roof that the great Stephen Crane was in the office. Editors, reporters, compositors, proof-readers crowded around him shaking his hand. It was a revelation of the commanding power of genius. When at last the tower is up and the lamp set and burning, how swiftly its light penetrates into all the highways and byways! It has a power like that of radium.

Soon Crane's book came out and was almost immediately the one literary theme of the English speaking world. A query was in all the wondering of critics and reviewers. He had been a mere boy not twenty-five years old who had never seen a battle-field when the book was written. How had he been able to write of war with a vividness unparalleled in English literature?[220]

Now there were certain young fellows on Park Row who had some skill in writing. They cherished the hope of winning literary fame. Crane's rise had stimulated their ambition. These were Willis Brooks Hawkins,—"a most cheerful companion, a man of playful whims and quaint and delightful fancies,"— Charles W. Hooke, a humorist and a successful writer of mystery tales; Post Wheeler, until lately Secretary of our Legation in London; Tom Masson, a delightful humorist and for many years the managing editor of *Life;* Edward Marshall then the most brilliant of the young editors on Park Row, and myself. Often we dined together, generally at Mouquin's.[221] Crane became one of us.[222]

. . . .

Stephen Crane, who had been sending us delightful sketches from Mexico,[223] had gone to Jacksonville[224] and was to seize the first opportunity—to get across to Cuba. We gave him seven hundred dollars in Spanish gold to be carried in a chamois-skin belt on his person. He was to send us articles from the island as often as possible and if war came he was to write of that. He was detained in Jacksonville more than a month. From what happened later I judge that he fell in love with a young woman there and married her.[225] We sent a number of drafts for his expenses in this period of waiting.

He got off at last with Scovel, the *World* correspondent in a tug-boat chartered by the latter.[226] She was either a rotten old hulk or else she was practically scuttled before she left shore so that her bottom dropped out of her as soon as she began to jump in heavy seas. Far out Stephen and Scovel[227] and the crew had to fight their way back in an open boat. They were overturned on the rocks offshore. Stephen had to throw away his gold and a part of his garments to get in and was near losing his life at that.[228] Soon the thrilling tale of "The Open Boat" came to us. We sold it to *Scribner's Magazine* for three hundred fifty dollars.[229]

We could afford to speculate no further on the chance of getting Stephen into Cuba. He was eager to go there and made a contract with William R. Hearst for whom his many war adventures were written. The last, great, shining star had fallen out of our sky.

∽

32 / Robert H. Davis

Robert H. Davis (1869–1942), journalist and playwright, began working on the *New York Journal* in 1896 after having worked as a newspaper reporter in San Francisco. He later wrote a column for the *New York Sun* under the name "Bob Davis" that was compiled into a series of books. Davis's reminiscence, written for Wilson Follett's edition of Crane's works, is a romanticized portrayal of Crane as a "modern Villon" and reveals his interest in Ambrose Bierce.

Source: Robert H. Davis, introduction to *Tales of Two Wars* (1925); vol. 2 of *The Work of Stephen Crane,* ed. Wilson Follett (New York: Knopf, 1925–27), ix–xxiv.

. . . [In the fall of 1895] I met Ambrose Bierce and William C. Morrow,[230] two distinguished men of letters who have since joined the shades, and spoke to them of *The Red Badge.* Both had read it. I do not recall Morrow's exact criticism except that it was reasonably laudatory. Bierce's observation remains with me: "This young man," said he, "has the power to feel. He knows nothing of war, yet he is drenched in blood. Most beginners who deal with this subject spatter themselves merely with ink."

. . . In 1896, having lost my copy of *The Red Badge,* to say nothing of numerous newspaper connections, and craving action in the Far East, I came to New York and went to work on the then *New York Journal.* . . . S. S. Chamberlain, Managing Editor of the *Journal,* conceived the idea of sending Crane abroad.[231] Some enterprising scout rounded up the author of *The Red Badge,* got him into the *Journal* office, and the deal was concluded.

After Crane had left the building I strolled into the Chamberlain office and heard the news. Curse on such misfortune. My desire to meet Crane flamed anew. Fortunately the following day I was commissioned to see him on the subject of transportation and certain matters with reference to the cabling of news. I made an appointment by telephone to meet him at the Hoffman House. This appointment he broke. Very well, I took it for granted that a superior power was protecting Crane against my enthusiasm. He was not, however, destined to escape me.

The same night. 11:30 P.M. Temperature falling. I was chatting with a reporter named William Dunlevy on the eastern front of that small iron-fenced triangle of land which forms the apex of Thirty-third Street and Broadway under the old Sixth Avenue "L." At the northern end of the triangle was a bronze statue of Horace Greeley seated comfortably in a cold bronze chair gazing northward. Horace was subsequently derricked out of his garden and set on the pavement so that subway operation could go forward. Down the street, about the middle of the block between Thirty-first and Thirty-second on Broadway, opposite the Imperial Hotel, I discerned a thin individual garbed in a loose rusty overcoat almost henna in tone. His gaze was bent upon the pavement. In a flash he seemed familiar. Yet in a counter-flash the suggestion vanished like a mist. Nevertheless I kept my eye upon him until he had passed me and come into the zone of Dunlevy's vision.

"Do you know the little fellow in the brown overcoat?"

"No!"

"Stevey Crane!" answered Dunlevy *sotto voce*.

"Introduce me!" My request was an importunity.

"Oh, Crane!" shouted Dunlevy in the direction of the receding figure. "Here's a man who can't sleep until he meets you.

"Mr. Davis, Mr. Crane."

I pressed his thin veal-like hand with unfeigned warmth. The pressure from his hand was indifferent. Fragments of the thousand and one things I wanted to say began crowding in upon me. His manner was cold; yet I resented the presence of Dunlevy. Nevertheless I delivered the instructions I had received from Chamberlain, imparted certain information about cable stuff, and wondered by what plan I could break the trio and establish a duet. There was much to be said. Dunlevy came to his own rescue by apologizing for an unavoidable hasty exit, and started alone up Broadway in the direction of the Herald Square restaurant, whither Crane, as he afterwards informed me, was bound in search of kindred spirits.

True to the combinations that guarantee stupidity on the occasion of first meetings I made some more or less banal remark about covering a war in the country for which the poet Lord Byron was prepared to shed his blood.

"No man," replied Crane, "should be called upon to report a war in a country that he loves. I shall do a better job than Byron could have done. Greece means nothing to me, nor does Turkey. After Cuba it will be cold over there, I imagine. By the way, this is a hell of a town. I never come here without feeling the necessity for taking immediate steps to go elsewhere."

"Hardly the place for a minister's son," I commented in the hope that he would appreciate the subtle reference to his paternal ancestor.

"Well, for that matter," he reflected, "is there any place exactly suited to a minister's son?"

"We are not understood," I observed.

"You, too?"

"Yes, Episcopalian. I was born on the Nebraska prairies where my father was a missionary after the close of the war."

Unwittingly I had uttered the one word that penetrated the shell of Stephen Crane: "War." . . .

In spite of my long reportorial training I found it hard to get anything out of Crane about himself. He seemed more interested in the fact that we were both minister's sons.

"Have you ever observed," said he, "how the envious laity exult when we are overtaken by misfortune?"

The cigarette that hung from his lips performed like a baton to the tempo of his speech.

"This is the point of view: The bartender's boy falls from the Waldorf roof. The minister's son falls from a park bench. They both hit the earth with the same velocity, mutilated beyond recognition."

There was a crescendo to this announcement that merited a long pull at the baton, followed by an exhalation of smoke.

Failing in my efforts to unchain Stephen Crane's tongue I made a careful examination of his characteristics. He wore a black felt hat pulled down rather closely over his eyes; the collar of his overcoat was turned up to protect his thin neck from the wind. I was struck by the weakness of his chin and the paleness of his lips. The nose, while quite thin, was delicately molded, the nostrils dilating slightly when he became animated. The eyes, about which I had heard much, did not seem to be in any way remarkable.

The bleak of the night, the sudden meeting, the apparent desire to get somewhere under warm cover probably contributed something to the lack of sparkle in Crane's manner, added to which I was a comparative stranger.

It seemed reasonable under the circumstances that I should invite him to have a drink. The Imperial bar was close at hand. A few days before I had visited the Lambs' Club with Edward W. Townsend, author of *Chimmie Fadden,* and received at his hands a new mixture.

"Would you mind trying a novelty?" I asked Crane. "It is a combination of one part amier picon and three parts ginger ale."

"Sure I'll try it," replied Crane—"with your belly."

Crane led a loud explosion of laughter and seemed quite delighted with his own flash of humour.

This gust of mirth was interrupted by the approach of a girl who had evidently come under the Sixth Avenue Elevated structure and crossed into Broadway in front of the Greeley statue. Crane saw her first and gave all his attention to the direction from which she was approaching. Regardless of the fact that my back was turned I felt that she had suddenly stopped behind me and that Crane had secured her attention.

In the middle nineties traffic at that particular hour and on that particular cold night was rather light on lower Broadway, but this girl of the shadows had come out of them, stopped, and looked at Stephen Crane. Straightway he detached himself from my side, tossed his cigarette into Greeley Square, placed his left hand upon his heart, removed his hat, and made a most gallant bow. I have never seen a more exquisite gesture of chivalry than this youth sweeping the pavement with his black felt.

Under the flickering shadows of the arc-lights which at that time illuminated Broadway I got for the first time a blinding flash of the romantic Crane. A lock of soft hair lay upon his high, white, and shapely forehead. There was a fullness about the temples, and over the eyes; the modelling exquisite. Crowning the cheek-bones was a tone of light coral accentuated against the sallow dominant tone. It may have been because of the high light reflections but there seemed to be a tawny note in his hair, which was soft and long and in disarray. Around the mouth hovered an elusive smile, while the whole posture of the body suggested the dancing master about to begin a minuet.

I was not a hero-worshipper. My whole newspaper training had been toward the development of composure. Nevertheless at that moment I discerned an almost indescribable luminous beauty in the eyes of this modern Villon. They were large, the iris seemingly out of proportion to the pupil, blue in general tone, brilliant, flashing.

All else was sombre, dull, chilled. I can still see the small hand pressed against his coat, a network of blue veins, the thin index and middle fingers and the ball of his thumb stained with nicotine. But from that forehead and those eyes quivered an aurora.

The moment was embarrassing to me because I became aware that neither Crane nor the girl was conscious of my existence.

"A stranger here?" inquired Crane with the utmost delicacy in his speech as though addressing one lost in a great city.

The girl stood there with her lips parted and a queer expression of indecision on her face. I do not know to this day whether she was lured by the beauty of his eyes and forehead or startled by the weakness of his chin and the poverty of his garb. She caught her breath.

"Well, suppose I am a stranger. Can you show me anything?"

"Yes," replied the author of *Maggie,* "I can show you the way out, but if you prefer to remain—" Crane made another gesture with his felt and bowed with an air of magnificent finality.

The girl suddenly found an extra button at the throat of her coat and fastened herself in. The light seemed to go out of Stephen Crane's eyes as though some one had turned down a lamp from within.

"You shouldn't hang out here, kid," said Maggie in a throaty voice. "You look cold. You can't stand it. This fat guy can."

At last I was recognized.

The girl sauntered off utterly indifferent in the direction of Shanley's, Burns's, Delmonico's—

"This is a long cañon," said Crane. "I wonder if there *is* a way out. Come, now you can have your picon and ginger ale. I'll *not* take the same."

In due course a pair of clergymen's sons found a brass rail that fitted their feet. It was there, jostled by all sorts and conditions of laymen, that I told Crane what Bierce had said of him. He made no comment whatever but seemed content to slide his glass of whisky up and down a wet spot that glistened on the walnut bar.

In one corner of the room there was a group of rubber plants in tubs.

"If we were in Cuba now," observed Crane, "there would be five murderers with drawn machetes behind those Brooklyn palms. Two of them would be candidates for office."

His glass continued to glide up and down the bar while his mind shifted back to an earlier subject.

"Read Bierce's 'Occurrence at Owl Creek Bridge'!"

I informed him that I had.

"Nothing better exists. That story contains everything.[232] Move your foot over."

He then asked me for particulars concerning Bierce's personality. I supplied the information to the best of my ability.

"He will not be appreciated until long after he is dead," I prophesied.

"Has he plenty of enemies?" asked Crane.

"More than he needs," was my reply.

"Good. Then he will become an immortal."

Crane's liquor remained untouched. He smoked innumerable cigarettes. Suddenly he stepped back from the bar, extended his palm, and shook hands warmly.

"Good night! I hope to see you when I get back from Greece."

With my hand still in his I made a gesture toward the still filled glass upon the bar. He merely shook his head. Together we passed out into the cañon of the night. Crane went up-town, possibly toward the Herald Square restaurant, and I back to my quarters on Ninth Street. The last glimpse I had of him was when he was passing the Horace Greeley statue in the direction of the Tenderloin.

The next day I told a mutual friend how Crane had left an untouched drink on the Imperial bar. A raucous guffaw greeted my statement and thereafter whenever I made any reference to that occasion some one went into a fit of laughter. Had a single individual accepted the statement as true I would have rewarded him with the story of the girl who came out of the shadows and spoke with Crane, but the man who could not believe one story would not believe the other, yet both are equally true. . . .

~

33 / Kenneth Herford

Kenneth Herford wrote a literary column "Heard Here and There" for the *Detroit Free Press* and visited Crane in 1899 at Brede Place. In all likelihood, Crane told Herford about the origins of *The Red Badge of Courage* at that time.

Source: Kenneth Herford, "Young Blood—Stephen Crane," *Saturday Evening Post* 172 (18 November 1899): 413.

On a winter afternoon about six years ago a boy of twenty-two lolled upon a divan in the New York studio of an artist friend. While the artist painted, the boy read the stories in the current number of an American magazine. Finishing the last, he tossed the periodical aside, and, picking up a guitar, twanged the strings idly. He was thinking.

"Huh!" he exclaimed disgustedly.

"What's the matter, Steve?" asked the artist, turning from his easel.

"I've just read a battle story in that magazine," was the reply, "and I was thinking I could write a better one myself."

"Why don't you, then?" The artist dabbed a little spot of paint on his canvas and stepped back to observe the effect.

The boy was silent for a moment, then suddenly he exclaimed, "By jove! I believe I will. Good-by." And he was off.[233]

The artist did not see his friend again for more than a year, and then he was asked to a reception "to meet Mr. Crane."

The boy went directly home—to his little hall bedroom on an obscure street off Broadway. As the crisp air cut his cheeks he seemed to see the first glow of a roseate future dawning for him. He thought of his college days at Syracuse, and how a certain professor said to him once, "Crane, you'll never amount to anything. Why don't you let up on writing and pay a little more attention to conic sections?" But he had been unable to, so had left the college. His father, the rector of a little church over in New Jersey, had not looked with favor upon his son's going to New York to enter upon a career of journalism, but when he learned the determination behind the desire he offered Stephen five dollars a week for such a time as he might need more than his writing would bring him.[234] As the boy unlocked the door of his little hall bedroom he remembered that the last five dollars from home had gone to pay the rent.

Sitting down at his writing-table, he took up a soft lead pencil, sharpened it, and wrote the first sentence of his battle story—that was to be better than the one he had read in the magazine.

The first paragraph written, he read it over three times, then pushed the sheet away from him to think. The result of that moment's hesitation was that the next morning he searched through a friend's library until he found a history of the Civil War. In the book he ran across a chapter having to do with the battle of Chancellorsville. The weather of the day was noted, also the topography of the country and the positions occupied by the troops. "That will do," said Crane, and, returning to his hall bedroom again, he began work in earnest.

He was not discouraged by the fact that he did not know a musket from a repeating rifle. He thought of what a musket ought to look like. He had never heard a volley fired, but he imagined what the noise would resemble; he had never seen a man stopped by a bullet, but he was sure a man thus struck would fall a certain way, then writhe a certain way. So the boy wrote about another boy, a farmer's son, in battle for the first time, and analyzed his every thought and emotion as he heard the rattle of musketry and saw his comrades fall around him. He asked old soldiers concerning their own emotions in battle. But apparently they had had none. So, failing thus to learn at first hand, the boy imagined. Finally the story worked out to an end. The words were counted. There were fifty-five thousand of them. That amount of writing had been accomplished in nine days.

The boy spent his last five cents for carfare to the office of one of the largest magazines in New York.

"What you got, Crane?" asked the editor.

"A novel—battle story. Call it *The Red Badge of Courage.* Fifty-five thousand words."

The editor contracted his brows.

"Pretty unlikely, but leave it," he said.

After a month's waiting the story was refused. "It won't do," said the editor. During that month the boy had lived on less than the parental five dollars a week. The sketches he had peddled among the newspapers had not gone very well. There had been a rush of news and no space for "specials." Then the manuscript was taken to the editor of a certain newspaper syndicate. It was read a second time. "Cut it down to eighteen thousand words and we'll take it at five dollars a column" was the verdict. Ninety dollars for nine days work! Ten dollars a day! Crane could hardly realize the sum in all its immensity.

He cut the book down to the required length. The syndicate sold the abridgment, as a serial, to papers all over the country. It proved one of the most successful stories the company had ever offered. Crane was tendered a position, writing regularly for the syndicate.

Meanwhile the story as printed had been examined by a New York publisher. A letter was sent the author asking permission to reissue it, this time between covers. It was the original story of fifty-five thousand words that was published in book form. No one bought the book until a copy had been sent to England. A great critic wrote a review of it that awoke London to its worth.[235] Crane was advised by his American publisher to sell the English rights for twenty pounds. He did. The book jumped into fourteen editions in England. America detected the note of approval. Twenty-three editions were reached in a few months. . . .

[Herford concluded with brief comments on Crane's career and on Brede Place.]

⌒

34 / Henry McBride

Henry McBride (1867–1962)—artist, illustrator, and art critic—offered a lively account of Crane's association with artists in New York between early 1895 and late 1896. McBride was an early advocate of modernism and founder and director of the Educational Alliance of New York City. He worked for the *New York Sun* for almost four decades.

Source: Henry McBride, "Stephen Crane's Artist Friends," *Artnews* 49 (October 1950): 46.

One of the chief requisites of a memoir-writer is a memory—of which I have little and never did have much—and so the venturesome reader of the following little chapter in the life of the novelist Stephen Crane is hereby requested to supply the dates for the episodes himself and even to supply the locations for them although, of course, enough hints will be given implacable daters and locaters to enable them to do their deadly work with a fair degree of accuracy.

The tale concerns Crane's relationship with a group of artists in the early days of his career and since it is said that we are known by the kind of friends we make, his evident pleasure in association with artists may explain some of his own essential artisticness. The fact that none of these painters ever achieved celebrity doesn't minimize the fact that Crane loved the atmosphere that artists, good or bad, always seem to be able to create for themselves and he dined regularly every night for two or three years with a certain coterie which had managed to incorporate a little bit of France into a dingy but quite clean tenement somewhere in the Thirtieth Streets west of Broadway.[236] This coterie revolved around the Pike brothers, two husky giants built on the style of our modern professional football players. Both I think were architects, and Charley Pike, the elder of the two, had gained a certain prestige among his fellows because Charles Dana Gibson had featured him in drawings illustrating art-student life in Paris, just then published in the *Century Magazine*. Both the Pikes were rollicking, good-natured, social types, always the center of a crowd wherever they were; and not long after their return from abroad—homesick for Paris, the café evenings and the good food—they somehow found two oldish French peasant women and persuaded them to cook a dinner which they guaranteed should be for twelve every night; and if any of the promised twelve customers failed to show up they would be paid for just the same. This was the agreement faithfully lived up to but seldom put to the test, for we always did show up, the food being good, the company delightful and the price of the dinners so low that you people now living in the inflationary Truman period would scarcely believe it were I to set it down. We ate in the kitchen which was one flight down from the street in the rear with windows giving upon an area-way, the two cooks plumping the dishes hot from the range directly upon our very plates. It was great fun. Who the convives were I don't completely recall. I remember, in addition to the Pike boys and Stephen Crane, only my two especial friends, Edward S. Hamilton and Gustave Verbeek, but most of the twelve were artists. Hamilton was already an Academy exhibitor and destined but for his early death to have become an out-and-out academician. Verbeek, born in Japan of a missionary father, was, so we were all convinced, a genius; but he never actually flowered into fame, although he sometimes came near it both in Paris and New York. We three occupied adjoining studios on lower Fifth Avenue near Fourteenth Street, but usually most of us assembled for dinner in the studio of a commercial artist named Newman on Twenty-third Street just west of Sixth Avenue, which is what leads me to think that our dining place could not have been far up in the Thirties. The region was a much more bohemian neighborhood then than it is now. Just across the street was Proctor's Theatre where Miss De Wolfe (Lady Mendl to you) was doing a fairly good job as an actress in a melodrama by Sardou, and nearby was the music hall of Koster and Bial's to which ladies high in society went, heavily veiled, in order to see Carmencita dance, the same Carmencita who later on got immortalized in a portrait by John Singer Sargent.

The Pike brothers sat at the head of the table nearest to the source of food, and with them sat Stephen Crane and the livelier members of the party. The conversation was, of course, mighty free but not particularly outrageous. We never, in those pre–Greenwich Village days, went to the lengths of behaviorism that you behold in the paintings of Paul Cadmus[237] (although I for one never believe the half of what Paul Cadmus puts into his records of the Village goings-on). Once a cellist of some note came to dinner with us, fetching his cello along and favoring the company during an interval between dinner courses with a sturdy fugue by Bach to which we all, including the two cooks, gave serious attention. A shade more restraint was put upon us one evening by the advent of Jesse Lynch Williams,[238] a highly successful novelist of the day who was a bit of a stuffed shirt. However, every one behaved civilly and treated him very nicely. He never came again though.

At the conclusion of dinner the dishes were taken away and the Pike boys and Stephen Crane invariably threw dice for unpretentious stakes. The French hostesses, being French, showed no aversion to calling it an evening and were never in a hurry about shooing us out. On one occasion, the Pike brothers being absent and no other candidate available, Stephen Crane insisted upon my taking their place with the dice. Not much of a sport and nothing of a gambler I hesitated to comply but finally, after a few instructions from Stephen, I was persuaded to rattle the bones. To my surprise I won. I continued to win. I had beginner's luck. I couldn't lose. After a while the thing became such a farce that Stephen suggested that we play "double or quits," and I agreed. I knew he could no longer pay and he knew he couldn't pay, but with "double or quits" if he should accidentally win once, the whole indebtedness would be cancelled with one fell throw. It wasn't cricket, of course, but we did it and so the game ended. As we were laughing about it, and saying good night to the hostesses, Stephen said: "Just the same I think I do owe you something," and with a flourish he produced from his pocket a very grand cigar, all wrapped in tin-foil, and encased in a special box of its own. "It's a dollar cigar," he added, impressively, explaining that the Lantern Club had honored him that day with a banquet-luncheon[239] and this cigar was a relic of the occasion. Not being keen on cigars I gave it next day to Tappan Adney, one of my writing friends, and meeting him again some days later, asked him it if had been any good. Slightly embarrassed, Tappan confessed that he in turn had given it away, passing it on to John Clark, a Wall Street broker; and with that, of course, it went quite out of my world and I never did learn of its quality. A dollar was a dollar in those days. It was thought a prodigious sum to pay for a smoke.

Crane had already written *Maggie,* which had been discovered and highly commended by William Dean Howells, but had not yet written, or at least not published *The Red Badge of Courage.* In an offhand, careless way he had given me a copy of *Maggie* but without putting a *dedicace* on the title page, the vogue for that sort of thing not being so prevalent then as now. In the spring of that year I returned home one afternoon only to find that my studio had been on fire and most of my possessions ruined. The fireman still in charge of the debris pointed to a pile of books and canvases which had been rescued from the conflagration and on the top of the heap lay my copy of *Maggie,* a bit torn and besmirched but still *Maggie*—a genuine first edition. The next day, riding up Broadway with Crane on the rear platform of one of the horse-drawn street cars of the period, I told him of the incident. He thought it a great joke and, assuming a caricatured posture of importance, said: "Who knows, maybe in the years to come that may be considered the most valuable item to have been rescued from your fire." Many a true word is spoken in jest, and this one unquestionably became true. . . .

[McBride concluded with an anecdote about his attempt to sell his copy of *Maggie.* For a discussion of *Maggie* as a collector's item, see Bruccoli.]

35 / John Northern Hilliard

John Northern Hilliard (1872–1935), a journalist and freelance writer, met Crane when they were reporters in New York City in 1892–93. In 1895 he became the literary editor, drama critic, and editorial writer for the *Rochester Union and Advertiser* and the *Rochester Post Express.* His articles on Crane in these papers (Stallman, *Bibliography* 102–4, 281) and in the *New York Times* (Wertheim and Sorrentino, *Correspondence* 99, 195–96, 322–23) are important statements on Crane's ancestry and literary beliefs. Hilliard mentioned in the following letter that he owned about 150 Crane letters, manuscripts, and inscribed first editions in storage, but his collection has since disappeared. Only four of Crane's letters to Hilliard have surfaced, and three of them exist only in printed form. The letters were written to be used in articles by Hilliard on Crane. For a discussion of the text of the letters, see Wertheim and Sorrentino, *Correspondence* 693–96.

Source: John Northern Hilliard to Thomas Beer, letter, 1 February 1922, Thomas Beer Papers, Beer Family Papers, Yale University Archives.[240]

Carmel, [Calif.] February 1, 1922.
My dear Mr. Beer:—
. . . I will do my best to answer your questions.[241] As to your data on Mrs. Crane, I can't help you there. I never met the lady; and in such few letters as I received from Crane after his marriage, and in the latter years of his life in England, he never mentioned his wife or referred to personal matters. I have a recollection of about as many conflicting and unreliable statements concerning her as has been your misfortune. Do you know if she is still alive? As to the silence of Crane's relatives, I suppose that they are not particularly enamored of the way he looked at life and lived it, though it is difficult to think this in this age. But they were ministerial folk. Crane lived the life of the bohemian in those days—a bit too fever-ishly, perhaps, for his own good, that is to say, for his physical health. He drank and he smoked and like Robert Louis Stevenson he had a hankering after the women. He took up with many a drab, and was not overly par-ticular as to her age, race or color. Many a time I have heard him say that he would have to go out and get a nigger wench "to change his luck." Time and again he would bring a lady from the streets to his room. He had no eye for women of his own class or station. He preferred the other kind. I can understand this. Women of his own class could have given him nothing. In the slums he got life. He got the real thing, and that was what he was always looking for—the real, naked facts of life. And in seeking them, in living them, he was tolerant and absolutely unashamed. This was because essentially he was big. He knew nothing about cant; he was no more of the Pharisee than the animal seeking food and answering the call of the female. And young as he was in those years, he had a fine and great contempt for the conventional hypocrisy of his fellows. He never minced matters in his speech. He spoke right out as nakedly as he wrote *The Black Riders*. And he tried no more to hide his relations with the women of the underworld than an animal would. So I can understand that he must have

shocked his relatives. I know they practically disowned him. I not only understand this, but I experienced it myself; for at that time (I was about Crane's age) my own people had given me up to the devil. I just touch upon these things, for it may help you in getting at an estimate of the man. It is a big thing you have to, my friend. Crane was a big man as well as a big writer—the biggest writer, to my mind, this country has produced. He lived his own life, a free, untrammeled life; he had great courage (he was the most utterly fearless man I have ever known); he faced poverty blithely, and he wrote absolutely to please himself. And always he had a gay spirit, even when, as often happened in those days, we sat together in Union Square and speculated on the flapjacks and coffee we would eat and drink if we had two-bits between us. And then when the gods were kind, and a newspaper editor gave us a check, it was ho! for fleshpots and an all-night session at poker. It is those days, those play times that remain freshest in my memory, for Crane was always playing. He played all his life. He was the Playboy of the Western World.[242] He was always imagining himself something, from Hell-Devil Dick of the Deadwood Range to the Red Rover of the Spanish Main. He was exactly as he delineated Jimmy Trescott in the Whilomville Stories. He was Jimmy Trescott. That book comes pretty near to being autobiography. In my *Bookman* article[243] I give some data concerning his *Maggie: A Girl of the Streets.* One thing I did not mention—I didn't think of it at the time—was that many of the characters in the book were drawn from people he knew in Middletown, N.Y. I understood later that many of the people whose portraits he drew with that uncanny knack of his, didn't like it. But Maggie herself he drew straight from life, from the girl I describe in my article. As to *The Red Badge,* I also give one or two fragments that you may find to throw light upon that extraordinary book. Also the same with *The Black Riders. . . .*

One thing before closing, do please, take a fall out of that nonsensical Ford Madox Hueffer stuff he wrote about Crane in the *New York Evening Post Literary Review.*[244] He meant well, but he has no humor. And no one without at least a modicum of humor ought to write about Crane, for Crane was bubbling over with fun and, as I said, was always playing. He didn't have wit, but he had a great gift of fun and a sardonic humor. Remember, I am tremendously interested in your work. I can very well believe that with you it is a labor of love. How I should like to do it myself, but alack! the gods gave me no critical faculty, as our friend Van Wyck Brooks can tell you. . . .

∽

36 / Harry B. Smith

Harry B. Smith (1860–1936) was a music critic and author of numerous musical plays and comic operettas. Among his collaborators were Victor Herbert, Irving Berlin, and Jerome Kern. Smith was also known as a collector of rare books and manuscripts.

Source: Harry B. Smith, *First Nights and First Editions* (Boston: Little, Brown, 1931), 177–78.

One afternoon[245] I happened to be in the Hoffman House bar where art lovers used to go to look at Bouguereau's painting, "Satyr and Nymphs," and I found myself standing beside Willis Hawkins, sending himself to an early grave by imbibing a silver fizz. Hawkins I had known as a member of the editorial staff of the *Chicago Daily News*. He had with him a book which he asked me to read. We had lunch together the next day, and he asked:

"What do you think of 'The Red Badge of Courage'?"

I praised the vividness of the battle scenes but diffidently suggested that the author might have read Zola's "La Débâcle."

"I don't think so," said Hawkins. "I don't believe he reads French."

"Then," I suggested, "he must have been a soldier to be able to describe battle scenes so realistically."

"Oh, no." Hawkins laughed at the idea. "Steve Crane is just a kid. I'm going to his place to play poker this evening. Come on along."

I intimated that I was not ambitious to lose much money at the national indoor game.

"Nobody will lose much," he promised. "It will be something like the games we used to play at the Chicago Press Club to see who would lose if anybody had any money."

That evening Hawkins acted as guide and deputy host. It was after dark and I was a comparative stranger in Gotham; but my impression is that the building to which he conducted me was somewhere in the West Twenties. We went to the top floor, an extensive loft. In one corner was a bedroom partitioned off. The loft contained just about furniture enough for a small poker game. There were some odd things around, Indian blankets and a Mexican saddle. A curious piece of pottery was used as a depository for tobacco ashes. "Some kind of an Aztec damned thing," Crane drawled, when asked what it was. The supply of Pilsener was plentiful. There was no literary pose about Crane. He seemed to be what Hawkins had said—"just a kid"; but thin, pallid, looking like a consumptive. We played cards till two or three o'clock in the morning and, as we started for home, we passed the window of the partitioned bedroom. A girl was asleep in the bed.

"Gosh!" said Crane. "I didn't hear her come in."

There were facetious comments. "Is it *Maggie*?" asked one of the ribald, referring to Crane's story.

"Some of her," said Crane.

~~

37 / Willis Brooks Hawkins

Willis Brooks Hawkins (1852–1928) was Crane's closest friend in 1895 and 1896. A respected New York City journalist at the time, he was a founding member of the Lantern Club. Almost twenty years older than Crane, he often gave him fatherly advice and played an important role in convincing a reluctant Crane to attend the Philistine banquet in December 1895. When Crane prepared to go to Cuba in late 1896, he named Hawkins as one of his literary executors and asked him to manage a fund of five hundred dollars to be distributed in small amounts as requested by Crane himself and by a prostitute named Amy Leslie, with whom he had been living. When circumstances between Crane and Leslie became complicated, Hawkins became frustrated and stopped acting as a middleman between them. Crane's move to England essentially ended his frequent contact with Hawkins. Toward the end of his career, Hawkins wrote a newspaper column titled "All in a Lifetime" that recounted his life in journalism; three of the twenty-five columns dealt with Crane.

Source: Willis Brooks Hawkins, "All in a Lifetime," typescript, article 10, "The Genius of Stephen Crane" (3 pp.); article 30, "Stephen Crane Struggles" (3 pp.); article 31, "Stephen Crane Flinches" (3 pp.), Willis Brooks Hawkins Collection, University of Virginia Library.[246]

The Genius of Stephen Crane

. . . Once I asked Stephen how he managed to write so graphically about things of which he knew nothing from either experience or observation. It was a silly question, and it got the answer it deserved. With that funny little shy smile of his, as if trying not to show annoyance at the foolish query, he insisted that he had done nothing to warrant "all this damn hullabaloo" over the book. "Hell!" he exclaimed. "Anybody could have written *The Red Badge*." He believed just that. Repeatedly he told me that in writing he merely put into his own words what he saw as distinctly as if he had always lived in the midst of the scene and actions.

When nearly every critic and paragraphist in this country was poking fun at his little volume of free verse *The Black Riders,* Crane laughed with them.

"Why," he told me, "I wrote all that stuff in one evening, while my two roommates were frolicking about and joshing me. I never thought of the verses again until those two Indians put the Boston chap up to publishing them."[247]

I asked him how he came to hit upon that peculiar form of verse, for that was before "verse libre" had come into fashion.

"I don't know," Stephen answered. "It just seemed to be the perfectly obvious way of expressing what I felt at the moment. There was no special reason for breaking it up into lines, except that I felt sort of poetic that night; and I have a sneaking idea that those feelings which cannot be expressed satisfactorily in prose should be put into verse. I couldn't have written those things in prose form that night any more than I could have chewed up green paper and spit out ten dollar bills."

At that time Crane and two young artistic chums occupied a single room on Second Avenue in what was anything but a deluxe section of New York City. None of the trio could find a market for his pen or pencil products, so they had to depend on the indulgence of a generous landlord who did not press for rent money.

Later all three achieved fair fame and fortune, but Stephen once told me that the morning after he had written *The Black Riders* he and his mates pooled their entire pecuniary resources and spent the whole ten cents for three inadequate breakfasts, after which they faced what they diagnosed as triple starvation.

Stephen Crane Struggles

. . . He once told me that his father's family always had looked upon him as the black sheep of the flock. This saddened him, in a way, though he bore it with fortitude; and if there was a streak of cynicism in him, as some critics of his writings have seemed to discover, it may have been due to this false estimate of him by those of whom he was really fond. He never, to my knowledge, sought for the reason of this estimate. I did, and concluded it may have been because he was profoundly interested in all degrees and shades of life and found it largely made up of what many of us are pleased to call the lowest strata of society. His predominant hobby was to know life as it was; and if he found it more freely expressed in those strata than in the more conventional circles, it is not for me to say that he approved all he saw. Indeed, after years of intimate association with him, I could truthfully testify that he was exceptionally clean in thought and deed. As for the stories of his drinking and doping that have been bruited about, they were probably originated by people who did not know him and who properly come under the ban of the commandment about bearing false witness. The short word is none too ugly. I know and do not hesitate to say that all these stories are a lie.

I first met Crane in 1892 or 93, through Irving Bacheller, who showed me a portion of the manuscript of *The Red Badge of Courage,* which he was about to send out to a syndicate of newspapers, for Bacheller was the first editor, it seemed, to recognize the exceptional quality of Crane's writings.[248] That story, destined to make its author famous, had then been rejected by all the many publishing houses to which it had been submitted. After the first meeting Stephen and I were veritable cronies until 1899, when he went to England,[249] where he lived for about a year before going to Germany to die.

Maggie: A Girl of the Streets, his first published story (1891),[250] was a financial failure. For some years both before and after that time Crane often went hungry, yet, with the courage of his convictions, he continued to depict life as he found it and in his own way—the only way he knew or cared about.

Meantime *The Red Badge* was going its unsuccessful rounds, Stephen sacrificing many a meal to pay the necessary postage. As a last resort he sent it to D. Appleton & Co. He afterward assured me that he would have burned the manuscript if it had come back again. How narrowly that misfortune was averted was related to me by Ripley Hitchcock when he and I were pall bearers at Stephen's New York funeral.

One day in 1896[251] Hitchcock, then an Appleton reader, chanced to look at the first page of a manuscript that had been rejected by another reader and dumped on the table for wrapping and return to its author. The large, plain, rather amateurish handwriting caught Hitchcock's eye and he read a few sentences. These so impressed him that he took the manuscript to his room and read it through, with the result that he told Mr. Appleton, head of the house, that he deemed it a remarkable work. Mr. Appleton, after reading it, agreed, and in due time the most successful book of its day was published.

Crane, with a few hundred dollars of advanced royalties in his pocket, came to me, joyously declaring that he had more money than his hand had ever clutched before. At once he began speculating on how he was going to spend it. "First," said he, "I am going to have two pairs of trousers and, by gosh, a pair of suspenders for each." What he really did buy first was a complete and expensive outfit for horseback riding—a Mexican saddle, elaborately decorated bridle, etc.

It was early in November, 1895, when Stephen received at Hartwood, N.Y., where he was visiting relatives, a letter from Elbert Hubbard, saying that the Society of Philistines wished to give a dinner in his honor, to which two hundred of "the best known writers, publishers and newspaper men of the United States and England" would be invited. Crane at once sent that letter to me and begged me to invent a decent form of refusal for him. His letter and its enclosure are before me as I write this. He was in the blue funk of which I have spoken above. His letter and the whole story of that dinner are so characteristic of Stephen that I am tempted to give them to you but want of space compels me to defer them to another time.

Stephen Crane Flinches

In previous articles of this series I have told of Stephen Crane's mental and moral courage and promised to tell of the panic that seized him when Elbert Hubbard and the Philistines proposed to give a dinner in his honor.

On November 8, 1895, when Crane was visiting relatives at Hartwood, N.Y., he received a letter from Hubbard. . . . [252]

This letter, written and signed by Hubbard's hand, was also signed by H. P. Taber, Managing Editor of the *Philistine;* William McIntosh, Managing Editor of the *Buffalo News;* E. R. White of the *Buffalo News* Editorial Staff; and I. G. Blythe of the *Buffalo Express.*

Stephen at once wrote to me, enclosing the Philistine letter with some commendatory clippings from reviews that Hubbard had sent to him. . . . [253] I immediately wrote, telling him he absolutely must accept the invitation and that I would provide suitable attire for him.[254]

A day or so later I received a long letter from him. . . . [255]

Thursday evening, December 19, 1895, Stephen and I sat next each other at that dinner. He was in immaculate evening clothes, but he was ill at ease. The many speeches lauding his literary work had double effect on him. Nothing in his outward behavior indicated whether they pleased or displeased him, but every now and then he would nudge me and utter a nearly suppressed groan or half-whispered word of disapproval of what I knew he regarded as kindly-intended bosh; for he had repeatedly assured me that he had done nothing to warrant any part of this praise.

When Hubbard, who presided, had, in glowing terms, extolled the honored guest as man and genius, he called on Crane for a few words. Stephen, with manifest reluctance, rose. Evidently he was panic-stricken. Wetting his pale, parched lips, he seemed for a moment unable to utter a word. At last his innate courage came to his relief, but he could say only that he had done nothing in a literary way but to tell in his own poor words what he saw and as he saw it.

Hubbard later wrote for a special number of the *Roycroft Quarterly:* "Crane was the youngest individual at the board, but he showed himself the peer of any man present. His speech was earnest, dignified, yet modestly expressed. His manner is singularly well poised, and his few words carry conviction."

The fact is, Stephen was in a blue funk.

⤳

38 / Claude Bragdon

Claude Bragdon (1866–1946) was an author, architect, and set designer of theatrical productions who attended the Philistine Society dinner for Stephen Crane.

Source: Claude Bragdon, *Merely Players* (New York: Knopf, 1905), 61–70. Rpt. as "The Purple Cow Period," *Bookman* 69 (1929): 475–78.

Hubbard's now historic dinner tendered to Stephen Crane,[256] whose star was just then rising above the horizon, provides a perfect example of [Hubbard's] method of getting publicity for himself by means of others. I do not impeach Hubbard's sincerity: he admired Crane's talent as sincerely as a lover the woman he desires, but that dinner, held in a private room of a Buffalo hotel, is still a distressing memory—like the sight of young ox led to the slaughter. At first the dinner was dominated by a lot of drunken pseudo-reporters, who had come there with the evident intention of turning the whole affair to ridicule by their ribald and irrelevant interruptions, much to the distress, naturally, of Hubbard and us others. When these men were finally cowed into some semblance of order[257] Crane was forced to his feet to respond to Harry P. Taber's tribute to "the strong voice now heard in America—the voice of Stephen Crane." What he said and the impression he made were thus succinctly reported in the *Buffalo News* the following morning: "Mr. Crane responded modestly and gracefully, saying he was a working newspaper man who was trying to do what he could 'since he had recovered from college' with the machinery which had come into his hands—doing it sincerely, if clumsily, and simply setting forth in his own way his own impressions. He is a young fellow—twenty-four—with a smooth face and a keen eye and doesn't take himself over seriously."[258]

4
The West and Mexico

39 / Willa Cather

Willa Cather (1873–1947) met Crane in February 1895 in Lincoln, Nebraska, in the office of the *Nebraska State Journal*. A student at the University of Nebraska, she was working as a drama critic for the *Journal* and in December had copyedited *The Red Badge* for the newspaper, which subscribed to the Bacheller, Johnson, and Bacheller syndicate. Crane arrived in Lincoln on 1 February to cover a story that had been receiving national attention. A combination of drought and wind storms during the previous summer and the extremely cold winter of 1894–95 had devastated the state and left it impoverished. Though Cather's reminiscence, published under her frequently used pseudonym at that time, "Henry Nicklemann," is partly fictionalized, it remains an important commentary by one of America's outstanding writers and is the only eyewitness account of Crane during his Western trip.

Source: Willa Cather [as Henry Nicklemann], "When I Knew Stephen Crane," *Library* [Pittsburgh] 1 (23 June 1900): 17–18; rpt. in *Prairie Schooner* 23 (1949): 231–36.[1]

It was, I think, in the spring of '95,[2] that a slender, narrow-chested fellow in a shabby grey suit, with a soft felt hat pulled low over his eyes, sauntered into the office of the managing editor[3] of the *Nebraska State Journal* and introduced himself as Stephen Crane. He stated that he was going to Mexico to do some work for the Bacheller Syndicate and get rid of his cough, and that he would be stopping in Lincoln for a few days. Later he explained that he was out of money and would be compelled to wait until he got a check from the East before he went further. I was a Junior at the Nebraska State University at the time, and was doing some work for the *State Journal* in my leisure time, and I happened to be in the managing editor's room when Mr. Crane introduced himself.[4] I was just off the range: I knew a little Greek and something about cattle and a good horse when I saw one, and beyond horses and cattle I considered nothing of vital importance except good stories and the people who wrote them. This was the first man of letters I had ever met in the flesh, and when the young man announced who he was, I dropped into a chair behind the editor's desk where I could stare at him without being too much in evidence.[5]

Only a very youthful enthusiasm and a large propensity for hero worship could have found anything impressive in the young man who stood before the managing editor's desk. He was thin to emaciation, his face was gaunt and unshaven, a thin dark moustache straggled on his upper lip, his black hair grew low on his forehead and was shaggy and unkempt. His grey clothes were much the worse for wear and fitted him so badly it seemed unlikely he had ever been measured for them. He wore a flannel shirt and a slovenly apology for a necktie, and his shoes were dusty and worn gray about the toes and were badly run over at the heel. I had seen many a tramp printer come up the Journal stairs to hunt a job, but never one who presented such a disreputable appearance as this story-maker man. He wore gloves which seemed rather a contradiction to the general slovenliness of his attire, but when he took them off to search his pockets for his credentials, I noticed that his hands were singularly fine; long, white, and delicately shaped, with thin, nervous fingers. I have seen pictures of Aubrey Beardsley's hands that recalled Crane's very vividly.

At that time Crane was but twenty-four,[6] and almost an unknown man. Hamlin Garland had seen some of his work and believed in him, and introduced him to Mr. Howells, who recommended him to the Bacheller Syndicate. "The Red Badge of Courage" had been published in the *State Journal* that winter along with a lot of other syndicate matter, and the grammatical construction of the story was so faulty that the managing editor had several times called on me to edit the copy. In this way I had read it very carefully, and through the careless sentence-structure I saw the wonder of that remarkable performance. But the grammar certainly was bad. I remember one of the reporters who had corrected the phrase, "it don't" for the tenth time remarked savagely, "If I couldn't write better English than this, I'd quit."[7]

Crane spent several days in the town,[8] living from hand to mouth and waiting for his money. I think he borrowed a small amount from the managing editor. He lounged about the office most of the time, and I frequently encountered him going in and out of the cheap restaurants on Tenth Street. When he was at the office he talked a good deal in a wandering, absent-minded fashion, and his conversation was uniformly frivolous. If he could not evade a serious question by a joke, he bolted. I cut my classes to lie in wait for him, confident that in some unwary moment I could trap him into serious conversation, that if one burned incense long enough and ardently enough, the oracle would not be dumb. I was Maupassant mad at that time, a malady particularly unattractive in a Junior, and I made a frantic effort to get an expression of opinion from him on "Le Bonheur." "Oh, you're Moping, are you?" he remarked with a sarcastic grin, and went on reading a little volume of Poe that he carried in his pocket. At another time I cornered him in the Funny Man's room and succeeded in getting a little out of him. We were taught literature by an exceedingly analytical method at the University, and we probably distorted the method, and I was busy trying to find the least common multiple of *Hamlet* and greatest common divisor of *Macbeth,* and I began asking him whether stories were constructed by cabalistic formulae.[9] At length he sighed wearily and shook his drooping shoulders, remarking:

"Where did you get all that rot? Yarns aren't done by mathematics. You can't do it by rule any more than you can dance by rule. You have to have the itch of the thing in your fingers, and if you haven't,—well, you're damned lucky, and you'll live long and prosper, that's all."—And with that he yawned and went down the hall.

Crane was moody most of the time; his health was bad and he seemed profoundly discouraged. Even his jokes were exceedingly drastic. He went about with the tense, preoccupied, self-centered air of a man who is brooding over some impending disaster, and I conjectured vainly as to what it might be. Though he was seemingly entirely idle during the few days I knew him, his manner indicated that he was in the throes of work that told terribly on his nerves. His eyes I remember as the finest I have ever seen, large and dark and full of lustre and changing lights, but with a profound melancholy always lurking deep in them. They were eyes that seemed to be burning themselves out.

As he sat at the desk with his shoulders drooping forward, his head low, and his long, white fingers drumming on the sheets of copy paper, he was as nervous as a race horse fretting to be on the track. Always, as he came and went about the halls, he seemed like a man preparing for a sudden departure. Now that he is dead it occurs to me that all his life was a preparation for sudden departure. I remember once when he was writing a letter he stopped and asked me about the spelling of a word, saying carelessly, "I haven't time to learn to spell." Then, glancing down at his attire, he added with an absentminded smile, "I haven't time to dress either; it takes an awful slice out of a fellow's life."

He said he was poor, and he certainly looked it, but four years later when he was in Cuba, drawing the largest salary ever paid a newspaper correspondent, he clung to this same untidy manner of dress, and his ragged overalls and buttonless shirt were eyesores to the immaculate Mr. Davis,[10] in his spotless linen and neat khaki uniform, with his Gibson chin always freshly shaven. When I first heard of his serious illness, his old throat trouble aggravated into consumption by his reckless exposure in Cuba, I recalled a passage from Maeterlinck's essay, "The Predestined," on those doomed to early death: "As children, life seems nearer to them than to other children. They appear to know nothing, and yet there is in their eyes so profound a certainty that we feel they must know all.— In all haste, but wisely and with minute care do they prepare themselves to live, and this very haste is a sign upon which mothers can scarce bring themselves to look."[11] I remembered, too, the man's melancholy and his tenseness, his burning eyes, and his way of slurring over the less important things, as one whose time is short.

I have heard other people say how difficult it was to induce Crane to talk seriously about his work, and I suspect that he was particularly averse to discussions with literary men of wider education and better equipment than himself, yet he seemed to feel that this fuller culture was not for him. Perhaps the unreasoning instinct which lies deep in the roots of our lives, and which guides us all, told him that he had not time enough to acquire it.

Men will sometimes reveal themselves to children, or to people whom they think never to see again, more completely than they ever do to their confreres. From the wise we hold back alike our folly and our wisdom, and for the recipients of our deeper confidences we seldom select our equals. The soul has no message for the friends with whom we dine every week. It is silenced by custom and convention, and we play only in the shallows. It selects its listeners willfully, and seemingly delights to waste its best upon the chance wayfarer who meets us in the highway at a fated hour. There are moments too, when the tides run high or very low, when self-revelation is necessary to every man, if it be only to his valet or his gardener. At such a moment, I was with Mr. Crane.

The hoped for revelation came unexpectedly enough. It was on the last night he spent in Lincoln.[12] I had come back from the theatre and was in the *Journal* office writing a notice of the play.[13] It was eleven o'clock when Crane came in. He had expected his money to arrive on the night mail and it had not done so, and he was out of sorts and deeply despondent. He sat down on the ledge of the open window that faced on the street, and when I had finished my notice I went over and took a chair beside him. Quite without invitation on my part, Crane began to talk, began to curse his trade from the first throb of creative desire in a boy to the finished work of the master.[14] The night was oppressively warm; one of those dry winds that are the curse of that country was blowing up from Kansas. The white, western moonlight threw sharp, blue shadows below us. The streets were silent at that hour, and we could hear the gurgle of the fountain in the Post Office square across the street, and the twang of banjos from the lower veranda of the Hotel Lincoln, where the colored waiters were serenading the guests. The drop lights in the office were dull under their green shades, and the telegraph sounder clicked faintly in the next room. In all his long tirade, Crane never raised his voice; he spoke slowly and monotonously and even calmly, but I have never known so bitter a heart in any man as he revealed to me that night. It was an arraignment of the wages of life, an invocation to the ministers of hate.

Incidentally he told me the sum he had received for "The Red Badge of Courage," which I think was something like ninety dollars, and he repeated some lines from "The Black Riders," which was then in preparation. He gave me to understand that he led a double literary life; writing in the first place the matter that pleased himself, and doing it very slowly; in the second place, any sort of stuff that would sell.[15] And he remarked that his poor was just as bad as it could possibly be. He realized he said, that his limitations were absolutely impassable. "What I can't do, I can't do at all, and I can't acquire it. I only hold one trump."[16]

He had no settled plans at all. He was going to Mexico wholly uncertain of being able to do any successful work there, and he seemed to feel very insecure about the financial end of his venture. The thing that most interested me was what he said about his slow method of composition. He declared that there was little money in story-writing at best, and practically none in it for him, because of the time it took him to work up his detail. Other men, he said, could sit down and write up an experience while the physical effect of it, so to speak, was still upon them, and yesterday's impressions made to-day's "copy." But when he came in from the streets to write up what he had seen there, his faculties were be-numbed, and he sat twirling his pencil and hunting for words like a schoolboy.

I mentioned "The Red Badge of Courage," which was written in nine days, and he replied that, though the writing took very little time, he had been un-consciously working the detail of the story out through most of his boyhood. His ancestors had been soldiers, and he had been imagining war stories ever since he was out of knickerbockers, and in writing his first war story he had simply gone over his imaginary campaigns and selected his favorite imaginary experiences. He declared that his imagination was hide-bound; it was there, but it pulled hard. After he got a notion for a story, months passed before he could get any sort of personal contract with it, or feel any potency to handle it. "The detail of a thing has to filter through my blood, and then it comes out like a native product, but it takes forever," he remarked. I distinctly remember the illustration, for it rather took hold of me.

I have often been astonished since to hear Crane spoken of as "the reporter in fiction," for the reportorial faculty of superficial reception and quick transfer-ence was what he conspicuously lacked. His first newspaper account of his ship-wreck on the filibuster "Commodore" off the Florida coast was as lifeless as the "copy" of a police court reporter. It was many months afterwards that the liter-ary product of his terrible experience appeared in that marvellous sea story "The Open Boat," unsurpassed in its vividness and constructive perfection.

At the close of our long conversation that night, when the copy boy came in to take me home, I suggested to Crane that in ten years he would probably laugh at all his temporary discomfort. Again his body took on that strenuous tension and he clenched his hands, saying, "I can't wait ten years, I haven't time."

The ten years are not up yet, and he has done his work and gathered his reward and gone. Was ever so much experience and achievement crowded into so short a space of time? A great man dead at twenty-nine![17] That would have puzzled the ancients. Edward Garnett wrote of him in *The Academy* of December 17, 1899[18]: "I cannot remember a parallel in the literary history of fiction. Maupassant, Meredith, Henry James, Mr. Howells and Tolstoy, were all learning their expression at an age where Crane had achieved his and achieved it triumphantly."[19] He had the precocity of those doomed to die in youth. I am convinced that when I met him he had a vague premonition of the shortness of his working day, and in the heart of the man there was that which said, "That thou doest, do quickly."

At twenty-one this son of an obscure New Jersey rector, with but a scant reading knowledge of French and no training had rivaled in technique the foremost craftsmen of the Latin races. In the six years since I met him, a stranded reporter, he stood in the firing line during two wars, knew hairbreadth escapes on land and sea, and established himself as the first writer of his time in the picturing of episodic, fragmentary life. His friends have charged him with fickleness, but he was a man who was in the preoccupation of haste. He went from country to country, from man to man, absorbing all that was in them for him. He had no time to look backward. He had no leisure for *camaraderie*. He drank life to the lees, but at the banquet table where other men took their ease and jested over their wine, he stood a dark and silent figure, sombre as Poe himself, not wishing to be understood; and he took his portion in haste, with his loins girded, and his shoes on his feet, and his staff in his hand, like one who must depart quickly.

1. Stephen Crane on the New Jersey Coast, ca. 1879 (Courtesy of the Stephen Crane Collection (#5505), Clifton Waller Barrett Library, Special Collections, University of Virginia Library).

2. Stephen Crane seated at right in student group, probably at Syracuse University, spring 1891 (Courtesy of the Stephen Crane Collection (#5505), Clifton Waller Barrett Library, Special Collections, University of Virginia Library).

3. Corwin Knapp Linson's oil portrait of Stephen Crane, 1894 (Courtesy of the Stephen Crane Collection (#5505), Clifton Waller Barrett Library, Special Collections, University of Virginia Library).

Fort Plain, N. Y.
Oct 1--1944

Dear Mr. Herzberg--

I am very glad you liked my Steve Crane blurb and that you put it in such good permanent repository as the Newark Library--fitting as Crane was a Jersey native.

Steve always had a cigar--when he could get one and a cup of black coffee.

Yours truly
Nelson Greene

Wrote with a   pen
like this on foolscap paper and
ink. I was a cartoonist on the
old Puck 1913-1915. after which
I tried to get a job as cartoonist
on the newark News--didn't get
same

Steve Crane
Writing the "Grey Sleeve"
In my Studio in New York City
1894

4. Nelson Greene's Sketch of Stephen Crane, 1895 (misdated as 1894, Courtesy of the Newark Public Library, New Jersey).

5. Stephen Crane in Athens, Greece, May 1897 (Courtesy of the Stephen Crane Collection (#5505), Clifton Waller Barrett Library, Special Collections, University of Virginia Library).

Mrs Stephen Crane as war
correspondent during the Graeco-Turkish
Scrap.

6. Cora Crane in Athens, Greece, May 1897, inscription in Cora's hand (Courtesy of the Stephen Crane Collection (#5505), Clifton Waller Barrett Library, Special Collections, University of Virginia Library).

7. Stephen Crane in his study at Ravensbrook, Oxted, Surrey, England, with mementoes of his western trip on the desk and walls, 1897 (Courtesy of the Stephen Crane Collection (#5505), Clifton Waller Barrett Library, Special Collections, University of Virginia Library).

8. Stephen Crane aboard the *Three Friends* during the Spanish-American War, 1898 (Courtesy of the Stephen Crane Collection (#5505), Clifton Waller Barrett Library, Special Collections, University of Virginia Library).

BREDE PLACE, 1858.

9. Chapel end of Brede Place (Courtesy of the Stephen Crane Collection (#5505), Clifton Waller Barrett Library, Special Collections, University of Virginia Library).

Last photo taken of Stephen Crane with his dog "Spongie" –

10. Last photo of Stephen Crane, inscription in Cora's hand, Brede Place, 1900 (Courtesy of the Stephen Crane Collection (#5505), Clifton Waller Barrett Library, Special Collections, University of Virginia Library).

5
Florida and the *Commodore*

40 / Ralph D. Paine

Ralph D. Paine (1871–1925) served as the correspondent for the *Philadelphia Press* during the Cuban War. Paine later gave up his career as a journalist and became a historian of the sea and a writer of fiction. His autobiography, *Roads of Adventure,* which is dedicated to Crane and Ernest W. McCready, chronicles his experiences during the Cuban War, the Boxer Rebellion, and World War I. Paine and Crane first met in Asbury Park, where they were local reporters for metropolitan newspapers, and met again in Jacksonville, Florida, in December 1896, when both were attempting to secretly enter Cuba. Though Crane failed to reach there, Paine was successful. As reporters of the Cuban War, they encountered each other for the last time.

Source: Ralph D. Paine, *Roads of Adventure* (Boston: Houghton Mifflin, 1922), 162–63, 168–70, 192–93, 222–38, 243–46, 251–54.

[When Paine and Ernest W. McCready (No. 41) entered a café in Jacksonville in mid-February 1897, they noticed that Crane was showing a draft of "The Open Boat" to Edward Murphy, captain of the *Commodore*.]

Two men were dining in another curtained alcove adjoining, and the voice of one sounded vaguely familiar. It was not identified, however, until he began to read aloud to his companion something which was evidently in manuscript. He stopped reading to say:

"Listen, Ed, I want to have this *right,* from your point of view. How does it sound so far?"

"You've got it, Steve," said the other man. "That is just how it happened, and how we felt. Read me some more of it." . . .

A silence in the alcove and Captain Edward Murphy commented:

"The *Commodore* was a rotten old basket of junk, Steve, but I guess I did feel something like that when she went under. How do you wind it up, when poor old Billie was floating face down and all those people came running down to pull us out of the breakers?" . . . [1]

"Do you like it or not, Ed?" asked Stephen Crane.

"It's good, Steve. Poor old Billie! Too bad he had to drown. He was a damn good oiler."

When there came a lull in their talk, Paine and McCready pushed the curtain aside and made a party of it. Here were four of us, all in the same boat, as one might say, foregathered by a singular chance, and our combined experiences embraced all the vicissitudes of filibustering. And so we sat and wove together those recent voyages of the *Three Friends* and the *Dauntless* and the *Commodore*.[2] Young Captain Murphy was a man without a ship, but he hoped to get another one and play the game again.

Stephen Crane had never been robust and there was not much flesh on his bones, at best. Sallow and haggard, he looked too fragile to have endured his battle for survival with the furious sea, but his zest for adventure was unshaken. His thin face, mobile and very expressive, brightened when he talked of attempting another voyage. His indifference to danger was that of a fatalist. In appearance, in the careless indifference to conventions, in a manner of speech extraordinarily brilliant when his interest was aroused, there were many suggestions of Robert Louis Stevenson.

Incessantly smoking cigarettes, the long fingers straying to the straggling brown mustache, Crane sat slumped in his chair and discussed the fine art of filibustering in a drawling, unemotional voice, now using the slang of the street and the bar-room, again flashing in some bit of finished prose like this. . . . [3]

[By April 1898 Key West was filled with reporters and naval personnel eagerly waiting for Adm. William T. Sampson's fleet, which was blockading the Cuban coast, to intercept the Spanish fleet of Adm. Pascual Cervera y Topete, making it safe to leave for Cuba. Crane arrived in Key West on 25 or 26 April.]

. . . The Key West Hotel was a bedlam of a place while we waited for the war to begin. And when other diversion failed, you could stroll around the corner to the resort known as the "Eagle Bird" where a gentlemanly gambler, as well-groomed and decorous as Jack Oakhurst,[4] spun the roulette wheel. And there you would be most apt to find Stephen Crane, sometimes bucking the goddess of chance in contented solitude, a genius who burned the candle at both ends and whose spark of life was to be tragically quenched before he was thirty years old. With his tired smile he would drawl these cryptic lines, when about to take another fling at the "Eagle Bird":

> "Oh, five white mice of chance,
> Shirts of wool and corduroy pants,
> Gold and wine, women and sin,
> All for you if you let me come in—
> Into the house of chance."[5]

[On 14 May Paine, McCready, Harry Brown of the *New York Herald,* and Crane sailed to Haiti aboard the *Three Friends* to send their dispatches.]

The sea was rough all the way. The correspondents endeavored to write, braced in the bunks with pads of papers on their knees, and found that they were performing acrobatic feats. The scene lacked that composure essential to literary production. As a rule, not much good prose is turned out by a man who persists in standing upon his head.

However, these correspondents solved it by lying flat on their stomachs, having discovered that they could not fall off the floor, and although they slid about more or less they managed to write many hundred words describing the glorious feat of Lieutenant Hobson and the *Merrimac*.[6]

In the midst of his exhausting labors, Harry Brown, dean of the "Herald" staff, paused now and then to inform all hands, in a melancholy baritone, that he would rather sing a song to a harp of one string than to hear the water gurgle or the nightingale sing. Stephen Crane occasionally expressed the opinion that the sun was over the yardarm and that there were times when the corkscrew was mightier than the pen! He abominated this drudgery of grinding out news dispatches, with an eye on the cost of cable tolls. And seldom could he be coaxed to turn his hand to it. His was the soul of the artist, slowly, carefully fashioning his phrases, sensitive to the time, the place, and the mood.

[Upon arriving at Mole St. Nicholas, site of a French cable station, they met resistance from armed inhabitants, who, speaking in their native dialect, frightened the correspondents with repeated outbursts of *"Qui vive."*]

. . . Of the quartet, only Stephen Crane was enjoying the experience. As usual, he refused to take the responsibilities of daily journalism seriously. He had been known to shorten the life of a managing editor. A night in Mole St. Nicholas had its appeal for the artistic temperament.

"It is your move, Crane," said McCready. "Fiction is your long suit. Here it is. Things like this don't happen in real life. Let us have a few remarks from the well-known young author of "The Red Badge of Courage.""

"Me?" grinned Crane. "If I caught myself hatching a plot like this, I wouldn't write another line until I had sobered up. Steady, boys, the night is still young, and I have a hunch that there'll be lots more of it. This opening is good."

Harry Brown, in charge of the "Herald" war service, was an older man and less frivolous, who kept an eye on the ball. He began to issue commands.

"There must be some way of breaking through this silly blockade of armed ragamuffins. You come along with me, Steve Crane, and we'll work along the beach and try to get by at the western end of the town. Paine and McCready can scout in the other direction. If we are still out of luck, we can meet down at the boat landing so as not to lose each other."

The youthful deck-hand from the *Three Friends* listened to this counsel and wandered off alone. He was having the time of his life. Half an hour later, the four correspondents were reunited down at the boat landing. Their strategy had been futile. They merely had more tales to tell of sentries and little fires and *"Qui vives."* It was their opinion that Mole St. Nicholas was enjoying another revolution. Certainly it was well guarded against surprise. Martial law was rampant.

"I tried to bribe the last nigger soldier that stopped me," sadly said Harry Brown, "but when he saw me stick my hand in my pocket he jabbed at me and, say, I had no idea I was so fast on my feet. I don't know but what we shall have to go aboard ship and wait for morning. This seeing Haiti by moonlight is getting too dotty for me."

"Stick around, Harry," advised Stephen Crane. "Age has dulled your feeling for romance. We can beat this game yet."

After some more useless conversation, the solitary deck-hand came sauntering to the beach, wearing the air of a young man immensely well pleased with himself. His serenity was inexplicable. To the disgruntled group he announced:

"Sure, I busted the jam. It was dead easy. I went sailin' through them nigger soldiers, one bunch after another of 'em, with a fair wind and tide. They saluted me like I was a brigadier-general with a feather in his hat. After a while I come to the big, two-decked shack with a piazza on it, and I got a couple more salutes outside, and they woke up a hefty smoked ham of a man that was the first mate or something, and he came rollin' out in sky-blue pajamas, and—"

"Stop it, Bill," broke in Stephen Crane. "You make us dizzy. Unravel yourself, for God's sake! Go back to the salutes and start again."

"Oh, didn't I tell you? It was comical. One of them nigger obstructions in the channel had fetched me up all standing—you know, a little fire in the road and those walleyed boys *qui-vivin'* like hell—and I went around the corner and leaned against it to study what next—when along come a shiny big buck of an officer, and the soldiers hopped to attention, and he gave 'em the password. I could hear it plain as anything, and so I slid along to the next outfit of sentries—"

"And tried the password on them?" exclaimed McCready. "Look here, Bill, how could you wrap your tongue around this Haitian French lingo? It stumps us, and we went to college one time."

"French, nothin'," replied the astute deck-hand. "It was good United States. All I had to do was to parade up to these chocolate drops, and say to 'em, 'I-AM-THE-BOSS!' Just like that!"

"I-AM-THE-BOSS" slowly echoed the bewildered correspondents. It was beyond them to guess what phrase of this bastard French dialect could have sounded like the deck-hand's magic sesame.

"And he said it just like that, Bill?" demanded Harry Brown.

"Didn't I tell you? 'I-AM-THE-BOSS.' Mebbe he thought he was talkin' French, but I knew better."

"Bill, you are a wonder," solemnly declared Stephen Crane. "But, darn you, you are too impossible for fiction. I shall have to get good and drunk to do you justice. And you told them you were the boss and got away with it?"

"Come along and see," readily answered the deck-hand. "I'll show you. And, listen, I met an awful pretty girl, and there was mighty little tar baby about her, I could see that, an octoroon, mebbe, and I made a date with her—"

"That will do for you, Bill," chided Harry Brown, as the official chaperon. "Forget your immoral love affairs and lead us to the palace."

Young Bill moved on ahead with a touch of swagger in his gait. He had this town eating out of his hand. Boldly he approached the nearest flickering fire and the loafing soldiery. Throwing out his chest, he sharply proclaimed:

"I-AM-THE-BOSS! Salute, you black sons-of-guns."

At his heels marched the four correspondents, chanting in unison: "I-AM-THE-BOSS! Salute, you black sons-of-guns."

The effect was as magical as the astute deck-hand had foretold. The slouching sentinels rolled their eyes and bobbed their heads in recognition of the password. One or two even attempted to present arms, but the result was sketchy. Their hands strayed to their straw hats. A salute was evidently intended. Past them strode the conquering deck-hand and the admiring correspondents. Crane was murmuring aloud:

"I wonder if we could blast the secret out of a French dictionary. Probably not. We shall never know. It is just one of those things."

The cordon was broken. We were inside the lines. Unimpeded, the advance was continued to the pretentious frame building, in front of which a sentry bawled a challenging *"Qui vive"* but Bill told him even more loudly who was the boss and there was no argument. In the light of a lantern hung on the piazza stood a large, round man of a saddle-colored complexion, clad in blue pajamas and straw slippers. He beamed cordial good nature and welcomed the strangers as his guests. To their profound relief, he spoke English, racily, as though perfectly familiar with it.

"Ah, ha, it is a pleasure, gentlemen, you bet your sweet life," he cried, shaking hands effusively. "I am the Chief-of-Staff to the Governor of the Arrondissement of Mole St. Nicholas who is the General of the Army also. He is fatigued and have hit the hay. In the morning he will be dee-lighted, *n'est pas*? You found some trouble with the brave soldiers of *mon général*? There is a war, a little one, in Haiti. Pouf, we will win in a walk. The soldiers were on the job? You found them awake? Two of them had to be shooted yesterday for sleeping too much on guard. It made the army buck up, you bet."

The urgent errand was explained, concerning the French cable office, and the rotund Chief-of-Staff was all sympathy and action. The two cable operators would be in bed at this hour, but he himself would summon them *vitement,* in a jiffy. He slipped on a blue coat adorned with tarnished gold lace and fringed epaulets, and yelled at a colonel or something, the officer of the guard, who paraded five soldiers as an escort. Thus honored, the correspondents ambled along with the Chief-of-Staff who imparted the following information: "You admire how I speak English, eh? Pretty smooth! I twist her by the tail. Why not? Four years I was a butler in New Rochelle, New York!"

Stephen Crane made gestures with both hands, then propped himself against a tree while he gurgled:

"Hooray for the Chief-of-Staff! *He buttled in New Rochelle!!* My hunch was a winner. This is a purple night with spangled trimmings."

Thereafter Crane insisted upon addressing our host as Alice-in-Wonderland. We yearned to know what fantastic nudge of destiny had thrust the butler into this martial niche. It could have happened only in Haiti. But he prattled of other things until the procession halted in front of a low-roofed house which, nevertheless, could boast of an upper story and windows therein. The colonel of the guard was tripped by his sword which was too long for his stature, but he yanked it from between his legs and sternly commanded the five soldiers to stand at attention, all in a row.

[The colonel forced two tired French cable operators to open up the cable station at gunpoint.]

The march was resumed, the colonel now and then becoming entangled with his sword. A path had been cut through the jungle, almost half a mile to the building near the shore of the bay where the cable had been landed. There was a sense of gloomy isolation in this jungle trail which caused McCready and Paine some uneasiness. They were not wholly trustful of the Haitian Soldiery, but Stephen Crane expressed all the confidence in the world in the saddle-colored ex-butler of New Rochelle. We were perfectly safe with Alice-in-Wonderland.

And so it turned out. The cable operators were in a ruffled mood, but they consented to start sending the dispatches without delay. While we lingered to make sure of this, McCready wandered to the beach to explore the ruins of an ancient stone fort. One of the soldiers followed him, it seems, and clutched him by the arm. As McCready told it later, he was scared and confessed it without shame. The black ruffian had led him some distance away, beyond the ruined fort, until they were remote from succor.

"He had a bayonet and a machete," said Mac, "and it looked like dirty work, me with a money belt on, and this ferocious nigger had seen me take it off to slip the cable operators a gold piece as a tip. But he didn't unlimber the deadly weapons, and I guess I was curious or paralyzed, for I let him tow me way down yonder, where my screams could not have been heard. Then he spoke for the first time, in English, mind you:

"'Gib me one dollah, white man.'"

"Did he get it? I shucked him out two silver ones and clawed my pockets for small change. It was cheap ransom, a regular bargain. Don't mind that rattling noise. It's only my knees knocking together. I can't make 'em stop."

With happier minds the correspondents returned to the town of Mole St. Nicholas, having done their duty by their several newspapers. It occurred to them to try, in some small degree, to display their appreciation of the courtesy of the Chief-of-Staff and the soldiery. The courteous impulse was to buy the Haitian Army a drink. This desire was conveyed to the Chief-of-Staff, who replied that all the rum-shops were closed, for the hour was past midnight, but he would be glad to open one of them.

The invitation was comprehended by the colonel and the five soldiers. Presently, by some kind of telepathy, the news seemed to spread throughout the army. Instead of five men, more than twenty trooped along as a guard of honor, and the mobilization was increasing rapidly. It looked as though the reserves had been turned out as a compliment to the four correspondents. The column turned into one street after another, and the impression was that it grew longer in passing the groups of sentries at the little fires.

A halt was ordered at the door of a stone-walled hut, and the Chief-of-Staff shouted one of those mandates of his. The response was too laggard to please him. *Nom de Dieu!* He spoke to the colonel, and the foremost file of soldiers shuffled up, reversing their muskets. With the steel-shod butts they battered that door in and made kindling wood of its stout planks. It was one way to open a door.

The landlady of the grog-shop was in the act of descending from a sort of loft in which she slept. When the door crashed from its hinges, she was so startled that she missed the ladder and hit the floor with a mighty thud, being a negress of ample proportions and chastely clad in a brief chemise. It was an unusual welcome to an inn, so we thought, and she appeared to agree with us.

The Chief-of-Staff, however, made no comment. It was all in the night's work. Stephen Crane admired him more than ever. It was an affinity. They were becoming like brothers.

The dazed and ponderous landlady was requested to produce rum. Harry Brown laid three dollars upon the rude counter. There was a row of bottles on a shelf. It was expected that the money would buy one or two of these. But the landlady passed them by and turned elsewhere. In a corner stood one of those huge glass carboys in which acids are stored. It was empty. She began to fill it with rum. Gallon after gallon gurgled into it. We were learning how to sluice the dusty throats of an army.

"Rum is forty cents a gallon, it seems," said Crane, who had conferred with the Chief-of-Staff. "A unique experience, this—entertaining an army at a cost of three dollars. By golly, boys, she intends to fill that carboy. And the night is still young. Was it a winning hunch? I ask you."

Two muscular soldiers slung the carboy from a pole, in a rope netting, and the army moved in the direction of the beach. You could not have separated it from that carboy short of a drumhead court-martial. There had been no pay-days in several months. It had been a long time between drinks.. Soon after this, the white beach of Mole St. Nicholas was a scene of life and animation, all of that.

The correspondents began to wonder whether three dollars' worth of rum was not too much. They felt this way after the army began firing salutes as a token of its esteem. The guns wobbled too much at random. The Chief-of-Staff had tarried until the merriment was more like a riot. Then he excused himself, mindful of his dignified station and exalted rank, and promising to meet us in the morning. At that time His Excellency, the Governor, would expect us for an audience at the palace, you bet.

In the morning? It was morning already, with a flush of dawn in the sky, while the enthusiastic soldiery danced on the beach and the astute deck-hand taught them to sing, "There'll he a Hot Time in the Old Town To-night." And, between choruses, this useful young man danced with the pretty girl who "had mighty little of the tar baby about her, let me tell you."

There were hoarse cheers for the grand Republic of the United States, and eloquent eulogies of the peerless Republic of Haiti, jewel of the Antilles, as voiced with deep emotion by the younger correspondents. Never was an *entente cordiale* in better form. Harry Brown, having attained years of discretion, and realizing his responsibilities as manager of a newspaper war staff, forsook the party before sunrise and went off to the *Three Friends* to snatch a few hours of sleep.

The other correspondents remained as hosts to the army. Courtesy demanded it. They were hailed as eternal friends of Haiti, as long as a drop of rum was left in the carboy. When there was no more rum, the guests began to disperse, leaving wavering tracks in the sand as they moved away, still singing.

The three correspondents, rather weary, returned to the *Three Friends* for breakfast. The social whirl had not yet released them. They remembered the engagement with the Governor at the palace. They sat on deck in a row, holding their heads in their hands. The obligations of hospitality had been exhausting. The astute deck-hand, as blithe as a daisy, was scrubbing down decks.

They were aroused by a noise in the town, the blare of bugles, the squeak of fifes, the roll of drums. They asked the skipper for a boat. Mole St. Nicholas was calling them. They were good for a farewell appearance.

To the palace they trudged, collecting many a friendly but blear-eyed salute *en route,* and found the vivacious Chief-of-Staff awaiting them. He was very much in uniform, crimson breeches and cavalry boots, gold cords on the blue coat, a plumed cocked hat. In Crane's opinion, the ex-butler would have knocked New Rochelle cold. While we chatted with him, a tall and dignified black man came out on the piazza. He wore a frock coat, with a sword belt buckled on. His face was serious and intelligent. In French the Governor greeted the visitors with a courtly ease of manner.

He took himself and his position with deep seriousness. He wished it to be understood that a review of the troops was to be held. It was a tribute to the distinguished journalists who had so cordially fraternized with his own people, as citizens of sister republics. It was open to remark that His Excellency was either deaf or had slept like a dead man. Otherwise he would have mistaken the cordial fraternizing for an attack by the enemy in force. Revolutions have been started with much less racket than that moonlit party on the beach.

The military band straggled past, an odd assortment of musical talent oddly arrayed, and banged and tootled its way to the parade ground. The Governor, the Chief-of-Staff, and the correspondents walked in that direction, but when you tried to step in time with the martial music of Haiti, your feet pranced in a cake-walk. It couldn't be helped. Back of the town was a cleared field in which the army awaited its commanding general. A shrill fanfare of bugles, and the troops began to march in review.

There were perhaps two hundred of these black infantrymen, with brigadiers, colonels, and majors sprinkled as thick as huckleberries in a pudding. For uniform most of the privates were lucky to have a shirt and breeches and a big straw hat. The officers strutted in extraordinary remnants of military trappings, but it would have been unkind to laugh at them. It was like children playing a game in absorbed imitation of grown-ups. Solemnly the army straggled past in review, guns of all vintages carried at all angles while the officers waved their swords and yelled strange orders. In justice it should be said that the army was conscious of feeling a difference in the morning. It was not quite up to par.

Then the zealous brigadiers attempted to maneuver the infantry, and got in trouble with it. Across the field, beyond the parade ground, the ragged files loped at the double to charge the imaginary enemy, but the pace soon slackened and there occurred a perplexing phenomenon. Every few steps the army halted and many men stooped over to pick up one foot in their hands, and then the other.

Stephen Crane was appealed to, as an expert in the tactics of war. The literary critics had given him credit for a rare insight into the psychology and impulses of battle-fields.

"You can search me, boys," said he. "I never knew an army to stop and take its feet in its hands that way."

"You poor stupids," exclaimed McCready, who had solved it. "If you steer a barefooted army into a field covered with cactus bushes, can you blame it for stopping to pull the thorns out?"

"Quite so," agreed Crane. "I have no doubt you will find it included in the Haitian drill regulations."

From the harbor echoed three long, impatient blasts of the *Three Friends'* whistle. It was time to return to the blockade of Santiago. We bade His Excellency, the Governor, a warm farewell, but he urged us to wait a little. A dozen soldiers had laid hold of a rope and were dragging an antique cannon which may have been left in Haiti by the artillery forces of Napoleon. They were about to fire a salute with this interesting curio. It was, indeed, time to put for the open sea.

Ralph Paine hurriedly addressed his comrades: "When that thing busts, it's going to scatter far and wide. Without hurting anybody's feelings, I suggest that we waive this final ceremony."

The Governor understood. He had heard the steamer blow her whistle again. It was the call of duty which must be obeyed. The Chief-of-Staff came down to the beach with us. Stephen Crane, reluctant to part from him, was asking him for the story of his life, and what about that four years as a butler in New Rochelle, when again Captain Montcalm Broward jerked the whistle cord. We shook hands with our genial host and friend, who said:

"It was a hot time in Mole St. Nicholas, you bet your sweet life. *Au revoir,* but not good-bye, and stay longer next time. Those cable operators, they will be on the *qui vive, n'est pas?* I think so, by jingo."

Before the ship sailed we sent off to him, in a skiff pulled by the astute deck-hand, a case of sardines, a ham, and a tin of cigarettes, as slight tokens of our gratitude and affection. The *Three Friends* steamed out of the bay set between the lofty green mountains. Three correspondents kicked off their shoes and crept into their bunks to fall asleep. McCready murmured his favorite bit of Kipling:

But I would n't trust 'em at Wokin',
We're safer at sea again.

Harry Brown was humming to himself that mournful ditty of his own invention:

> . . . Than to hear the water gurgle,
> Or the nightingale sing,
> A bottle o' rum, the ship's a-sinking,
> *Two* bottles o' rum, we'll all be drowned,
> *Three* bottles o'—

Stephen Crane raised his voice in tired protestation:

"Please don't sing that, Harry, old man. The words offend me. Rum is poison. Think what you did to an army with your vile three dollars. You ought to have known better."[7]

[On 10 June 650 marines landed at Guantánamo Bay from the USS *Panther* in order to establish a coaling station for the blockading ships that previously had to make the eight-hundred-mile voyage to Key West to recoal in port. Crane, McCready, and Paine watched the landing from the *Three Friends*. In the evening Crane went ashore while the other correspondents took the dispatch boat to Port Antonio, Jamaica, to cable their stories.

When fighting intensified, Capt. Henry Bowman McCalla of the *Marblehead* sent in reinforcements. The marines' headquarters, which they called Camp McCalla, overlooked Guantánamo Bay. Months later Crane vividly reported the intense fighting on the evening of 11 June in "Marines Signaling under Fire at Guantanamo," *McClure's Magazine,* 6 February 1899.]

Meanwhile the *Three Friends* had left in a hurry for Port Antonio, Jamaica, to cable the news of the landing and the opening skirmish. This was the first attempt of an American armed force to seize and hold enemy territory in Cuba, a curtain-raiser in advance of the grand entrance of the Army. Stephen Crane stayed ashore with the marines because he foresaw much personal enjoyment. A hawser could not have dragged him away from the show. As I have said, the haste to file cable dispatches never troubled him. It was his business, as he viewed it, to gather impressions and write them as the spirit moved.

The *Three Friends* wasted no time during that run of a hundred and ten miles to Jamaica. It was the intention to return to Guantanamo Bay as soon as the Lord would let her. The weather was unusually favorable, but after reaching Port Antonio she was delayed several hours for engine-room repairs. As a result, it was in the middle of the night when the *Three Friends* approached the Cuban coast and then went more cautiously lest she become entangled with the blockading fleet or with scouting cruisers. Also, she had been told by crisp and emphatic naval commanders not to go blundering into Guantanamo Bay until after sunrise.

In the early morning, therefore, she passed in from the sea and dropped anchor not far from the *Marblehead* and within a short distance of the marines of Camp McCalla upon the hill. They were still there, and Old Glory stirred in the faint breeze that breathed with the dawn. The petulant pop of rifles indicated that the fight was unfinished. For more than thirty hours there had been no cessation. The marines had taken their punishment. Between the tents they had laid their dead in a row on the grass and decently covered them with blankets. There had not yet been leisure for digging graves.

Stephen Crane came down to the beach and waved his hat in token of his desire to be taken aboard the *Three Friends*. He was dirty and heavy-eyed and enormously hungry and thirsty. It was all he could do to drag himself into the ship's galley where he gulped down food and black coffee. Then he sprawled on deck, rolling cigarettes and talking in a slow, unemotional manner as was his wont, but the thin, pallid face kindled and the somber, weary young eyes brightened when he told us how it had fared with the battalion of marines. And as he went on, he used words as though they were colors to be laid on a canvas with a vigorous and daring brush.

What had particularly impressed him was the behavior of the four signalmen, who, through the night, had kept the *Marblehead* informed of events upon the hill. These marines had a cracker-box, placed on top of a trench. When not signaling, they hid the lanterns in this box, but as soon as an order to send a message was received, it became necessary for one of the men to stand up and expose the lights.

"And then—oh, my eye!" drawled Crane, "how the guerrillas hidden in the gulf of night would turn loose at those yellow gleams. How in the name of wonders those four men were not riddled from head to foot and sent home more as repositories of Spanish ammunition than as marines is beyond my comprehension. To make a confession, I, lying in the trench, invariably rolled a little to the right or left in order that, when he was shot, he would not fall on me. . . . Whenever the adjutant, Lieutenant Draper, came plunging into the darkness with an order, such as 'Please ask the *Marblehead* to shell the woods to the left,' my heart would come into my mouth, for I knew that one of my pals was going to stand up behind the lanterns and have all Spain shoot at him.

"The answer was always upon the instant, '*Yes, sir.*' Then the bullets began to snap, snap, snap at his head while all the woods began to crackle like burning straw. I could lie near and watch the face of the signalman, illumined as it was by the yellow shine of lantern light, and the absence of excitement, fright, or any emotion at all, on his countenance was something to astonish all theories out of one's mind. The face was in every instance merely that of a man intent upon his own business, the business of wig-wagging into the gulf of night where a light on the *Marblehead* was seen to move slowly."

Crane had joined the daylight sortie of a hundred and sixty marines under Captain Elliott who had burned the headquarters of the guerrilla forces at Cusco.[8] Small incidents had impressed him, for it was of such that he had builded "The Red Badge of Courage," and this bit from his novel, written before he had seen a man killed in war, was precisely what he had found on the trail to Cusco. . . .[9]

Rested and refreshed, Stephen Crane was eager to go ashore from the *Three Friends* and rejoin his pals, the marines, but McCready made vigorous objection.

"For heaven's sake, Steve, sit down and write some of this stuff. We left you here to cover the fight, and you've got it all. As soon as we catch up with the story, I must run this vessel back to Port Antonio and keep the cable busy. Duck into the cabin and write."

Crane paid no attention, but continued to talk about the marines. These practical, uninspired newspaper men were a confounded nuisance. They and their absurd demands were to be brushed aside. McCready tried bribery—beer and cigarettes—and Crane consented to dictate a dispatch, although very much bored. It was a ridiculous scene—McCready, the conscientious reporter, waiting with pencil and paper—Crane, the artist, deliberating over this phrase or that, finicky about a word, insisting upon frequent changes and erasures, and growing more and more suspicious. Finally he exclaimed:

"Read it aloud, Mac, as far as it goes. I believe you are murdering my stuff."

"I dropped out a few adjectives here and there, Steve. This has to be news, sent at cable rates. You can save your flub-dub and shoot it to New York by mail. What I want is the straight story of the fight."

Ralph Paine left them wrangling bitterly, with small hope of a satisfactory adjustment.

[During a skirmish between the Spanish and the marines at Guantánamo Bay, the Spanish sniper that Paine thought he was shooting at turned out to be a piece of dried palm branch. Caught in crossfire, he hid in an abandoned sugar boiler until the fighting stopped. Crane recounted the incident in "The Lone Charge of William B. Perkins."]

. . . [T]he perfidious Stephen Crane wrote for "McClure's Magazine" a story cast in the fictional form which he labeled "The Lone Charge of William B. Perkins: A True Story." I read it with embarrassment. As a disciple of realism,

Crane had been conscientious. In order that you may visualize the incident as he saw it, and to save the chief actor from talking about himself for a few minutes, I quote, in part. . . . [10]

This is how Stephen Crane interpreted it. To the reader it will be obvious that he pinned a leather medal, as a booby prize, on William B. Perkins. And the verdict will not be disputed. And yet it seemed a perfectly logical thing at the time, to shoot up the Spanish army as a token of hearty coöperation with the battling marines. Had it occurred a generation later, the students of psychoanalysis would be demanding to know what was the matter with the young man's complexes. But he would have had Dr. Freud and his disciples guessing, because the explanation was so simple. This was merely another attack of *damfoolitis!*

✍

41 / Ernest W. McCready

Ernest W. McCready (1869?–1950) was a correspondent for the *New York Herald* during the Cuban War. In May 1898 he, Crane, Ralph D. Paine (No. 40), and Harry Brown of the *New York Herald* visited Haiti aboard the *Three Friends,* and in June McCready reported on the marine landing at Guantánamo Bay and the march to Siboney. Crane depicted him as Shackles in "God Rest Ye, Merry Gentlemen," "The Revenge of the *Adolphus*," and "Virtue in War" and as McCurdy in "War Memories." Besides referring to Cora Taylor, McCready recounts Crane's reluctance to leave the fighting at Guantánamo Bay on 11–12 June in order to write a dispatch. McCready eventually lured him back to the *Three Friends* and took his dictation for the dispatch "In the First Land Fight Four of Our Men Are Killed" (*New York World,* 13 June), which was published unsigned most likely because McCready considered it the result of joint authorship.

Source: Ernest W. McCready to Benjamin R. Stolper, letter, 22 January 1934, Stephen Crane Papers, Rare Book and Manuscript Library, Columbia University.[11]

. . . Stephen, on the afterdeck of a stout dispatch boat, in the Caribbean moonlight, told me repeatedly, vehemently, imperatively, loftily, sarcastically,—in fact he *told* me, precisely how to write a short story; and hence how to write any story. He told me, also, with equal force, variety, and even seeming interest, that he knew I wouldn't grasp the notion, and that he was wasting his time. He was right, of course, as to that last; but I *couldn't* see why he needed to be so damned *triumphant* about it.

. . . .

I'm wondering much if anyone ventured really into Crane's one big romance—the origin of the lady who "saw him first" when she met him—in whose living room he picked up a copy of one of his early books of short stories[12] after the *Commodore* sank under him & Cap. Murphy; or if she still survives him. Ralph Paine professed to know the ins and outs of this angle.[13] I encountered the lady, along with Paine, one wild night in our filibustering days. The house was on the outskirts of Jacksonville. There was a semi-circular sign of generous size over the door, bearing in great letters of gold the inviting legend "Hotel de Dream." It was hers. She was hostess—in the later euphemism. The non-coms & privates numbered some 12 or 15—of unusual comeliness and youth—especially considering the Jacksonville of 1897. The lady was handsome, of some real refinement, aloof to most—to all, indeed, until Steve & Cap. Murphy arrived—newly come from death and the sea,[14] eager for drink, and drowsy ease or whatever the phrase is in the "I-have-a-Rendezvous-with-Death"-thing. Paine and I were in one section of the house and did not that night encounter Crane—whom P already knew—but only heard distantly the Murphy party. But we returned some nights later—Christmas eve[15]—sojourned—and sat in at the "family" board next day for *Christmas dinner*—Paine carving the noble bird. As the very admirable Mrs. P. and a charming family survive, in & about Durham, New Hampshire, where the Paine literary home is "Shankhassick"—among whose trees Ralph is buried, being at heart a Romantic—or thinking of R. L. S.'s self-written epitaph,[16]—I'm very cautious in approaching the subject. However, P. learned then & thereafter, between sessions at the roulette wheel, that our Mr. Crane had discovered the lady reading his book. Murphy & Crane were thinly incog. Presently, as the skipper hoisted a few more and a few more, he revealed his friend's identity. The news pierced the lady's very liver. *Paine told* me he heard of the subsequent exodus or hegira, after the Porto Rico campaign, I think, to London & the society of Harold Frederic et al of the Bohemian literary set in London & Surrey or Sussex. There they were in a country house. My impression of the Dame aux Camillias (or whatever it is) is still vivid. Fact is, she was a cut above us in several ways, notably poise and surety of command of herself and others. If she had any false notes I was then all too unskilled in recognizing authentic "class," or lack of it, to detect any. One carries gold in war time, or on campaign, and there was drink a-plenty, of course. Yet even before we knew that Crane had not only staked the claim but that there was instantaneous mutual attraction (I'm no bio-chemist, you'll guess) we never proposed to her that a little love interlude would be profitable to her and quite irresistible to us. Why? It was after all, the "Hotel de Dream." I'll have to go to one of De Maupassant's yarns to match my reflections on this encounter as reviewed from this distance—say 37 or 38 years along the road. Stephen took her in his stride—and as it turned out, in some very solid respects, the gray mare proved to be the best horse. I'll confess this piece of the Crane analysis beguiles me a lot. Again I regret having missed out on "Ulysses." I wonder. . . .

[The *Philadelphia Press* and the *New York World* had made arrangements with the *New York Herald* for their correspondents to use the *Three Friends,* one of the *Herald's* three boats, to make the twenty-hour round trip to Mole St. Nicholas to deliver dispatches to the cable station. As correspondent for the *Herald,* McCready decided when the boat would make the journey. He discovered, however, that Paine and Crane were preoccupied.]

. . . My boat was empty of both Paine & Crane. It developed that Paine, instead of going up front after Steve, had "gone American" or patriotic—which is sheer poison to newspaper work in war time—& had harnessed himself in with a crew who were dragging a gun from the *Texas* up the bluff, and thereafter had seized the rifle of a soldier who had fallen out from sunstroke. . . . At long last I found Crane—dirty, sleepless from the night attack, bleary from the preliminaries and reviews of his Marine hosts, disgusted with life in some aspects, particularly in having smoked the last of his, or their, cigarettes, but somehow gloomily elated over the scenery and the prospect that presently it would be a whole lot worse. The shells from the cruisers were still going over our heads, the Marines were still going up the ravines, & extending in less rugged but more heavily-brushed ground, and the Spanish rifle fire was evidently slackening. The Americans were pushing up more automatics and 3-inch field pieces.

Crane was sitting on a rock. There was some smoke drifting over and around us from the firing, and while at the moment we did not seem to be directly in line with any bullets from either side, I had already heard some talk about wrongly fused or otherwise ill-directed shells from the cruisers, and was afraid, too, that a shift of the Spanish, or the arrival of their supports would result in the ridge being swift to cripple American runners from the base to the advancing front line. I ignored the artist's gruff greeting—as long since we had dispensed with any but free, frank, & highly colorful forms of conversation, the sky being the limit so far as terms of compliment or complaint were concerned.

Rapidly and perhaps a bit roughly I told him there wasn't a minute to lose, that the dispatch boat was under the hill, that the show was over & complete in the newspaper sense, until the after-dark developments, for which I had made arrangements; that he could go to the Mole with me if he liked, and thus get to a cable some hours earlier than by any other course.

"Come on" I said. "Let's hustle like hell down to the boat. It's under the hill, covered from the firing, and we can start her the minute we're aboard!"

He regarded me with visible dislike.

"Gimme a cigarette!" he commanded. "Do you think, for God's sake, that I'm going away now on your damned boat, and leave all this?"—and he waved a hand in a sweeping gesture covering the battle picture. I knew what he meant. This, outside the torpedo boat attack at Cienfuegos where the Spanish had the ranges marked, & the venture with mosquito craft was unwise in view of the probable or possible profit to be had, was the first action, & the first landing; the first infantry encounter; the seizing and establishing of a naval base, preparatory to taking Santiago by combined land and sea attack. He'd been in camp with the Marines throughout the night attack and seen their dead and wounded, shared their in [*sic*] councils; loved the picture before him, and saw an artist's profit in it; it was hoarding a hundred impressions for his own peculiar treatment, the methods in which he had most faith—his own.

For me there was only one point that stood out. To go at once, with all possible speed to the Mole, was indicated as the right newspaper tactic, beyond dispute. Magazine stuff, Sunday stuff, atmosphere. They were not for plain and garden variety reporters in whose faith there was no God but Bennett whose prophet was Reick. My temper was short, and it was slipping; but I thought Crane already had a detailed list of casualties, and as we were working in common—Paine, Crane & myself—for the time being, and as I commanded our transportation, I was in one hell of a hurry, and again explained why—somewhat explosively. And I urged him to forget the scenery & the "effects" and remember that in Broadway and in Park Place edition was following special edition, extra following extra, and that he had been the only newspaper man in the show who had means of getting to a cable station.

But Crane was not a newspaper man. He was an artist from crown to heel, temperamental, undisciplined in the narrow sense of the word—careless of any interest that did not march with his own private ones, contemptuous of mere news getting or news reporting; thinking of his *World* connection as a convenient aid rather than as one imposing sharp and instant responsibility upon him.

He explained, briefly enough, that as he had shared the adventure thus far with the officers, had eaten their bread & salt, and wanted to see the end, as he had seen the beginning and all the rest up to that minute, & seen it in his own way, from vantage points of his own choosing, he'd be damned if he'd stir from his rock. As for me, I could do what I damned well liked—and I was simply distracting his attention.

Right there I nearly lost the game. I somehow had a thought that choked back the blistering reply I had on my lips. If I couldn't lure him to the boat, I'd have to lose more time in getting the casualty list, having another shot at the Colonel, trying to rout Paine out of the underbrush whence he was warring with "Alphonso Docy." My aim was speed. So I played a little poker with my friend Mr. Crane, meantime cursing him inwardly, & promising myself that in due course I would make him acquainted with some language and some lines of thought that had never got within the survey or the purview of the gallant author of *The Red Badge of Courage;* a species of direct narration and confrontation wearing the flower and shot through with the essence of a certain neck of the woods in distant New Brunswick. This man Crane was detaining me under fire, wasting time that I should be employing in cutting down that 110 miles to the black Mole where I knew a mahogany General of Division and a black chief of staff who had once been a waiter in New Rochelle—and was proud of it. Darkly I wished we were in the Haytian bush. I might be a bit short on artistic values; but in the bush, and for practical purposes in some other capacities, I could row my weight in the boat when a stylist, however intrepid, would find his sense of values challenged if not shaken.

I proffered more cigarettes—the olive branch—and spoke him fair. He took all the cigarettes—making sure of so much. Presumably I could get more on board, or at the base in passing. As for him, he was of MacMahon's mind, & fixedly: I said J'reste, and all that.

"Listen a minute," I said, rather mournfully. "Here's where you get it both ways. Come on down aboard. Either come on to the Mole with me, or dictate your stuff to me before I start. I'll take full notes and extend it in full on the trip. We'll be ten hours, or more if the wind's head on or there's a heavy sea. Paine may or may not be on the ship now. Anyhow, if you'd prefer to dictate it, so you can get back here quicker, that'll suit me too."

He had been frowning at the brush up ahead where the shells still pitched occasionally, singly now, by salvos again, by two & threes anon, and where the American skirmishers seemed to be making slower progress—whether of design, or because resistance had stiffened, or because they were awaiting protection for their flanks, being uncertain from our O.P.[17] And he shifted impatiently. But he turned his gaze on me for a moment, & his eyes flickered as if in momentary uncertainty.

"Oh, be damned to it!" he said gratingly. "Er"—and then with a sudden shift of purpose—"Have you got a drink on the damned boat? Or did you and the Armored Cruiser (Paine) lap it all up?"

That was better. It was surrender—or half surrender—disguised as something else, or masking some further notion to be developed in due course.

"There's three or four bottles of ale," I said, "and I think there's a drink or two of Scotch. Come and get it. It's yours. The Armored Cruiser and I will have to rustle some more, if he hasn't already, or wait ten or 12 hours for a drink at the Mole—and that'll be White Mule too."

I wanted one of my own cigarettes; but I didn't ask for it.

Yes, he was coming. I had an Indian's stride in the bush or across the open. Besides, I was scared, whenever I had time to think about it; but Crane wasn't. There was no fear in him so far as battle murder or sudden death was concerned— in the observation of anyone who saw him in places where the average man feels a chill wind momentarily or is afraid he's about to get the wind up.

"What the hell's the rush?" he asked. "Do you realize that I've not had a damned wink of sleep for 48 hours? Besides all this mess last night—that was a real mess compared with this"—and now in contempt of me, my fears, my haste, and perhaps in disgust, too, that in part he had seemed to allow himself to be persuaded from his purpose, he waved briefly toward the front where the skirmishers had disappeared. The popping of rifle fire & the crash of shell fire were becoming less intrusive. Contrariwise, we were moving toward the Bay, and the cruisers were talking more plainly. That irascible old man McCalla on the *Marblehead* seemed to be particularly irritated, judging by the volume of his fire as compared with that of his consorts.

I professed a growing concern about Paine, saying that he had some information that made it necessary for me to find him, or get his particular facts at the base hospital or elsewhere. That was not true. The Armored Cruiser—my best friend—had moved his bed, & must lie in it.; I was not going to wait for him. I was thinking of Bennett and Reick in the Doge's Palace in the little triangle at Broadway and Sixth[18] whose front elevation was crowned by the two giant bronze strikers of the hours irreverently—yea, blasphemously—named "Stuff and Guff" by *Town Topics* on the very day after the current was turned on and Minerva's birds began to wink at the passing minutes.

"Hi, Steve," I said, grinning, "You know about that A.P.[19] bird out in Newark don't you?"

"What about him?" he asked, in the tone of one discouraging suspected efforts at levity.

"Well, I expect to be reminded of him by cable right soon if I don't hit the Mole pronto"—meaning that I expected Stephen would be reminded of him by Mr. Joseph Pulitzer's pushful *World,* later if not sooner. Anyhow, there was a big labor riot in Newark, and troops out, ball cartridge, the riot act read, and all that.

The resident A.P. man got off an early bulletin to New York, and then went at the job of collecting his facts. New ones kept cropping up in flocks, and he was young. Very soon the A.P. wired, on receipt of his bulletin:

"Rush 5,000 words!"

And he replied, concisely:

"Can't now. All is excitement!"

"Yes?" said young Mr. Crane, with menace, "And what's the particular point in that?"—though well he knew.

We were now close to the top of the bank under which lay the old *Three Friends,* a stone's throw away from the *Texas* & its attendant collier.

"It means," I said, "That Mr. Paine is going to be told by several people—me first of all, that this isn't his private war; that if he's a war correspondent or a reporter he can't go soldiering as a side line; and if he's a soldier he's no damned use to the *Philadelphia Press* & Emory Smith, or, incidentally, to me."

"Likely he's there and's drunk up all the rum," quoth the brooding novelist, darkly.

A deckhand rowed quickly ashore for us when we hit the beach; but Mr. Paine was still singeing his Catholic Majesty's beard.[20]

I produced with all speed, such ale as there was, denied that there was any Scotch left—though I thought in that matter there was an ace in the hole, albeit a modest one—was generous of cigarettes, and noted with some satisfaction that Crane was already some what more at peace with his world. I set out a little table on the after deck, saw that the skipper was all set to go at any moment, asked him to have the beach watched for Paine, so that a boat might put off for him instantly if he were sighted—and resumed the business of staying Mr. Crane with flagons and comforting him with bananas and such placating speech as might avail. I produced copy paper and pencils, and seating myself amanuensis-like invited him to fire when ready, Gridley—for Gridley went before Lafayette in those brave days as the surviving members of the Society of the Carribean will testify cheerfully.

Stephen, pacing his quarter deck slowly, presently spoke the opening sentence of his cable to Mr. Pulitzer ("Accuracy! Terseness! Accuracy!"[21] say those big placards all through the *World* news room, I was thinking, as mechanically I wrote to his dictation). I have no idea what that sentence was. When it was half written an explosion thumped my ear drums, and I sprang up and turned all in the one motion to face the *Texas.* But the smoke blast had come from the collier—& it bellowed outward toward the opposite shore of the Bay.

Young Mr. Crane had come suddenly alive. He was radiant. Here was hell burst loose again, apparently in a fresh quarter. The notion washed him clean of fatigue and of fret in a twinkling. His grip had tightened on the bottle neck, and instinctively he had raised the container somewhat, as if, mayhap, to prevent a fracture and catastrophic leakage in case anything blew off the pilot house or dashed him to the deck.

In that instant, as we were scanning the opposite shore of Guantanamo Bay seen between drifting wisps of smoke from the collier's 6-inch, the *Texas* opened with her starboard battery, and young Mr. Crane refreshed his hold upon the bottle. How I subsequently got caught in the very act of faking a verbatim taking of his dictation of his masterpiece-of-the-moment, recaptured the Armored Cruiser who, as he afterwards related in his "Bright Roads of Adventure," had taken refuge in an abandoned sugar factory boiler he found while seeking Spaniards in the underbrush,[22] returned Stephen to his Marines and his battle setting, and fled to the Mole—writing Crane's cable story from my sketchy notes and thus committing all the literary butchery he had charged me with meditating— is an extension of this too long to glance at here. I had some voyages elsewhere in the war zone with Stephen,—but more than enough for this nonce. Yes? Yes.

Source: Ernest W. McCready to Benjamin R. Stolper, letter, 31 January 1934, Stephen Crane Papers, Rare Book and Manuscript Library, Columbia University.

. . . [M]y Night in Puerta Plata with S. Crane,[23] in the course of which he went native, and, perhaps in recoil from the adventures in having successfully invited a seduction, joined me in debunking two gentlemen who had so indulged in the Stars and Stripes and Haytian "white mule" that they emerged in due course as a twin saturated solution. Stephen was holding his liquor nobly on this occasion and it *was he* who engineered the really machiavellian device for robbing them of a Vast Container of Rum, though as he plotted against it—and them—the Jug lay in the womb of a barque anchored ¾ of a mile away, across a shark-infested harbor. In the black hills the nigger fires were winking, and the drums gave out that woodeny sound which some one likened to the music produced by a bevy of folk thumping distantly on a flock of wooden piss-pots. Steve went adventuring on this occasion in his bare feet, clothed only by exceedingly soiled blue-striped pajamas, an equally soiled brown beard of a week's well-fertilized herbage—and his circumbient Breath. This last was protection enough for all ordinary purposes. Indeed, it would have sufficed in the then still undiscovered stratosphere. But the purposes in view were very other than ordinary. So he had his due reward.

. . . .

The Cora lady (lives she yet? Or died she where, when, and how?) gives me considerable pause. A rare friend of mine, sired and damned hereabout, often used to say: "After all, there *is* such a thing as *class*." Well she had it, but to me the quality didn't lend itself readily to definition. The Christmas feast was lavish as to victual and drink, but not vulgar; and the Hostess' authority and *standard* ran through the whole stable, imposing a decorum that yet escaped any constriction of natural spirits and wasted no inspiration due to licker. That Irishman we lost a couple of years since in a motor smash—Donn Byrne[24]—he *nearly* caught her in "The Wind Bloweth." But she was several of his attractive females—and a touch like the marble awaiting a Crane to impart the glow with his particular Something. . . .

Source: Ernest W. McCready to Benjamin R. Stolper, letter, 3 March 1938, Stephen Crane Papers, Rare Book and Manuscript Library, Columbia University.

[Henry R. Cary managed the affairs of the *New York World* field staff in Cuba and was thus] Stephen's supposed boss. . . . Crane seemed never quite able to deal with him as he would have liked.[25] Stephen frowned and sometimes even fumbled at his dirty silk brown whiskers (he was dirtier than the main of a mainly dirty lot); but Cary was Stevie's Field *Paymaster,* being O.C. [officer commanding] then of Pulitzer's Shock Troopers in and about Key West—Havana—Santiago "axis"—(yep, a *crooked* axis that) and that sordid circumstance also had Stephen stopped. Cary had a way with a faro bank or a 36-wheel, or a certain type of confessed or potential Cyprians that Crane never acquired. One to have known—Cary—one sort of touchstone as to C., but of course not to be lugged into the Opus unless in the narrative he is cued in naturally re Ulysses.

6
Cuba, Haiti, Puerto Rico

~

42 / Charles Michelson

Charles Michelson (1869–1948), a journalist and later publicity director for the Democratic Party, first met Crane in Jacksonville in December 1896, when Michelson was en route to Cuba as a reporter for William Randolph Hearst's *San Francisco Examiner.* He and Crane met again during the Spanish-American War as fellow reporters for the *New York Journal.* Though Michelson spent most of his time on dispatch boats during the war and thus was not with Crane during combat, his reminiscence offers a striking portrayal of him during this period.

Source: Charles Michelson, introduction to *"The Open Boat" and Other Tales* (1927); vol. 12 of *The Work of Stephen Crane,* ed. Wilson Follett (New York: Knopf, 1925–27), ix–xxiv.

. . . Crane always disappeared on his arrival at a new town. He dived into the deep waters of society and stayed under. His associates knew where to find him and haled him forth when the time came, but he never was to be looked for about his hotel or in the bright cafés where the rest of us sunned ourselves during the waiting-time. Of all the businesses in the world none is less subject to schedule than that of getting munitions to an insurgent army. Waiting is the biggest part of it. The mere appearance of an unidentified man around the dock, a rumour of a loitering craft outside the harbour, the circumstance that one of the engine-room force was seen talking to a stranger—and the expedition is off *sine die.* Night after night Stephen loitered in the back room of a grimy waterfront saloon, partially, doubtless, because it was close to the dock, but largely because there people did not talk to him about his books—book, rather, for *The Red Badge of Courage* was the only one people knew about then.

This was the period he was supposed to be sunk in debauchery. Actually he was consuming innumerable bottles of beer—I never knew him to take anything stronger—and listening to the talk of oilers, deck hands, sponge fishermen, wharf-rats and dock thieves, and all the rest of the human flotsam that is washed into a port that has the West Indies for a front yard. This was his way of soaking in knowledge of the reactions of the kind of men he loved to write about, and while he was at it he was one of them—a sombre, silent member, contributing no adventure of his own, never flushing his quarry with a word that was not in their vocabulary.

He liked small gambling—dice or poker—but never seemed to get much of a thrill out of it; his luck was usually bad; so bad that on one occasion a tugboat mate suggested that he must be the very devil with the women. That started Stephen on a whimsical lament of his unsuccess with the sort of women they were talking about.

"If the five of us started out and gathered in four girls, I'd be the odd man ten times out of ten."

It was not hard to believe, on the deck of a tugboat, for Crane on his way to war was one of the most unprepossessing figures that ever served as a nucleus for apocryphal romances; shambling, with hair too long, usually lacking a shave, dressed like any of the deck hands, hollow-cheeked, sallow, destitute of small talk, critical if not fastidious, marked with ill-health—the very antithesis of the conquering male.

Actually there was plenty of poise and an abundance of solid qualities about him, despite the shadowy picture that has developed of Stephen Crane as an erratic, abandoned, unreliable whirling dervish of a fellow only redeemed from total depravity by the possession of one splendid gift.

The tugboat was carrying us from Pensacola to Ponce[1] to report the Porto Rico campaign. There was a head-wind most of the way, and the nose of the boat was under water with every wave, and somebody discovered that by standing far forward with a tight grip on the stays the Atlantic Ocean could be turned into an acceptable shower-bath. Crane revealed the wreck of an athlete's frame—once square shoulders crowded forward by the concavity of a collapsed chest; great hollows where the once smooth pitching muscles had wasted; legs like pipestems—he looked like a frayed white ribbon, seen through the veil of green as the seas washed over him.

Yet he apparently suffered none at all from the rough passage. The landlubbers generally gave way to seasickness, but Crane never had a qualm. He told me, as we sat on a midget deck before the pilot-house through the purple afternoons and velvet evenings, that the sea never had bothered him, not even when he met it in a tumbling dinghy that stood on end as each pouncing wave sprawled it nearer to the breakers off Neptune light.

That's when he told the story of the wreck of the *Commodore*. Whether he had written the story and was simply reciting the composition, or whether he was actually marshalling the words to be put later in type, I do not know; but when I got "The Open Boat" in print there it was, phrase for phrase, for entire paragraphs, as he told it on the Pensacola tug as she wallowed in the cross current of the Gulf Stream.

Some of our people were ghastly ill on the deck (where the motion was not nearly so appalling as up by the pilot-house), and he drew attention to the convulsive jerk of their shoulders as they bent miserably over the low rail, mentioning that men died with just such a spasm—he had been to the Greek-Turkish war in the interval between the filibustering period and our going to war. It was not lack of sympathy, or callousness, for he was as merry and considerate a shipmate as anybody could ask. It was simply that motion-picture mind of his registering impressions. It was an instinct, stronger than pity, or love, or fear. I don't know that he was a braver man than those who went through the same experiences in war-reporting, but I do know that while these were wondering if the next volley would spatter their way he was commenting on the rigidity of men in columns of four, and the imperturbability of birds scolding each other while the bullets cut the bushes on which they perched. . . .

There were few thrills to the tugboat journey. Once an American cruiser, the *Minneapolis,* I believe, swept up to us. We were none too sure of our status—a cargoless civilian boat in the blockade zone—but we hailed her cheerily with some question that revealed our character, and that she ignored, sheering off; her stern seeming to show her indignation at the impertinence.

"Like a fat dowager duchess," commented Stephen, "who has been asked by a scrubwoman where she had bought her hat."

Off San Juan[2] we found the improvised cruiser *Prairie,* while far inshore a Spanish destroyer was strutting to and fro under the guns of the land batteries trying to decoy the American warship within range of the heavy shore forts. The *Prairie* mentioned to us, hopefully, that if we went in close enough the Spaniard might make a try for us and so give the cruiser an opportunity of cutting her out. Presently we did veer inshore. The chaperon of our war party went to the pilot-house to learn the reason for the turn. There he found Stephen baiting the captain to run in close. Asked why he was doing it, the seaman answered fervently: "You don't think I'm going to let this damned frayed tholepin think he's got more guts than me, do you?"

Until the joke staled, Stephen was Lord Tholepin. He had taken the Morton Frewen House, Brede, and had told us something of its spaciousness.[3] Promptly the fiction was created of Stephen as a liverish British squire, with an East Indian background, and the ancestral mansion was christened Mango Chutney. Innumerable variations of the theme were suggested, and Lord Tholepin of Mango Chutney had more fun out of it than anybody else. It doesn't take much to amuse half a dozen men jailed together in a tugboat for a week.

Only once more were our expectations aroused on that cruise. A ship none of us recognized, except as differing from the American type, signalled us to lay to. There was nothing to do but to obey. When she got within hailing distance she megaphoned an inquiry that told us she knew who we were and why we were there, and went about her business. Later in referring to the incident Crane called it an "onion."

"Why onion?" I asked, knowing that he did not pick his figures of speech at random. In explanation he told us about an episode in which he had figured on another dispatch-boat in those waters. A ship nobody aboard recognized, except as differing from any American naval type with which they were familiar, signalled them to lay to. She had an American flag, but the wiliness of Spain was in everybody's mind. Spain turned out to have no war guile at all, but in those days, when Cervera's[4] fleet was being reported daily off every port from Maine to Mexico, she was credited with having all sorts of strategy up her sleeve. Moreover, word had come that some Spanish admiral had announced that any newspaper correspondents he caught in the war zone would be hanged as spies forthwith. Probably no such statement was ever made, but in the early days of a war, any tale of barbarism by the enemy finds credence. The strange ship came within megaphone range, and a voice boomed across the water: "Can you let us have some onions?" It was only one of the nondescript craft that had been converted to war purposes for blockade duty, whose supply of vegetables had run short. Thereafter "onion" was Stephen's private code-word for any adventure that missed fire.

Mention has been made of Stephen Crane's habit of losing himself in every new town. It happened again at Ponce, Porto Rico. There was every opportunity for a comfortable, clean campaign; decent hotels and cafés, cabs that took you to the front for *quatorze reales,* shops in which to buy souvenirs, men you knew at home, in bright new uniforms, a cable office, a censor, and all the rest of the war trimmings that were required at that archaic date, when wireless and air navigation were yet unborn, and poison gas an unmentionable military sin. We were hardly ashore when we missed him.[5] We found him, where we knew to look for him, in a back-street cantena, with the wastrels of Ponce—drunkards, drabs, and tin-horn gamblers. They did not know a word of his language nor he a word of theirs. Moreover, this was a conquered city and he was one of the invaders. That made no difference. He was accepted into the easy brotherhood of the thriftless without question.

"*Todos son ladrones,*" said our guide, the Porto Rican policeman whose beat had been taken over by an American soldier, waving us toward the group in the midst of which sat Stephen drinking bottled beer and local colour. Perhaps they were all thieves, but neither this nor any other group of the sort, that I ever heard of, exercised their professional skill on him, though his loose-fingered way with his money was a constant invitation.

The Army and Navy officers made a great deal of the literary lights. Richard Harding Davis was always the star of their parties—this was all in back of the lines, of course—but they were intensely curious about Crane. It was hard to get him to the dinners. Maybe he resented the contrast between himself and

Davis—the latter always a full-page illustration by Gibson of a war correspondent,[6] immaculate in a tailored uniform, his deep chest striated with service ribbons. In these gatherings Davis glittered not only by his accoutrements but by his accomplishments. He would borrow a banjo and to its accompaniment sing "Mandalay" and other ballads, and between times carry his full share of the burden of conversation, always ready, always interesting, while Stephen, in his old campaign clothes, sat tongue-tied. They would try to talk to him about his books, but Crane was willing to talk shop only with shop people. It was neither sullenness nor diffidence, nor self-deprecation; he had a normal appreciation of his achievements and endowments, and was reasonably militant and loquacious in verbal battles over the true and false in literature, but it was not his kind of company.

Later on, in the English environment, evidently he displayed a sufficiency of entertaining graces, but at Ponce he seemed a social bankrupt. Possibly the explanation is that he wanted to hear about the reactions of these men under their adventures, while they wanted to hear a literary lion roar, and, the ground being respectively distasteful, their minds never met.

Porto Rico was no flaming corner of the war. The Spaniards had crowned the peaks along the steep road to San Juan with vicious little forts, setting the stage for a real drama; but General Miles[7] sent his troops along parallel lines, so that the wasps' nests had to be abandoned one after another, most of them without ever having a chance to fire a shot. On this account the road was open for leagues. A flock of correspondents rode along this line early one morning vainly seeking breakfast. All the inns were pre-empted by hungry officers. At Juana Diaz, however, there was better fortune. We got there ahead of the army, but realized that we were likely to be ranked out of our breakfasts before we could get them, for the innkeepers had a most discreet and discriminating respect for official insignia.

Then came Stephen Crane's inspiration. He rode ahead and announced that the American governor of Porto Rico was on his way and ordered breakfast for His Excellency and staff. The most imposing member of the party, fortunately in immaculate whites, took the part of governor. He gave instructions to advise anybody who appeared that he did not wish to be disturbed during his meal. The preposterous strategy worked. Presently there came a brigadier-general and his aides. He was not one of the big generals, who would necessarily have known of the arrival of a civil dignitary, and had a soldier's idea that the civil side of Washington was capable of anything, even to sending out a provisional governor in advance of the capitulation of the island. Stephen almost lost his breakfast, for he could not tear himself away from the shuttered window, whence he whispered gleefully back descriptions of the general on his horse, pulling his moustache with impatience. Afterwards he went out and greeted the general, and, when the inevitable question came, lied glibly to this effect: "Governor? Oh, I guess the people here heard us call Jack Mumford governor, he looks so much like one. There's nobody here but a bunch of newspaper correspondents."[8]

In one of his stories that concerns a fugitive fleeing for his life,[9] Crane brings in the telepathic sympathy of the rider and the horse on whose endurance the result of the race depends. That was no literary abstraction. His horse was always a full partner in Crane's adventures. If it had been possible he would have gathered every animal he ever rode and kept them by him as long as they lived. A spavined moth-eaten menagerie they would have been, for good horses are not to be picked up in the wake of armies. Most of those who rode with him exchanged their mounts whenever opportunity for betterment presented itself, but Crane took his horse for better or for worse, until the campaign was over. His sense of the loyalty due a companion banned any desertion. He knew horses and helped the less sophisticated in making their trades. The shortcomings of his own steed were patent to him, but he no more thought of abandoning an animal because it was slow or bad-tempered than he would have quit a brother because he was lame or ill-favoured.

During the Porto Rico campaign he rode a hammer-headed, spur-scarred, hairy-hoofed white beast hardly bigger than a goat, with all the bad habits that could be grafted on original sin by ignorance and bad treatment. "El Dog" was his name while Crane had him. He was always picketed apart from the other horses, for he was both a biter and a kicker, but he and Crane got along together like sweethearts. There came the day when we were due to sail for home. The embarcadero is four miles below Ponce, and there we were all assembled except Crane. It fell to me to go in search of the missing member of our company. Half-way back to the town I found the horse-dealer from whom we had bought our chargers, and to whom we resold them at an adequate reduction when we were through. In his string he had all the animals except El Dog. To my inquiry he made response by shrugging a shoulder towards a gully filled with an all but impenetrable thicket. In this jungle I found Crane. His arm was over the bowed neck of the disreputable pony, and the face he turned to me was stained with tears. At the same moment the horse rolled a white and menacing eye at the disturber, showing that, so far as he was concerned, the softness of the moment extended none beyond the man who was bidding him good-bye. It sounds maudlin and mawkish in the telling, but somehow it did not appear either that afternoon in Porto Rico.[10]

Stephen made neither apologies nor explanations as we tramped together to where the steamer was impatiently waiting.

. . . Perhaps nothing differentiated his way from the newspaper way of recording facts or registering impressions so clearly as this. Uncorrelated incidents and unrelated pictures filtered into him; in the subtle chemistry of his mind they were resolved into the tales he was to tell. He could no more be hurried than a hen could be hurried in egg-laying. He did, of course, write his press dispatches, inconsequential alike in their subject matter and in literary quality, but hinting at both importance and rhetoric. In a way they resembled the battle ode he composed in this period,[11] that was intended to tell of the rousing of America to the power and fury of war. There was something of the church-organ roll of Kipling's Recessional,[12] something of Ambrose Bierce's poem of despair[13] in which "a wolf sat howling on a broken tomb"; but it misses fire somehow. . . .

〰

43 / Cecil Carnes
(writing about James H. Hare)

James H. Hare (1856–1946) had a long and illustrious career as a news photographer of world events. In spring 1898 he went to Cuba as a photographer for *Collier's Weekly*, covering the siege of Santiago and the Battles of San Juan Hill and El Caney. He met Crane at the end of May 1898 aboard the dispatch boat *Somers N. Smith*, which the *New York World* and the *New York Herald* had jointly chartered to search for the Spanish fleet. Crane gave Hare a tour of the Las Guásimas battlefield on June 30, and they spent time together during the momentous events of July 1.

Source: Cecil Carnes, *Jimmy Hare, News Photographer: Half a Century with a Camera* (New York: Macmillan, 1940), 60–63, 70–78, 128–29.[14]

[Hare arrived in Siboney on June 29.] He took it as a good augury that he discovered himself immediately among friends. A short distance inland from the beach, a group of tumble-down shacks were being used as headquarters by a coterie of correspondents. Jimmy found Scovel,[15] his assistant, Nichols, and Stephen Crane, all representing the *New York World*, housed in one of the huts. The others mostly sheltered correspondents from Hearst's *New York Journal*. . . .

Jimmy was interested in knowing Stephen Crane, who had already achieved fame in the literary world with his book, "The Red Badge of Courage." He proved a charming fellow, fond of a drink and not too fond of work. Lighting one cigarette from another, he confided to Jimmy his only reason for signing up with the *New York World* had been to get a military pass, his present ambition being to do a book about the war. Scovel, in charge of the *World* correspondents in the field, usually found it very difficult to get Crane's copy. . . . [16]

Crane led Jimmy on a tour of the Las Guasimas battle ground—the skirmish that had been deftly puffed up into a major engagement.[17] Then the two parted, for the wiry little photographer was ready and eager to follow the mean, tortuous trail that led over the mountain toward the actual front. . . .

Battle, it appeared, was to be joined on the morrow at dawn.[18] General Lawton was to take El Caney, and Scovel assigned Crane to cover that phase of the general advance.

. . . [A]lthough [Hare] had walked twenty-five muddy miles that day, he was on his feet with a suggestion that they had better get going. Crane stared at him and fingered his whiskey-glass nervously. Why, he demanded, should they start now when four o'clock in the morning would do? They should rest while a chance was offered them. "It'll be the soldiers who do the fighting," added Crane; "all we have to do is report afterward what they did."

That argument won over the others and they climbed into their hammocks. But Crane refused even to do that yet; he would "sit up awhile with a sick friend," he told them, and poured himself another drink.

Crane's solicitude for his ailing friend resulted in difficulties the next morning. Jimmy was up promptly, but there was no rousing Crane from his slumbers. He had promised faithfully to partner the photographer on the trip to El Poso, and Jimmy was pardonably annoyed. His most vigorous shaking of the unconscious form brought only a mumble of excuses. Fairly losing his temper, Jimmy shouted he was off "to cover the blarsted war alone!" And he added a number of the uncomplimentary thoughts he was thinking about Crane, and stormed out of the shack.

In two moments Crane was trotting at his side, striving to make amends and apologizing for his lethargy. He forgot he had shown Jimmy the Las Guasimas battlefield already, and in his anxiety to be restored to favor, volunteered to take him over the scene. Jimmy thanked him coldly, said he'd been there once, and was now looking for a fresh battlefield, not something warmed over. They went on in silence except for the *squushing* mud beneath their feet. But it was still too hazy to use his camera effectively, and Jimmy presently softened. Nobody, he explained afterward, could stay angry with Stephen Crane for very long. They were chatting amiably by the time they reached the vicinity of El Poso, where their paths diverged and Crane continued his way in search of Lawton's force.

[After leaving Crane, Hare spent several hours photographing battle scenes.] With a sigh of relief, he packed up his kit and began to think again of returning to El Siboney and its heavenly calm. But as he decided to do so, a horse's head came over his shoulder from behind.

It was not the sort of thing you'd expect to see just then and there, so he raised his eyes curiously and found himself in the presence of another lunatic. It was Stephen Crane, mounted on a pinto pony and wearing, of all incredible garments, a gleaming white raincoat. He and the horse made a shining target that fairly cried aloud for the attention of some Spanish marksman; but of the pair, only the horse was showing any trace of nervousness. Crane was cool and unconcerned as if he had been at a garden party.

"Hullo," he said casually, and raised his chin toward the crest of San Juan Hill. "I'm going on up. Want to come?"

"Up there?" demurred Jimmy. "I've just come down from up there. It's not very—attractive."

"Oh, well, come along anyhow. Maybe I'll get a story."

"More likely an epitaph," said Jimmy crossly, looking at the conspicuous pair. "All right, I'll come if you want, but do get down off that pony! If you must take *him* with us, walk behind him."

"Nonsense. If they aim at me, so much the better; no Spaniard ever hits the thing he aims at."

"Well—d'you mind if *I* walk behind him?"

"Not at all. Only sorry he isn't larger."

They started off, but by a different route than Jimmy had taken before. Thoughtful of his horse's comfort, Crane selected a narrow trail which afforded better footing than the slippery grass. They made good time, though they had to turn aside every so often to let a stretcher party pass them on the way to the rear.

Thus it was, the strange combination of a reckless writing genius, an innocent pony and an equally innocent photographer came to that elbow of the San Juan River which was later nicknamed "The Bloody Bend."

There they stopped short, immobilized by horror at the sight before them. A hundred broken men, the human wreckage brought from a few square yards of the battlefield, were receiving first aid though still under fire. The slight overhang of the river's bank afforded only partial shelter; many of the wounded were hit again as they lay there, and many a doctor fell across the body of the man he was helping. A ghastly business. . . . [Carnes's ellipsis]

Crane dismounted and began to talk with some of the wounded men. A sudden exclamation from him caught Jimmy's quick ear; the writer had been startled at recognizing among the injured an old schoolmate, Reuben McNab, whom he had not seen since those early days.[19] It was rather a bizarre setting in which to renew an old acquaintanceship, thought Jimmy, as he snapped the reunion, and he could see Crane was deeply impressed by the incident.

There was a temporary shortage of stretchers, and Crane insisted on turning over his pony to Reuben McNab so the wounded man would not have to walk the weary miles back to the base hospital at Siboney. And as the writer appeared fairly bemused by the encounter and anxious to stop for a chat with McNab, Jimmy unobtrusively left them and slipped away. . . .

It was after he had replenished the soldier's canteen and gone to earth in the trench[20] that Stephen Crane turned up once more. The stubborn fellow was still unwounded, still indifferent to danger, still wearing that infernal white raincoat. He saw Jimmy, came up to where he was cuddled in the ditch, and remained standing erect, staring toward the Spanish lines. Colonel Wood—he had more trouble that afternoon with noncombatants than with the enemy—spoke sharply to him, ordering him down. Crane ignored the command. Wood spoke again in terms unbecoming an officer and a gentleman but quite forgivable under the circumstances. Still Crane held his statuesque pose while bullets sang by his charmed person. It was Jimmy who finally brought his friend to earth. He remembered the two Hearst reporters, Edward Marshall and James Creelman, who had recently been wounded and had thereby gained much glory and publicity for the Hearst organization. Jimmy plucked at the hem of the white raincoat.

"What's the idea, Steve?" he yelled. "Did you get a wire from Pulitzer this morning reading: 'Why the hell don't *you* get wounded so we can get some notices, too?'"

There was a roar of laughter from the soldiers within hearing, and Crane, blushing, got down meekly and stayed there.

San Juan Hill had been definitely taken by late afternoon, and the firing, though still heavy at intervals, became spasmodic. It was time to start home, and reasonably safe to do so. Crane in the meantime had found a friend—a large man whose broad-brimmed felt hat sported a vivid puggaree and whose English-tailored costume was of a cut designed for the "romantic" type of war correspondent. Jimmy had never seen the fellow before, but when Crane explained he was suffering acutely from an attack of sciatica, the friendly little cameraman was prompt in offering his assistance to get the invalid back to camp. He possessed himself of the big man's tiny box camera and binoculars, then somehow got a shoulder under one of his arms while Crane did the same on the other side.

White with pain, the crippled reporter protested against the arrangement. They presented too large a target, he said, and would surely draw the enemy's fire. He begged his colleagues to leave him there, insisting he could make the camp by himself after dusk. "We'll all get shot!" he pleaded, doubling over in a sharp seizure of pain. "Aw, those Spaniards can't hit a haystack!" retorted Jimmy. So they went on in their clumsy, reeling fashion till they were out of the danger zone and finally at Sevilla. While the victim of sciatica was freshening up in his tent, Jimmy seized the occasion to question Crane.

"Who's this pal of yours we just brought down the hill?"

"Beg pardon, Jimmy," said Crane, "I thought you knew him. That's Richard Harding Davis."

That gave Jimmy food for reflection. He had heard stories to Davis' discredit, but they had been told by newspaper correspondents who were satisfied to stay miles in the rear and get their battle yarns from returning soldiers; Davis, it seemed, covered his subject at the front, even when in agony from sciatica. It entirely changed his conception of the "big writer."

Dick Davis in turn sensed that Jimmy was the genuine article, too, for he ever afterward named him as one of his closest friends.

On this occasion, Davis revived sufficiently to scout around and find the pack of a well known Rough Rider who had been killed in battle that afternoon. He gave it to Jimmy with the suggestion he and Crane camp with him overnight near the battlefield and so avoid the long hike back to Siboney. Jimmy and Crane were both so tired it was almost out of the question to do anything else. After a heartening meal from Davis' well stocked larder, the correspondents lay down in their blankets and wrote. Jimmy noted his captions for the day's photographs, then went and peeked over Stephen Crane's shoulder. This is what he read: "Many years ago I went to a school at a place called Claverack. . . . 'If you're going by the hospital, step in and see me,' said Reuben McNab. That was all."[21]

[On a train trip in 1902] Cortelyou[22] had a copy of Stephen Crane's newly published "Wounds in the Rain" on board.

. . . He took the book from his secretary and scanned its title page reflectively. "You knew this fellow Crane rather well, didn't you, Jimmy?"

"Yes, sir, very well indeed."

Again the Roosevelt teeth clicked decisively.

"I remember him distinctly myself. When I was Police Commissioner of New York I once got him out of serious trouble."[23]

"Oh, yes," said Jimmy slowly. "I recall the occasion. It was while he was collecting data for his book, 'Maggie: A Girl of the Streets.'"

"Nonsense!" retorted Roosevelt vigorously, careless that Jimmy had come to his feet with a face anything but pale as paper. "He wasn't gathering any data! He was a man of bad character and he was simply consorting with loose women."

Bristling at every whisker, a hundred pounds of human dynamite exploded.

"That is absolutely not so!" flared a man who defended his friends. "Nothing could be farther from the truth!"

Roosevelt stared, and Cortelyou gasped. Admittedly, it was no way to talk to the President of the United States, even if the incumbent himself happened to be a two-fisted wielder of words. Jimmy knew instantly he had been guilty of a lapse in good taste; he forced down his choler and spoke more calmly.

"I'm sorry," he said, a trifle too shortly to be convincing. "You see, I happen to know the story behind that incident. My friend, Crane, was merely taking the part of an unfortunate young woman who was being hounded by the police; that was the whole reason for his getting into a scrape with the law."

Roosevelt was still staring, but a fiery gleam that had lighted his eyes now died away. He nodded understandingly.

"All right, Jimmy," he said. "Have it your own way."

~

44 / Edward Marshall

Edward Marshall (1869–1933) had an extensive career as a journalist and playwright. He and Crane became close friends in 1894 when Marshall, Sunday editor of the *New York Press* and a staunch advocate for attempts to improve tenement housing, hired Crane to write New York City tales and sketches. As an early supporter of Crane, Marshall read *The Black Riders* in manuscript, encouraged him to show Irving Bacheller the manuscript of *The Red Badge of Courage,* and championed Crane's originality in reviews of *The Red Badge, Maggie,* and *George's Mother.* During the Spanish-American War Marshall served as a correspondent for the *New York Journal.* When he was wounded at Las Guásimas, Crane took Marshall's dispatch to Siboney to cable it to the *Journal,* an act resented by Crane's employer, the rival *New York World.*

Source: Edward Marshall, "Loss of Stephen Crane—A Real Misfortune to All of Us," *New York Herald,* 10 June 1900, sec. 6, 8. Reprinted with minor changes as "Stories of Stephen Crane" in *Literary Life* n.s., no. 24 (December 1900): 71–72.

. . . [Crane] was a correspondent for one New York newspaper during the war with Spain. I was a correspondent for another New York newspaper. On June 23 I was told that a battle would occur the next day. I asked Crane if he intended to go to the front. It was insufferably hot, and we had all learned to distrust rumors. He decided not to go. I was amazed by his apparent indolence. I went to the battle and was badly hurt by a bullet. When I regained consciousness, hours after the fight had ended, one of the first faces I saw was that of Stephen Crane. The day was hot. A thermometer—had there been such an instrument in that God-forsaken and man-invaded wilderness—would have shown a temperature of something like 106 degrees. Yet Stephen Crane—and, mind you, he was there in the interests of a rival newspaper—took the dispatch which I managed to write five or six miles to the coast and cabled it for me. He had to walk, for he could get no horse or mule. Then he rushed about in the heat and arranged with a number of men to bring a stretcher up from the coast and carry me back on it. He was probably as tired then as a man could be and still walk. But he trudged back from the coast to the field hospital where I was lying and saw to it that I was properly conveyed to the coast.[24]

One day in 1890[25] a young man came to my office with a letter of introduction.[26] He was thin—almost cadaverous. He wanted work and got it. His article—written for a ridiculously low price—on tenement-house fire panics, was one of the best things that he or any other man ever did.[27] It was followed by other strikingly strong stories.

One day he said to me most modestly: "I have written some verse." He handed me a package of manuscript. The next day I left the package on an elevated railroad train. I never told him about it, for within twenty-four hours I had recovered it from the lost property office of the Manhattan L. The manuscript was that of "The Black Riders," which had a tremendous vogue in England.

We were both members of a club made up of writers. The best part of its furnishings was a great open fireplace. Four or five of us sat before it one night and Crane read us parts of a story full of fighting. It was "The Red Badge of Courage." Afterward, when we had really seen fighting together, I marvelled because his stories of actual battles were less realistic than his descriptions of imaginary conflicts in this book. It was that faculty which would have made of Crane a great novelist. He had an accurate and logical imagination. . . .

45 / Burr McIntosh

Burr McIntosh (1862–1942), a prominent actor at the turn of the century, created the role of Taffy in *Trilby* and appeared in many Broadway plays. In 1909 he toured the country, playing the leading role in *The Gentleman from Mississippi* and left the stage in 1910 to start his own movie company in California. In 1898 he went to Cuba for *Leslie's Weekly* as a correspondent and photographer to report the siege of Santiago, but yellow fever caused him to return to the United States soon thereafter.

Source: Burr McIntosh, *The Little I Saw of Cuba* (London: F. Tennyson Neely, 1899), 124–27, 132–33.

[On 23 June 1898 McIntosh, Crane, and Edward Marshall (No. 44) of the *New York Journal* marched to Siboney, which had been abandoned by the Spanish, behind the First Volunteer Cavalry, the Rough Riders, commanded by Col. Leonard Wood and Lt. Col. Theodore Roosevelt. The following day the troops and the correspondents headed for Las Guásimas, where the Spanish were entrenched. En route they were ambushed, and Marshall was severely wounded. By the morning of 1 July Crane, McIntosh, and other reporters were on the hill of El Pozo, which allowed them to observe the decisive Battle of San Juan Hill.]

That hill was soon as barren as a desert, with the exception of those who manned the guns. . . . Here I found Remington,[28] Crane, Whigham,[29] Bengough,[30] Captain Paget of the English Navy, the Japanese attaché, and several other foreign representatives. . . . After remaining for an hour and a half on the hill, where we witnessed the earlier charges, Remington started off alone, while Whigham, Crane, and myself went up the road together, to where the firing was then at its height. As we passed by the ford at the foot of the hill, we saw Scovel[31] sitting under a tree writing rapidly, while a man with a horse stood near, waiting to carry his despatch. As Scovel saw us pass he shouted: "Don't go up there! Sharpshooters!" We stopped and inquired what he meant, and were informed that the trees on both sides of the road were full of sharpshooters, who had been picking off men ever since they started to go up the road. He himself had just returned, having seen much of the famous charging. As we proceeded on our way, the road seemed to be literally strewn with blanket rolls and bits of clothing which had been thrown aside in the rush to get to the front. We met a number of the wounded coming down and saw some really pitiable sights. After proceeding for half a mile, two men were noticed ahead of us, assisting a man who had received a very severe wound in his ankle; he had paused and was bending over to adjust the bandage, when we heard the sharp whir-r-r of a bullet. With a low moan he fell forward. We rushed up to find that his whole left jaw had been shattered. I took a picture of the group as he lay there, but it did not develop. We looked about into the trees, but could not see any sign of life; the smokeless powder rendered detection impossible and we could not judge the direction from the sound.[32] Another two hundred yards or thereabouts were traversed, when suddenly there came the most piercing shriek I ever heard in my life. Looking back some twenty-five feet, toward a spot which we had passed but a few seconds before, we saw a young man bending over and feeling his knee; as he did so, the blood spurted out at both sides. He had been shot directly through the knee-joint. I "snapped" a picture of him, which was also unsuccessful. We all sought to be of any possible service, but he had friends near by who said they would take care of him. We three resumed our march, passing several others, and occasionally a dead body lying by the roadside, when, while in a broad open spot, we heard the whir-r-r of two bullets within a distance of two or three feet in front of us. As we halted, I ventured the remark that it was a little bit warm and getting more so, and that in a very short time we were liable to be targets, in a manner which might be very disagreeable. Consequently, we retraced our steps and returned to near El Poso. Whigham and Crane went back in a few moments,[33] but this for me was a physical impossibility. The fever by this time had taken a very firm hold.

. . . .

At nine o'clock we went our various ways to seek shelter for the night. Crane bunked on a pile of saddles and provender, with a blanket over him, and Scovel, also, slept within a few feet of our camp fire. Davis and I had been told that there were several empty tents which had been pitched by the Rough Riders early that morning. We went in search of them, but without success. Returning to the one covered ruin, we were told by the sentry that there was room for a couple more to lie on the stone floor. Accordingly, we were soon stretching our weary bones upon a blanket, which was the only thing between us and the hardest floor that ever was given to mortal man to lie upon.

↬

46 / Richard Harding Davis

Richard Harding Davis (1864–1916), son of the influential journalist Lemuel C. Davis and the realistic writer Rebecca Harding Davis, was one of the most popular journalists and writers of romantic fiction of his generation. Davis met Crane in London in March 1897, when both were en route to report the Greek-Turkish War, and later in Cuba, where Davis was reporting the Spanish-American War for the *New York Herald*, the *Times* of London, and *Scribner's*. Davis may have characterized Crane as Channing in the short story "The Derelict" (*Scribner's*, August 1901).

Source: Richard Harding Davis, "Our War Correspondents in Cuba and Puerto Rico," *Harper's New Monthly Magazine* 98 (1898–1899): 938–48.

. . . It is impossible to designate one correspondent as being better than another, because what is important to one does not seem to be of value to his rival, and their ideas as to their duty differ. One may prefer to stand on the firing-line in order to see what is going forward close at hand, but while he is in greater personal danger, another who watches the battle from an elevation in the rear can obtain a much better view, and a much more correct idea of what is being done in all parts of the field. So the presence of a correspondent on the firing-line, or his absence from it, does not prove that he is not doing his full duty to his paper. The best correspondent is probably the man who by his energy and resource sees more of the war, both afloat and ashore, than do his rivals, and who is able to make the public see what he saw. If that is a good definition, Stephen Crane would seem to have distinctly won the first place among correspondents in the late disturbance. . . .

Near the close of the war, a group of correspondents in Puerto Rico made out a list of the events which, in their opinion, were of the greatest news value during the campaign, and a list of the correspondents, with the events each had witnessed credited to his name. Judged from this basis, Mr. Crane easily led all the rest. Of his power to make the public see what he sees it would be impertinent to speak. His story of Nolan, the regular, bleeding to death on the San Juan hills, is, so far as I have read, the most valuable contribution to literature that the war has produced.[34] It is only necessary to imagine how other writers would have handled it, to appreciate that it could not have been better done. His story of the marine at Guantanamo, who stood on the crest of the hill to "wigwag" to the war-ships, and so exposed himself to the fire of the entire Spanish force, is also particularly interesting, as it illustrates that in his devotion to duty, and also in his readiness at the exciting moments of life, Crane is quite as much of a soldier as the man whose courage he described.[35] He tells of how the marine stood erect, staring through the dusk with half-closed eyes, and with his lips moving as he counted the answers from the war-ships, while innumerable bullets splashed the sand about him. But it never occurs to Crane that to sit at the man's feet, as he did, close enough to watch his lips move and to be able to make mental notes for a later tribute to the marine's scorn of fear, was equally deserving of praise.

Crane was the coolest man, whether army officer or civilian, that I saw under fire at any time during the war. He was most annoyingly cool, with the assurance of a fatalist. When the San Juan hills were taken, he came up them with James Hare,[36] of *Collier's*. He was walking leisurely, and though the bullets passed continuously, he never once ducked his head. He wore a long rain-coat, and as he stood peering over the edge of the hill, with his hands in his pockets and smoking his pipe, he was as unconcerned as though he were gazing at a cinematograph.

The fire from the enemy was so heavy that only one troop along the entire line of the hills was returning it, and all the rest of our men were lying down. General Wood, who was then colonel of the Rough Riders, and I were lying on our elbows at Crane's feet, and Wood ordered him also to lie down. Crane pretended not to hear, and moved farther away, still peering over the hill with the same interested expression. Wood told him for the second time that if he did not lie down he would be killed, but Crane paid no attention. So, in order to make him take shelter, I told him he was trying to impress us with his courage, and that if he thought he was making me feel badly by walking about, he might as well sit down. As soon as I told him he was trying to impress us with his courage, he dropped on his knees as I had hoped he would, and we breathed again.[37]

After that, in Puerto Rico, we agreed to go out together and take a town by surprise and demand its surrender. At that time every town in Puerto Rico surrendered to the first American who entered it, and we thought that to accept the unconditional surrender of a large number of foreigners would be a pleasing and interesting experience. But Crane's business manager, who guarded him with much the same jealousy as that with which an advance-agent guards the prima donna, did not want any one else to share the glory of the surrender, and sent Crane off by himself. He rode into Juana Diaz, and the town, as a matter of course, surrendered, and made him welcome.[38] He spent the day in establishing an aristocracy among the townspeople, and in distributing largesse to the hungry. He also spent the night there, sleeping peacefully far beyond our lines, and with no particular interest as to where the Spaniards might happen to be. The next morning, when he was taking his coffee on the sidewalk in front of the only café, he was amused to see a "point" of five soldiers advance cautiously along the Ponce road, dodging behind bushes and reconnoitering with both the daring and skill of the American invader. While still continuing to sip his coffee he observed a skirmish-line following this "point," and finally the regiment itself, marching bravely upon Juana Diaz. It had come to effect its capture. When the commanding officer arrived, his sense of humor deserted him, and he could not see how necessary and proper it was that any town should surrender to the author of the *Red Badge of Courage*.

A week later, Millard of the *New York Herald*, "El" Root of the *New York Sun*, Howard Thompson, and myself, with some slight assistance from four thousand soldiers, captured a much larger city than the one Crane attacked; but as we stumbled into the town first, under the impression that it was filled with American cavalry, the town of Coamo surrendered to us. The question is, whether it is more creditable to take a town of five thousand people with three other correspondents, supported by four thousand soldiers, or to take a town of two thousand inhabitants single-handed. I fear that in the eyes of history Crane's victory will be ranked higher than that of Millard, Root, Thompson, and myself.
. . . .

The great proportion of correspondents sent home ill was out of all proper relation to their numbers. . . . One of the best known of the correspondents, who was on the firing-line at Guantanamo, Guasimas, and San Juan, was sent home, desperately ill with fever, in the same clothes he had been forced to wear for three weeks. He had forded streams in them, slept on the bare ground in them, and sweated in them from the heat and from fever, and when he reached Fortress Monroe he bought himself a complete new outfit at the modest expenditure of twenty-four dollars. For this his paper refused to pay. This was the same paper that discharged Sylvester Scovel for telling the truth about the Seventy-first New York Volunteers and for returning a blow. . . . [39]

Source: Richard Harding Davis, "How Stephen Crane Took Juana Dias," in *In Many Wars by Many War-Correspondents,* ed. George Lynch and Frederick Palmer (Tokyo: Tokyo Printing, 1904); rpt. (La Crosse, Wisc.: Sumac Press, 1976), 43–45.

[Knowing that Puerto Rican towns along the roads to San Juan were eager to surrender to advancing Americans, Richard Harding Davis saw] a chance for great entertainment, and much personal glory, especially as one would write the story oneself. It would be a fine thing I thought to accept the surrender of a town. Few war correspondents had ever done so. It was an honour usually reserved for Major Generals in their extreme old age.

Half way between Ponce and Coamo there is a town called Juana Dias which, at that time, seemed ripe for surrendering and I accordingly proposed to Stephen Crane, that at sunrise, before the army could advance to attack it we should dodge our own sentries, and take it ourselves. Crane was charmed with the idea, and it was arranged that on the morrow our combined forces should descend upon the unsuspecting village of Juana Dias. We tossed to see who should wake the other, and I won the toss. But I lost the town. For in an evil moment Crane confided the strategy of our campaign to the manager of his paper, the *New York World,* Charlie Michelson, and Michelson saw no reason why in this effort to enlarge our country's boundaries, a man representing a rival newspaper, should take any part. So, no one woke me, and while I slumbered, Crane crept forward between our advance posts, and fell upon the doomed garrison. He approached Juana Dias in a hollow square, smoking a cigarette. His khaki suit, slouched hat and leggings were all that was needed to drive the first man he saw, or rather, the man who first saw him, back upon the town in disorderly retreat. The man aroused the village and ten minutes later the alcade, endeavoring to still maintain a certain pride of manner in the eyes of his townspeople, and yet one not so proud as to displease the American conqueror surrendered to him the keys of the cartel. Crane told me that no general in the moment of victory had ever acted in a more generous manner. He shot no one against a wall, looted no churches, levied no "forced loans." Instead, he lined up the male members of the community in the plaza, and organized a joint celebration of conquerors and conquered. He separated the men into two classes, roughly divided between "good fellows" and "suspects." Anyone of whose appearance Crane did not approve, anyone whose necktie even did not suit his fancy, was listed as "suspect." The "good fellows" he graciously permitted to act as his hosts and bodyguard. The others he ordered to their homes. From the barred windows they looked out with envy upon the feast of brotherly love that overflowed from the plaza into the bystreets, and lashed itself into a frenzied carnival of rejoicing. It was a long night, and it will be long remembered in Juana Dias. For from that night dates an aristocracy. It is founded on the fact that in the eyes of the conquering American, while some were chosen, many were found wanting. To this day in Juana Dias, the hardest rock you can fling at a man is the word "suspect." But the "good fellows" are still the "first families."

In the cold grey dawn of the morning, as Crane sat over his coffee in front of the solitary cafe, surrounded by as many of his bodyguard as were able to be about, he saw approaching along the military road from Ponce a solitary American soldier. The man balanced his rifle alertly at the "ready," and was dodging with the skill of an experienced scout from one side to the other of the long white highway. In a moment he was followed by a "point" of five men, who crept close to the bushes, and concealed their advance by the aid of the sheltering palms. Behind them cautiously came the advance guard, and then boldly the Colonel himself on horseback and 800 men of his regiment. For six hours he had been creeping forward stealthily in order to take Juana Dias by surprise.

His astonishment at the sight of Crane was sincere. His pleasure was no less great. He knew that it did not fall to the lot of every Colonel to have his victories immortalized by the genius who wrote the *Red Badge of Courage.*

"I am glad to see you," he cried eagerly, "have you been marching with my men?"

Crane shook his head.

"I am sorry," said the Colonel, "I should like you to have seen us take this town."

"*This* town!" said Crane in polite embarrassment. "I'm really very sorry, Colonel, but I took this town myself before breakfast yesterday morning."[40]

Source: Richard Harding Davis, *Notes of a War Correspondent* (New York: Scribner's, 1910), 125–28.

[Davis recalled an incident also recorded by Carnes (No. 43) in which Crane and Jimmy Hare helped an ailing Davis.]

. . . [A]s I had a bad attack of sciatica and no place to sleep and nothing to eat, I accepted Crane's offer of a blanket and coffee at his bivouac near El Poso.

On account of the sciatica I was not able to walk fast, and, although for over a mile of the way the trail was under fire, Crane and Hare each insisted on giving me an arm, and kept step with my stumblings. Whenever I protested and refused their sacrifice and pointed out the risk they were taking they smiled as at the ravings of a naughty child, and when I lay down in the road and refused to budge unless they left me, Crane called the attention of Hare to the effect of the setting sun behind the palm-trees. To the reader all these little things that one remembers seem very little indeed, but they were vivid at the moment, and I have always thought of them as stretching over a long extent of time and territory.

⤸

47 / Don Carlos Seitz

Don Carlos Seitz (?–?) probably first met Crane at the Lantern Club, where Seitz was treasurer. Business manager of the *New York World*'s staff in Cuba, Seitz characterized Crane as a lazy, irresponsible correspondent. Although he misrepresented Crane and distorted facts surrounding him, his reminiscence has influenced numerous accounts of the Spanish-American War.

Source: Don Carlos Seitz, "Stephen Crane: War Correspondent," *Bookman* 76 (February 1933): 137–40.

[Crane signed a contract with the *New York World* on April 22 for three thousand dollars to report the Spanish-American War.]
. . . The first word we got from Stephen Crane was on July 1. He had taken a leisurely stroll with a scouting party of Marines, which resulted in the death of two recruits and of Dr. Gibbs, the Army surgeon.[41] The dispatch was a dull one, undoubtedly true to facts. Stephen was evidently dead tired when he wrote it. The story ended:—

As we neared the camp we saw somebody in the darkness—a watchful figure, eager and anxious, perhaps uncertain of the serpent-like thing swishing softly through the bushes.

"Hello," said a Marine. "Who are you?"

A low voice came in reply: "Sergeant of the Guard."

Sergeant of the Guard! Saintly man! Protector of the weary! Coffee! Hard-tack! Beans! Rest! Sleep! Peace![42]

This was printed on the day Major-General William R. Shafter moved against the Spanish commander, Toral. The *World*'s account was mostly Associated Press with sundry illicit gleanings from other sources. F. H. Nichols, a lazy but able reporter who was to shed much light on China in *Hidden Shensi*[43] and to die there on a return trip with Thibet in view, had been in Mole St. Nicholas where the cable from Jamaica touched, and by arrangement with the cable operator he helped himself to the best news that came along. There was no trace of Crane in it.

El Caney had been stormed and victory, with a considerable casualty list, perched on Shafter's banners. Then on the Fourth of July Admiral Cervera's Spanish fleet stole out of Santiago Harbour, past the collier *Merrimac* (sunk in the wrong spot by Lieut. Richmond Pearson Hobson), and was duly smashed by Commodore Winfield Scott Schley with Admiral Sampson's fleet—to the great annoyance of the Admiral, who was absent inspecting something. This filled all news space, and we forgot about the Army. The Army was not heard from for nearly a fortnight, and then in came a dispatch from Crane—not signed, for obvious reasons. We planted it in the middle of the front page on July 16th. . . . [44]

It required no great discernment to read charges of considerable cowardice between the lines against an important local regiment. Hearst lost no time in making the discovery and in vigorously denouncing the *World* for "slandering" heroes. This he blew into a storm that mightily disturbed Joseph Pulitzer, who was summering at Narragansett Pier. I was summoned to the Pier and consulted about the best course to follow. I advised standing by our guns. Mr. Pulitzer seemed to agree, but on the next Sunday called Nelson Hersh, City Editor, to Narragansett Pier, and sent him back with a plan for raising a monument to the fallen men of the aspersed regiment. The *World* subscribed $1,000 in an announcement made Monday morning, July 25. The only result was a redoubling of the Hearst fire. The public response was languid—about $900—and this stopped when an official report proved Crane's story true—in fact too lenient.

When the fund, such as it was, came to be tendered to the regiment, it was hotly refused. It lay in the bank for years, until Major Lewis L. Clarke asked that it be given to improve the regimental lot in Kensico Cemetery.

No more was heard from Crane until he made his way back to New York and turned in a column describing the killing of a Marine from ambush, as he wig-wagged a message to the ships on the redoubt at Guantanamo.[45] Crane brought out the fact that he had a sister who was a chambermaid in Omaha. The story got into a spare spot on the editorial page and was very striking. Delighted, I went to William H. Merrill, Chief Editor, and complimented him on getting in so good a thing. He did not know it was there! It was agreed that he would give space to more. On my way downstairs I met John Norris, the Financial Manager, coming out of his office, rubbing his hands gleefully.

"I have just kissed your little friend Stephen Crane good-bye," he said with a full-face grin. "He came here asking for another advance. 'Don't you think you have had enough of Mr. Pulitzer's money without earning it?' I asked. 'Oh, very well,' he said, 'if that is the way you look at it, by-by.' So we're rid of him."

This was the last of Stephen Crane as our War Correspondent.[46]

◡

48 / Walter Parker

Walter Parker (?–?), correspondent for the *New Orleans Times Democrat,* met Crane in spring 1898 and was with him in Havana during the final phase of the Cuban War. His reminiscence is the only extended eyewitness account of Crane during this period.

Source: Walter Parker, "Memorandum by Walter Parker, Re: Stephen Crane, New Orleans, March, 1940," typescript, 8 pp., H. L. Mencken Papers, Manuscripts, and Archives Division, New York Public Library.[47]

After the fall of Santiago and the peace protocol in the spring of 1898,[48] the correspondents were permitted to enter Havana, Stephen Crane among the group.[49] The hangout was the American Bar on a corner of the Prado. Most of us had rooms at the Pasaje Hotel next door. The only fighting going on was between the Spanish soldiers and the Cubans who drifted in contrary to orders. These conflicts occurred only at night.

The correspondents began gathering at the American Bar at 10 A.M., and for the most part remained there until 10 P.M. or until a riot broke out. Crane was usually the last to show up in the morning. He drank tropical beer only but consumed many bottles of beer in a day.

Apparently Crane was not engaged in any serious work and never referred to his newspaper connections. We had to clear all our cable stuff through a Spanish censor, but had free access by mail whenever we could catch a steamer. Not once did any of us ever run into Crane at the Censor's office.[50]

Crane was never hurried, and was always quite reserved. Apparently he was not in funds because the boys not infrequently had to pass a gold *centén*[51] to him to enable him to pay his American Bar bill.

Crane was of very great value to all of us because of his Cuban revolutionary affiliations. He had saved one Cuban from drowning when a blockade runner was wrecked,[52] and the Cuban had constituted himself a slave to Crane, and would kneel and kiss his hand or the hem of his coat every time they met.

This Cuban was an inside figure in the Cuban revolutionary movement, and had real influence and access everywhere, especially to forbidden places. Through him we were able to circumvent the Spanish authorities at nearly every turn.

Each night, at about 10 o'clock the five or six chaps, Crane included, who fraternized at the American Bar, would wander out on the Prado looking for the nightly excitement. Usually we had some hot tip from Crane's Cuban friend.

There were 200,000 Spanish troops in and near Havana. There were no United States troops there until fall, and they were not to take charge until January 1, 1899, when the Spanish evacuation would be completed.

Under the protocol none of the Cuban revolutionaries were to come into Havana until after January 1, but were supposed to come no nearer than the Cuban camp of generals, colonels, majors, captains, and lieutenants ten miles away.

But they drifted in anyhow, and frequented the restaurants and cafes most frequented by the Spanish officers, where they would make insulting remarks about Spain and the Spanish officers.

At first the Spanish officers personally resented not only these offenses but the presence of the Cubans, and personal difficulties resulted.

The Comandante then issued orders requiring his officers merely to blow a whistle to bring strategically located Spanish troops to deal with the situation. The method employed was to begin shooting as soon as they came in sight of any revolutionary Cubans.

Since these were nightly occurrences, our little group had plenty to do after 10 P.M., including keeping out of the line of fire.

The favorite gathering place at night of the Spanish officers was in a cafe adjoining the Inglaterra Hotel, and there the Cubans would come to insult the Spaniards.

We watched that place closely.

The first night of the effectiveness of the Comandante's order, the offending Cubans ran out of their cafe into the Inglaterra Hotel, up the stairs, and claimed protection from the American peace commissioners.

These latter gentlemen stood at the head of the stairway, with pistols drawn. The Spanish troops, not desiring to restart the war, gave up the chase.

With ready harborage so closely available, the Cubans flocked in from Marinao. Among the number was Senor Julio Sanguili, whose life had once been spared through banishment and a promise never to return to Cuba so long as the Spaniards were there.[53]

With Julio was a French engineer who hated all things Spanish and who had joined the Cubans.

Upon spying Senor Sanguili, the guards did not await an insult, but just blew their whistles, and the troops began to close in.

Sanguili and the Frenchman ran to the Inglaterra. Sanguili fleeter of foot, gained the stairway first, and mounted five steps at a time.

Half way up, the stairway turned. A great mirror, back of the turn, faces the street. As the Frenchman made the turn a Mauser bullet caught him on the hip, passed through, and into the mirror. He stumbled upward. The American peace officers, with drawn revolvers, came to his assistance, and the Spanish guard retired.

Friends carried the Frenchman to the roof, across several buildings, and passed him down through a skylight.

Crane's Cuban friend came to us and told us that he could take us to the wounded man. He led us through a back alley, up a ladder and into a window. There the Frenchman lay on the floor.

Soon a Cuban surgeon arrived.

"We must clean the wound with burnt linen. It will be painful. I shall give you an anesthetic."

"No. Never. No! Go ahead. I want to feel the pain," replied the Frenchman.

The operation proceeded. Beads of perspiration gathered on the engineer's forehead. He suffered great pain.

Later, when the pain had abated, Crane inquired why he had refused the anesthetic.

"I am an enemy of Spain, gentlemen. I desire to feel all the pain so that I should never forget that I am an enemy of Spain."

He recovered.

On another occasion, Crane's Cuban friend led us to a Cuban danza where money was being raised for the Cuban cause, all of which was prohibited by the Spaniards.

The day before, a correspondent of a New Orleans afternoon paper had blown into Havana, looked me up, and I had introduced him to the group in the American Bar. This chap spent the day taking Cognac aboard and when time to go to the danza came, we took him along because we did not know what else to do with him.

Down the center of the room there were two lines of chairs, back to back. Our group were assigned seats in one row. Crane's Cuban friend and his lady love, a really beautiful girl, sat in the row just back of us. Our inebriated companion kept tilting his chair which knocked against the back of the chair occupied by the lady. She complained that she was being annoyed.

Up leaped the Cuban, knife in hand, and made for the offender, intending to stab him to the heart.

Crane jumped to the rescue and caught the sharp glittering blade in his right hand. The Cuban dropped to his knees and kissed the hem of Crane's coat. Crane's hand was bleeding. He wrapped it in a handkerchief and thrust it in his coat pocket. We made apologies to the lady through the Cuban and retired.

Next day we shipped the offender back to the United States. Havana was no place for him in those days.

Crane failed to show up in the morning as was his custom. His hotel door was locked and we could get no answer from him. Later we climbed over the half-wall partition and found Crane in high fever, unconscious and with a terrible wound in his hand. The Cuban procured a doctor who gave him treatment. Many days had to pass before Crane's hand was completely cured. Even then he kept his hand in his pocket most of the time as though desirous of hiding it.

He was not the same after the incident, was more reticent and less regular in his habit of joining us every morning. When several days elapsed and he did not turn up, we investigated and found that he had had a personal shock. The affair was wholly personal and the details are nobody's business.[54]

Anyway, he went into complete retirement, and there wrote a poem, "The Ashes of Love,"[55] which was the last work of his that we knew of.

One day the British Consulate in Havana called on us for information as to Crane's whereabouts. We feigned ignorance until the consul told us that he had money for Crane. We then gave him the desired information.

Soon the hullabaloo incident to the formal transfer by the Spaniards of Cuba to the United States came[56] and we all were all busy and forgot all about Crane.

I returned to New Orleans and to my old job on the *Times Democrat* in February, 1899, and so never saw Crane again.

He was a calm and companionable fellow. Never talked much, and rarely discussed himself, and never his own experiences.

Our group included men whose experiences had been very much out of the ordinary, and Crane would listen to them with close attention.

One day he and I crawled through the tunnels under El Morro fortress.[57] Another day we gained entrance into Cabanas fortress by a ruse. Four thousand

Spanish soldiers who had mutinied were held prisoner there. They had gone on strike because they had not been paid, and called off the mutiny when they were promised the equivalent of 9 cents a month for cigarette money.

Still another day we inspected the Spanish defenses of Havana, which an American army of 17,000 strong expected to capture by storm, and found a completely coordinated system of trenches, bomb-proof and connecting tunnels, in an ever narrowing circle. Our non-military opinion was that those defenses would not be taken so long as the Spaniards and their ammunition held out except at the expense of the lives of far more than 17,000 United States troops.

Shortly after the peace protocol in 1898 was signed, Crane and I set out to find and interview the Cuban patriot army, about which the world had been hearing much.[58] At Marinao we located forty generals, a hundred colonels and an uncounted number of captains and lieutenants, but there were no privates there.

The generals were evasive when questioned as to the whereabouts of the Cuban armies and gave several locations.

We decided to visit all the locations and to begin with a plantation some twenty miles in the interior. We obtained a carriage and an armed guard and set out early in the morning.

We found the place—a ruined plantation; the house in bad repair. On our approach a tall, yellow negro sentry changed his gun and bayonet with a small black negro and blocked the entry of the approaching party.

Asking for the general in command, we were conducted to the house where a very dignified Cuban told us he was the general, and introduced a doctor as his surgeon major.

It developed that the two negro sentries alternated between the kitchen as cooks and the gate as sentries. The general and the surgeon major were the only others there.

Asked, "Where is the Cuban army?" the general explained Cuban tactics thus:

"We have plenty of officers. When we need privates we just round up the peons and country folk, arm them and proceed.

"Afterward, we disarm them, they scatter, the officers go into retirement, and when the Spaniards come to find us there is nobody to find.

"Such tactics baffle the enemy.

"Weyler[59] tried to solve the problem by driving 200,000 reconcentrados into Havana to starve."

And such was the Cuban army which had done so much harm to the Spanish army, but which no one could ever locate in a body.

~

49 / Otto Carmichael

Otto Carmichael (?–?), Washington correspondent for the *Minneapolis Times,* was in Cuba during the fall of 1898. His reminiscence offers a rare glimpse of Crane during the four months from mid-August to late December 1898 during which he isolated himself in Havana while he wrote dispatches for the *New York Journal,* Cuban war stories, and the remainder of the poems that would make up *War Is Kind.*

Source: Otto Carmichael, "Stephen Crane in Havana," *Prairie Schooner* 43 (1969): 200–204.[60]

Stephen Crane to a certainty was a Bohemian. He was absolutely worthless except for what he did. The city editor of a modern newspaper would not have had him around the city room for a week. He was irresponsible and unmanageable. There was nothing vicious about him or even reckless; he was serenely indifferent; trifles would change him and big things would not stop him; fancy would hold him to a place and money would not move him from it.

The first time I ever met Crane was when General Wade, then chairman of the American Evacuation commission in Havana, asked me to carry word to him that he had a London cablegram for him. I told him in a cafe. He said "Thanks," and it passed out of his mind. The next day General Wade told me he had another cablegram asking if the first had been delivered and would I kindly tell Mr. Crane that the cablegram seemed important and that he should call at the offices of the commission and get it. I delivered the second message at the same place. Crane said:

"Say, didn't you tell me something about a cablegram yesterday?"

"Yes, I told you about one, and this second is an inquiry as to whether the first was delivered."

"Yes. I see. Using the government to find me. Anyway, I'm much obliged."

And again he forgot all about it. Or at least he never paid any attention to my notices. Some time later, after I had become acquainted, I told him that the message was still in Wade's hands.

"Oh, it's some tradesman I owe a bill to, I suppose," and that is the last I ever heard of it, although I saw a great deal of him afterwards.[61] It is not likely that a London tradesman would spend 60 cents a word to find out about a tailor bill, even if Crane did owe one. He was not extravagant, or in the habit of owing large sums. It simply struck him as nothing worth bothering with and he let it go at that.

I have heard many army officers say he was the bravest man they ever saw. He apparently did not think of danger. Death to him was nothing more than the next breath, or the next breakfast or sleep. Bullets were nothing to him, moving or in cartridges, except something to make copy about. This was not affected. It was the quality of the fellow. To see others suffer tore his tender heart. He was almost girlish in his sympathies. But it apparently did not bother him to be hungry himself or to be in pain. He never grumbled about taking his share. I heard many stories of his matter-of-fact fearlessness, but, as I was not there, will not try to tell of them. Others will.

He was mixed up more or less intimately with the Cuban war from the start to finish. He knew Jose Marti, had been with Maceo, Gomez, Garcia, Rabi and others.[62] The whole thing to him was never anything more than a big "story." He knew it just the same as a police reporter knows all about a big case, with its star criminals, its vital witnesses, lost clues, big lawyers, involved law points, ruined reputations, death scenes and hangings and its human sorrows and miseries. Into this he was picking and picking for copy. As the city editor would define it, he was looking for things of human interest. He knew every fiber of these leaders and fighters.

So far as I could note, courage was the only thing he admired. If he cared anything for the Cuban cause he never showed it. He had a boundless admiration for the men who did the real fighting. The only time I ever saw him really enthusiastic was when he was trying to prove to a cafe crowd that the filibusters who landed on the enemy's shores had more courage than any of them.

Crane had seen all kinds of fighting. It had a fascination for him. Danger was his dissipation. He was really grieved when he learned he had left a cafe just a few minutes before a noisy shooting scrape.

A strong man could not help feeling sorry for Crane. He seemed on the verge of collapse for lack of strength. His arms were as thin as one who had been ill for a long time. In a dim light Crane's face was handsome to the point of being exquisitely beautiful. In the full light his face had a sick and a miserable look. His drawn lips, his yellowish, haggard face, his tired eyes and generally wornout appearance combined to make a picture not particularly attractive. But he was so simple and genuine that one soon forgot all about these and could see the wan, half-pleading smile on the frank, boyish face. This little smile went for everything with Crane. It was his thanks for a light, his approval of an act, his delight over a story, his acknowledgement of distress, his pity for weakness. In fact, that sensitive little smile was always flitting about his face.

He did nothing with regularity. He ate and slept when he could no longer do without these necessary comforts. He would remain in the streets and in the cafes until his friends and chance acquaintances were tired out. He lived with a former filibustering associate in a pair of rooms not far from the downtown hotels and when other places were closed to him he would go there in hopes of finding some stragglers. If he did he would sit and listen to their chatter until they were tired out. Then he would go to work. When I saw him he was doing 600 words a day. This was the only thing he did with regularity. He was very particular about his work. He wrote somewhat slowly and was whimsical about words. He would spend a long time in trying to find what suited him. Inasmuch as he had no dictionary or books of reference, his search for words and information consisted in chewing his pencil and waiting until they came to him.

When his 600 words were written he would rouse some of his straggling guests—if they would stand for it—and if not he might read or go to bed. To take care of his health never occurred to him. He had the Cuban fashion of drinking light drinks and coffee, but he did not indulge to excess in alcohol. This was somewhat remarkable at a time and place of excessive drinking. This was two years ago and his health then was wretched. There was no chance for him to live unless he mended his ways. It was nothing more than thoughtlessness. He simply refused to think about himself. He was wafted over and around that island with each passing breeze and gust of excitement, attracted to where there was danger or something doing. All of this may have concealed a sort of a rudimentary business instinct and possibly he was making it profitable, but it is hardly likely.

I remember one time where he was drumming up some friends to play hearts with him. Finally he made up his party and they went to a club. The usual stakes were 5 cents a heart. Even 5 cents a heart is sufficient to make this game interesting. The counters were being distributed when Crane suddenly said: "Let's play for *centéns*."

This was startling. *Centéns* were $5 gold pieces. With such stakes it would be possible to lose $65 on a hand, and very easy to get rid of a few hundred dollars at a sitting. Not a member of the party had any right to be playing for such stakes, but for some reason they did. They just fell into a helpless sort of way.

And no one would have thought that Crane was not used to playing friendly games of hearts for gold *centéns*. It was to be seen, however, that he was taking keen note of the nerve of the others. Courage was always in his mind. He was looking for it in big and little ways.

The only man who lost much was his friend, the bartender and ex-filibuster.[63] He was the one who could least afford it. That pleased Crane immensely. A book could be written about the camaraderie of these two. They had been in all sorts of tight places together. The "bartender" knew the Cuban coast by night and day. He had been the Pilot on the *Three Friends,* and later on the *Dos Hermanos*—the *Two Brothers.* He was no bartender, but Crane called him that because he once got him a position in a cafe and then had him discharged because he was late in the morning in getting to work.

We had breakfast together the morning I left Havana.

"Not because I particularly cared for the breakfast," he explained, "but to make sure that you give those shirts to my friend."

"Now, the bartender here will help you get out of town," he said, after the shirts had been selected to his satisfaction, "for there are a great many things to do with your passports, health certificates and God knows what. You might get uppish with your high-sounding letters. He will keep you poor and you'll get off cheap."

And with his happy, sunny little smile he was gone—nowhere.[64]

50 / Edwin J. Emerson

Edwin J. Emerson (1869?–1959) was a correspondent in Cuba for *Leslie's Weekly* and later *Collier's* as well as a spy for the Military Information Division of the U.S. Army during the Spanish-American War. Later, Emerson continued his career as a journalist for the *New York World.* In *Pepys's Ghost,* a burlesque diary that imitates *The Diary of Samuel Pepys,* he recounted humorous events involving Crane during the fall of 1898.

Source: Edwin J. Emerson, *Pepys's Ghost* (Boston: Richard G. Badger, 1900), 149–51.

To the Inglaterra for my daily draught of Xeres wine and there beheld Señor Sanguilly,[65] the Cubano rebel, lately returned, with black ugly looks flashing 'twixt his friends and highly wrathful souldiers of the Spanish King his forsaken army. So lingered until nightfall and after supper back again for trouble was surely brewing.

Of a soddain, we having quaffed our third round of wassail cups, bursts forth an angry quarrell 'twixt Cubanos and Spaniards, and one man striking 'tother in the face, tables be overturned, and flashes of drawn swordes. Anon cometh the loud noyse of a blunderbuss and other souldiers running up, all fall to shooting their arquebuses this way and that, we hiding away into an ingle nook, whilst bullets and broken glass flew hither and thither. The Cubanos flying up the stairway, with Spanish souldiers shooting after them, I out into the square and there beheld Mr. Mott[66] upon a balcony watching the Spanish souldiers assault the hostelry. Then did I see poor Veloce shot dead, and one fierce Spanish trooper hot spur after a Cubano flying for his life before the sharpe point of his sworde, and anon come upon Stephen Crane, who standeth with both his hands held aloft, lest he be shot for a Cubano, and I accosting him, he did waggishly shake his head and proclaim, *'Tis another night of St. Bartholomew*.[67]

[Emerson's entry for 16 December described the arrival of American troops in Havana.]

They have come back in the nick of time quoth Steven Crane, we coming upon him in the midst of the town, for he hateth all Spaniards as they were poison. He most cocksure how more frays and mayhap bloody rebellion must soon follow, and so gave but scant heed when I did bid him go with us to behold them unearth the bones of great Sir Cristopher Columbus in the church of La Habana on the morrow, but in the end gave me a hearty yea.

[Emerson's entry for 20 December described the cortege supposedly bearing the remains of Columbus as it proceeded to the wharf where the casket was trans-ferred to a Spanish warship. Emerson then continued:] [H]ome to dinner, deep in meditacion on the vanity of all things, which I seldom am, but tarried at the *Three Friars,* Stephen Crane his chosen tap room, to uprayed him for so light a breach of his solemne promise, but he so far gone in dalliance with two morena damozels and at such losse what to plead in his owne behalfe that he did feign to be too deep in drink to know my face, and so left him, nor knew how to explain his ill manners to my wife, waiting for me below in her hackney coach.

7
England

51 / Joseph Conrad

Joseph Conrad (1857–1924) was Crane's closest literary friend in England; they and their families spent much time together during Crane's final years. The two writers admired each other's work and developed a symbiotic relationship based on what Jessie Conrad (No. 52) called "easy terms of complete understanding." Conrad's impressionistic reminiscence re-creates one of the most memorable events in Crane's life, the day he and Conrad first met.

Source: Joseph Conrad, "Stephen Crane: A Note without Dates." *London Mercury* 1 (December 1919): 192–93. Rpt. *Notes on Life and Letters* (London: J. M. Dent and Sons, 1921), 49–52.[1]

My acquaintance with Stephen Crane was brought about by Mr. Pawling,[2] partner in the publishing firm of Mr. William Heinemann.

One day Mr. Pawling said to me: "Stephen Crane has arrived in England. I asked him if there was anybody he wanted to meet and he mentioned two names. One of them was yours."[3] I had then just been reading, like the rest of the world, Crane's "Red Badge of Courage." The subject of that story was war, from the point of view of an individual soldier's emotions. That individual (he remains nameless throughout[4]) was interesting enough in himself, but on turning over the pages of that little book which had for the moment secured such a noisy recognition I had been even more interested in the personality of the writer. The picture of a simple and untried youth becoming through the needs of his country part of a great fighting machine was presented with an earnestness of purpose, a sense of tragic issues, and an imaginative force of expression which struck me as quite uncommon and altogether worthy of admiration.

Apparently Stephen Crane had received a favourable impression from the reading of the "Nigger of the *Narcissus*," a book of mine which had also been published lately.[5] I was truly pleased to hear this.

On my next visit to town[6] we met at a lunch.[7] I saw a young man of medium stature and slender build, with very steady, penetrating blue eyes, the eyes of a being who not only sees visions but can brood over them to some purpose.

He had indeed a wonderful power of vision, which he applied to the things of this earth and of our mortal humanity with a penetrating force that seemed to reach, within life's appearances and forms, the very spirit of life's truth. His ignorance of the world at large—he had seen very little of it—did not stand in the way of his imaginative grasp of facts, events, and picturesque men.

His manner was very quiet, his personality at first sight interesting, and he talked slowly with an intonation which on some people, mainly Americans, had, I believe, a jarring effect. But not on me. Whatever he said had a personal note, and he expressed himself with a graphic simplicity which was extremely engaging. He knew little of literature, either of his own country or of any other, but he was himself a wonderful artist in words whenever he took a pen into his hand. Then his gift came out—and it was seen then to be much more than mere felicity of language. His impressionism of phrase went really deeper than the surface. In his writing he was very sure of his effects. I don't think he was ever in doubt about what he could do. Yet it often seemed to me that he was but half aware of the exceptional quality of his achievement.

This achievement was curtailed by his early death. It was a great loss to his friends, but perhaps not so much to literature. I think that he had given his measure fully in the few books he had the time to write. Let me not be misunderstood: the loss was great, but it was the loss of the delight his art could give, not the loss of any further possible revelation. As to himself, who can say how much he gained or lost by quitting so early this world of the living, which he knew how to set before us in the terms of his own artistic vision? Perhaps he did not lose a great deal. The recognition he was accorded was rather languid and given him grudgingly. The worthiest welcome he secured for his tales in this country was from Mr. W. Henley[8] in the *New Review* and later, towards the end of his life, from the late Mr. William Blackwood in his magazine.[9] For the rest I must say that during his sojourn in England he had the misfortune to be, as the French say, *mal entouré*. He was beset by people who understood not the quality of his genius and were antagonistic to the deeper fineness of his nature.[10] Some of them have died since, but dead or alive they are not worth speaking about now. I don't think he had any illusions about them himself: yet there was a strain of good-nature and perhaps of weakness in his character which prevented him from shaking himself free from their worthless and patronizing attentions, which in those days caused me secret irritation whenever I stayed with him in either of his English homes. My wife and I like best to remember him riding to meet us at the gate of the Park at Brede. Born master of his sincere impressions, he was also a born horseman. He never appeared so happy or so much to advantage as on the back of a horse. He had formed the project of teaching my eldest boy[11] to ride and meantime, when the child was about two years old, presented him with his first dog.

I saw Stephen Crane a few days after his arrival in London. I saw him for the last time on his last day[12] in England. It was in Dover, in a big hotel, in a bedroom with a large window looking on to the sea. He had been very ill and Mrs. Crane was taking him to some place in Germany, but one glance at that wasted face was enough to tell me that it was the most forlorn of all hopes. The last words he breathed out to me were: "I am tired. Give my love to your wife and child." When I stopped at the door for another look I saw that he had turned his head on the pillow and was staring wistfully out of the window at the sails of a cutter yacht that glided slowly across the frame, like a dim shadow against the grey sky.

Those who have read his little tale, "Horses,"[13] and the story, "The Open Boat," in the volume of that name, know with what fine understanding he loved horses and the sea. And his passage on this earth was like that of a horseman riding swiftly in the dawn of a day fated to be short and without sunshine.

52 / Jessie Conrad

Jessie Conrad (1873–1936) wrote two reminiscences, *Joseph Conrad as I Knew Him* (1926) and *Joseph Conrad and His Circle* (1935), about her husband and his friends. Her memories of the Cranes complement those of her husband and offer additional details about life at Ravensbrook and Brede Place.

Source: Jessie Conrad, "Recollections of Stephen Crane," *Bookman* 63 (April 1926): 134–37.

My first meeting with Stephen Crane came one evening early in November,[14] 1897, a little more than seven weeks before our eldest boy, Borys, was born.[15] My husband, who had met him perhaps twice, had in a way prepared me for someone at once unusual and with a charm peculiarly his own. He must have been then about six and twenty, and appeared to my maternal mind very slight and delicate. He and Joseph Conrad were on the easy terms of complete understanding, I saw at once; his manner to me was slightly nervous and not a little shy. I don't remember much of the evening that followed after that dinner—I left them together and did not see him before he left early the next morning. The most lasting impression I have is of our taking our coffee, when Stephen, balancing himself on his tilted chair, discoursed gravely on the merits of his three dogs, Sponge, Flannel, and Ruby. The former two had the distinction later of being the parents of the dog he insisted on presenting to the baby. I believe this puppy was known as Soap until he became a member of our household, when Conrad christened him Escamillo, Millo for short.

When the boy was two days old I was deeply moved to receive from Stephen's wife Cora a beautiful box of flowers and a warm invitation to spend a week with them in their home Ravensbrook as soon as the baby was old enough to travel. This visit we made when Borys was exactly five weeks old.[16] The royal preparations for the small person's arrival touched me very much—since we came without a nurse, a huge easy chair was placed by the side of mine at the table for him to lie in. Stephen had brought with him from Greece two brothers, one of whom he retained in his own household as butler.[17] This youth was most assiduous in his attentions on the young gentleman, and would creep into my room when I was bathing the baby if I forgot to lock the door against him. His English amused us not a little on more than one occasion. One day he was sent by Stephen with a message for my husband and this is the form in which he delivered it: "Mr. Conrad, Mr. Stokes, he come, he want you Mr. Crane." I fear that, owing to my inexperience, the baby must have disturbed the peace of the household not a little; his food decidedly disagreed with him and he voiced much of his dissatisfaction in the night, a habit most infants have. However, we spent a very pleasant week and left with a warm invitation to repeat the visit someday soon. Stephen declared he had some distinct claim to our precious baby. Cora too was very much taken up with the child, but in a different way.

Our next meeting with Cora, then staying alone while Stephen was in Cuba, was marred by her very real anxiety as to his whereabouts, and a fierce jealousy as to his possible fancy for someone he might meet. In vain I assured her of my complete conviction that Stephen was deeply attached to her, and that his thought as soon as he was able to get a letter through would be of her.[18]

A few weeks afterward he returned, a changed man. Exposure and his experiences in Cuba had set their mark on a constitution never very good, and we looked apprehensively at each other. It was about this time that we saw the most of Stephen. His chief delight was to lie on the grass smoking and watching the small boy's efforts to move along alone. I often caught a wonderful gleam in his eyes as he watched so intently his little friend. He and the boy's father made plans far ahead when it should be time to put the child on horseback. "I shall teach your boy to ride, Joseph," he would say, "and he must have a dog, a boy ought to have a dog."

We stayed for more than a fortnight on our first visit to Brede Place, which had been lent him by some friends.[19] Here it was that Stephen would sit in the window of the big drawing room, twanging a guitar and singing in a low voice some haunting Neapolitan air, his wonderful eyes fixed on space. He never varied his tune but I always noticed an expression of serenity and quiet satisfaction on his face at these times. . . .

One vivid recollection I have of both Stephen and Cora. I had been talking to her while she made her preparations to retire, and after I had kissed her good night I withdrew toward the door at the far end of the room and looked back. She had chosen for her bedroom the ballroom, and her big four post bedstead standing on the raised dais (where the musicians were meant to sit) looked like a tiny doll's bed. All the necessary bedroom furniture was grouped close together in a small island and the light from the two tall candles threw the rest of the vast apartment into ghostly shadow. At the extreme end of the big room appeared a small opening like a tube railway; far in the distance I saw Stephen and my husband seated in close conclave. From where I stood their animated faces seemed to hang in the air, independent of their bodies. From that tiny room there was no exit except through Cora's bedroom. I remember thinking that when Stephen escorted his friend through as they parted for the night, Cora would be sleeping too far away to be visible, even with the light of the candles burning close beside her. Hardly a comfortable room to have chosen for sleeping, especially in winter. There were plenty of more manageable bedrooms which could have been made extremely cosy. Numbers of the rooms were empty, no servant then would ever consent to sleep the night in Brede Place which was supposed to be haunted. The long array of really slatternly girls and women who appeared in the morning and faded away at sunset must have been depressing in the extreme to a man as highly strung and sensitive as Stephen. It was this peculiarity on the part of Cora that gave rise to much unfavorable gossip. This and her strange fancy for inviting people in such shoals to visit the house that even Brede Place could not accommodate them each with a bedroom.[20] Cora therefore made the vast rooms into dormitories, and all day long a wagonette, drawn by two horses, plied between Brede Place and Rye Station for the convenience of those friends and acquaintances who might desire to call on the Cranes. I fancy Cora's idea was that this lavish hospitality would bring to Stephen much popularity; and all the while he wrote, feverishly anxious, too anxious to get the best out of himself. There were days when he would appear unexpectedly driving his two horses, Glenroy and Gloster, down the steep hill road above the old farmhouse where we lived.[21] Stephen, Cora, and a friend— seldom more, and always unexpected. Those visits were at all times a delight, and Stephen and my husband seemed to get much mutual benefit from the close interchange of ideas.

Our small boy had now attained the age of fifteen months or so, and our next visit to Brede Place[22] was marked by the fact that Borys took his first two or three steps all alone, down the steep bank outside the study window, in full view of his admiring friend and his proud father. The child became a regular rival to those dogs to whom Stephen had become so devoted. Time after time I have seen him raise the thin face bent low over his work and, without the least impatience, open the door for one of those spoiled animals to pass through. Then when he had almost returned to his seat he would have to repeat the performance. Sometimes, when he was too ill and languid to attend to their demands himself, he would request the old servitor (an elderly manservant who had been lent with the house[23]) to do so. Many times I watched the solemn farce, sorely tempted to interfere. The old ruffian, his face set in the most benevolent expression, would escort the dogs to the head of the stone steps and then solemnly kick each one down the steep flight.

Those dogs were the source of much tribulation in the village and were also very destructive to the sheep and lambs in the surrounding park.[24] It happened unfortunately that Stephen either could [not] or would not consent to pay for the damage, and the shepherd more than once threatened dire consequences. All this Stephen disregarded in a somewhat lofty manner. Then one day when we were returning from a long drive (we had been absent two days) we all gasped and held our noses as soon as the horses turned into drive. A sheep's carcass hung from each of the four or five biggest trees bordering the drive in the park. Stephen's face turned deathly pale with anger while he muttered curses under his breath. The horses shied violently at the ghastly objects swinging on a level with their heads. Next morning when I went out the carcasses had all disappeared, and I never heard that Stephen did more than roundly curse the shepherd.

It was something like eighteen months later, and some few months since we had heard from him. We had, indeed, no idea that he was much worse; but one night I woke my husband to tell him of a very vivid dream I had had. I saw the man for whom we had so great an affection being conveyed to some seaport town a long distance from Brede Place. I distinctly saw the invalid carriage, which I recognized as an ambulance being driven at a gentle pace along the road. I seemed to be present at the inn where the horses were changed, and my impression was so strong that I had to speak of it at once. By the next morning's post came a letter from Cora requesting us to go at once to Dover, as Stephen wished to see us once again before he completed his journey to the Black Forest.[25]

We went early in the day, taking the small boy Borys with us. Conrad told me afterward how he had sat talking to the sick man, who was able to answer only by signs and by a few panting words scarcely above a whisper. That parting glimpse of Stephen lying on the bed with his wonderful eyes fixed on the ships that showed through his open window, the feeble voice, and the stretcher on which he was to make this final journey, made a deep and lasting impression on my husband's mind. I recall his words when he rejoined me in the hotel, where I sat endeavoring to comfort poor Cora. We took a sorrowful farewell of her and anxiously requested a wire to let us know which day they were to leave. The weather was too rough for them to cross for nearly a week, and even then they had to spend two days on the way because of his increased weakness. My husband's words ring in my mind now: "It is the end, Jess. He knows it is all useless. He goes only to please Cora, and he would rather have died at home!"

Source: Jessie Conrad, *Joseph Conrad and His Circle* (New York: E. P. Dutton, 1935), 56–58, 72–75.

[After repeating comments in her earlier reminiscence, Jessie Conrad briefly described Brede Place and supplied additional details.]

Stephen, after riding one of his two horses along the edge of a narrow terrace past the drawing-room windows, would come into the drawing-room with an old violin and accompany himself singing some ditty in a thin but tuneful voice. Robert Barr was also a guest and had shown an excess of nervous apprehension when he once slept in the same room I used afterwards that opened into the picture-gallery, because of the ghost.[26]

Brede Place was supposed to be haunted, and it was impossible to persuade local servants to spend the night there. The only two who would sleep there were the old butler, who fortified himself with liberal potions, and an excellent cook—who did likewise.[27] She had often to be bribed to function in the evening with a bottle of brandy. The chances of dinner—at eight—were often very small, especially when there were many people expected. The cook would appear and announce in the most truculent tone that she was even at that moment departing. Cora Crane, at her wits' end for the moment, would wring her hands and appeal to Stephen. He in turn would give her one glance and solemnly ring the bell. Like clockwork the old butler appeared and handed a bottle of brandy to the thirsty woman, who retired with no further comment to her kitchen, and an hour or so later a perfect dinner would be served, complete in every detail. One night the old butler, who had primed himself a trifle early, knocked over the lamp and set the table alight.[28]

Stephen Crane was also a frequent visitor while we lived in that farmhouse.[29] There was a curious telepathy between this young man and myself. I remember once, when we had not heard anything for some months of him and did not know he was desperately ill, I had a most vivid dream one night which I told my husband in the morning. I had had a vision of dear Stephen lying on a stretcher being placed in an ambulance with two nurses in attendance and Cora Crane, and of the ambulance being driven to the coast as quickly as possible.

The dream was curious because we had not spoken of the Cranes or seen anyone connected with them for some months. When the post arrived an hour later a letter told us the exact substance of my dream and begged us to go that morning to the "Lord Warden" in Dover, where the poor fellow lay awaiting a calm sea to cross and try to reach the Black Forest in search of health. For poor Cora it was a pitiful business, she had not the means to pay for meals in the "Lord Warden." The nurses were fed outside, but I know that the wife often went without.

The small boat we shared with Stephen had been in Rye for months. That arrangement was not very satisfactory as far as we were concerned, and Cora Crane's illogical request made to my husband rather took his breath away. We had bought the boat, *La Reine,* from Mr. Hope[30] on the understanding that Stephen and my husband were to be joint owners, and half the time we kept it in Folkestone and the other half of the time Stephen had her in Rye. But he had never paid his half-share,[31] and his wife's proposition was that she should allow their local wood merchant to take her over in payment for their wood account.

A few days after that this queer telegram arrived for their man of business, who was not aware that they had taken the favourite dog with them to Germany: "God took Stephen at 11.5, make some arrangement for me to get the dog home."

I always thought that it was a terrible pity the poor corpse should have to lie in a London mortuary waiting for a passage to America for so long. There was a glass let in the lid of the coffin, and people were allowed to take a last look at poor Stephen, and leave their card at the mortuary.

⌒

53 / Ford Madox Ford

Ford Madox Ford (1873–1939), born Ford Hermann Hueffer, dropped his middle name in 1915 before entering the British Army, and changed his last name to Ford in 1919, partly as a reaction to World War I and partly because of his complicated marital affairs. A masterful impressionist and storyteller, Ford wrote a number of reminiscences in which "[w]here it has seemed expedient to me I have altered episodes that I have witnessed but I have been careful never to distort the character of the episode. The accuracies I deal in are the accuracies of my own impressions" (*Return* viii).[32]

Despite the unreliability of his accounts, they have significantly influenced biographers of Crane. As with Beer, Ford is the only source for a number of colorful stories, for example, Crane's dislike of Robert Louis Stevenson, his lecture on flag waving, and his swatting flies with his pistol. Compounding the problem of the reminiscences is the fact that though Ford repeats the same anecdotes throughout his reminiscences, he recasts them with different details each time they are told. In addition, a descriptive bibliography of Ford's reminiscences is complex. Publication titles of the same book vary; for example, *Memories and Impressions: A Study in Atmospheres* (1911) was published in America and simultaneously appeared in England as *Ancient Lights and Certain New Reflections: Being the Memories of a Young Man* (1911); the American publication *Portraits from Life: Memories and Criticisms* (1937) appeared in England as *Mightier Than the Sword* (1938). Also, a supposed reprint of a reminiscence is actually a silently revised version of the original text. The reminiscence of Crane in *Return to Yesterday: Reminiscences, 1894–1914* (1931) has been listed in bibliographies as a reprint of "Stevie," which appeared in the *New York Evening Post Literary Review* (12 July 1924) but is a variant account. Further complicating the issue is the fact that the reprinting of *Return to Yesterday* (no subtitle) in America (1932) contains additional silently made variations. Though a number of the changes between the magazine and the two book versions are matters of house style (e.g., changes in punctuation and spelling), a few of the changes affect the meaning of the text.

Reprinted below is Ford's reminiscence in *Thus to Revisit*, the first extended account of his relationship with Crane. This is supplemented with lengthy excerpts from *Return to Yesterday: Reminiscences, 1894–1914* (1931) and *Portraits from Life* and with additional details in the endnotes from other reminiscences.

Source: Ford Madox Ford, "Two Americans: Henry James and Stephen Crane." *New York Evening Post Literary Review.* 19 March 1921, 1–2; 26 March 1921, 1–2. Rpt. *Thus to Revisit: Some Reminiscences* (London: Chapman and Hall, 1921), 106–13, 118–20; rpt. (New York: Octagon Books, 1966), 106–13, 114, 119–20.

It was perhaps in 1896[33]—I am never very certain of my dates, but it was about then—that Mr. Garnett brought poor, dear, "Stevie"[34] to call upon me.[35] I was then living a very self-consciously Simple Life at Limpsfield in a newly built cottage of huge lumps of rough stone.[36] These Crane, fresh from the other side of the world, muddledly took to be the remains of an ancient fortification. He put in, I remember, a rose tree beside the immensely thick, oaken front door—for all the world like a king planting a memorial oak!—and looking at an outside fire-place remarked:

"That's a bully ol' battlement!"[37]

He told me afterwards that, although he did not, in the ordinary way set much store by corner lots and battle-fields I and my establishment had pretty well seen him for the jack-pot. But the literary point about the interview was this:

At a given moment Mr. Garnett said that Crane—he was then the all-famous author of the *Red Badge of Courage*—must have read a great deal of French imaginative literature. Crane said defiantly that he had never read a word of French in his life. (I dare say the defiance was to my address far more than to Mr. Garnett's.) He had been dragged up in the Bowery,[38] he had, and he hadn't any use for corner lots. When Mr. Garnett persisted and pointed out the great resemblance of his handling of a story to Maupassant's, Crane said:

"Oh well, I've read ol' man James's. . . . " I forget what it was he confessed to having read, but it was one of James's French critical works.

Later, I was requested—this will seem an improbable story—to go one evening to Crane's house at Oxted, near by, to give Mrs. Crane a lesson in dress-making. The request had been made by a local lady[39] who liked to "bring people together," I not having, out of shyness, I dare say, pursued the acquaintance of Crane. I found Mrs. Crane alone and she did not want a lesson in dressmaking—of the medieval variety. But she begged me to await Crane's return: he had gone up to town on business and she expected he would be nervous and glad of distraction. I think this was the only unsolicited call I ever paid—and that was due to a misapprehension!—and I was nervous enough myself!

He came back[40]—nervous and distracted, truly, and very late—but extraordinarily glad. I have never again seen such gladness as was displayed on that Oxted-night by that great and elf-like writer. For me, Crane came nearer to the otherworldly being than any human soul I have ever encountered: he was indeed what Trelawny has made us believe Shelley was—the Author of emotionalised fiction.[41]

He kept it exaggeratedly beneath the surface. Superficially he was harsh and defiant enough: his small, tense figure and his normal vocabulary were those of the Man of Action of dime drama—very handy in a Far Western fashion, with a revolver. He loved, indeed, to sit about in breeches, leggings, and shirt-sleeves, with a huge Colt strapped to his belt. And he would demonstrate with quite sufficient skill how, on a hot day, he could swat a fly on the wall with the bead foresight of his "gun"—all the while uttering Bowery variations on his theme of giving no fancy prices for antiquities. He meant by that that he was not a Poet. . . .

He was glad, that night at Oxted; he was astonishingly glad, the joy shining out of him as heat glows sometimes through opaque substances—because his agent, Mr. Pinker, had given him a contract to sign which guaranteed him £20 per thousand words[42] for everything that he chose to write and had advanced him a sum of money sufficient to pay his Oxted debts.[43] So he could get away from Oxted. The motive may seem materialistic to the official-poetic among readers. But Crane had hated his suburban villa with a hatred comprehensible enough—and he hated debts with the hatred of a high-strung, nervous but realistic poet.[44]

With the falling from his shoulders of that intolerable load he desired, as Mrs. Crane had foreseen, to talk. And he talked. He kept me there listening, right through the night, until breakfast time.[45] He had the most amazing eyes; large, like a horse's; frowning usually with the gaze of one looking very intently—but shining astonishingly at times. And a deep voice. When he became excited[46]—as that night he was—the studied Americanisms disappeared from his vocabulary, or nearly so, and he talked a rather classical English.[47] He planned then, his glorious future.

They were, his plans, not so much a matter of the world over which he intended to travel, flinging coins from the purse of Fortunatus that had been put by Mr. Pinker into his hands: it was a question, rather, of how he would render that world when he had roved all over it. He talked, in fact, about his technique.

I do not flatter myself that it was to me that he talked; that night he would have talked like that to a broomstick. . . . [Ford's ellipsis] I had, I suppose, in those days a Pre-Raphaelite or Aesthetic aspect[48] and he seemed to make me responsible for the poems of Rossetti and the prose of Mr. Legallienne.[49] So that, beginning by telling me, like Mr. Conrad, that I could not write and never should be able to write, he went on to tell me how writing should be done—and from time to time denouncing me.

And his formulae were those of the Flaubert-Maupassant-Turgenev school. He had read, naturally, a great deal more French than he had chosen to acknowledge in my unsympathetic presence, to Mr. Garnett. I do not mean to say that his native talent and inspiration did not make him a peculiarly good subject for that contagion. He would no doubt have written simply and forcibly and in the most economical of forms if Maupassant had never written a line. But, under that stimulus he had arrived much more quickly at a "method" and he knew quite well "what he was doing."[50]

And what particularly interested me was his projection before me, then, of a great series of heroic poems that he was planning to write—in Vers Libre. Of these he wrote only one volume[51]—*The Black Riders*, and, if, in this verse he did not attain to the quietness and colloquialism, at which he aimed theoretically—and to which I fancy that even at that date I had attained—he certainly showed some of the way for a whole school. He hated both rhyme and formal metre and at one point he shouted at me—he had never seen a word of mine:

"You ruin . . . ruin . . . ruin . . . all your work by the extra words you drag in
to fill up metres and by the digressions you make to get at rhymes!"[52]

He possessed, in fact, in a remarkable degree not only the Literary Gift but
the Literary Sense—and a devouring passion for words.

The contacts of Henry James and poor Stevie were peculiar. I do not remember to have heard the two of them discuss together anything of material interest.
Indeed I only remember to have seen them together at large social functions like
the flower shows that Crane and his family interested themselves in, at Brede in
Sussex.[53] But I heard the two men discuss each other, often enough.

Crane's attitude toward the Master—except for occasional lapses of irritation
in which he would talk of James as Henrietta Maria[54]—was boyishly respectful
and enthusiastic. I dare say that, with his marvellous insight, he valued the great
man very sufficiently, and when his defiant mood was off him and he was not
riding about the country on one of his immense coach-horses, he would readily
enough acknowledge himself to be, if not a disciple, at least an attentive scholar
of the Old Man's works.

By that time he had taken Brede Place—an immense, haunted and un-
restored Elizabethan manor house, lying, unhealthily beshadowed and low in a
Sussex valley.[55] I fancy I was responsible for introducing him to the Place;[56] at
any rate I had known it for many years before he came there. And, with characteristic enthusiasm, though he would still declare that he had no use for
battle-fields[57]—he led there the life of an Elizabethan baron. Rushes covered the
floors; dogs lay beneath the table to gnaw the bones that fell; a baron of beef and
a barrel of ale stood always ready near the back door for every tramp to con-
sume. The house was filled with stray dogs, lost cats, and, as if in tides, indis-
criminately chosen bands of irresponsible guests, would fill and recede from, the
half-furnished rooms. . . .[58] [Ford's ellipsis] And in a small room over the great
porch of the house Crane would sit writing, to keep it all going.[59]

. . . [W]hat most appalled [James] was Crane's life of the moment: his
aping, so that he seemed to reduce to absurdity, the semi-feudal state of a Tudor
lord—on the poor "£20 per thousand." It was as if the Old Man shuddered at
seeing a mock made of a settled and august mode of European life; and shuddered all the more because that very mockery was the sincere expression of admiration by a compatriot. In much the same way he spoke with bitter hatred of
Mark Twain's *Yankee at the Court of King Arthur.*

. . . He would, if he never talked of books, frequently talk of the personali-
ties of their writers—not infrequently in terms of shuddering at their social
excesses, much as he shuddered at contact with Crane.

. . . .

Stevie used to rail at English Literature, with its Stevenson and the interjected
finger,[60] as being one immense, petty, Parlour Game. Our books he used to say

were written by men who never wanted to go out of drawing-rooms for people who wanted to live at perpetual tea-parties. Even our adventure stories, colonial fictions and tales of the boundless prairie were conducted in that spirit. The criticism was just enough. It was possible that James never wanted to live outside tea-parties—but the tea-parties that he wanted were debating circles of a splendid aloofness, of an immense human sympathy, and of a beauty that you do not find in Putney—or in Passy! . . .

[Ford's reminiscence in *New York Essays,* 22–24, 26, elaborated on Crane's relationship with James.]

. . . I remember . . . walking along the Rye road with Crane when we perceived approaching us James, then bearded and much more majestic than he appeared later in life when he was clean shaven. He was riding his bicycle almost more slowly than I thought it was possible to do, wearing a curious square black felt hat. And behind him duly rode his butler. There went past Crane and myself a young woman in the very earliest stages of bicycle riding. The inevitable happened. No sooner was that young woman level with the master than she let go the handles of her machine with a shriek. The machine immediately swerved to the right and her front wheel struck his exactly at right angles. My emotions and Crane's were of such agitation that we neither of us saw what happened immediately next. For we both by one accord stepped behind a large bush on the roadside, not wishing to let the great man see that we had witnessed his downfall. But when we emerged James and the girl were both still sitting in the road regarding each other whilst the butler was picking up the bicycles. And the words that the master was addressing to that young woman surpassed all imagination. I do not mean to say that he used profanity; of that he was incapable. He only expressed the sentiment that that young woman's friends should not have allowed her out on the road until she had attained a greater proficiency with her wheel, but he expressed that simple sentiment with an incredible variety of locutions and in short, cruel sentences alternated with others of almost incredible length. And when Crane and I arrived and assisted him to rise—the butler by then supporting the sobbing girl—he repeated all those sentences over again to Crane and myself.

He had in him a singular vein of cruelty, which very seldom came to the surface, and I can assure you that listening to what he said to that young woman was every whit as painful as reading *The Turn of the Screw,* which is the most cruel story in our language. But the point I want to make with this tale is that neither Crane nor myself saw anything comic in the incident. Usually, I imagine, one would laugh if one saw a nice old gentleman knocked off his bicycle and sitting in the road, but Crane uttered exclamations of intense concern as if he were witnessing a catastrophe of the most terrible importance, and for the rest of the day he talked straight English in his natural character, which was that of a singularly refined and studious human being. That was a great tribute to James!

He had moreover a deep reverence and a great affection for the master. Of that I am convinced. It is always difficult exactly to define human relationships, and I have been astonished to find several writers who knew Crane, asserting that he regarded the old man as a comic or a disagreeable figure. But that was not, not, *not* the case.

. . . .

That James had a very great admiration for Crane I know. He constantly alluded to Crane as "that genius," and I have heard him say over and over again, "he had great, great genius," always repeating the word "great" twice, and emphasizing the second "great" as if he were italicizing it in writing. Crane, of course, shocked the old man,[61] but he was just a naughty boy who, on purpose, delighted to shock his uncle, and toward the end of his life he no longer even shocked the master. For, as I have put on record elsewhere, James's perturbations and agitated concern when Crane lay dying at Brede were painful indeed to witness.

Early in their relationship Crane, I think, was pained by the thought that James did not take him and his work very seriously, and I remember having quite frequently assured him that James did take his work at least very seriously indeed. And so did Crane take the work of James. He used at first to talk of James and even to write of him in letters as "the old man," but one day he astonished me by talking of some one whom I didn't immediately identify, as "the master." When I asked him whom he meant he turned on me with a look almost of contempt, and said with deep agitation, "Why, the old man, of course. He's the master of us all! Don't you know *that*?"

[Ford's reminiscence in *Return to Yesterday: Reminiscences, 1894–1914* (1931), 29–31, offered additional comments on the relationship between Crane and James.]

The effect on James of poor Steevie was devastating. Crane rode about the countryside on one of two immense coach-horses that he possessed. On their rawboned carcasses his frail figure looked infinitely tiny and forlorn. At times he would rein up before the Old Man's door and going in would tell the master's titled guests that he was a fly-guy that was wise to all the all-night pushes of the world. The master's titled guests liked it. It was, they thought, characteristic of Americans. . . . James winced and found it unbearable. . . .

And the joke—or, for the Old Man the tragedy—was that Crane assumed his Bowery cloak for the sole purpose of teasing the Master. In much the same way, taking me for a pre-Raphaelite poet, at the beginning of our friendship, he would be for ever harshly denouncing those who paid special prices for antiquities. To Conrad or to Hudson,[62] on the other hand, he spoke and behaved as a reasoning and perceptive human being.

And indeed the native beauty of his nature penetrated sufficiently to the Old Man himself. I never heard James say anything intimately damaging of Crane, and I do not believe he ever said anything of that sort to other people.

. . . [James] suffered infinitely for that dying boy. I would walk with him for hours over the marsh trying to divert his thoughts. But he would talk on and on. He was for ever considering devices for Crane's comfort. Once he telegraphed to Wanamaker's for a whole collection of New England delicacies from pumpkin pie to apple butter and sausage meat and clams and soft shell crabs and minced meat and . . . [Ford's ellipsis] everything thinkable, so that the poor lad should know once more and finally those fierce joys. Then new perplexities devastated him.[63] Perhaps the taste of those far off eats might cause Steevie to be homesick and so hasten his end. James wavered backwards and forwards between the alternatives beneath the grey walls of Rye Town. He was not himself for many days after Crane's death.

[Ford's reminiscence in *Portraits from Life,* 31–36, concluded with an account of a 2 January 1900 meeting between the two writers as well as additional comments on Crane's personality and literary influence.[64] Unless otherwise noted, all the ellipses are Ford's.]

The last time I drove that way was on the second day of January, 1900, and that time I did not see him in his workroom. I was led instead by an imposing maid to a hide-hole in a summer house up the bank behind that lugubrious place. It seemed a singular spot for a consumptive to choose on a January afternoon. But when I approached him, he sprang out, his face radiant, and exclaimed:

"Hueffer, thank God, it's you! . . . I always say you bring me luck. . . . "

The luck I had brought him was that of not being the tax collector from whom he was hiding. He had the theory that if, in England, you did not pay your taxes on New Year's Day, you went to prison.

I certainly had happened upon him usually at his more fortunate moments— on the occasion of his glorious visit to Pinker, the agent; on that day when I had certainly brought him all the good wishes of the season; several times when he had received unexpected payment checks—and once that he certainly regarded as miraculous. I had been driving along the Udimore road which was unduly domed and with a glassy perfection of surface. At a little distance I saw him coming along on one of his immense horses and a second later I saw him on the ground with the horse lying on his leg. The horse's legs had shot out sideways on the treacherous surface. I suppose they were both a trifle stunned; for he said I had all the aspect of a fabulous deliverer, appearing in a dogcart and dragging him forcibly from under his horse. . . .

On that second of January, after I had assured him that he need not fear the tax collector for two or three months . . . and alas, a more grim visitor reached him before that functionary . . . on that second of January he led me delightedly into his drawing-room where there was someone rather nice talking to Mrs. Crane and Mrs. Rudy [Ruedy]. . . . It might have been Robert Barr or James or Conrad—or possibly Owen Wister. I suppose an English visitor would have reassured him as to the habits of the collectors of Her Majesty's revenue. . . . At any rate, it was someone nice and probably American, and we sat and had tea and muffins before blazing logs and talked composedly about the house party which had so lately been swept out of the place that the drawing-room was as yet the only habitable apartment in the house—a great room with warm shadows and rather good bits of furniture that Mrs. Crane picked up here and there. It might have been the tea hour at Henry James's Lamb House. . . .

But when I was getting into my dogcart on the steps before the arched porch, Crane took hold of my arm suddenly; with an air of the deepest gravity, his avenger's face lit by my cart lamps against the January darkness, he exclaimed:

"Mr. Hueffer, you have been intimate with me in several places: in Limpsfield; in Oxted; in London a little . . . and here. . . . Now tell me on your honour. . . . "

He asked me whether I had ever seen him drunk; or drugged; or lecherously inclined; or foul-mouthed; or quarrelsome even. He said—and that struck me as shrewd—that we had lived in the same villages for several years; our servants knew each other. Had I ever heard a word of housemaids' or village gossip against him? In any particular or on any occasion?

Poor Steevie; poor dear fortunate youth. . . . If you nourish broods of vipers for long periods in your bosom, it is likely that you will be stung. He had been.

Of course I had never heard a word said against him. If it did not seem so fantastic I should be inclined to say that I am certain that he was as pure in heart—and almost as naïve—as his mother, the wife of a Non-conformist minister.

. . . [my ellipsis] Crane would assert that he had been in all sorts of improbable spots and done all sorts of things,[65] not vaingloriously lying, but in order to spin around his identity a veil behind which he might have some privacy. A writer needs privacy, and people talked so incessantly about poor Steevie that he had to keep his private life to himself.[66]

. . . [my ellipsis] He had a curious deference for the opinions of those older than himself and a curious necessity for their approval. So that, because he knew I approved of him and his work, he had to regard me as vastly his senior, though actually I entered the world two years and forty-five days after he did.[67] But I wore in those days a beard and was known as the last of the pre-Raphaelites, and Crane insisted that to be the last of a race one must be tremendously aged and dim-eyed and wise. So except on moments of deep emotion he always called me Mr. Hueffer and insisted that his friends should be silent so that I could speak. . . . [my ellipsis]

To say that he was completely ignorant of Zola or Maupassant would probably be untrue. He would state at one moment, with expletives, that he had never heard of those fellows and, at the next, display a considerable acquaintance with their work. Indeed, he said that it was after dipping into Zola's novel about the Franco-Prussian War that he determined to write a real war novel, and so sat down to *The Red Badge*. . . . [my ellipsis][68]

54 / Edward Garnett

Edward Garnett (1868–1937), who succeeded his father and grandfather as Keeper of Printed Books in the British Museum and who was married to Constance Garnett, renowned for her English translations of nineteenth-century Russian novelists, was a critic and reader for the London publisher T. Fisher Unwin at the time that he met Crane. Later he was a literary adviser for Heinemann and Jonathan Cape and helped to further the careers of Joseph Conrad, William Butler Yeats, John Galsworthy, and D. H. Lawrence. According to Garnett's son, David, the Cranes moved to Ravensbrook to be close to Garnett (David Garnett 62). Crane, Conrad, and Galsworthy often met at Garnett's home, the Cearne, for literary discussions (Bates 1950, 21).

Source: Edward Garnett, *Friday Nights: Literary Criticisms and Appreciations* (London: Jonathan Cape, 1922), 202–4.[69]

. . . Crane, when living at Oxted, was a neighbour of mine, and one day, on my happening to describe to him an ancient Sussex house, noble and grey with the passage of five hundred years, nothing would satisfy him but that he must become the tenant of Brede Place. It was the lure of romance that always thrilled

Crane's blood, and Brede Place had had indeed, an unlucky, chequered history. I saw Crane last, when he lay dying there, the day before his wife was transporting him, on a stretcher bed, to a health resort in the Black Forest, in a vain effort to arrest the fatal disease, and I see again his bloodless face and the burning intensity of his eyes. He had lived at too high pressure and his consumptive physique was ravaged by the exhausting strain of his passionate life, and sapped by the hardships of the Cuban campaign, which he suffered as a war-correspondent. Crane's strange eyes, with their intensely concentrated gaze, were those of a genius and I recall how on his first visit to our house I was so struck by the exquisite symmetry of his brow and temples, that I failed to note, what a lady pointed out when he had left, the looseness of his mouth. Yes, the intensity of genius burned in his eyes, and his weak lips betrayed his unrestrained temperament. Crane's genius, his feeling for style were wholly intuitive and no study had fostered them. On first reading "The Red Badge of Courage," I concluded he had been influenced by the Russian masters, but I learned when I met him, that he had never read a line of them. Would that he had! For Crane, as Conrad reminded me, never knew how good his best work was. He simply never knew. He never recognized that in the volume "The Open Boat,"[70] he had achieved the perfection of his method. If he had comprehended that in "The Bride Comes to Yellow Sky" and in "Death and the Child" he had attained then, his high water mark, he might perhaps have worked forward along the lines of patient, ascending effort; but after "The Open Boat," 1898, his work dropped to lower levels. He wrote too much, wrote against time, and he wrote while dunned for money. At first sight it appears astonishing that the creator of such a miracle of style as "The Bride Comes to Yellow Sky" should publish in the same year so mediocre a novel as "On Active Service."[71] But Crane ought never to have essayed the form of the novel. He had not handled it satisfactorily in *The Third Violet*, 1897, a love story charming in its impressionistic lightness of touch, but lacking in force, in concentration, in characterization. My view of Crane as a born impressionist and master of the short story, I emphasized in an Appreciation in 1898. . . .

Source: Edward Garnett, *Letters from Joseph Conrad* (Indianapolis: Bobbs-Merrill, 1928), 11–12.

Conrad's moods of gay tenderness could be quite seductive. On the few occasions that I saw him with Stephen Crane he was delightfully sunny, and bantered "poor Steve" in the gentlest, most affectionate style, while the latter sat silent, Indian-like, turning inquiring eyes under his chiseled brow, now and then jumping up suddenly and confiding some new project with intensely electric feeling. At one of these sittings Crane passionately appealed to me to support his idea that Conrad should collaborate with him in a play on the theme of a ship wrecked on an island. I knew it was hopelessly unworkable—this plan—but Crane's brilliant visualization of the scenes was so strong and infectious I had not the heart to declare my own opinion. And Conrad's skeptical answers were couched in the tenderest, most reluctant tone. I can still hear the shades of Crane's poignant friendliness in his cry "Joseph!" And Conrad's delight in Crane's personality glowed in the shining warmth of his brown eyes.[72]

55 / H. G. Wells

H. G. Wells (1866–1946) probably first met Stephen and Cora shortly after they moved to Ravensbrook, but their friendship did not develop until Crane's last year. Before meeting Crane, however, Wells was aware of his work. Though he was ambivalent about *Maggie* ("Another View of *Maggie*," *Saturday Review*, 19 December 1896, 655), criticizing Crane for striving too hard "self-consciously" to achieve a particular mood, he had praised *George's Mother* and compared Crane to Tolstoy for his narrative strength and recognized that he was "much more of a theoretical product than critics here have recognized" ("The New American Novelists," *Saturday Review*, 5 September 1896, 262–63). When the *Academy* conducted a literary symposium at the end of 1896 and asked prominent authors to name the best books of the year, Wells's list included *Maggie* and *George's Mother*. Unlike Edward Garnett (No. 54), who considered Crane unable to evaluate his own work, Wells concluded that he was a self-conscious literary craftsman experimenting with new ways of perceiving reality. Though Wells advocated the novel of ideas, he admired Crane's artistry and saw in him a kindred soul who defied literary tradition and helped to build the foundation for modernism.

Source: H. G. Wells, *Experiment in Autobiography: Discoveries and Conclusions of a Very Ordinary Brain since 1866* (New York: Macmillan, 1934), 522–25.

Another very important acquaintance of my early Sandgate[73] time, now too little appreciated in the world, was the American Stephen Crane. He was one of the earliest of those stark American writers who broke away from the genteel literary traditions of Victorian England and he wrote an admirable bare prose.[74]

. . . I forget the exact circumstances of our first meeting but I remember very vividly a marvellous Christmas Party in which Jane[75] and I participated. We were urged to come over and, in a postscript, to bring any bedding and blankets we could spare. We arrived in a heaped-up Sandgate cab, rather in advance of the guests from London. We were given a room over the main gateway in which there was a portcullis and an owl's nest, but at least we got a room. Nobody else did[76]—because although some thirty or forty invitations had been issued, there were not as a matter of fact more than three or four bedrooms available. One of them however was large and its normal furniture had been supplemented by a number of hired truckle-beds and christened the Girls' Dormitory, and in the attic an array of shake-downs was provided for the men. Husbands and wives were torn apart.

Later on we realized that the sanitary equipment of Brede House dated from the seventeenth century, an interesting historical detail, and such as there was indoors, was accessible only through the Girls' Dormitory. Consequently the wintry countryside next morning was dotted with wandering melancholy, preoccupied, men guests.

Anyhow there were good open fires in the great fireplaces and I remember that party as an extraordinary lark—but shot, at the close, with red intimations of a coming tragedy. We danced in a big oak-panelled room downstairs, lit by candles stuck upon iron sconces that Cora Crane had improvised with the help of the Brede blacksmith. Unfortunately she had not improvised grease guards and after a time everybody's back showed a patch of composite candle-wax, like the flash on the coat of a Welsh Fusilier. When we were not dancing or romping we were waxing the floor or rehearsing a play vamped up by A. E. W. Mason, Crane, myself and others. It was a ghost play,[77] and very allusive and fragmentary, and we gave it in the School Room at Brede. It amused its authors and cast vastly. What the Brede people made of it is not on record.[78]

We revelled until two or three every night and came down towards mid-day to breakfasts of eggs and bacon, sweet potatoes from America and beer. Crane had a transient impulse to teach some of the men poker, in the small hours, but we would not take it seriously. Mason I found knew my old schoolfellow Sidney Bowkett and had some anecdotes to tell me about him. "In any decent saloon in America," said Crane, "you'd be shot for talking like that at poker," and abandoned our instruction in a pet.

That was the setting in which I remember Crane. He was profoundly weary and ill, if I had been wise enough to see it, but I thought him sulky and reserved. He was essentially the helpless artist; he wasn't the master of his party, he wasn't the master of his home; his life was altogether out of control; he was being carried along. What he was still clinging to, but with a dwindling zest, was artistry. He had an intense receptiveness to vivid work; he had an inevitably right instinct for the word in his stories; but he had no critical chatter. We compared our impressions of various contemporaries. "That's Great," he'd say or simply "*Gaw!*" Was so and so "any good"? So and so was "no good."

Was he writing anything now?

His response was joyless. Pinker the agent had *fixed* some stories for him. "I got to do them," he said, "I got to do them."

The tragic entanglement of the highly specialized artist had come to him. Sensation and expression—and with him it had been well nigh perfect expression—was the supreme joy of his life and the justification of existence for him. And here he was, in a medley of impulsive disproportionate expenditure, being pursued by the worthy Pinker with enquiries of when he could "deliver copy" and warnings not to overrun his length. The good thing in his life had slipped by him.

In the night after the play Mrs. Crane came to us. He had had a haemorrhage from his lungs and he had tried to conceal it from her. He "didn't want anyone to bother." Would I help her get a doctor?[79]

There was a bicycle in the place and my last clear memory of that fantastic Brede House party is riding out of the cold skirts of a wintry night into a drizzling dawn along a wet road to call up a doctor in Rye.[80]

That crisis passed, but he died later in the new year, 1900. He did his utmost to conceal his symptoms and get on with his dying. Only at the end did his wife wake up to what was coming. She made a great effort to get him to Baden-Baden. She conveyed him silent and sunken and stoical to Folkestone by car, regardless of expense, she had chartered a special train to wait for him at Boulogne and he died almost as soon as he arrived in Germany.

56 / Karl Edwin Harriman

Karl Edwin Harriman (1875–1935), a journalist and writer of fiction, was sent to England as a correspondent by the *Detroit Free Press* in the spring of 1899. He met Crane through Robert Barr and spent several weeks at Brede Place as a guest during the summer of 1899. He is the only source in Crane biography for a number of anecdotes, including the erroneous statements that "The Monster" was written and revised at a single sitting, that Hall Caine refused to contribute to the fund for

Harold Frederic's children, and that Crane's brother Wilbur visited Brede Place in 1899.

Source: Karl Edwin Harriman, "A Romantic Idealist—Mr. Stephen Crane," *Literary Review* 4 (April 1900): 85–87.

. . . Now and again a few friends come down to him for a week, but mostly he is alone. Each morning sees him up in his little study in the tower of Brede House writing, writing. He works methodically, and at the same time by jerks, if the expression is allowable. . . . He goes to his study when he feels the spirit quickening, locks the door and writes, writes, writes, until he has done. Once, to my knowledge, he lingered in that little turret-room three days, and at the end of that time, before lolling upon the divan for a little sleep, he poked out under the door four stories, which Mrs. Crane ran off on the typewriter for him and sent to his agent in London.

That splendid story, "The Monster," was written in this way. It was finished, polished, and revised at a sitting, and it is a tale of some twenty-five thousand words.[81]

The Red Badge of Courage, the least valuable from any standpoint, but the best known of this author's books, the one that brought him fame—if not fortune— was written in nine days with a soft lead-pencil on pulpy copy paper, such as every reporter in the land uses quires of every day.

This story was the result of a conclusion arrived at by Stephen Crane after reading a battle story in a certain monthly magazine[82]—that he could write a better one—he who had never seen even a sham battle by his state militia, who did not know a Maxim from a Krag-Jorgensen.[83] He selected the battle of Chancellorsville. From records he learned the topography of the country, the atmosphere of the battle, the position of the troops, and then he wrote his story without mentioning a name, a locality, a troop, and at the same time he presented accurately, picturesquely, vividly, the problem of war resolved to an equation of battle.

And for this tale, running as it did into edition after edition, he received in all one hundred and ninety dollars, ninety for the syndicate rights in America, and twenty pounds for the same rights in England.[84]

But one hundred and ninety dollars was indeed a fortune to a boy who for months had lived in New York City on five dollars a week and had, the while, peddled manuscripts up and down Newspaper Row in a basket.

That little volume of lines that the newspaper parodists love, *The Black Riders,* written simply as exercises in word placing, was completed in three days, and on the next the printer set up the first type of the book.[85]

It is interesting to know Stephen Crane's own opinion of his work. He does not hold, with the mass of readers, that *The Red Badge of Courage* is the best of his performances. He places first "The Monster"—splendid self judgment—and second *George's Mother*, after these, in order of merit, a tiny tale entitled "An Old Man Goes a-Wooing,"[86] and *Maggie: A Girl of the Streets;* which latter, by the way, was written before *The Red Badge,* and published without the publisher's imprint. That worthy feared, at the last moment, the volume would not reflect sufficient of credit upon his house, and withdrew his mark. . . .

Stephen Crane's power of observation is astonishing. Allow me to cite an instance. Last summer[87] I happened to be one of a certain party at the Henley Regatta,[88] of which Mr. and Mrs. Crane were also members. I think Trinity was rowing. Her opponent I do not remember. But in the stern of her long, slim boat, crouched a tiny coxswain, a lad of perhaps ten. He leaned forward, shouting to the straining oarsmen.

The veins of his neck were like cords where they were like ropes on the necks of the men he urged. He swore at them like forty pirates. On the bank of Bucks we heard him. We cheered, shouted, screamed for that little coxswain. He never wavered. Curse after curse rang out. Trinity was pulling ahead. In another moment it was all over. Trinity had won. And that little ten-year-old coxswain had made it possible. The big, half-naked fellows knew this. They lifted him up, kissed him, fondled him. He lingered around the lower reach of the course on shore. Crane, taken with his actions while in the boat, sought him out. He found him, a child, buying a little tin rooster, a simple, tinsel toy, from a vender in the street of Henley. The General had become a Boy again. No further oaths fell from his lips, because no further oaths were needed.

And Stephen Crane noted all this, understood the nature, the duality of nature, if you will, in that child. It impressed him. How many of the thousands who had witnessed the race would have learned anything, do you suppose, from seeing a little boy buy a tin, tinsel rooster from a street vender?

And, too, it impressed Crane, because a bond of sympathy linked that child's heart to his.

He is a General, a mighty General when he takes up a pen; and his Army is composed of Words. But when that pen falls from his hands he becomes again the Boy, the frank, open-hearted, genial, joking, mischievous Boy, whom to know is to love.

Source: [Untitled commentary in "The Lounger"], *Critic* 37 (July 1900): 14–16.

. . . Mr. Karl Edwin Harriman, of Ann Arbor, Michigan, who, last fall, spent several weeks with Mr. Crane in his English home, scouts the idea that the story-writer contracted tuberculosis in Cuba. "His home killed him," writes

Mr. Harriman. "The old manor house, in which he lived for the past two years, was loaned him by Mr. Frewen, the owner, and was built in the thirteenth century of almost porous stone.[89] The chill, damp, and draughts of the old house were terrible, believe me. The floors are of flagging, with great deceptive fireplaces, and the wind whistled through the casements every moment of the day and night. Crane's study was in the tower,—the draughtiest of all." Mr. Harriman caught severe colds every time he visited the place. Late in April last, before Mr. Crane was taken down with the illness which was the immediate cause of his death, Mr. Harriman had a long letter from him in which he told of his work. "I've finished 56,000 words on a romance of Ireland—George II.'s time; some folks call it rippling,—but I don't know; tell me what you think of it when you get your copy." Mr. Harriman, judging from the way he worked, thinks that Mr. Crane must have finished the story before his death.[90] He would write ten or twelve thousand words at a stretch, then rest for a day or two and go at it again.

Mr. Crane estimated his work in this order: "An Old Man Goes Wooing," "The Monster," "George's Mother," "The Red Badge of Courage." Mr. Harriman, who got his figures from the author, says that he received from Heinemann for all English rights in "The Red Badge" £20.[91] From the syndicate that printed the story first in this country,—cut from 55,000 to 18,000,—$90. His profits came when Messrs. Appleton published the story in book form.

Source: Karl Edwin Harriman, "The Last Days of Stephen Crane,"[92] *New Hope: A Record of the Contemporary American Arts* 2 (October 1934): 7–9, 19–21.

[Sent for three months as a London correspondent for the *Detroit Free Press*, Harriman was introduced to Crane by Robert Barr.]

"Then I shall meet Stephen Crane?" I asked.

"Sure," Barr replied lighting a fresh cigarette from the stub in the apple-wood holder. "You'll like him."

It never entered my twenty-three-year-old head that Crane might not like me. He did though. He told me as much with one of those pale smiles of his, that first afternoon, as we walked through the ghostly garden of Brede Place, the hand of a lovely little girl in his and the hand of a lovely littler boy, her brother, in mine.[93] I didn't know whose those charming children were, then. I only knew that they were not Stephen's. Cora Crane was to tell me their tragic story later, as I shall tell it to the reader later.

Stephen had met us at the railway station. I hadn't known there was to be any "us" till I stepped down from the third-class carriage and moved along the platform. I had picked him out at once from the few there. I'd seen any number of pictures of him. Approaching him, too, was a man older than he, accompanied by a young girl. Stephen shook hands with the man and kissed the girl. Then he held out his hand to me. You see, I'd never met him. I had been asked down at the suggestion of Barr. But that didn't make any difference. He made me one of the family immediately, for that is what the group really was—the three of them, I mean—Stephen's indifferent brother Wilbur, and the latter's daughter Helen.[94] As I recall, Helen was going to school in Switzerland, and, with her father, had stopped over a few days in England to call on Uncle Stephen.

... Stephen took up the reins and we were off. ... He seemed a lot older than I, though his seniority was only a matter of four or five years. He was so *quiet*—I guess that was the reason. He wore riding-breeches and puttees, like a stable-boy, a flannel shirt, belt, and no coat—the sort of costume that so shocked Henry James.[95] When Stephen learned *that* he always affected the rig when he called on James as we frequently did that summer, or whenever James, with official warning, so to speak, descended for tea on the lawn at Brede Place.

As we drove on, Stephen would indicate with the whip this or that patch or covert, or bridge, or stream, and Helen would "oh" and "ah." ...

As the brake stopped and Heather, the most amazing house man that ever served a Scotch and soda, took the horses' bits, there came out into the sunlight of that early June day, through the Gothic arch of the ancient portal, a woman whose appearance took my breath away. What it did to Helen I was not to know, but Wilbur, as I recall, gasped.

What a woman was Cora Crane! Later I was to adore her; still later I was to learn all about her. At the moment I could only look!

She was dumpy, and the dumpiness was enhanced (which is not at all the word but it will do) by the costume she was wearing. This consisted of a plaid skirt and a mandarin blue smock, though in those days they called them middy blouses, I believe. On her feet were some sort of strapped sandals. Perhaps she was not wearing stockings. But all that didn't matter. It was her face—her head—that clutched one's eyes—the eyes, at least, of a boy of twenty-three who was even then a good bit of a sentimentalist.

Her hair was the honeyist I have ever seen, and finer than any floss as real blond hair is likely to be. And Cora Crane's was real—no greenish grey at the roots. Honey all the way down and into her scalp, and through it, and on. Her eyes were just such eyes as her hair demanded. ...

"Now that I've seen you," she said as presently we strolled across the lawn, "I'll tell Heather he can bring out the spoons!"

From that moment I was never anything but Karl to Cora and Stephen. Honest face!

A little later on they became Stephen and Cora to me.

"We'll not dress tonight," Cora said as we crossed to where the tea-table stood beneath the canopy of a gorgeous beech, "Wilbur didn't bring his evening things." How I had happened to, God only knows, but young men were rather dressy in those days, you will recall—frock coats, toppers, gibuses and what not. I made a mental note to keep my feet on the floor whenever I should don my dinner-jacket, (My evening shoes had holes in their soles!) for that was the type of evening garment worn at Crane's, never tails. In fact I never saw Stephen in tails but once, and that was when I dined with Cora and him and two others in London some weeks later.

But our tea is cooling. One must get on. There was no one else there, that afternoon and evening, that is no one else but the children, and lovelier children than little Héloïse and her younger seven-year-old brother, Barry, never hunted fairies in the hedgerows of Sussex. . . .

It was quite a month before Cora Crane, with Stephen, in the flagged kitchen, which was the dining-room of Brede, told me all that those children meant to them both and whence they had come.

Their father was Harold Frederic, their mother his English wife,[96] to employ Cora's phrase. Frederic, beloved of Stephen and Robert Barr—for all he was old enough to be Stephen's father[97]—had fallen ill, so ill that the other two musketeers knew he would never recover. His "wife" was strong in the faith of Mrs. Eddy and Frederic was too ill to combat her disinclination to summon medical service. He told Cora Crane as much as she told me, but when he came to die Cora perjured herself in a British court and testified that Harold had been one with his wife in her faith.[98] You see the British Medical association had set out to make a case of it, a test case, and if Cora Crane had testified to the truth as, according to her story to me, she knew it, the end of "Mrs. Frederic" would doubtless have been quite different from what it was.

"You liked her, then?" I suggested.

She sneered.

"I have never disliked another woman more," was her reply.[99] "But" she went on, while Stephen watched her from the shadows (it seems to me now, in memory, that mostly Stephen lurked in the shadows) "when, after a sleepless night, during which I saw her in prison, I finally made up my mind to lie for her, I felt vastly better. And Stephen thought it best." (Was there a smile at that, a smile of infinite patience on the long, thin face, there in the shadows behind the candle-light?)

Cora took the children unto herself, and pillowed their brown heads on her abundant bosom and set her own honey head a-thinking as to what she could do for them. Stephen hadn't much to offer inventively. That was Stephen— detached—always. Finally Cora decided to write all Harold's friends and solicit them to contribute to a fund that would assure the babies' well-being as long as might be.[100] Notes were sent to Barrie[101] and Conrad, and Barr[102] and A. E. W. Mason, Frank Mathews, Jerome,[103] Clement Shorter[104]—Kipling—everyone, doubtless, who had known Frederic.

Among these, and many more, she wrote a very great man,[105] a novelist who had made for himself a place in late Victorian letters, a place one may add, now overgrown with weeds, but then widely in the sun. He was a Savior come back; his spirit of the new Brotherhood, the benign and all-forgiving; "Christ on the Mount of Man," as Stephen called him, showing me the photograph, framed, on the wall of Brede, revealing the Master in his Quaker hat and his enveloping cape, the wind of the channel blowing his Buffalo Bill hair. . . . [Harriman's ellipsis]

"God! how I loathe him!" snarled Cora—the only time I ever heard her speak thus of any living soul. And this is why.

In response to one of her letters of solicitation for little Héloïse and Barry she received the following reply; (I read the thing, held it in my hands, read it again, committing it to memory and the years have not yet been sufficient to erase that memory!)

> Dear Mrs. Crane:
>
> I have your note and am sorry. As I never approved of Mr. Frederic's course in life I do not feel called upon to contribute to the support of his illegitimate children now that he is dead.
>
> > Very sincerely,
> > Hall Caine[106]

I can still hear Cora Crane's "God, how I loathe him!" and see the sneery curl of Stephen's thin lips as I passed the note back to his wife. I wonder if it is still among the papers Stephen left!

Let's turn the medal over.

One afternoon Stephen, Cora and I drove over to ancient Rye to call on Henry James, Stephen in his breeches and puttees, much to Cora's amused embarrassment. Her mission was to solicit a contribution from the then master of Lamb House.

I shan't concern myself with that call save to record that when she had stated her mission James cocked his head to one side, a listening mannerism, *tch-tch-tched* a few times and said: "My dear Mrs. Crane, I am so sorry; I shall write you." And thereupon other things were spoken of—the coming mud-boat regatta held annually in those days in Rye, and which James always refereed in a Homburg hat, knickerbockers and ghillie shoes; the rise of a new man named

Knut Hamsun whose "Hunger"[107] I had carried down to Stephen from London and which he had passed on in turn to Henry James, theretofore unknowing of the "Swede," as Stephen called him; and of cabbages and kings, and of Mrs. Humphrey Ward, whom Stephen cordially disliked without ever having read a line she wrote, for he told me that himself.[108] "It's just instinct," was his smiling explanation—smiling, for I never heard him laugh.

And later Henry James *did* write, and out of his letter dropped a crossed check for fifty pounds.[109] "I only wish I could do more," he wrote.

Cora Crane cried when she read that note, and Stephen smiled.

"Did you expect anything less?" he asked.

And forthwith Cora wrote Henry James a note filled with gratitude poured warm from her heart. Came another note from the master of Lamb House in the ancient Cinque Port of Rye, and it said:

Dear Mrs. Crane:

All thanks for your note. I am glad any sort of sum has been raised for the poor little mortals

Most truly yours and his
Henry James

That note, given me by Cora Crane, hangs over my desk. I have just looked up to copy it.

Mr. Thomas Beer in a recent piece[110] about Cora Crane refers to the first letter I have presented here, but he hesitated—although crediting me with personal knowledge of it—to make known its authorship beyond an indefinite Mr. Z. I have not so hesitated. Nor is my taste to be impugned for in such circumstances it seems to me there is no such thing as taste.

(to be continued)

Source: Karl Edwin Harriman, "The Last Days of Stephen Crane," pt. 2, typescript, 8 pp., Box 20 (Folder "Crane 1899"), Melvin H. Schoberlin Research Files, Special Collections Research Center, Syracuse University Library.

"We call your room the pint-pot," Stephen said. "Come on; I'll guide you."

And a guide was necessary. Stephen himself had to pause a moment at the top of the wide stairs and think.

"As I recall," he said, "it's off one corner of the banquet-hall."

I followed on through the long room with its immense oaken table, midway down the length of which one perceived the wells for the salt cellars. When, in the ancient days that table was set for service, the lord of the manor had sat above, the retainers below the salt. Huge hooks were sunken into the outer wall beneath the casement window.

"The story is they used to hang 'em from those hooks when they were naughty," Stephen explained. "They'd run the hooks through their gills and let 'em dangle, but of course that's a lie. The hooks were more likely used to run ropes over when milord wanted to raise anything from outside to this floor. Easier than lugging it up-stairs."

The pint-pot was about ten feet square fitted with a chair, a chest of drawers, a wash-stand, and a camp bed. There was no floor covering. The house had not been opened for years until Stephen took it, you understand, and Cora had furnished it with a hodge podge of things picked up here and there.

Stephen had some difficulty in opening the casement and when he finally managed it a half dozen bats revealed their annoyance.

"You see," he cheerfully explained, "the pint-pot hasn't been occupied since a couple of days before Columbus discovered America and it's a little musty. It'll be all right, though, now that the windows are open."

I wondered.

On the bed lay my things that Heather had unpacked. So he had probably discovered the holes in my shoes after all. Oh, well!

"We dine at seven-thirty," Stephen said; "Cora probably told you we're not dressing." At the doorway, giving into the banquet-room, he paused and added: "And, oh yes, you should know that the pint-pot is supposed to be haunted. I've never slept in it so I don't really know."

He was gone, leaving me there. And at once I began to feel the goose-pimples rising on me like hives. I leaned out the window. It overlooked that ghostly garden, I observed, and I wondered if men shod in scale steel could climb a ladder, or did they just pull themselves up by their own boot-straps. Time—a night, perhaps—would tell. I closed the door and found my way downstairs as speedily as might be. I do not recall that I paused long enough to stow away my scant belongings in the slim chest of drawers or even to wash my face.

The great hall was empty save for three dogs that came sniffing with friendliness as my footfall sounded on the stairs. Two of them were black spaniels, the larger Sponge, as I was later to learn, the smaller, Flannel. The third dog, to which the spaniels paid not the least attention was Powder-Puff, a Pekinese I think she would be called now, but not then.

Stephen thought more of those dogs, I was presently to learn, than of almost any other living thing; more even than he did of his two horses. They alone were privileged to scratch for entrance into his red study during the morning hours. No other living creature was, not even Cora. But that's not quite correct. I spent one morning there and was myself witness to such a scene as Joseph Conrad described.[111] There came a scratching at the door. Without a smile Stephen rose, opened the door and into the study filed Sponge and Flannel and Powder-Puff in that order. Their movements were always in that order. Powder-Puff, apparently, was merely suffered to tag along. They ranged themselves beside Stephen's chair and he reached down and petted each in turn and pulled their several ears, mumbling affectionate words of dog-talk, the while, deep in his throat. Thereupon, with Sponge leading the way, they moved with dignity to the door, which Stephen opened for them and closed on Powder-Puff's curled and feathery tail.

"They come in each morning," he explained without the trace of a smile on his sensitive lips, "to let me know things are all right; I shouldn't see them till luncheon, or later, otherwise."

For Stephen never appeared for breakfast, sometimes not till tea-time, even when there were guests in the house—"Indians" he called most such. In point of fact it was the plentitude of "Indians," who were always descending upon Crane to partake of Cora's amazing cooking, that prevented him, for all his seclusion, from accomplishing what he should have accomplished during that last summer of his life.

At the moment of my descent upon him, he was doing his Whilomville stories, perhaps high among the best pieces of writing ever done by him. As a souvenir of our friendship he gave me the complete manuscript of one of those stories, written in his violet ink on four sheets of shiney foolscap. Returning to America in the autumn I framed the manuscript in four panels and it hung on my library wall until faded to blankness. As another souvenir he gave me a copy of *War Is Kind,* his second volume of poems. This, he autographed to me and it is still one of my most cherished possessions. Also, at this time there was rolling around in his head the basic idea of a novel he was never to finish, a swashbuckling yarn to be called *The O'Ruddy,* which, after he had gone, his well-beloved Barr was to bring to an indifferent conclusion.

Stephen's method of writing was the method of spontaneity if that term may signify anything. Perhaps an illustration will make clearer what I mean.

One week-end among other "Indians" were Joseph Conrad and A. E. W. Mason. Stephen adored Conrad; in fact that was his attitude toward most artists older than himself who showed the least interest in him, and mostly they did. Artists I mean, not merely writers. He was never through talking of *The Nigger of the "Narcissus,"* but I think Mason's amazing monocle fascinated him more than that novelist's *Courtship of Morrice Buckler.* (Have I the title correct?)[112]

At any rate we were seated about the dining-table in the old flagged kitchen, and the whiskey and siphons had been set out by Heather. All afternoon the thunder heads had been gathering; the atmosphere was leaden; the stillness that of a dead world. Frantically the "farmer" about the place had sought to gather the cocks of hay that sentinelled the meadow running down toward the River

Brede from the garden. At nine o'clock the storm broke with cannonading and ripping riflery that must have swung Stephen's mind back to Cuba. The discussion had been about methods of composition. Stephen had told of Frederic's "adverb screen," which, he explained, was a long window shade on which Frederic had lettered all the adverbs he could think of that might reasonably, or unreasonably, for that matter, qualify the verb "said." How Conrad laughed, but Stephen swore it was the truth.

"He was a stickler for adverbs and adjectives," explained Stephen. (Where a greater stickler than himself?) "And it was his custom to go over the first draft of a manuscript and underline each adjective in red and each adverb in blue, so that with one blow of the eye he could determine whether the nuance he sought had been achieved."

Conrad thought that not a bad idea at all. Mason shook his head and poured himself another drink. Stephen's cigarette had died between his yellow fingers.

"The only way is to know exactly what you're going to do before you attempt anything," Mason declared. "I always make a complete outline, the frame first, as to speak, and then I paint my picture."

Stephen's explosion of dissent synchronized with a new cannonading outside.

"Can't agree with you at all," he retorted. "My belief has always been that the whole business is a matter of technique. If a man is master of his particular technique he can write a story about anything."

Mason had risen and gone to the casement where he stood peering out into the swirling night. As a wide sheet of lightning illuminated as of noonday the meadow before the house, he turned and glowering through his glass at Stephen, exclaimed, "If that is true, write a story about those hay-cocks out there. I challenge you!"

"I accept," Stephen returned with one of his whimsically patient smiles, and we all laughed and the chatter took another groove.

I think it was Mason, also, who expressed himself rather frankly concerning certain American novelists, Howells in particular. Stephen held up his hand in gentle reproof. "Here! here!" he protested, "I can't allow Mr. Howells (not Howells, mind you) to be derided at my table. If he hadn't blazed the way, there'd be no sort of decent writing in America in our day. And the same may be said of Hamlin Garland." Thus the unforgetting Crane of the two men who did more for him in the beginning than all others combined. Rather unusual I thought then, and still do.

Stephen then poured himself a final drink and flung on the hearth the tenth or twentieth cigarette that had gone out in his fingers. His drinks were always few and sparse—perhaps a tablespoon of whiskey in a sea of seltzer; and though called a tremendous smoker, he was not. I never saw him finish a cigarette. Two puffs and he'd hold them between his fingers till they went out. He never re-lighted one, either: would fling the three-quarter unburned portion away and light another. Quite the antithesis of Robert Barr who used to buy his Virginias by the thousand at Salmon and Gluckensteins (always with a short applewood holder in the box as a sort of premium) and light one from another all day long. But he was a brown-bearded ox and no harm ever came of it. His cigarette smoking was like Mason's monocle—continuous. I was with Mason one whole day from breakfast until dressing-time for dinner and not for an instant was the rimless, cordless disk out of his eye.

"If I could wear a monocle the way Mason does," said Stephen to me as we drove, one day, to Rye, "I'd wear *two.*"

And so to bed.

Stephen didn't appear at luncheon the day following the storm, but at dinner time when the rest of us were seated and Heather was beginning service he came into the room with a roll in his hand tied with a blue ribbon. Cora laughed for she had been a party to what was coming.

"You see," she said, "Stevie has just graduated and he's brought his diploma to show you. Haven't you, Stevie?"

He nodded, sheepishly and unsmiling.

After dinner, when again the siphons and decanter were placed, Stephen said, as he untied the blue ribbon, "I'm going to prove something to you Indians."

Arranging two candles, he smoothed the sheets of manuscript, and, in his rather monotonous voice, read to us the story he had written that day in acceptance of Mason's challenge. Its period was Cromwell's and under each of those hay-cocks in the meadow was concealed a soldier of the Commonwealth, awaiting the signal for attack upon the house.[113] And what a commotion he pictured as going on within the very house where we were listening. The monks had crawled into their holes and lay a-tremor in the deep cellar as the attack began. I don't recall the details of the story, only the impression it made. Across the table in the shadow, as Stephen read on, I saw Conrad fumbling his beard, and caught the red reflection on Mason's monocle. The reading finished, Stephen thrust the manuscript from him (it was quickly gathered up by Cora) as Mason's hand went out to him across a corner of the table.

"I stand corrected," he said.

As for Conrad, he merely grunted—a Polish expression of approval perhaps— pulled at his beard and nodded, as if he were thinking things of wonder.

From: Mrs. Karl Edwin Harriman, Dangerfield House, Jenkinton, Pa.

Source: Karl Edwin Harriman, "The Last Days of Stephen Crane," pt. 3, typescript, 8 pp., Box 20 (Folder "Crane 1899"), Melvin H. Schoberlin Research Files, Special Collections Research Center, Syracuse University Library.

[The bracketed comments below concerning missing material are in the original typescript. Other bracketed comments are my summations of deleted passages.]

[After James B. Pinker sold one of Harriman's short stories to an English magazine, Harriman told Crane,] "I have six guineas and I am going to Paris," I announced with the scant breath left me.

"It's too much to take to Paris," Stephen said," "but where did you get it?"

I passed over to him the check, and Jimmy Pinker's letter.

"We must have champagne for dinner," Cora declared, clapping her hands.

[In Paris Harriman visited an apartment containing a collection of objects once owned by Victor Hugo. When he told Crane about the collection,] . . . Stevie became vastly excited. He was for leaving the next day for Paris, with a note of introduction to my friend. The latter he insisted upon. I gave it him at dinner and he placed it in his bill-fold. But he never went to Paris to view those souvenirs of Victor

[One page of manuscript missing.]

[H]e didn't care, for he knew then, in the soul of him, that his end was approaching. He told me as much on one of those evenings by the river as the moon floated above us, silvering the Abbey ruins and flooding the facade of the little Georgian hotel with its ghostly light.

"I've long known I shan't live to be thirty-one," he said with that wistful smile, as he lit another cigarette.

"But why thirty-one?" I asked, assuming, at the moment, that his prophecy had been made in humor.

"Oh, I don't know," he replied, "unless it's because thirty-one is thirteen, tail-end foremost, and thirteen has always really been my unlucky number. I could tell you stories, you Indian you"—But he never did.

During the four days we stopped at Medmenham[114] none of us was permitted to spend a farthing on our own. I recall a little incident illustrative of Stevie's pecuniary thoughtfulness, so to speak, of his guests at that time. I had asked Bennett, I think it was, to join me in a drink when we had returned to the hotel one evening. We had Scotch and soda and they cost two and six each, even then. You see Henley lived for a year on the Regatta profits of four days. It was a lot of money but my half-sovereign was produced, after a little search.

"I beg your pardon, sir, but aren't you with Mr. Crane's party?" the barman asked. (Not a barmaid, for some extraordinary reason.) I replied that we were. "I took you to be, sir," returned the man, sliding my half-sovereign back to me across the bar. "Instructions from Mr. Crane, sir; everything goes on his bill."

After that, for the period of our stay at the hotel none of us males had another drink save when Stevie himself was with us.

Our luncheons were always picnics on the river bank. Cora, it appeared, had ordered the Army and Navy Stores to send down by train each morning, a picnic hamper, which Heather would collect at the railway station, and bring to us at the luncheon spot selected for the day. We would proceed thither in the punts at mid-day and afterward, loaf about on the river bank till the races were re-sumed in the afternoon. And always there was a surprise in the hamper for Stephen. Once, it was a great pot of baked beans, the first, no doubt, ever pre-pared by the Stores.

"How in the world did you manage them, in this country?" I begged of Cora.

"When I was in town last week I went in and told them just how I wanted them," she explained. "Are they good?" They were. It might have been the Back Bay, as far as the beans were concerned, rather than a green-velvet curve of the river bank at Henley.

That was Cora's way. She was a woman of singular definiteness, in a manner of speaking. I don't know how long she might mull a thing over in her mind, but once she spoke of a contemplated action, not an instant was lost in effecting it. No doubt she knew Stephen liked beans: The moment it occurred to her, to London town she sped and sought the *chef de cuisine* of the Stores. That he knew no more about baking beans than he did about escaloping nightingale's tongues, would not dissuade Cora Crane from the end she had in mind. She'd *show* him. And she had done so. And we had our beans.

It was on this four day adventure that I saw Stephen angry for the first and only time. His sole remaining box of one hundred cigarettes the unfortunate Heather accidentally dropped into the water over the side of the punt as he was arranging the cushions, one morning, for our journey up the river. Stephen's face became porcelaine and all the little color went out of his thin lips beneath his wisp of mustache. Cora put her hand on his arm for she, too, saw murder in his glare. Heather, himself, who could have taken Stevie in his two hands, and broken him, quite readily, over his knee, shrank from the snake fangs in his master's eyes. For an instant not a word was said, then Cora spoke, quite calmly.

"Heather," she said, "please telegraph at once for a half dozen boxes. . . . " [Remainder of the manuscript is missing.]
From: Mrs. Karl Edwin Harriman, Dangerfield House, Jenkinton, Pa.

⌒

57 / Edith Richie Jones

Edith Richie Jones (?–?) was the nineteen-year-old niece of Kate Lyon and sister of Mark Barr's wife, Mabel, who came to Brede Place in July 1899 as a companion for Crane's niece Helen. She stayed there till January 1900. During this time she travelled with the Cranes to Ireland and Paris and took dictation for several of Crane's stories and sketches. Besides offering a glimpse of the Crane household at Brede Place, her reminiscence supplies details about the haunted room at Brede Place, Crane's association with Joseph Conrad and Henry James, and the origins of "Manacled," "The Ghost," and *The O'Ruddy*. Crane playfully named Major General Richie in the Spitzbergen Tales after her.

Source: Edith Richie Jones, "Stephen Crane at Brede," *Atlantic Monthly* 194 (July 1954): 57–61.

In June, 1899, my mother took me to call upon Mr. and Mrs. Crane, who were staying at a hotel in London. I had been away at school in Switzerland and now I was being introduced to a lot of my parents' and my sister's friends whom I had not met before. I did not know that Stephen Crane was a famous author. I only knew that he and Cora were family friends. In spite of the small difference between us in age (Stephen was twenty-seven and Cora a few years older, and I was nineteen), they at once began to "mother" and "father" me. I called them "Mr. Crane" and "Mummy Crane." They called me "Snubby" because of my short nose. They were darlings to me from that day until they went out of my life, more than half a century ago, leaving a hole that has never been filled. Who could ever forget Stephen and his whimsicalities, and Cora with her gleaming golden hair, exquisite skin, and humorous mind?

With them at the hotel was their niece, Helen Crane, who was eighteen. Her father, Stephen's brother, was a judge in some town in New York.[115] Before my mother and I left them that day, the Cranes decided that they wanted to have a party for Henley Regatta[116] and invited me to be there. I think the regatta is held around July 4, and it was then that I next met them. The Cranes and Helen, Karl Harriman, and several others and I all stayed at a little riverside inn. I remember that the old Marquis of Queensberry was also there.

[In mid-July the Cranes invited Edith and her friend Florence Bray, friends from the Henley Regatta, as well as novelist A. E. W. Mason and George Lynch, to a party at Brede Place. Crane and Lynch, war correspondent for the *London Chronicle*, had served together in Cuba.]

. . . The party left after a few days, but Florence stayed for two weeks and I stayed until January, 1900. While the crowd was there, we were all invited over to tea with Henry James in his house in Rye. The Cranes and I went frequently after that,[117] and Mr. James would bicycle the seven miles over to Brede at least once a week. One day Mr. James and Stephen were having a discussion about something, and Stephen was getting the better of the argument. Suddenly Mr. James said, "How old are you?" "Twenty-seven," said Stephen. "Humph," said Mr. James, "prattling babe!"

In those days, I used to sing a little and Stephen liked it. Whenever Mr. James came to call, I was made to sing for the poor man. Then Cora would say, "Now, let's have a concert." I would pick up the five puppies and, with three heads over one arm and two over the other, I would sing and play while five little muzzles rose howling in anguish. Mr. James and the Cranes would become limp with mirth.

Sometimes, when there was a crowd in the house, there would be a tap on my bedroom door soon after I had gone to sleep. Cora's voice would say, "Stephen wants some music. Slip into your dressing gown and bring your comb." We would all troop down to the huge old kitchen, to which we never had access in daytime because the servants were there. The party might consist of A. E. W. Mason, Joseph Conrad, Mr. and Mrs. H. G. Wells, and others. We would first raid the pantry, and then, with tissue over our combs and Stephen conducting with the toasting fork as his baton, we all would sing horribly and happily through the combs. Such foolishness amused those brilliant minds!

2

[Jones described Brede Place. For details on its history and appearance, see Wertheim and Sorrentino, *Crane Log* 308–9.]

. . . The Cranes always said that the "modern improvements" were made in Elizabethan days. There was no running water—it had to be pumped outdoors and brought in. No gas or electric lights, just lamps and candles. Huge open fireplaces. Many rooms in the house were left unfurnished. Cora had found a lot of lovely old four-poster beds being used as chicken coops in neighboring farmyards and had bought them for a song and had them rubbed down and fitted with mattresses. Cora had been clever in finding other odds and ends for the house. The big beautiful oak-paneled hall, where we lived most of the time, was full of comfortable couches and chairs and pretty tables with lamps and plants and books. The dining room had a long refectory table and rushes on the floor from the meadow by the brook. There was a chapel in the house, but it had long been used as a storeroom. The Cranes stored apples there.

. . . When Mr. Hueffer came to Brede, he read some of his poems to us. In one, there was a line about "birds in treetops," which he read "birds in the tea trops" and we three had much difficulty in concealing our giggles.

Stephen's workroom was an austere place with a not too comfortable chair and a long table in it, bare except for his papers. When he was in the writing mood, we would all stay away from him. But sometimes he would say that he could think better if he had company, and then he would bring his work down to the hall and write while Cora and I sewed. One day he told us that he had had a dream which he thought would make a good story. He dreamed that he was acting on the stage of some theater and in the play he was a prisoner. He had been handcuffed and his ankles were bound together. Suddenly there was a cry of "Fire!" In his dream, all the other actors and the audience ran for the exits and forgot that he was tied up and helpless. That was his dream. He wondered, in writing about it, how long it might take him to inch his way along a corridor to an outside door. So he got Cora and me to tie his hands and his ankles together and then he spent the morning trying, over a given distance, to hop or roll or work along like an inchworm, all in deadly seriousness. I don't know whether he published the story, but he lived it and wrote it.[118]

Heather, the butler, was pompous and typical, but devoted to the Cranes. When there was a crowd in the house, he would manage between courses to wash and dry the flat silver, for there was not a great amount of it.

Vernall, the cook, was half English, half Swiss. She had been my mother's cook for about ten years, and Mother had taught her to cook good American dishes. Mr. James loved her doughnuts. I have unfortunately lost a lovely photograph of him, eating Vernall's doughnuts at the church fair.[119] Vernall's husband, Chatters, did the outdoor work and the carrying of water. There were a couple of maids. And Pat, the coachman, and his wife lived over the stables. A big establishment, but they could not do with less.

The house was supposed to be haunted and no one from Brede village would work there after dark. I slept in the haunted room, and Stephen insisted that a dog or two should sleep there too. He was afraid someone might try to play practical jokes and scare me. Outside my windows was thick ivy in which white owls roosted, and their hoo-hoo-hoos were eerie if you didn't know where they came from. The room had three doors, leading to other rooms or halls. When I went up to dress for dinner, I would carefully close each door. A moment later I would look fearsomely over my left shoulder. Door number one would be open. Then, over my right shoulder, door number two open and, a little further to the right, door number three. I always turned slowly and always had the same spooky feeling. But the doors, I knew, were not really bewitched. They all had old slippery wooden latches which had to be pegged to stay shut.

When I was lying in bed at night, I seemed to hear babies crying, or a coach-and-four would come trundling from a distance, the horses' hoofbeats pounding louder and louder over my head. I loved it, because it was the wind making the rafters creak and groan.

3

Sometimes Cora, Stephen, and I would be alone; sometimes there was one guest, a couple, or a crowd. I have read articles about Stephen's frantic worry about money, about people who came uninvited and battened upon him, of his writing early and late to make enough to pay for all that was demanded of him. I never heard money mentioned while I was there. I never saw an uninvited guest.[120] The guests who came were invited by Cora at Stephen's suggestion. I have heard her protest to him that he should have a rest after a houseful over a weekend. But he loved to have people there. We never thought of him as being delicate. He was slight but wiry. People have said of him that he drank too much, smoked too much. That is nonsense. He always had a tumbler of whisky and soda by his side as he wrote, and he sipped it from time to time. I mixed his drinks for him and I did it the way he wanted, with about two teaspoonfuls of whisky in a tall glass of soda water. He might have three of these during the day. He always had a cigarette in his fingers, but most of the time it was out. Cora and I used to pick up dozens of cigarette stubs which had obviously been puffed once, then thrown away in disgust when he found they had gone out.

Mr. Frewen was the rector of Brede village. Soon after Florence Bray and I went to Brede Place, a fair was held in the rectory garden. Cora had a booth where she sold knickknacks; Florence played the piano and sang; everyone did what he or she could to help. I told fortunes. This I was chosen to do because I had long dark hair and could be dressed up to look like a gypsy. I sat in a little summer-house, with a table in front of me. On it were a lot of envelopes filled with sugar and spices which I sold as love potions to the "local yokels," as Stephen called them. Henry James insisted upon sitting there with me all after-noon, adding much to my confusion. I knew nothing about telling fortunes and I only hoped I was not raising false hopes in the bosoms of the young couples who came shyly in to consult me. I was shyer than they were.

The first month or so of my visit to Brede, Helen Crane was there too. Helen was sophisticated in some ways, childish in others, and Stephen thought she needed more education. My sister, Mabel Barr, and I had been at Rosemont-Dézaley in Lausanne and loved the school. Stephen wrote Helen's parents and got their consent to her going to Rosemont. The Cranes decided that Stephen would take Helen to Switzerland, and that Cora and I would accompany them as far as Paris and wait there for his return. I think it must have been the end of August when we four got into the omnibus (used as a rule to meet guests at Rye Station) and were driven by Pat, the coachman, to Folkestone, where we spent the night with the H. G. Wellses. That evening Mrs. Wells and I gave them some music of sorts; then we all played animal grab. I can still hear Stephen roaring like a lion, Cora twittering like a canary, Mr. Wells barking like a dog.

Next morning George Lynch joined us and we crossed to Boulogne. In our compartment on the train to Paris there was a stout middle-aged and very serious Frenchman. He slept most of the time, with his mouth wide open. We had a lunch basket with us, and while we were getting things out of it Mr. Lynch took a bottle of fizzy water, the cork of which was tied on like a champagne cork. From the corner of my eye I saw him aim nonchalantly, so that no one would notice, cut the string, and—pop! into the poor Frenchman's mouth went the cork and a generous supply of soda water. Fury! Rage! But George apologized so charmingly for his "carelessness" that the victim was soon mollified. Not so Stephen. He later gave Mr. Lynch the dressing-down he deserved.

We four stayed at the old Hôtel Louis le Grand, and Mr. Lynch went off on his own. The first night we were there, after we had all gone to bed, a note arrived from him saying he was going to fight a duel and he wanted Stephen to come at once and be his second. Stephen thought it was just one of George's jokes and refused to go. But, early next morning the Wild Irishman appeared, arm in arm with a delightful Frenchman, whose other arm was in a sling!

Cora and I were alone in Paris for a couple of days while Stephen took Helen to Lausanne. We saw the sights and window-shopped. Stephen returned and immediately did a lot of writing. One morning a page of his manuscript was missing and there was wild excitement in the hotel while chambermaids came into our rooms and emptied wastepaper baskets all over the place to see if the page had been thrown away by accident. It was not found and Stephen had to rewrite it.

We met various friends in Paris and had a gay time, with lunches, dinners, theaters, cafés-chantants, and sightseeing. We had meant to stay quite a while, but suddenly we all got homesick for Brede and the dogs and decided to go home. All the time we were away, both Cora and Stephen got small pieces of candy from penny-in-the-slot machines and mailed them home to the dogs.

One morning in October, Stephen came down to breakfast and said, "Edith has never been to Ireland. Let's go to Ireland." Bless him! He was writing *The O'Ruddy* and he wanted some local color and I was a good excuse.[121] So we packed our bags and off we went to London.

That evening there was a big party at the Frewens', where the Cranes were lionized. Next morning we went to the station to take the train to the boat for Ireland, but found that we had had an old timetable and that the train had gone. No matter. It was fun to have another day in London. We missed that train three days in succession. It sounds as if we were all morons. But we were just happy, carefree country bumpkins who had lost the habit of catching trains. And each day and evening was full of more parties—lunches, teas, dinners. Everyone wanted to entertain the Cranes. Finally we reached Ireland and went from Cork to Ballydehob to Skibbereen to Skull to Bantry, ending at Glengariff, staying at little country inns. We rode in low-back cars or in little trains which Stephen said leaped from crag to crag, and we made friends with people all along the way. We were to have gone to Killarney, but again we got homesick for Brede and the dogs.

4

Joseph Conrad came often to Brede, but his wife was not well at that time and I never met her. The Cranes gave the Conrads one of the puppies, named Pizanner because he was black and utterly mongrel in shape, with a leg on each corner, like an old-fashioned square piano. The Conrads renamed him and he was much loved by them. I liked Mr. Conrad the most of any of the Brede guests. He was charming, quiet and courteous. I was shy and inclined to listen rather than to talk. He would discuss books with me as seriously as with his fellow writers.

I wish I knew how to describe the atmosphere of Brede. I have never known two people more deeply in love with one another than were Stephen and Cora. Their sweetness and consideration each for the other were touching and charming. Each was extremely sensitive, each protective. Cora ran the household for Stephen's comfort and happiness. She followed his every change of mood. If he wanted silence, he had silence. If he wanted company and gaiety, he had them. They were fine people, both of them. They were *good*. Always they were good. Not only were they "good" to me. They were ethically good. They were kind. They were just.

Stephen had candid gray eyes and tawny hair and mustache, both rather shaggy. He was slender but not delicate-looking. Cora was short. She had great dignity and quiet charm. Her hair was pure gold, her skin exquisite. She was a woman of great distinction.

She used to say, "I haven't any more clothes than a rabbit." At Brede she wore a kind of tunic and skirt, which she made herself. Some were made of cotton, some of wool, some of silk or velvet. She always wore sandals. She had brought home the original pair from Greece and had them copied by the cobbler in the village. She had a suit and blouses and shoes which she wore when she went to town, and a lovely black evening gown. But she certainly never spent money on herself. Stephen usually wore knickers at home and he always forgot to put on his garters. Cora said his stockings were accordion-pleated.

One day Stephen was talking about his *Whilomville Stories*. He said most of them were founded on stories that Cora had told him of her childhood.[122] I asked her where she had been born and she told me some place in Massachusetts. I have forgotten the name. Later on, she told me a lot about her childhood and younger days. Her parents had died when she was a tot, and her grandfather had brought her up. He had made money out of some system he had devised for restoring old paintings. He died when she was fifteen and left her his money but did not name a guardian for her.[123] The first thing she did, after his death, was to buy herself a long black velvet dress and a string of pearls! Poor child.

I believe that at one time she was married to a young Englishman of title.[124] Her brushes and mirror and other toilet silver were marked with a coronet and initials. And her old trunks in the attic were marked with coronets. She must have been very young at that time. She and Stephen both told me that they met in Greece during the Greco-Turkish War[125] when Stephen was a war correspondent there and Cora was writing for some American newspaper.

When Mr. Conrad, the H. G. Wellses, A. E. W. Mason, Mr. Pugh, and others were at Brede, we would sit around the huge fireplace in the hall in evenings and everyone would have to tell stories. I remember one told by Mr. Mason. When he was a lad he went to stay with a classmate whom he had visited before. They arrived late at night when everyone had gone to bed. The young host showed Mason to the room he had had on other visits, and Mason went to bed and to sleep. He wakened to hear groans and to see a white figure floating between ceiling and floor. Terrified, he pulled the bed clothes over his head and finally went to sleep. In the morning he found that a poor young maid had hanged herself from the tester of his big four-poster bed. She had thought the room was empty.

For a long time my family had been clamoring for me to come home, but the Cranes would say they needed me—they would be all alone (alone! with endless guests) in the country, miles from anywhere. Finally, Christmas was in the offing and I *must* go home. "No" said Stephen. "Let's have a real party. We'll have all your family here and your friends and our friends. It will be your party. We'll have a ball and a play." "What play?" asked Cora and I. "Oh, you two can make up some sort of play and I'll get a lot of friends to send a scene or a sentence or even a word that you can work into it. Then we can say they wrote it." That was how "The Ghost" was born.[126] I think it was Edwin Pugh who contributed "He died of an indignity caught while chasing his hat down the Strand."[127]

Later, various actor-managers, among them Sir Herbert Beerbohm Tree,[128] reading in the newspapers the formidable list of "authors," wrote Stephen asking if we would give the play in one of their London theaters![129] The play was utter nonsense. Mr. Mason as the Ghost had the only real role.[130] The rest of us sang or danced or did what stunts we could. The cast had a good time but I do not know how much the audience enjoyed it.

Cora and I worked like dogs before the party—sending out invitations, hiring extra servants from London. The play had to be written and typed, each of us typing with two fingers. Music had to be copied and new words written for each song. I painted the scenery: the huge fireplace in the hall was the backdrop. Guest rooms had to be arranged for married couples. Erstwhile big empty rooms fixed up as dormitories, one for men, one for women. An orchestra had to be engaged, cots hired from a local hospital. Cora got the village blacksmith to make dozens of iron brackets, each holding two candles, to hang around the oak-paneled walls of the hall. We made long ropes of holly and greenery and festooned them around the walls. We wrote on cards who-should-take-in-whom to dinner every evening, and put them near each guest's bed.

The cast came a day before the other guests. After a sketchy rehearsal at home, we gave a trial performance of "The Ghost" that afternoon in the village schoolhouse for the school children. When the other guests arrived next day, we numbered about fifty. We had the real performance that night.

Next night was the ball. Then everyone left the following day and we three were alone again. But I had been told that now I must come home. Cora asked Stephen if he had enjoyed the party and he said yes, every bit of it.

I left them the first week in January, 1900, expecting to see them both soon again. Stephen had been his usual self, not tired or bothered in anyway. He seemed as vigorous as ever. Cora and I wrote every few days to one another and all seemed well. Then came a frantic letter saying Stephen had had a hemorrhage and that she was rushing him to the Black Forest. Then, the end.

Cora died just a few years later. I loved them both. . . .

⌒

58 / Mark Barr

Mark Barr (1871–1950), a scientist and engineer, occasionally visited the Cranes at Brede Place along with his wife, Mabel, who was the niece of Harold Frederic's mistress, Kate Lyon, and the elder sister of Edith Richie Jones (No. 57).

Source: Mark Barr, "The Haunted House of Brede," typescript, 5 pp., Berg Collection of English and American Literature, New York Public Library.[131]

Stephen Crane during his last years in England lived at Brede Place, the ancient manor house near Rye. I had met him through Harold Frederic in London, and on my first visit to Brede Stephen met me in a wagonette drawn by two very temperamental bay horses named Hengist and Horsa because, he explained, they were true "Kentishmen!"[132] The manor house amazed me. The Great Hall with its Linenfold panelling. the gallery, the winding stairways and the old kitchen now used as the dining room. But beyond all strange features was the underground secret passage which long ago had led to a smuggler's cavern. Rye, nearby, in early days was on the sea shore, many years before the waters had receded.

We went through the stone tunnel, running under the garden and now ending at a stone wall blocking the old passage which beyond Brede Place had long since caved in.

H. G. Wells was one of the week-end guests and as we went through the dark tunnel I told him that the place seemed ghostly. "Brede Place *is* ghostly!" he said, "Don't you know that it is haunted?" He smiled. I knew that he did not believe in ghosts. In fact, in those early years Wells took an infinitely factual view of the universe which bothered me for I felt more as Stephen Crane felt,—that the transcendental unknown far outreached the known although I disagreed with many people whose subliminal wish too highly colored their thought. Wells and I used to talk Science, but never with Stephen who took no interest in it. It is true that Crane once asked me to impregnate some wood with certain chemicals so that Henry James, who often came to Brede, seeing colored flames in the ingle-nook fireplace, would think it was ship-timber! The joke succeeded, but that was the only occasion on which Stephen Crane showed the slightest interest in laboratory work. Thomas Beer, who never met Crane, says in his book that I "took Science to Brede Place."[133] This is absolutely untrue. Apart from the joke on Henry James, I admit that when Stephen decided to have the walls, ceiling and carpet of his waiting-room colored bright scarlet I gave "scientific" reasons, determined by Charcot,[134] to dissuade him.[135] Apart from that, nothing. Even in regard to the ghost, Wells and I refrained from criticism.

Cora and Stephen Crane were delightful hosts. They lodged their friends in the unhaunted wing of the manorhouse. The ghostly visitations were said to occur chiefly in a circular room up in a little tower at the far end of the house where creaking footsteps were heard at night. Also, it was said, the door of the haunted room would mysteriously open,—the latch being lifted by invisible means, no investigation having revealed the presence of any person. . . . [Barr's ellipsis] No one was bothered by ghostly phenomena at Brede. We had very gay times, and at Christmas and New Years wonderful parties with many interesting and charming guests. Many things took one back in years and I often thought of Wells's wonderful book, *The Time Machine.* One day I asked Stephen why the stone floor of the entrance-hall was sunk three inches below the door sills and Wells at once explained that in the old days they were strewn thick with rushes. Stephen then suggested that we go off to the meadows and brooks and see if rushes still grew there,—so that we could put them in the hallway as of old. We found many green rushes and met Joseph Conrad who was delighted to hear Wells's explanation. He helped us to gather great bundles of the plants which were soon laid in the old hallway.

I noticed that on the oak panels of the Great Hall a number of very old wrought-iron candle holders were missing and I secretly asked the village blacksmith to make copies of one which I had taken from a dark corner. The copies were perfect and I told my host that I had found them in the haunted part of the house! At once a guest said: "I'm certain that the ghost put them there!"

Robert Barr, the novelist, a distant Scotch relation of mine, once slept in the haunted room and had a weird experience. I was not there at the time but I was told that the door unlatched and swung open and that footsteps were heard on the oak stairs. Robert piled up furniture against the door to keep out the ghost. . . . [136] [Barr's ellipsis] Stephen used to laugh when the ghost was mentioned and yet I was never sure that he disbelieved the stories. Wells and I never volunteered to investigate the weird phenomena, but a later event cleared up the mystery.

Occasionally we dined with Henry James[137] at Rye. He never spoke of the ghost at Brede. Later when his brother William became interested in Spiritualistic phenomena I wondered what Henry thought of it.

One day in the Summer I went to Brede Place for a quiet week-end when no one was there but Stephen and H. G. Wells. After dinner Stephen asked me if I would like to sleep in the haunted room and I said I would. Later I had the impression that Stephen and H. G. were up to some joke because I saw them grinning in the hall and whispering. At once I had an idea. At two in the morning they would probably come up in white sheets, open my door and groan. . . . [Barr's ellipsis] I filled a large tin pitcher with water and placed it near the door. I sat propped up in bed reading by the light of a beeswax candle (the only illumination at Brede), intending, if I heard footsteps, to put out the light and dowse the intruders when they opened the door. But I fell asleep!

I was suddenly awakened; I heard creaking on the stairs. My candle had burned out. I slipped out of bed and grabbed the pitcher. The door was wide open and I could see no one silhouetted against the dim light of the far-off hall windows. Still hearing creaks on the stairs to my left I pitched the water with a swing and shouted: "Yah, I've got you two ghosts!" No one answered. I then went in and shut the door and searched for a new candle. Suddenly the door opened wide. I lit the candle and rushed down to the first turn of the stairs. No one was there.

I went back to my room, shut the door and stood watching it. A high wind was blowing, it had come up after I went to sleep. I noticed that when a strong gust came the latch clicked and the door swung open! On examination I found that the iron rider-piece of the very old latch had been so worn down by the blade that the holding-detent was less than a thirty-second of an inch deep. Also, I found that if unlatched and not held, the door swung open of itself. I wish to remark that this is no tale of cleverness on my part for had it not been for my impression of joke-playing I might have been frightened.

I tied the latch to its rider piece and went to bed. Early in the morning I borrowed a screw-driver and file from the butler and told him not to mention it. I removed the hinge-wing at the bottom of the door frame and packed it out an eighth of an inch with lancer match strips. This made it impossible for the door to swing open of itself, and I also filed the latch-detent deeper, so that however hard the wind blew the strain on the old door frame would not release the latch. Thus I laid the ghost. The creaking of the stairway was not stopped but no one could hear the "footsteps" when the door was closed. At breakfast Stephen and H. G. were grinning but I had the fun of announcing that the ghost would never again open that door!

Stephen Crane! What memories. . . . [Barr's ellipsis] The personal character, talents and outlook of few famous people are known to the general reader. Crane was misunderstood by many newspaper men in his early days in New York. A rare characteristic was his dislike of praise and publicity. He made an enemy of the yellow press. He used to sit alone in Delmonico's and when a reporter approached him he would tell him to go to the devil![138] The result was that libelous gossip built up. Here is an example: One night Richard Harding Davis went into the Hoffman Bar and heard a young man say: "Stephen Crane has left America for America's good, he is a drug addict." Davis said: "That is untrue and I wish to add that you know it is untrue." The stranger made a threatening gesture whereupon Dick Davis hit him a terrific blow and knocked him down. The stranger did not get up and Davis quietly walked out.[139]

Everyone who knew Stephen Crane loved him. People of very different interests found him congenial. His clarity of expression, his wit and humour, his kindness and consideration charmed his many friends. He had no vanity of any kind. His writing was to him play, not work. He died at the age of twenty seven.[140]

⤳

59 / A. E. W. Mason

Alfred Edward Woodley Mason (1865–1948), actor, playwright, and writer of romance and detective fiction, was best known for the novel *The Four Feathers* (1902). He contributed to "The Ghost" and played the lead role. Following Crane's death, Cora asked him to complete *The O'Ruddy*, after several other writers had declined the offer; he kept the manuscript for two years before returning it unfinished. Harriman's reminiscence (No. 56) provides additional details concerning the relationship between Crane and Mason.

Source: A. E. W. Mason to Vincent Starrett, letter, 4 October 1945, Stephen Crane Papers, Rare Book and Manuscript Library, Columbia University. In Stallman and Gilkes 342–45.

51 South Street,
London, W1.
4th October, 1945
Dear Mr. Starrett,

I cannot remember when I first met Stephen Crane, but I became friendly with him and went down to stay for a week at Christmas with Cora and himself at Brede Place, six or seven miles from Rye, which the Cranes had taken from Moreton Frewen; in fact, Clare Sheridan, the sculptress, who is living there now, is Frewen's daughter. There was a large party of us that Christmas. The house, which frankly was not in a state to be occupied, was sketchily furnished and I think there was arranged a dormitory in which six or seven men slept. I know that I was given a room to myself but warned not to open, except very cautiously, two great doors which enclosed one side of it. There was no electric light and naturally enough I opened very carefully the two doors. I found that if I had taken one step forward, I should have stepped down about thirty feet into the chapel, this being the private pew or box of the owners of the house. We had, I remember, rushes on the floor instead of carpets, and there were other disadvantages which meant nothing to us, for we were all of us young.

One of the conditions of our visit was that we should each write a line for a pantomime which he proposed to produce in the village hall on one of the evenings: and, with one rehearsal, we did it and, apparently, to my infinite astonishment, with much laughter and success.[141]

Crane gave a ball on one night, to which he had invited the leading figures of the country-side, but there was a tremendous fall of snow, and this being the day before motors, hardly a local resident turned up. This was, perhaps, just as well for H. G. Wells arrived with his wife and he invented a game of racing on broomsticks over the polished floor, which I think would have staggered the local gentry if they had turned up.

Beyond Wells and a man who is now a most important Solicitor and a dramatic critic,[142] I have not one idea of the people who were staying there, but I do remember being greeted by Henry James, who was standing at the gate of his garden at Rye as I drove past him, and being warned by him that I might find an actress or two in the party and should be careful not to get caught.

After this, and fairly soon after, Stephen got ill. I can't remember what year this was but it was a year during which he had written twenty accounts of battles[143] in various magazines (I think chiefly in the *Cornhill*), and got £100 for each article.[144] You, of course, will have details. I think it was the Christmas before he died, unless my memory has played me very false.

From that time, I began to see a good deal of Stephen and went down fairly often to Brede Place. It wasn't really fit for him and he told me finally that he had been coughing up blood, which Cora wouldn't stand. Some time that last spring I have a recollection of seeing him in bed in the open air, under the shelter of a corner of Brede Place, and that he was looking forward—or pretending to look forward—to getting well in the Black Forest. The doctor had very little hope of his recovery and said that he should never have stayed in that house which had no proper plumbing or furniture. I remember that bats flew about my ceiling and walls until the candle was put out and they settled down then to share the room with me.

As to *The O'Ruddy*, during that last spring he asked me to read it. He told me its history. He had begun it, scoffing at some of us who were writing that sort of romantic tale, but, as he went on with it, he got bitten by the theme and the treatment and the period, and was enjoying himself writing it.[145] I read it very carefully. I think there must have been, even at that time, a suggestion or hint that if he did not come back, I should finish it, but of that I can't be sure. Certainly I read it carefully and inclined to realize that this was not his pigeon at all. However, I think I told him that he must get well and finish it himself. After he died, Cora wrote to me and asked me to undertake it. I didn't, for although I guessed that Stephen's affairs were not very flourishing, I did not think that *The O'Ruddy* would add either to his estate or his reputation. It was a little time afterwards that Barr finished the book and justified my reluctance. Stephen had left nothing whatever to guide you as to how the story was going to run. I think he was letting it go its own way.[146]

I think that's all that I remember. I liked Stephen very much. He was a great enthusiast and if he had been a little less "Early English,"[147] just to suit Brede Place, it is possible that he might have lived longer. But that I don't know. You couldn't heat the place and the winter could be pretty harsh. I think it is likely, from what I remember, that when he was alone, he was not out enough in the open air.

However, I see that I am beginning to guess; so I fall back upon a certainty, which is that I have a new Hanaud novel called *The House in Lordship Lane*[148] coming out next year. Yours sincerely,

A. E. W. Mason

60 / Edwin Pugh

Edwin Pugh (1874–1930) was a prolific novelist, literary critic, and writer of short stories who was also an outspoken member of the Fabian Society. He contributed a line to "The Ghost," and the character Suburbia in the play comes from Pugh's *Street in Suburbia* (1895), a collection of stories that portrays lower-class life in London.

Source: Edwin Pugh, "Stephen Crane," *Bookman* [England] 67 (December 1924): 162–64.[149]

[Pugh praised Thomas Beer's "admirable study" for the "daylight" it would shine on Crane, because "much that has been rumoured and written about him is largely mythical," but criticized Joseph Conrad's introduction for depicting Crane "as something of a simpleton."]

. . . What was [Crane] like? I wish I could describe him. But his face is so familiar to me as I write—the fine glowing splendour and triumphant beauty of this man who has been dead to this present world for a quarter of a century— that I cannot. To say that he was rather tall, inclined to stoop a little, very fair, with a slight moustache and resplendent hair of pale brown, seems trivial. To say that he was beautiful and brave and careless, that he was in short all those things the typical fool doesn't like, might be misleading. But . . . [Pugh's ellipsis] he talked with a lazy American accent, and he flopped and lounged about a good deal. His hands were miracles of strength and cleverness. He could play hand-ball like a machine-gun. He would fire the ball at me from every conceivable angle, in that green old damp garden of his,[150] with a sort of wild-cat fury.

It was from Brede Place in Sussex that he hailed me unceremoniously to come and stay with him as long as I liked. "Eternity's an entr'acte," he said in his first letter. And you bet—as he would say—I went. He met me at the station with a fly in attendance, and bent that pale Mephistophelian face of his close to mine and said: "This looks like Edwin Pugh." That seemed the queerest approach to friendship I had ever known: it embarrassed me considerably. Hardly a word passed between us on the long drive to his home, but from time to time he hummed, and the refrain of his humming was:

"I'll be there, I'll be there!
When the Hully Gee is calling I'll be there—
Sure as you're born!"

He was already very ill. He had contracted malaria in Cuba, where he had been war correspondent during the Spanish-American affair. Then he had gone to Greece on his own account,[151] and a tale he told me about his experiences there is just enticing.

"Say, when I planted these hoofs of mine on Greek soil I felt like the hull of Greek literature, like one gone over to the goldarned majority. I'd a great idea of Greece. One catches these fleas at Syracuse, N'Yark. So I said to the chocolate-box general of the Greek army: 'Can I go into the fighting line?' And he says to me like a Denver Method: 'Not in those trousers, sonny.' So I got back at him with: 'How near may I get to the fighting line, then?' And he says in his eloquent way, 'Not less that two miles.'" Then Stevie paused, filled, drained his glass, and said very solemnly in that extravagant Yankee accent which he affected when he was telling a story: "That commanding officer was right for sure. I never was within two miles of the fighting line.[152] But I was mostly two miles nearer the Turks than the Greek army was. Bekase they ran like rabbits."[153]

His wit was like liquid silver, his humour profound: so profound that usually he practised it merely to amuse himself.

And I never heard him say a cruel word of anyone. He was always full of love and praise, and yet, when the name of someone or some book he liked cropped up in the talk, he would break off in the midst of eulogy and say: "O hell! what's the use of words, anyway, when you want to say something?" . . .

॰

61 / C. Lewis Hind

C. Lewis Hind (1862–1927), novelist and art critic, was editor of the *Academy* when he met Crane in the summer of 1899. He was a guest at Brede Place for the production of "The Ghost."

Source: C. Lewis Hind, *Authors and I* (New York: John Lane, 1921), 71–73.

. . . I was spending my summer holiday at Winchelsea, and as I had been writing in *The Academy*, with admiration, of this young American who had captured literary England, it was natural that I should wish to see him.[154] So one day in full summer, when the hops were head high, and all the country decked with bloom and greenery, I cycled over to Brede Place.

Stephen Crane was seated before a long, deal table facing the glorious view. He had been writing hard; the table was littered with papers, and he read aloud to me in his precise, remote voice what he had composed that afternoon. One passage has remained with me—about a sailor in a cabin, and above his head swung a vast huddle of bananas. He seemed over-anxious about the right description of that huddle of bananas; and it seemed strange to find this fair, slight, sensitive youth sitting in the quiet of Brede Place writing about wild deeds in outlandish places.[155]

Our next meeting was amazing. I received an invitation to spend three days in Brede Place; on the second day a play was to be performed at the school-room in Brede Village a mile away up the hill. This play we were informed, sub rosa, had been written by Henry James, H. G. Wells, A. E. W. Mason and other lights of literature.

Duly I arrived at Brede Place. Surely there has never been such a house party. The ancient house, in spite of its size, was taxed to the uttermost. There were six men in the vast, bare chamber where I slept, the six iron bedsteads, procured for the occasion, quite lost in the amplitude of the chamber. At the dance, which was held on the evening of our arrival, I was presented to bevies of beautiful American girls in beauteous frocks. I wondered where they came from. All the time, yes, as far as I remember, all the time our host, the author of "The Red Badge of Courage," sat in a corner of the great fireplace in the hall, not unamused, but very silent. He seemed rather bewildered by what had happened to him.

Of the play I have no recollection.[156] The performance has been driven from my mind by the memory of the agony of getting to Brede Village. It was a pouring wet night, with thunder and lightning. The omnibuses which transported us up the hill stuck in the miry roads. Again and again we had to alight and push, and each time we returned to our seats on the top (the American girls were inside) I remarked to my neighbour, H. G. Wells, that Brede village is not a suitable place for dramatic performances.

62 / W. Pett Ridge

W. Pett Ridge (1860–1930) was a prolific novelist and author of numerous works. Despite his productivity, little is known about him and almost nothing about his association with Crane.

Source: W. Pett Ridge, *I Like to Remember* (London: Hodder and Stoughton, 1925), 210–11.

Many people looked doleful on Show Sunday,[157] both before starting out on the tour and after their return. But I never saw any visitor quite so depressed on the occasion as Stephen Crane, and this, I fancy, was mainly due to the circumstance that tea had no overweening attraction for him, or indeed, at that period, for any American. When, after he had written *Maggie,* and the still more wonderful *Red Badge of Courage,* Crane paid his visits to England, he never seemed to be closely accompanied by good health. Once, at Rye, he was taken ill, and the local doctor came in.

"Now, Mr. Crane," said the doctor breezily, "let us take the question of meals. What is your appetite like in the early morning, eh?"

"Fine, doc, fine."

"That's very good to hear. Tell me, what did you have for breakfast this morning?"

"Double the usual quantity."

"Oh, splendid!" cried the local man, with something like rapture.

"I had," Stephen Crane went on, "two brandies and soda instead of one!"

List of Reminiscences

See the bibliography for complete citation of works listed.

Part 1. Port Jervis, Hartwood, Asbury Park

Crane, Edmund B. "Notes on the Life of Stephen Crane."
Crane, Elizabeth (Mrs. George). "Stephen Crane's Boyhood."
Crane, Helen R. "My Uncle, Stephen Crane," 24–29.
Crane, Wilbur F. "Reminiscences of Stephen Crane," 3.
Johnson, Willis Fletcher. "The Launching of Stephen Crane," 288–90.
———. Letter to the Editor. *New York Evening Post Literary Review*, 14.
Oliver, Arthur. "Jersey Memories—Stephen Crane," 454–63.
Price, Carl F. "Stephen Crane: A Genius Born in a Methodist Parsonage," 866–67.
Sidbury, Edna Crane. "My Uncle, Stephen Crane, as I Knew Him," 248–50.
Wells, Anna E. "Reminiscences of Stephen Crane."
Wheeler, Post, and Hallie E. Rives. *Dome of Many-Coloured Glass,* 20–22, 98–101, 106–7.

Part 2. School and College

Chandler, George F. "I Knew Stephen Crane at Syracuse," 12–13.
French, Mansfield J. Letter to Melvin H. Schoberlin. 14 October 1947.
———. Note accompanying a baseball used by Crane. 20 February 1934.
———. "Stephen Crane, Ball Player," 3–4.
Goodwin, Clarence N. Letter to Max J. Herzberg. 3 November 1921.
McMahon, William. "Syracuse in the Gay '90s," 13.
Noxon, Frank. Letter to Corwin Knapp Linson. 14 April 1930.
———. Letter to Mansfield J. French. 29 June 1934.
———. "The Real Stephen Crane," 4–9.
Peaslee, Clarence Loomis. "Stephen Crane's College Days," 27–30.
Smith, Ernest G. "Comments and Queries." *Lafayette Alumnus,* 6.
Travis, Abram Lincoln. "Recollections of Stephen Crane."
Wickham, Harvey. "Stephen Crane at College," 291–97.

Part 3. New York City

Bacheller, Irving. *Coming up the Road,* 276–79, 292–93.

———. *From Stores of Memory,* 110–12.

Barry, John D. "A Note on Stephen Crane," 148.

Bragdon, Claude. *Merely Players,* 61–70.

Brown, Curtis. *Contacts,* 222–27.

Carroll, William Waring. Untitled reminiscence, with cover letter to Thomas Beer, 20 March 1924.

Davis, Robert H. Introduction to *Tales of Two Wars,* ix–xxiv.

Ericson, (Axel) David. Letter to Ames W. Williams, 4 November 1942.

Garland, Hamlin. *Hamlin Garland's Diaries.*

———. "A Recollection of Stephen Crane," 4–5.

———. *Roadside Meetings,* 189–206.

———. "Stephen Crane as I Knew Him," 494–506.

———. "Stephen Crane: A Soldier of Fortune," 16–17.

Gordon, Frederick C. Letter to Thomas Beer, 25 May 1923.

Greene, Nelson. Untitled reminiscence, with cover letter to Melvin H. Schoberlin, 4 September 1947.

———. Untitled reminiscence, with cover letter to Melvin H. Schoberlin, 3 October 1947.

Hawkins, Willis Brooks. "All in a Lifetime."

Herford, Kenneth. "Young Blood—Stephen Crane," 413.

Hilliard, John Northern. Letter to Thomas Beer, 1 February 1922.

Kauffman, Reginald Wright. "The True Story of Stephen Crane," 143–45.

Lawrence, Frederic M. "The Real Stephen Crane."

Linson, Corwin Knapp. "Little Stories of 'Steve' Crane," 19–20.

———. *My Stephen Crane.*

McBride, Henry. "Stephen Crane's Artist Friends," 46.

Smith, Harry B. *First Nights and First Editions,* 177–78.

Vosburgh, R. G. "The Darkest Hour in the Life of Stephen Crane," 26–27.

Part 4. The West and Mexico

Cather, Willa [as Henry Nicklemann]. "When I Knew Stephen Crane," in *Prairie Schooner,* 231–36.

Part 5. Florida and the *Commodore*

McCready, E. W. Letter to Benjamin R. Stolper, 22 January 1934.

———. Letter to Benjamin R. Stolper, 31 January 1934.

———. Letter to Benjamin R. Stolper, 3 March 1938.

Paine, Ralph D. *Roads of Adventure,* 162–71, 214–17.

Part 6. Cuba, Haiti, Puerto Rico

Carmichael, Otto. "Stephen Crane in Havana," in *Prairie Schooner,* 200–204.

Carnes, Cecil [writing about James H. Hare]. *Jimmy Hare, News Photographer,* 60–63, 70–78.

Davis, Richard Harding. "How Stephen Crane Took Juana Dias," 43–45.

———. *Notes of a War Correspondent,* 125–28.

———. "Our War Correspondents in Cuba and Puerto Rico," 938–48.

Emerson, Edwin. *Pepys's Ghost,* 149–51.

Marshall, Edward. "Loss of Stephen Crane."

McIntosh, Burr. *The Little I Saw of Cuba,* 124–27, 132–33.

Michelson, Charles. Introduction to *"The Open Boat" and Other Tales,* ix–xxiv.

Parker, Walter. "Memorandum by Walter Parker, Re: Stephen Crane, New Orleans, March, 1940."

Seitz, Don Carlos. *Joseph Pulitzer,* 240–42.

Part 7. England

Barr, Mark. "The Haunted House of Brede."

———. Letter to the Editor. *New York Herald Tribune.*

Conrad, Jessie. *Joseph Conrad and His Circle,* 56–58, 72–75.

———. "Recollections of Stephen Crane," 134–37.

Conrad, Joseph. Introduction to *Stephen Crane,* 1–33.

———. "Stephen Crane: A Note without Dates," in Conrad, *Notes on Life and Letters* 49–52.

Ford, Ford Madox. *Memories and Impressions,* 58–59.

———. "Stephen Crane," 36–45.

———. "Stevie," 881–82.

———. "Stevie and Company."

———. "Three Americans and a Pole," 379–86.

———. "Two Americans: Henry James and Stephen Crane."

Garnett, Edward. *Friday Nights,* 201–17.

———. *Letters from Joseph Conrad,* 11–12.

———. Review of Thomas Beer's *Stephen Crane,* 58.

———. "Stephen Crane," 320–21.

Harriman, Karl Edwin. "The Last Days of Stephen Crane." *New Hope,* 7–9, 19–21.

———. "The Last Days of Stephen Crane." Pt 2. Typescript.

———. "The Last Days of Stephen Crane." Pt. 3. Typescript.

———. "A Romantic Idealist-—Mr. Stephen Crane," 85–87.

———. [Untitled commentary in "The Lounger"]. *Critic,* 14–16.

Hind, C. Lewis. *Authors and I,* 71–73.

Jones, Edith Richie. "Stephen Crane at Brede," 57–61.

Mason, A. E. W. Letter to Ames W. Williams, 14 February 1946.

——. Letter to Vincent Starrett, 4 October 1945.
Pugh, Edwin. "Stephen Crane," 162–64.
Ridge, W. Pett. *I Like to Remember,* 210–11.
Wells, H. G. *Experiment in Autobiography,* 522–25.
——. "Stephen Crane from an English Standpoint," 233–42.

Notes

Introduction

1. See Wertheim and Sorrentino (1990), Clendenning (1991, 1995), and Sorrentino (2003).

2. Though sixty-two individuals are listed in the table of contents, several wrote more than one reminiscence. Excerpts from these and other reminiscences appear in the text and notes.

3. Linson corresponded with Beer (Stallman and Gilkes 326–28). He may also have been influenced by the confusing reminiscences of Hamlin Garland, with whom he corresponded (Richter).

4. Beer (1923, 93) spelled the name "Creegan."

Part 1

1. The typescript ends with the following note: "This is a copy of a typed paper found among papers and letters of my brother Thomas Beer for his book on Stephen Crane. I assume it was sent to him by Mr. Max Herzberg of Newark. A. B. Beer May 15 48."

2. Compare with Wilbur F. Crane's comments (No. 3) about young Stephen's fearlessness in water.

3. Stephen began school at the age of six but dropped out because of ill health. For confusion about the age at which he first attended school and first learned to read, see Wertheim and Sorrentino, *Crane Log* 16–17.

4. Cora Crane recorded in her notebook that Stephen's "greatest play as infant boy buttons which he would call soldiers & would manuevre his armies—never picked up buttons after play" (Crane, *Poems and Literary Remains* 345).

As an adult, Crane often played Halma, a board game invented around 1880 that was the precursor to Chinese checkers, with Corwin Knapp Linson: "There was a strategic interest in this simple game which engaged him. With great glee he marshaled his 'phalanx' as he termed it, and wedged past me into the winning corner—it was more sport to me to be the loser, he became such a boy over it" (Linson 1958, 86).

5. The Junior Order of United American Mechanics.

6. See the headnote to Oliver (No. 6).

7. Crane was nineteen.

8. In January 1888 Crane enrolled at Claverack College and Hudson River Institute, a coeducational preparatory school and junior college with a military training battalion for boys.

9. Mrs. Crane died in Paterson on 7 December 1891 at the age of sixty-eight.

10. Land owned by William Howe Crane.

11. The Philistine banquet, which occurred on 19 December 1895 at the Genesee House in Buffalo.

12. Hubbard sold the horse, Peanuts, for sixty dollars. See Wertheim and Sorrentino, *Correspondence* Letter 205.

13. Possibly an allusion to "One Dash—Horses." For problems in treating the story as autobiography, see Linson (No. 21), n. 72.

14. As a child in Hartwood, Judge E. J. Dimock recalled that he "never saw [Crane] walk when he could ride a horse. It was all the more remarkable in a stony country where even a tired ploughman returning with his horses from an outlying field would trudge beside them rather than mount one. Crane, on the other hand, if he had to go 100 yards in one direction and had a horse 95 yards away in an opposite direction, would walk to the horse, mount it and ride the 195 yards. While in Buffalo on the Philistine Dinner trip he bought his famous horse 'Peanuts' who was almost as temperamental as his master" (Dimock 17).

15. "Asbury Park as Seen by Stephen Crane," *New York Journal,* 16 August 1896. James A. Bradley (1830–1921) established three New Jersey shore resorts—Asbury Park, Ocean Grove, and Bradley Beach—and as mayor of Asbury Park enforced a strict moral code. Crane satirized Bradley's puritanical behavior in several sketches about Asbury Park.

16. Stephen was four years old when his father became pastor of the Cross Street Church in Paterson in April 1876.

17. Stephen was eight when his father died.

18. See Edmund B. Crane (No. 1), n. 4.

19. Claverack College and Hudson River Institute—which Crane attended from January 1888 to June 1890—was a coeducational preparatory school and junior college in Columbia County, N.Y., with a military training program. See Wickham (No. 12).

20. George Peck (1797–1876), Stephen Crane's maternal grandfather, served as a Methodist minister for more than fifty years and was an influential voice in the governance of the church. Besides his work as an editor, he published religious tracts, historical accounts, and an autobiography.

21. Jesse Truesdell Peck (1811–83), Crane's maternal great-uncle, was also a prominent Methodist minister and bishop and author of numerous publications pertaining to

church matters. Because Peck was a founder of Syracuse University, Stephen was entitled to a scholarship to the Methodist institution.

22. See also Edmund B. Crane's comments (No. 1) about young Stephen's experience in the Raritan River.

23. Crane may have used this fight in two of his Whilomville stories, "The Fight" and "The City Urchin and the Chaste Villagers."

24. Stephen left Pennington in late November–early December 1887 and transferred to Claverack College and Hudson River Institute in January 1888.

25. See Oliver (No. 6), n. 50.

26. In 1849 Dickinson College made Reverend Crane an honorary member of its Belles Lettres Literary Society and in 1856 conferred upon him the degree of doctor of divinity. His wife's uncle the Reverend Jesse Peck had been president of Dickinson from 1848 to 1852.

27. Although Reverend Crane's publications typically adhered to traditional Methodist orthodoxy, his objection to the Holiness Movement in *Holiness, the Birthright of All God's Children* (1874) resulted in the loss of his position as a presiding elder in the church. See Benfey.

28. Reverend Crane was presiding elder of the Newark district (1868–72) and the Elizabeth district (1872–76) in New Jersey.

29. Agnes named the shack, which the Cranes built in August 1878, and later made it the setting of her short story "Laurel Camp, and What Came of It" (*Frank Leslie's Illustrated Newspaper*, 64 [2 July 1887]: 322–23). See Sorrentino (1986, 109–11) and Gullason (2002, 221–29).

30. For Garland's opinion of his first meeting with Crane in August 1891, see Hamlin Garland (No. 20).

31. Peaslee (No. 18) also states that Crane wrote for the *Detroit Free Press.*

32. See Crane's letter to John Northern Hilliard, Wertheim and Sorrentino, *Correspondence* Letter 78.

33. Located near Wilkes-Barre, Pa., the Wyoming Valley was the site of the Battle of Forty Fort on 3 July 1778. Crane's maternal grandfather, the Reverend George Peck, wrote a history of the valley, *Wyoming: Its History, Stirring Incidents, and Romantic Adventures* (1858), the source for Crane's three Wyoming Valley tales, written in the fall of 1899.

34. A lake in mythology considered an entrance to the underworld.

35. The Lantern (also spelled "Lanthorn" or "Lanthorne") Club was a group of newspapermen, editors, and journalists who met regularly to discuss each other's work; Crane joined the club shortly after it was founded in May 1895. It was located in a shanty on the roof of an old house on William Street near the Brooklyn Bridge and Park Row, the newspaper center of New York. According to Irving Bacheller,

The shanty on the roof was occupied by an old Dutchman, who gladly gave up possession for the sum of $50. Then the organizers, among whom was Stephen

Crane, employed a cook and fitted up the shanty so that it looked like a ship's cabin. There, far above the madding crowd, the "Lanthornes" held high intellectual revels. A luncheon was served every day, and the members let their hair grow long and their minds grow high. Every Saturday night they held a literary banquet. Each week some member of the club was assigned to write a story, and it was read at the dinner. Encomium and favorable criticism were prohibited. After the reading of the story the members jumped upon it as hard as they could, pointed out the flaws in it and pooh-poohed it generally, if possible. The highest tribute that a story could receive was complete silence. That was the best any writer ever got. ("Authors' Associations" 32–34)

36. *The Lanthorn Book* (1898), which contains Crane's "The Wise Men," was limited to 125 copies, and all contributions were signed by their authors except for that of Willis Brooks Hawkins, whose signature was printed in facsimile.

37. Gustave Doré's engravings published in an 1875 edition of "The Rime of the Ancient Mariner" depicted a haggard mariner.

38. Pierre Loti (1850–1923), pseudonym for Louis Marie Julien Viaud, was a French naval officer and novelist; Patrick Lafcadio Hearn (1850–1940) was an author and expert on Japanese culture. As journalists, they, like Crane, went beyond mere reporting of factual details.

39. See Wertheim and Sorrentino, *Correspondence* 82.

40. If Wheeler is alluding to the aftermath following Crane's satirical article about JOUAM (Junior Order of United American Mechanics), which was published in the *New York Tribune* in August 1892, then his chronology is incorrect. Because the letter quoted from in the previous paragraph is dated 22 December 1894, the incident involving the *Tribune* could not have occurred "[l]ater."

41. Wheeler shared a loft at 165 West 23rd Street with Victor Newman; Crane often stayed there.

42. Wheeler's chronology is also problematic at this point. Given the date of Crane's 22 December 1894 letter that Wheeler cites, Wheeler is maintaining that Crane was writing *The Black Riders* and *The Red Badge of Courage* in the loft on 23rd Street in 1895; however, Crane was reading page proofs of his poems at the end of 1894, and from January to May 1895 he was in the West and Mexico and making final changes to the manuscript of his war novel. Because Wheeler was in the loft sometime in 1894, Crane conceivably worked on the two books then. Wheeler's reminiscence is also confusing because he says he was trying to entice Crane to New York; however, the complete text of Crane's letter makes clear that Wheeler was in Newark, N.J., in late December 1894.

43. "The tale was later published in *Hutchinson's Magazine* in London, whose readers, presumably, had no inhibition, and reached O'Brien's *Best Short Stories* of the year" (Wheeler's note).

44. Other contemporaries explained the pseudonym differently. Lawrence (No. 22) recalled that Crane wished to disguise the authorship of a book that would offend his prudish relatives, and the jest consisted in elevating the plebeian "John Smith" into a

more aristocratic pseudonym. According to Willis Fletcher Johnson (No. 7), Crane chose the two most common surnames in the New York City directory and whimsically added a "t" to the first. Crane told Corwin Knapp Linson that "[t]he alias was a mere chance. 'Commonest name I could think of. I had an editor friend named Johnson, and put in the 't,' and no one could find me in the mob of Smiths'" (Linson 1958, 21).

45. According to Garland, he told Crane to give the manuscript to Gilder, editor of the *Century Magazine* (Wertheim and Sorrentino, *Crane Log* 80).

46. Starting with *The Black Riders and Other Lines* (1895), Crane's poetry, fiction, and journalism were parodied until his death.

47. Wertheim and Sorrentino, *Correspondence* 588.

48. Scottish expression for "strictly moral," the phrase was popularized by Robert Burns in his poem "Address to the Unco Guid, or the Rigidly Righteous" (1786).

49. As founder and mayor of Asbury Park, Bradley was synonymous with the shore community. Ocean Grove was the summer campground for Methodist revivals.

50. According to Max Herzberg, "Crane's account was immediately seized upon by Reid's political foes and used to discredit him; and years later Reid himself remarked, more or less jokingly, to the man who had been Crane's superior as shore correspondent that the story had beaten him for vice-president and had elected Cleveland" (Herzberg xii).

51. See Paine (No. 40).

52. See Wheeler (No. 5).

53. See Ford (No. 53).

54. The Sullivan County tales and sketches.

55. See Herzberg. Although several of the biographical details in his introduction are incorrect—for example, that Crane attended Lafayette for two terms and is buried in Elizabeth, N.J.—it is an important early biographical sketch. As part of a celebration in Newark commemorating the fiftieth anniversary of Crane's birth, Herzberg wrote a number of people for reminiscences about Crane and included silently edited versions of their comments in his introduction. His edition of *The Red Badge of Courage* contains their original reminiscences.

56. Johnson probably knew Crane's father through their mutual connection with Pennington Seminary. Reverend Crane was the principal at Pennington from 1849 to 1858, and Johnson later graduated from there.

57. Johnson is referring to the Sullivan County tales, the first two printed by the *Tribune* being "Four Men in a Cave" (3 July 1892) and "The Octopush" (10 July 1892). Earlier in the year the newspaper had printed several of Crane's nonfictional or semi-fictional sketches about the county, but none of the tales or sketches appeared there in 1891.

58. Johnson's dating has been disputed. Given his reference to the Sullivan County sketches, fourteen of which were published between February and July 1892, it would seem that he saw a draft of *Maggie* in 1892; however, accounts about the writing of *Maggie* suggest that there was first a Syracuse version, followed by an 1891–92 revision, then a fall 1892 revision, which would suggest that the book was not initially "A Story

of New York." It is conceivable that in the summer of 1891 Johnson saw the first draft, a story about slum life and prostitutes in Syracuse, but confused it with the final version of the novel when he wrote his reminiscence.

59. According to Noxon (No. 14), Crane did research in 1891 for an early draft of *Maggie* by interviewing prostitutes in the Syracuse police court and by visiting the tenement districts of the city.

60. The sensational and melodramatic fiction of English novelist Hall Caine (1853–1931) made him an international celebrity in the 1890s.

61. John Podsnap is a smug, pompous, prudish philistine in Dickens's *Our Mutual Friend.* Mrs. Grundy, a character who is often referred to but who never appears in Thomas Morton's *Speed the Plough,* represents the self-appointed judge whose straitlaced opinions control the conduct of society.

62. See Post Wheeler (No. 5), n. 44.

63. Edgewood Publishing Co. in Philadelphia, which had published Johnson's biographies of Sitting Bull, William Tecumseh Sherman, and Jay Gould and his history of the Johnstown, Pa., flood.

64. Johnson suggests that this event occurred during summer 1891, but it more likely happened the following summer, when Crane showed him some of the Sullivan County tales. In his preface to the 1900 Appleton edition of *The Red Badge,* however, Hitchcock does not mention any meeting with Crane until December 1894 (Hitchcock v).

65. Richard Watson Gilder (1844–1909), editor of *Century Monthly Magazine.*

66. Crane's contemporaries disagree on the source of the money for printing *Maggie.* Helen R. Crane (No. 8) believed that Crane's brother William game him a small loan and bought his shares in the family-owned coal mine in Kingston, Pa. Lawrence (No. 22) stated that Crane inherited the money from his mother; Vosburgh (No. 24) believed it came from his father's estate. Another possible source was William's purchase of Crane's share in their mother's house in Asbury Park.

67. See Hamlin Garland (No. 20).

68. Crane gave a similar account in an interview: "In a conversation, recently, Mr. Crane said that he began the tale as a potboiler, intending to make a short story for a newspaper; that he selected a battle as his subject as affording plenty of "color" and range for the imagination, although he had, of course, never been in a battle in his life. But as he went on, the story grew under his hand, and he determined to put the best work into it of which he was capable. . . . And he went on to say that he had kept this story in hand for nearly a year, polishing and bettering it" ("The Rambler: Comments on Stephen Crane and His Work" 140). Crane also told his friend Louis C. Senger that the story began as a potboiler (Stallman and Gilkes 318–19).

69. The parade occurred not on 1 September but on 17 August.

70. Beer 1923, 89.

71. Herzberg (xi–xii). When Herzberg's introduction and *The Red Badge* were reprinted in 1959 by Washington Square Press, an editor silently made substantive changes

in Herzberg's paragraph dealing with the JOUAM article. The phrase quoted here was deleted.

72. Herzberg (xi–xii). This passage was also deleted from the 1959 reprint by Washington Square Press.

73. For the view that Crane was fired from the *Tribune,* see Garland (No. 20), Barry (No. 28), and Oliver (No. 6).

74. Between spring 1894 and the following winter, Crane wrote feature articles on street life in New York for the *New York Press.*

75. Whereas Jones (No. 57) and Barr (No. 58) also believed that Crane drank only in moderation, Ridge (No. 62) and Crane's own description of a drinking binge in Galveston, Texas, suggest otherwise (Wertheim, "Stephen Crane in Galveston").

76. In a letter to Thomas Beer, 30 December 1933, Edith F. Crane, one of Edmund's daughters, criticized Helen's characterization of Stephen as antisocial; she and other family members were also shocked by the depiction of Cora, for "[w]e always understood that Aunt Cora was reporting for a newspaper in Jacksonville and that was how Uncle Stephen met her" (Thomas Beer Papers, Yale University Library). According to Florence Crane, one of William's daughters, the reminiscence reflected Helen R. Crane's mother's resentment toward the Crane family. Martha Kellogg, a servant in William's house, married Wilbur Crane in 1888 but was never fully accepted by her sisters-in-law; the reminiscence became her way of "getting 'hunk' on the family" (letter to Edith F. Crane).

77. Crane was a stringer for the *New York Tribune* in 1891 while he was at Syracuse University.

78. During summer 1888, at the age of sixteen, Crane began helping Townley report shore news from Asbury Park, N.J., for the *Tribune.*

79. At various times in 1893–94 Crane lived with aspiring artists and illustrators in the old Art Students League building at 143–47 East 23rd Street.

80. Edmund had four children by 1894; twins were born in 1900.

81. According to Sidbury (No. 9), the wives of William and Edmund "were very fond of him."

82. To decrease economic inequality, Henry George (1839–97) proposed that a single tax be levied on land and on practically nothing else. For comments on Crane's attitude toward political issues, see Greene (No. 23), n. 136.

83. Beer (1923, 55, 168) claimed that Crane had read Flaubert, as did Ford (No. 53). Stallman (1972, 32) asserts that his reading of *Madame Bovary* at Syracuse University influenced the writing of *Maggie.*

84. On 24 January 1893 Crane sold his share of the stock to William (Katz, "Stephen Crane: Muckraker," 7).

85. See Johnson (No. 7), n. 66.

86. Beer (1923, 90) says William lent him a thousand dollars. According to Florence Crane (letter to Edith F. Crane), her mother said that the money was a gift, not a loan.

87. The book was bound in mustard paper wrappers.

88. Other copies of the book were burned as well. According to Florence Crane, one

of William's daughters, two of her sisters burned copies, "believing they were 'not nice'" (Bruccoli 160). Fewer than forty copies are known to exist, with one copy being offered for sale in 1995 for $12,500.

89. The letter has not survived.

90. A slight variation of what Crane wrote in the second paragraph of "The Open Boat": "waves . . . barbarously abrupt."

91. According to Gilkes (152–63), the Crane family inferred that Stephen was "married" when William unexpectedly received a cablegram in fall 1898 from a Mrs. Stephen Crane concerning the whereabouts of her husband in Havana, though the source for this story is Beer (1934, 291), who claimed that William wrote him about the cablegram. Somehow the family learned about the "marriage," and Stephen acknowledged it to William in January 1899 (Wertheim and Sorrentino, *Correspondence* 446).

92. Crane sailed from New York on 20 March 1897.

93. A lung specialist examined Crane at least twice, once in the summer of 1898 and sometime earlier (Wertheim and Sorrentino, *Correspondence* Letter 398).

94. Crane's bout with dysentery forced him to miss part of the second battle of Velestino during the Greco-Turkish War.

95. Although Cora may have sold or transferred ownership of her house, the Hotel de Dream (Gilkes 68), she left Jacksonville without paying her bills. A warrant was issued against her, and the sheriff seized furniture in the house as security (Wertheim and Sorrentino, *Crane Log* 147).

96. While in Havana in the fall of 1898, Crane was writing dispatches for the *New York Journal*, Cuban war stories, and the remainder of the poems that would make up *War Is Kind*.

97. For additional information on Crane's disappearance in Havana, see Parker (No. 48). and Carmichael (No. 49).

98. The Cranes moved to Port Jervis in April 1878.

99. Stephen started school in September 1878 at age six.

100. Gullason (2002, 17 n. 4) cites a passage in the *Minutes of the Thirty-Fifth Session of the Newark Conference of the Methodist Episcopal Church* stating that Mrs. Crane attended the Young Ladies Institute of Brooklyn; however, Robert Crane (17) says she graduated from the Rutgers Female Institute in 1847.

101. For an example of one of her sketches, "The Myers House," see G. Peck (192). Special Collections in the Butler Library at Columbia University has one of her paintings.

102. To commemorate the fiftieth anniversary of Crane's death, the Newark School-man's Club installed a tablet on 7 November 1921 in the library.

103. Corwin Knapp Linson recalled Crane's interest in "the processes of a child's mind" during a trip to Port Jervis in August 1894:

A kid, when he wants to do a thing[,] is like an Indian after a scalp, he fights and makes no excuse. If he gets into a scrap and gets a bloody nose, that's glory—until he gets home. Then he is up against Opinion, a Code of Ethics, a Mother. But his Dad is satisfied if he licks the other boy. He may be forced into lace collars and curls, but he doesn't know a fried bean from a turnip about Ethics. If they were smashable he'd get a hammer. They are for grown-ups, anyway. What a kid wants to do he just does, and that's all there is to it. And if we think of conduct all the time we are not sincere. We assume an intellectual attitude and use evasions and we call that good manners. Rank dishonesty! This goes through all one's work. If that is not sincere, it has no value as art. To know truth and side-step it by mental smartness is sheer hypocrisy. Better be sincerely mistaken. In matters of art, we are only responsible for what we see, eh, CK? (Linson 1958, 73–74)

Judge E. J. Dimock remembered from his childhood days in Hartwood Crane's "fondness for children. I remember the ostensibly rapt attention that he gave to my description of the extraction of a loose tooth and to my exhibition of a small pair of electrician's pliers with which I told him my father had performed the operation" (Dimock 18).

104. See the Whilomville story "Lynx-Hunting."

105. This anecdote may have its roots in Beer (1923, 40).

106. In a letter dated 30 October 1922, Beer asked Edmund Crane whether or not the monster was based on a "disfigured teamster in Port Jervis . . . named Levi Hume" (letter to Edmund Crane), but Edmund died before receiving the letter; Beer decided not to mention Hume in his biography. For the possibility that the source for the monster is John Merrick (the Elephant Man), see Petry.

107. See Conrad (1923, 21).

108. Beer (1923, 102) states that Crane described himself and other campers as "bobcats." It is unclear whether Beer is Sidbury's source.

109. That is, "An Experiment in Misery."

110. The Sullivan County tales are loosely based on the camping experiences of four teenage friends—Louis E. Carr Jr., Frederic M. Lawrence, Louis C. Senger Jr., and Crane himself—though the particular incident recounted by Sidbury is not incorporated into one of the tales.

111. Edna's mother.

112. The visit most likely occurred shortly after mid-May 1895, when Crane returned from Mexico.

113. See Linson (No. 21).

114. Wertheim and Sorrentino, *Correspondence* Letter 489.

115. Edna's mother may have been referring to the response of publishers to whom Crane sent the manuscript of *Maggie* in 1893; no response, however, survives. Shortly after Crane published it at his own expense, he sent a copy to John D. Barry, assistant editor of the *Forum*, whose comment on Crane's use of language probably typified the response of publishers: " . . . you give too complete a picture of the vulgar and profane talk of your characters; much less of this would be more effective and less offensive" (Wertheim and Sorrentino, *Correspondence* 50). In preparation for the 1896 publication of *Maggie*, Crane "dispensed with a goodly number of damns" and "carefully plugged at the words which hurt," ending up with a book that "wears quite a new aspect from very

slight omissions" (Wertheim and Sorrentino, *Correspondence* 197, 200). Despite Barry's criticism, he recognized Crane's potential as a writer.

116. A paraphrase of what Crane wrote to the journalist John Northern Hilliard: "To keep close to my honesty is my supreme ambition" (Wertheim and Sorrentino, *Correspondence* 196).

117. Crane began writing *The Red Badge* in June 1893 at his brother Edmund's home in Lake View, N.J.

118. Actually, five months.

119. Stallman appended a note to the reminiscence: "Received from Anna E. Wells of Poughkeepsie, NY, at my query for it, September 1956." Wells added the wording "written about 1951" at the end of the reminiscence. Although the typescript spells her first name as "Anne," it is uncertain whether this is a typographical error.

Part 2

1. Travis wrote the manuscript in response to Mansfield J. French's request for a reminiscence about Crane.

2. For biographical information on Crane's education at Claverack College and Hudson River Institute and later at Lafayette and Syracuse, see Katz ("Stephen Crane at Claverack College and Hudson River Institute"), Gullason (1992), O'Donnell (1955, 1956), Pratt, Starrett (1968), and Wertheim ("Why Stephen Crane Left Claverack"). For information on Crane's education at Pennington Seminary, see Cazemajou, and Gullason ("The Cranes at Pennington Seminary").

3. During a 1952 interview, Mansfield J. French (No. 15) told Thomas A. Gullason that Crane was interested in current affairs and was an avid reader of the newspaper (Gullason 1958, 238). The extent of Crane's knowledge of literature, however, has long been a point of disagreement. Peaslee (No. 18) also described Crane as "an omnivorous reader," but Joseph Conrad was surprised when Crane "demanded insistently to be told in particular detail all about the Comédie Humaine, its contents, its scope, its plan, and its general significance, together with a critical description of Balzac's style" because "Crane was not given to literary curiosities of that kind" (Beer 1923, 16–17; see also Lawrence [No. 22], leaf 2a).

4. Only Travis says that Crane began writing *Maggie* while at Claverack. This statement is probably based on his mistaken belief that Crane spent his childhood in New York.

5. Beer 1923, 53.

6. The Reverend Arthur M. Flack, principal of Claverack and commanding colonel of the school's student military battalion.

7. Wickham may be alluding to an apocryphal Crane letter quoted by Beer (1923, 53): "I was very happy, there."

8. Claverack's student literary magazine.

9. John B. Van Petten (1827–?), a Methodist minister and Union officer during the Civil War, was a professor of history and elocution at Claverack. His experience as chap-

lain of the 34th Regiment, a number reminiscent of Henry Fleming's fictional 304th Regiment, and his witnessing the fleeing of Union soldiers at the Battles of Antietam and Winchester may have influenced Crane's treatment of war in *The Red Badge of Courage*. See O'Donnell (1955, 1956).

10. A pun on the name of Claverack student Harriet Mattison, with whom Crane was infatuated.

11. Beer 1923, 38.

12. Mrs. Leslie Carter (1862–1937), an American actress known for her highly dramatic style and often called "the American Sarah Bernhardt."

13. Beer (1923, 97–98) conflated Corwin Knapp Linson's 1903 reminiscence (No. 21) and fiction in his account of the origin of *The Red Badge*. Linson recalled that Crane read the series "Battles and Leaders of the Civil War" in the *Century* in his studio and criticized it because it recounted only what happened during the war, not what it felt like to fight in it. Beer shifted the scene from Linson's studio to the home of a Mrs. Armstrong.

14. That is, "The Five White Mice."

15. A set of rules for amateur boxing was first adopted by the Amateur Athletic Club in England in 1872. Because John Sholto Douglas, the eighth Marquis of Queensberry, endorsed them, they were known as the Marquis of Queensberry Rules.

16. The Dora Clark affair.

17. Despite Crane's poor academic performance in college, no evidence exists to support the often-held assumption that he was forced to leave Lafayette or Syracuse. He disliked the mining engineering curriculum at Lafayette, and with the support of his mother, he transferred to Syracuse, where she thought he would be given a scholarship because he was the great-nephew of Bishop Jesse Truesdell Peck, one of the founders of Syracuse University. As he wrote to a news reporter, he quit college after one year because "the cut-and-dried curriculum of the college did not appeal to me. Humanity was a much more interesting study. When I ought to have been at recitations I was studying faces on the streets, and when I ought to have been studying my next day's lessons I was watching the trains roll in and out of the Central Station. So, you see, I had, first of all, to recover from college" (Wertheim and Sorrentino, *Correspondence* 99). For additional information on Crane at Syracuse, see C. Jones.

18. Poem 67 in *The Black Riders and Other Lines*.

19. Though Beer (1923, 57) is often cited as the source for this anecdote, it comes from Elbert Hubbard's "As to Stephen Crane," *Lotos* 9 (1896): 676.

20. Crane's own mother and his brother Townley may also be models for the two main characters.

21. See Johnson (No. 7), n. 61.

22. In February 1890 Lillian Russell opened in Jacques Offenbach's operetta *The Grand Duchess* in New York.

23. An early title for *George's Mother*.

24. Wickham's cousin W. W. Young.

25. School records at Lafayette pertaining to Crane "reveal a student who was popu-

lar with classmates and who participated in virtually every extracurricular activity the college offered" (Robertson 4). For additional information on Crane at Lafayette, see Sloane.

26. In a letter to Lyndon Upson Pratt, Smith slightly revised his reminiscence:

> Steve roomed by himself in East Hall, one of the old college buildings, now demolished to give place to a new dormitory. Steve tried to play possum by not answering a loud summons and the usual practice followed by battering in the door. The sophomores crowded in, lighted a lamp and both Ormsby and I also gained entrance to the room. Steve was petrified with fear and stood in a grotesque nightgown in one corner of the room with a revolver in his hand. His usual sallow complexion seemed to me a ghastly green. Whether he ever pointed the revolver or not, I do not know, but when I saw him, both arms were limp and the revolver was pointed to the floor. As a matter of fact, the boy was so frightened that cooler heads prevented any further hazing of him (quoted in Pratt 468).

For two different accounts of the significance of the hazing of Crane, see Gullason (1994) and Robertson. Whereas Robertson downplays the significance of the incident, Gullason argues that Crane left Lafayette at least partly because of it.

27. The reminiscence was originally written as a 7 December 1926 letter to Max J. Herzberg (Stephen Crane Collection, Newark Public Library) and is reprinted in Stallman and Gilkes 334–39.

28. "A Foreign Policy, in Three Glimpses," Crane, *Tales, Sketches, and Reports* 574–78.

29. "Jack," Crane, *Poems and Literary Remains* 95–97. The story survives only as an incomplete manuscript.

30. Lawrence (No. 22) confirms that *St. Nicholas* rejected the story.

31. The Dora Clark affair.

32. Lawrence (No. 22) and Goodwin (No. 16) think that Crane began the book in fall 1892 in New York, but Peaslee (No. 18) believes that he was interviewing prostitutes in the tenement district of Syracuse and writing a first draft of *Maggie* in the spring of 1891. Henry Phillips, another Delta Upsilon fraternity brother and editor of the *University Herald*, also recalled that Crane was writing the book at Syracuse. In a 1926 newspaper article an anonymous writer recorded that "Phillips remembers one Sunday in the D. U. Chapter house when Crane was away for the week-end one of the boys found the manuscript of 'Maggie: A Girl of the Streets,' Crane's first novel, and read it aloud to a group of the fraternity brothers amid great hilarity. 'Crazy stuff,' was the verdict of the students . . . " ("Library Exhibit to Honor Novelist Trained on Hill" 20–21). A number of years later, Phillips wrote in a letter to the editor of a local paper that Crane "conceived his story 'Maggie: A Girl of the Streets,' at this period and I recall the reading of some of that original manuscript which was saturated with obscenity and profanity" (Phillips 6).

A letter dated 3 June 1941, from Lester G. Wells, former curator of rare books at Syracuse University, to Rees Frescoln suggests that Crane not only wrote a version of

Maggie at Syracuse but also tried to publish it. Wells recounts the story of William J. Peck, one of Crane's cousins, who attended Syracuse shortly after Crane left:

> I believe I told you that I had a legand [*sic*] that a manuscript of C's, was somewhere in the D. U. House at 426 Ostrom Avenue, Syracuse, but always believed it to be pure fiction. However, Mr. Peck tells this:—When with another classmate he was, when in college, exploring the attic of the fraternity house they came across a manuscript of C's, with the original wrapping in which it had been returned to him by some publisher; the two students tossed it down between the open beams of construction of the attic. Since then this attic was sealed up and a sleeping loggia made of it. Many years later, when some construction work was going on there and Peck was present he had workmen remove some construction to try to find the manuscript. They were unsuccessful. He believes that it may still be therein and asked me to endeavor to be present when and if the house is ever razed. This is the most reputable evidence I have ever had on this "lost manuscript" and you may accept it for what it is worth on face value. (Lester G. Wells)

If Crane is the author of the unsigned sketch "Where 'De Gang' Hears the Band Play" (*New York Herald*, 5 July 1891, 21)—which strongly resembles *Maggie* in terms of character, dialect, and setting—it would lend credence to the belief that he was working on his first novel while at Syracuse.

33. See Goodwin (No. 16).

34. Noxon is conflating the time sequence. After privately printing the book in late February–early March 1893, Crane sent a copy to Howells at the suggestion of Hamlin Garland. On April 8 Howells praised it in a letter written to help Crane get work on the *New York Evening Post* (Wertheim and Sorrentino, *Correspondence* 54) and publicly restated his enthusiasm on 8 June 1895 in *Harper's Weekly.*

35. Thomas W. Durston, a bookstore owner in Syracuse and a Goethe enthusiast, introduced Crane to *Faust* and most likely Charles L. Eastlake's translation of Goethe's *Farbenlehre,* which discusses the symbolic use of color.

36. After retiring from the soap business in 1892, Hubbard briefly attended Harvard in 1893.

37. In June 1895 Hubbard and Harry P. Taber founded *The Philistine: A Periodical of Protest,* the most successful of the iconoclastic little magazines of the 1890s. It challenged the conservative literary tastes of the established magazines—*Harper's, Century,* and *McClure's.*

38. Besides cofounding the *Philistine,* Harry Persons Taber (1865–?) established the Roycroft Shop, dedicated to fine printing in the tradition of William Morris's Kelmscott Press. In February 1896, after disagreeing with Hubbard on how to run the journal, Taber and several associates arranged to buy the *Philistine* from Hubbard and to set up a new publishing firm. When Taber met with Crane at the Hotel Imperial in New York to discuss being his publisher, he promised him one of his forthcoming books, probably *The Little Regiment;* but when Hubbard decided to keep the *Philistine,* Taber abandoned

the idea of being a publisher. For more on Taber's involvement with the *Philistine,* see Stallman (1972), 298–301, 310–12, 356–58.

39. By November 1895, with the critical controversy surrounding *The Black Riders and Other Lines* and the acclaim given to *The Red Badge of Courage,* Crane was seen as a rising literary star. To honor him and to publicize his own publishing ventures, Hubbard invited Crane to be the honored guest at a banquet in Buffalo, N.Y., in December hosted by the Society of Philistines. For additional information on the banquet, see Hawkins (No. 37); Bragdon (No. 38); comments by, and about, Harry P. Taber in Stallman's critical bibliography (1972, 242–45, 298–301, 310–12, 356–58); and Sorrentino (1982).

40. See Bragdon (No. 38).

41. Hubbard, who affected the title of "Fra Elbertus," did not pay for contributions to the *Philistine,* telling Crane that "we are not running this little magazine with any hope of a financial return—simply making a plea for liberty in Letters . . . " (Wertheim and Sorrentino, *Correspondence* 114).

42. John Clendenning, a reader for this book, suggested that this may be an allusion to Milton's "Lycidas."

43. Following the *Commodore* incident, Hubbard published a mock obituary of Crane in the February 1897 issue of the *Philistine.* Crane's near-death experience may be the "particularly startling occurrence" that Frederic M. Lawrence alluded to in an 8 November 1923 letter to Thomas Beer: "I recall Noxon's comment after some particularly startling occurrence: 'Oh, Stevie is just making biography for himself'" (Stallman and Gilkes 331)

44. In a 29 June 1934 letter to Mansfield J. French (No. 15), Noxon reiterated the anecdote: " . . . now and again of a Sunday night Crane and I used to attend St. Paul's, sitting in the rear pew. Crane was the son of an Episcopal clergyman and a choir boy. He said he had had such a dose of piety in his youth that the reaction was unfavorable to religious consecration in later years. It was the choir that drew him to St. Paul's."

45. French may also have been interviewed for a newspaper article on Crane's life at Syracuse ("A 'Varsity Boy," *Syracuse Standard,* 26 January 1896, 6). As with French's reminiscence, the article focuses on Crane's love of baseball and dislike of school. For the article see Sorrentino (1985).

46. Crane enrolled in the English literature class and attended Prof. Charles J. Little's class on the French Revolution. Though Syracuse did not give grades at the time, Crane would have had little interest in striving for high grades.

47. A month after the article appeared, French gave Syracuse University a baseball used in a game between Syracuse and Hobart College on 23 May 1891 in which Crane played shortstop. Syracuse lost the game because the centerfielder, named Wright, dropped a fly ball. "Poor Wright was unmercifully upbraided by his teammates. To my great surprise, Steve Crane refrained from saying anything to Wright, probably fearful of a future reprimand that might follow from his senior Fraternity brothers. However, I distinctly remember the look of absolute disgust on Crane's face that, in this instance,

spoke louder than words" (Mansfield J. French, note accompanying a baseball used by Crane).

48. Melvin H. Schoberlin wrote French for biographical information.

49. French is alluding to Max J. Herzberg's introduction to *The Red Badge of Courage* (Herzberg).

50. Herzberg's source for the anecdote about the pennant is a letter from Clarence N. Goodwin (No. 16); however, Herzberg (xiii) does not say that Crane accused French of stealing the pennant.

51. For Mansfield J. French's comment on this anecdote, see French (No. 15).

52. In October 1892 Crane moved into the Pendennis Club, a rooming house at 1064 Avenue A in Manhattan inhabited by a group of medical students. He shared a room with Frederic M. Lawrence (No. 22) overlooking the East River and Blackwell's Island.

53. See Noxon (No. 14).

54. This reminiscence, included in a series of articles dealing with Syracuse in the 1890s, was reprinted in Sorrentino (1985). It is unclear when McMahon wrote the reminiscence.

55. The music hall setting and the name "Madge" offer hints about the composition of *Maggie* (Wertheim and Sorrentino, *Crane Log* 62).

56. McMahon is mistaken; Reverend Crane died in 1880.

57. Crane was nineteen years old when he attended Syracuse.

58. Though not enrolled in a class on the French Revolution at Syracuse, Crane attended the class. See Peaslee (No. 18), n. 46.

59. Wertheim and Sorrentino, *Correspondence* 97. The wording is similar to that in another letter in Wertheim and Sorrentino, *Correspondence* 99. For a discussion of newly discovered letters from Crane to Peaslee, see Wertheim ("Stephen Crane to Clarence Loomis Peaslee").

60. See Travis (No. 11), n. 3.

61. Peaslee's comment may be the basis for Beer's assertion that Crane "sold sketches to the *Detroit Free Press*" (Beer 1923, 57).

62. He was born in 1871.

63. Peaslee's observation about Crane's heritage is echoed in Prof. Charles K. Gaines's published account of his interview of Crane (Gaines). Crane appreciated the account (Wertheim and Sorrentino, *Correspondence* 215) and spoke proudly of his ancestry in a letter to John Northern Hilliard (Wertheim and Sorrentino, *Correspondence* 165–68).

Part 3

1. Garland's three other reminiscences are "Stephen Crane: A Soldier of Fortune," 16–17; "Stephen Crane as I Knew Him," 494–506; and "Roadside Meetings of a Literary Nomad," 523–28.

2. Garland presented a series entitled "Lecture—Studies in American Literature

and Expressive Art" at the Seaside Assembly in Avon, N.J., 11–25 August 1891 (Åhne-brink 442–43).

3. Although Garland states that Crane asked for the notes to the lecture on "the lo-cal novel," he is confusing two lectures. Crane reported on Garland's lecture on William Dean Howells in "Howells Discussed at Avon-by-the-Sea," *New York Tribune,* 18 August in Crane, *Tales, Sketches, and Reports* 507–8. The *Tribune* does not contain a report on Garland's next lecture, "The Local Novel."

In "Stephen Crane: A Soldier of Fortune" there is no mention of Crane's borrow-ing notes, and Garland learns of Crane's identity not from Crane but from Mr. Alberti after the article appears in the *Tribune.* The two accounts, however, may be reconcil-able. Although Garland was "not particularly impressed with [Crane] in this short inter-view" (*Roadside* 189), the published report changed his mind. Perhaps not remembering Crane's name from the previous day, he asked Alberti for it. This explanation would reconcile the two accounts of how Garland got to know Crane's name.

4. At this point Garland is confusing his 1891 trip to Avon with his late August 1892 trip to Asbury Park, when Crane told him that the *Tribune* had fired him because of the recent JOUAM article. See the headnote to Oliver (No. 6).

5. Garland and his brother, Franklin, moved into an apartment at 107 West 105th Street in late December 1893.

6. Whereas this account and the *Yale* and *Bookman* accounts say that Garland re-ceived a published copy of *Maggie* in winter 1892, the *Post* account incorrectly dates the event in summer 1891; however, the book was published late February–early March 1893.

7. Compare Item 22 in Wertheim and Sorrentino, *Correspondence.*

8. In this paragraph and the next, Garland misquotes the opening of *Maggie.*

9. Garland's identification of Crane as the author strongly suggests that he had seen a manuscript version of the novel.

10. The copy sold for $2,100 in 1930. During the same year, an inscribed copy (Wertheim and Sorrentino, *Correspondence* Item 21), advertised as "the rarest book in modern American literature," sold for $3,700. As evidence of what Garland called "the unpredictable trend of literary taste," a copy of *Maggie* auctioned off in 1917 brought only $7.50 (Bruccoli 155).

11. The Art Students League building.

12. Between 10 and 15 March 1894.

13. Following Commodore Matthew Perry's expedition to Japan in 1854, the French became especially interested in Japanese culture.

14. The South African novelist Olive Schreiner (1855–1920) was best known for her novel *The Story of an African Farm* (1883). Crane was attracted to its rebellion against puritanical orthodoxy and its lyrical and innovative style. After reading it, he told Lin-son (1958, 34), "She is a woman of sense and an artist." For the possible influence of Schreiner's work on Crane's poetry, especially her allegorical *Dreams* (1890), see Kin-dilien, and Hoffman.

15. Garland's interest in Crane's assertion that his poems were simply unconscious

projections, composed without effort, owes much to his belief in psychic phenomena. He contributed to the *Psychical Review* and became the second president of the American Psychical Association in January 1892.

16. Garland expressed this sentiment to Crane by inscribing a copy of *Prairie Songs* "To Stephen Crane, a genius. Hamlin Garland" (Linson 1958, 81). The date would have been around the third week of April 1894, when Crane was showing him the manuscript of *The Red Badge*.

17. Garland's recognition of Crane's originality is similar to his assertion in *Crumbling Idols* that the new writers of America did not imitate the literary masters of the past. This would suggest another reason for Crane's indebtedness to Garland—and thus his dedication of *The Black Riders* to him—as an important inspiration for his poetry.

18. The *Yale Review* reminiscence identifies the poem as "I stood musing in a black world."

19. That is, 21 or 22 April 1894.

20. Despite inconsistencies in Garland's reminiscences, he maintained from the outset that the manuscript was untitled when he first saw it. See Garland's 1900 reminiscence in the *Saturday Evening Post* (17) and his December 19 [1923 or 1924] letter to Beer, in which he reiterates that "[t]he novel was not named at all when I read it first."

21. Carroll (No. 29) recalled an amount of twenty-five dollars.

22. Crane returned with the second half of the manuscript on 24 April.

23. Garland penciled in corrections and word changes and questioned the inconsistent use of dialect. In late April Crane revised the manuscript by substituting epithets for names ("the loud soldier" for Wilson and "the tall soldier" for Conklin), making stylistic changes, and recasting the dialect—though this recasting is inconsistent—and changing the title from "Private Fleming/His Various Battles" to "The Red Badge of Courage/An Episode of the American Civil War."

Besides these revisions, Crane made others: deleting chapter 12 in the manuscript as well as the endings of chapters 7, 10, and the original chapter 15. The timing of these excisions as well as the exclusion in the 1895 edition of the novel of uncanceled passages in the manuscript has led to much critical debate. Did Crane revise the manuscript on his own accord, or did his Appleton editor, Ripley Hitchcock, pressure him into making changes? If the latter, did Hitchcock see the manuscript or a typescript made from it? For a summary of the arguments, see Wertheim and Sorrentino, *Crane Log* 104–5.

24. Garland gave Crane "a letter to a Syndicate Press Company [i.e., S. S. McClure's syndicate], and with them he had left the manuscript of his war novel" (Garland 1900, 17). In early January 1894 Garland had sent Crane to McClure once before with a recommendation that he hire him as a writer.

25. Most likely "An Ominous Baby" (*Arena* [May 1894]: 819–21) and "The Men in the Storm" (*Arena* [October 1894]: 37–48). Benjamin Orange Flower, editor of the *Arena,* a crusading journal devoted to social amelioration, published a number of Garland's articles and stories. That Garland, rather than Crane, mailed the sketches suggests that Crane's statement in April 1893 to Lily Brandon Monroe, an unhappily married women with whom Crane was in love—that Flower "has practically offered me the

benefits of his publishing company for all that I may in future write" (Wertheim and Sorrentino, *Correspondence* 55)—was an attempt to impress her.

26. See Bacheller (No. 31).

27. Garland's 1900 reminiscence adds details concerning the discussion about "the bread lines":

> "Why don't you go down and do a study of this midnight bread distribution which the papers are making so much of? Mr. Howells suggested it to me, but it isn't my field. It is yours. You could do it beyond anybody."
> "I might do that," he said; "it interests me."

Sometime after 26 February 1894, when Crane observed a breadline during a heavy snow, he recorded the experience in "The Men in the Storm." See also Linson (No. 21).

28. *Arena* 8 (June 1893): xi–xii. The French novel is Paul Bourget's *Cosmopolis*.

29. The only other review of *Maggie* in 1893 appeared earlier on 13 March in the *Port Jervis Union* (Gullason, "The First Known Review" 301).

30. Garland slightly revised the wording in the original review. Of special interest are his additional comments in the review. Garland recognized in Crane "almost unlimited resource" and contrasted his *"technique"* and view of New York with that of Richard Harding Davis in *Van Bibber and Others* (1892), which depicted the lighthearted adventures of a handsome socialite in high society. As wartime correspondents, both would continue to be compared in terms of technique and point of view.

Garland praised *Maggie* because "it voices the blind rebellion of Rum Alley and Devil's Row . . . [and] creates the atmosphere of the jungles," but it "fails of rounded completeness. It is only a fragment. It is typical only of the worst elements of the alley. The author should delineate the families living on the next street, who live lives of heroic purity and hopeless hardship." Garland may have discussed his criticism with Crane before the review appeared, for Crane began writing *George's Mother*, a novel that strives for "rounded completeness," in late March 1893. Unable to complete it and almost penniless because of the printing of his first novel, he decided to write a potboiler to make money quickly. The potboiler would evolve into *The Red Badge of Courage*.

31. Barry sent them to Copeland and Day in early April 1894.

32. Garland saw Crane occasionally in early 1894 before leaving for Chicago in April.

33. Wertheim and Sorrentino, *Correspondence* 68–69. Garland, not Crane, was in Chicago.

34. *George's Mother*.

35. Gerhart Hauptmann's dream play, which premiered in New York in 1894.

36. Wertheim and Sorrentino, *Correspondence* 79.

37. Ibid., 65.

38. Ibid., 94.

39. On 17 June 1895 Crane signed a contract with D. Appleton and Company to publish *The Red Badge of Courage*. The contract stipulated that after Appleton's publication costs were covered, Crane would get a royalty of 10 percent but unlike other Appleton authors would be paid annually, not semiannually; the contract also had no provision for foreign rights. As Katz ("*The Red Badge of Courage* Contract," 5) observes, the contract raises several questions: Did Appleton have little faith in the book, and had Crane's brother William, a lawyer, not given him legal advice? If he did, did Stephen ignore it?

40. The most astute critic was George Wyndham ("A Remarkable Book").

41. Wertheim and Sorrentino, *Correspondence* 259.

42. Ibid., 260.

43. The Dora Clark affair.

44. Crane and Conrad first met on 15 October 1897. See Joseph Conrad (No. 51).

45. Moreton Frewen.

46. Garland implies he is quoting from his 1900 *Post* reminiscence. In actuality, he quotes the final three paragraphs but revises them stylistically, deletes the last sentence in the penultimate paragraph of the *Post* reminiscence—"I have never known a man whose source of power was so unaccounted for"—and adds the paragraph at the end of the *Roadside* account that begins "To send him to report actual warfare was a mistake." In putting this paragraph in quotation marks, Garland implies he wrote it in 1900, when in fact he added it in 1930. The paragraph attributes Crane's "source of power" to his vivid imagination and reiterates his irresponsibility.

Garland remained ambivalent throughout his career about Crane's work and personality, perhaps most clearly reflected in the *Yale Review* reminiscence:

> There was something essentially unwholesome about his philosophy, something bitter, ironic, despairing; and it may be that his work, so powerfully individual, and his diction, so striking and so vivid, worked against his advancement in the end. . . . His work did not change except for the worse. It remained fragmentary and severe. *The Red Badge* in its printed form did not in my judgment have the quality that was in the manuscript which came to me in the boy's pocket. . . . A strange, short-lived, marvellous boy! He never seemed to be other than a boy to me. He never arrived at full responsibility and citizenship. He was a genius, as erratic as he was unaccountable, a rocket whose very speed assisted in the wasting of his substance, and yet the work he did will live long in the libraries of those who esteem the man who is able to create original characters and to make old words seem new (504–6).

For additional comments by Garland on Crane, see Garland, *A Son of the Middle Border* 441–42; Pizer, *Hamlin Garland's Diaries* 121; Monteiro, "A Capsule Assessment of Stephen Crane by Hamlin Garland"; and Garland's "Recollection of Stephen Crane" in

Wertheim, *Studies in* Maggie *and* George's Mother 4–5. For an analysis of the relationship between the two writers, see Pizer, "The Garland-Crane Relationship"; Mane, "Une recontre littéraire: Hamlin Garland et Stephen Crane"; and Wertheim, "Crane and Garland."

47. Linson (1958, 13) later recalled Crane's use of humor to alleviate frustration at his inability to sell his work and to see the drivel being published. When one of Crane's illustrator-roommates showed him the pulp fiction he was illustrating, Crane responded, "It seems that my opinions and the opinions of the powers that pay for this stuff are not in agreement. Else I would be asking you out to dinner at the Astor House." Crane poked fun at his impoverished condition by writing the poem "Ah, haggard purse, why ope thy mouth" in the tradition of Chaucer. "He wrote it in my studio and then crumpled it up and threw it in a waste basket. I rescued it . . . " ("An Artist in His Hilltop Aerie" 1).

48. "We took to each other immediately and from that time he was a daily visitor" ("An Artist in His Hilltop Aerie" 1).

49. Crane complained, "no one would sell it, not even the jays who otherwise would sell their souls for a nickel" (Linson 1958, 21).

50. Crane told Linson,

> I sent copies to some preachers who were maniacs for reform—not a word from one of 'em.
>
> I wrote across the cover [see Wertheim and Sorrentino, *Crane Log* 89] so they couldn't miss it, that if they read it, they would see its sense. I knew they'd jump at first, but I hoped they were intelligent. You'd think the book came straight from hell and they smelled the smoke. Not one of them gave me a word! Icebergs, CK, flints! (Linson 1958, 21)

When a woman challenged Crane about his intention in the book, he retorted, "you can't find preaching on any page of *Maggie*! An artist has no business to preach. . . . A story must have a reason, but art is—oh, well, not a pulpit" (Linson 1958, 21, 18).

51. Howells and Garland.

52. Though Garland thought that "[t]he story fails of rounded completeness," it "is the most truthful and unhackneyed study of the slums I have yet read" ("An Ambitious French Novel," xi–xii); and though Howells "could not agree with [Crane] on all points of theory, [he] thoroughly respected [his] literary conscience, and admired [his] literary skill" (Wertheim and Sorrentino, *Correspondence* 54).

53. Late March–April 1893.

54. In Linson's later account of the writing of "The Pace of Youth," Crane explained his headgear: "Yeh! the towel? This thing got me going and I couldn't sleep, so I got up. Been at it all night. A wet towel cools the machinery all right. And I work better at night. I'm all alone in the world. It's great!" (Linson 1958, 29).

55. "'How do you feel all these people so long after you've seen them? It's months since you were down there [Asbury Park].' He smiled. 'Can't you make sketches from

memory? Of course. Well, haven't I known these types since I was a kid? Certainly'"
(Linson 1958, 28).

56. "The Reluctant Voyagers."

57. For another example of the vagaries of the publishing industry, given by Linson's cousin Walter Corwin Senger, see Linson 1958, 90.

58. After Crane submitted "The Reluctant Voyagers" to a magazine, the publisher held it for six months, then returned it for minor revisions. When it was resubmitted, the publisher lost Linson's illustrations. The story remained unpublished until 1900 (Linson 1958, 18–20).

59. Between November 1884 and November 1887, the *Century Magazine* published the series "Battles and Leaders of the Civil War," which included graphic accounts of the Battle of Chancellorsville and the series titled "Recollections of a Private"; all the articles were subsequently published in four volumes by the Century Publishing Company. See Linson 1958, 36–38.

60. "An Ominous Baby," "A Great Mistake," and "A Dark-Brown Dog."

61. At the Art Students League building, 27 February 1894.

62. See Garland (No. 20) and Linson 1958, 58, 62–63.

63. Linson was now living in a studio on West 22nd Street near Sixth Avenue.

64. Later Linson gave a more detailed summary of the events, which included comments by the painter Emile Stangé (1863–1943) on Crane (Linson 1958, 48–53). Stangé's reminiscence is not extant.

65. Frederic M. Lawrence (No. 22) and Lucius Button also attended the Uncut Leaves Society event on 14 April 1894. Besides John D. Barry's reading of several of Crane's lines, other works were read by the guest of honor Francis Hodgson Burnett, Kate Jordan, and Gilbert Parker (Linson 1958, 54–56).

66. Linson (1958, 52) cited the parody, written by one of Crane's roommates. Following the publication of *The Black Riders,* Crane's poetry elicited a number of parodies called "stephencranelets."

67. Linson (1958, 52) later clarified the statement: "The mutts yowl like bobcats when I try to write, but I'll get my innings. I'll put 'em in a book [i.e., *The Third Violet*], the lobsters. They're a husky lot."

68. The Boeuf-a-la-mode on Sixth Avenue, also known as the Buffalo Mud (Linson 1958, 16).

69. Linson's landscape painting later displayed in a 1926 Society of American Artists Show (Richter). It is unclear whether it was being displayed in another show in 1903, the date of the reminiscence.

70. Crane's harsh criticism of the Pennsylvania coal mines, "In the Depths of a Coal Mine," appeared in *McClure's Magazine* in August 1894; Linson illustrated it. See Linson 1958, 64–70.

71. "Steve used to borrow from me, tho I had mighty little myself. They were only small amounts, ranging mostly from a nickel to a quarter or half dollar. I remember once when I was strapped and Steve owed me a half dollar. He came in, fussed around a bit, smoked a lot of cigarets and then started to leave.

" 'Hey, Steve,' I called, 'have you got anything?'

" '*Not* a red, Ceek, not a red,' and off he went.

" 'Ceek' was my nickname, derived from my initials C and K" ("An Artist in His Hilltop Aerie" 14).

72. Linson (1958, 87–89) recalled Crane's adventure in Mexico that led to the short story "One Dash—Horses," but it is unclear to what extent he was influenced by Beer's fictionalized account (Beer 1923, 116–17) of the same adventure. For Beer as Linson's source for the name of the person who gave Crane opals in Mexico, see Sorrentino (2003, 192).

73. The Lantern Club, 7 April 1895, according to Linson (1958, 89n).

74. When Linson was surprised to hear this, Crane responded, " 'You might have had the lot but I wasn't sure you wanted 'em.' So like him!—and he chanted [a parody of a current song:]

I had fifteen pebbles in my inside pocket,
Don't you know, I gave you warnin'—
I wint to make a call
On my friends, who took them all,
An' divil a pebble had I in th' morning'! (Linson 1958, 89)

During an interview Linson recalled Crane's penchant for singing and another version of the song: "Steve was quiet rather than melancholy when I knew him. He was always cheerful and would sit and sing to himself as he worked. One of his favorite songs, as I recall it, went something like this: 'I went to make a call upon a man of Tammany hall and devil a cent had I in the morning'" ("An Artist in His Hilltop Aerie" 14).

75. That is, 14–15 March 1897.

76. Crane asked Linson, who had recently returned from covering the first modern Olympic Games in Greece, "Willie Hearst is sending me for the war. What I'll do among those Dagoes I don't know. What are they like, CK? How did you chin their lingo?" (Linson 1958, 99)

77. For additional comments on their last evening together, see Linson (1958, 99–102). Linson's letter to Thomas Beer in Stallman and Gilkes (326–28) discusses the evening, during which Crane told Linson "he was intending to marry a girl and go to England, giving me to understand that she had suffered from unfortunate circumstances," as well as other details pertaining to Crane.

78. L. S. Linson was captain of Company D in the 71st Infantry Regiment, New York Volunteers. Later he told his brother about "how animated and jolly [Crane] appeared, the spirit of the fighter in him. When I met him in your studio he seemed of an entirely different disposition, rather somber" (Linson 1958, 106).

79. A different version of this reminiscence was published as *The Real Stephen Crane*, edited by Joseph Katz (Lawrence 1980). Lawrence also briefly discussed Crane in two letters to Thomas Beer (Stallman and Gilkes 331–33).

80. Actually, 1891.

81. Easton, Pa., location of Lafayette College.

82. See Oliver (No. 6), n. 49.

83. See Noxon (No. 14), who also recalls that *St. Nicholas* rejected the story.

84. Lawrence went into greater detail in his 20 November 1923 letter to Thomas Beer:

> The plain truth is that Crane, in spite of his devotion to realism in literature, was incurably romantic about women, and this extended even to the girl of the streets. Many unkind things said about him were justifiable, for he was absolutely irresponsible in money matters; but whatever the stories about women, you can always find in Crane's behavior a curious trace of chivalry. If you know the real story of "Mrs." Crane, you will find it there—but I can readily understand why no biography came from her hand. Crane lived with Mayhew the year after I left New York, and that was, I fancy, his wildest period. (Stallman and Gilkes 333)

For information about Mayhew, see Greene (No. 23), n. 140.

85. Syracuse University is situated on a hill overlooking the city.

86. Professor of history and logic at Syracuse University (1885–91) and later president of the Garrett Biblical Institute, Evanston, Illinois. See Wertheim and Sorrentino, *Correspondence* Letters 459 and 474.

87. Jonathan Townley Crane Jr. began operating a summer news agency in Asbury Park, N.J., for the *New York Tribune* and the Associated Press in 1880.

88. Louis C. Senger Jr. and Louis E. Carr Jr.

89. Lawrence is the "pudgy man" in the Sullivan County tales; the "tall man" is modeled after Senger; the "little man" is Crane; and the "quiet man" is a composite of Crane and Carr.

90. The first Sullivan County tale, "Four Men in a Cave," appeared in the *New York Tribune* on 3 July 1892; "The Octopush" appeared on 10 July.

91. See Crane, *Tales, Sketches, and Reports* pt. 2.

92. Crane, with Senger's cooperation (Katz 1983), wrote *The Pike County Puzzle,* a four-page humorous mock newspaper based on their camping experiences and the return trip. Dated 28 August 1894, it was privately printed by the *Port Jervis Union.*

93. The publication of "A Tent in Agony" in *Cosmopolitan* marks Crane's first appearance in a popular magazine.

94. Because this paragraph follows a discussion about the *Pike County Puzzle,* the chronology is misleading. "A Tent in Agony" appeared in 1892 when, as Lawrence says, "Crane was twenty-one"; the *Pike County Puzzle* appeared in 1894.

95. Formerly known as Eastern Boulevard, Avenue A is now the site for Sutton Place.

96. Named after Thackeray's novel *Pendennis.* In a letter to Lester G. Wells, Lawrence stated that Crane suggested the title "Pendennis Club" (Lawrence 1953).

97. See Hamlin Garland (No. 20).

98. In an 8 November 1923 letter Lawrence told Thomas Beer that *Maggie* and

George's Mother were based on his and Crane's "own observations and adventures" (Stallman and Gilkes 331).

99. Located at 34th and Broadway, Koster and Bial's music hall was a popular entertainment center in New York City. The Vitascope movie projector made its debut there on 23 April 1896.

100. French phrase for "comic opera."

101. Carmencita, a belly dancer, was immortalized in Edison's short film *Carmencita Dancing.* Considered scandalous at the time, the film led to early discussions of film censorship.

102. The leading comedy team of the day, Weber and Fields opened the Weber and Fields Music Hall on Broadway in 1896.

103. Loie Fuller (1862–1928) revolutionized dance by experimenting with electric light, mirrors, and silk to portray things in nature. In the 1890s her choreographic highlights were the "Serpentine Dance" (1891), "Butterfly" (1892), "Clouds" (1893), "Lily" (1895), and "Fire" (1895). By the time Crane and Lawrence would have seen her, she had been a star with the Folies Bergère; she would become the personification of art nouveau.

104. Although Goodwin (No. 16) and Lawrence date the composition of *Maggie* to the autumn of 1892, Peaslee (No. 18) and Noxon (No. 14) recall a draft of the novel written in spring 1891.

105. Although Lawrence suggests that Crane wanted to disguise the authorship of a book that would offend his family, Wheeler (No. 5) recalls proposing the nom de plume as a joke; Johnson (No. 7) states that Crane took the two most common surnames in the New York City directory and added a "t" to the first one; Linson (No. 21) recalls that Crane based the name "Johnston" on an editor friend (in all likelihood Willis Fletcher Johnson).

106. See Johnson (No. 7), n. 66.

107. Ferdinand Ward, known as the "young Napoleon of finance," and Ulysses S. Grant Jr. formed a brokerage firm that included Grant's father, former President Grant, as a silent partner. In 1884 the firm collapsed as a result of Ward's embezzlement. The catastrophe damaged the Grant family's reputation and left them bankrupt.

108. Though largely ignored by the literary establishment, *Maggie* was reviewed in Crane's hometown newspaper, *Port Jervis Union,* on 13 March 1893, 3; Hamlin Garland's review, "An Ambitious French Novel and a Modest American Story," appeared in June in the *Arena* (8 [June 1893]: xi–xii).

109. The price of fifty cents was printed on the front wrapper. According to John Winterich, "This was high for a day when the newsstands were thick with novels in wrappers at twenty-five and ten cents each—novels much longer than 'Maggie,' and written by men and women much better known than Johnston Smith" (Winterich 1305).

110. Chapters 8 and 9 in *George's Mother.* Linson (1958, 27) adds additional details about the party: "Steve was ever fond of the hum and twang of a guitar. He began thrumming chords, and soon the 'Indians' were chanting to the rhythmic pound of a war dance. It was near midnight when from below came a warm protest: 'One couldn't

sleep down stairs; one rented rooms to gentlemen, not animals.' The sarcasm caught Steve's fancy. He called through the door while waving a frantic hand behind, compelling quiet, 'The animals apologize and will return to their cages at once!' And to us, 'Cheese it!" We did. After all, we were not rowdies, just youthfully forgetful of the world. I think that even the abused landlady had forgotten us within the week." Linson also states that Brentano's bookstore accepted twelve copies of *Maggie* but sold only two; that Mrs. Armstrong, who had spanked Stephen when he was a child, had several hundred copies; and that Jennie Cregan (spelled "Creegan" by Beer), the maid in the boarding-house, had used copies of the book to start a fire; but the source for these anecdotes is Beer's biography (1923, 91, 97, 102, 93–94).

111. It appeared in the 18 March 1893 issue of the weekly humor magazine *Truth*.

112. In 1894.

113. The Bacheller, Johnson, and Bacheller newspaper syndicate commissioned Crane to write feature articles while traveling through the West and Mexico. Crane left New York for the trip on 28 January 1895. See Katz (1970, ix–xxv) for an account of the trip.

114. Cather (No. 39) and a telegram from the Bacheller, Johnson, and Bacheller syndicate (Wertheim and Sorrentino, *Correspondence* 102) support the belief that Crane constantly ran out of money on the trip.

115. Lawrence's chronology is incorrect in this paragraph. Although he states that Crane went to Fredericksburg, Virginia, before he finished *The Red Badge,* the trip occurred in January 1896. The McClure Syndicate had asked Crane to tour Civil War battlefields for a projected, but not completed, series of historical pieces on the major battles. The "Civil War article" referred to by Lawrence is the short story "The Little Regiment," which Crane began writing before leaving on the trip.

116. Lawrence is the only source for the statement that Crane visited Civil War battlefields before writing *The Red Badge:* "I remember also his first trip to Fredericksburg and other Virginia towns[,] his delight in the reminiscences of the old soldiers whom he met there and his determination to write a real story of the Civil War . . . " (Stallman and Gilkes 332). If Lawrence is correct, the trip most likely occurred in spring–summer 1893.

117. See Bacheller (No. 31).

118. A department store in Philadelphia.

119. Sometime in early October 1895.

120. Crane's Revolutionary War namesake (1709–80) served two terms as a delegate from New Jersey to the Continental Congress in Philadelphia. He was captured by the British in June 1780 around the time of the Battle of Springfield and died of bayonet wounds.

121. One of the Revolutionary Stephen's sons, Jonathan, was also killed around the time of the Battle of Springfield for refusing to reveal the location of General Washington's army.

122. In April 1896 Crane moved back into the studio apartment he shared with Post Wheeler at 165 West 23rd Street.

123. See Linson (No. 21), n. 68.

124. Lawrence is confusing two or more dinners. The Lantern Club hosted dinners honoring Crane on 7 April and 22 September 1896 (the latter also honoring Garland and Abraham Cahan). The Philistine Society honored him on 19 December 1895.

125. The reminiscence is now back in 1895; *The Black Riders* was published in May.

126. "In the Depths of a Coal Mine" was syndicated by McClure in a number of newspapers under different headlines on 22 July 1894 and appeared in August in *McClure's Magazine* with Corwin Knapp Linson's illustrations.

127. Less than a month before his death, Crane said to Robert Barr: "Robert, when you come to the hedge—that we must all go over—it isn't bad. You feel sleepy—and— you don't care. Just a little dreamy curiosity—which world you're really in—that's all" (Wertheim and Sorrentino, *Crane Log* 440).

128. Lawrence had moved to Philadelphia in 1895.

129. Crane arranged with the Bacheller, Johnson, and Bacheller syndicate to send him to Cuba to report on the growing insurrection.

130. The 4 September reminiscence is not strictly chronological; Greene divided it into three parts of unequal length covering his early experiences with Crane at the old Art Students League building, the dating of *The Red Badge,* and the later experiences at the building. This reminiscence and the second one sent to Schoberlin were reprinted with an extended introduction and additional supplementary material in 1998 (Sorrentino, "Nelson Greene's Reminiscences").

131. That is, R. G. Vosburgh (No. 24).

132. Crane re-created the setting in *The Third Violet,* which included "the tousled bed . . . a little dead stove and the wonderful table." Visitors sat "upon the divan, which was privately a coal box" (Crane, *The Third Violet* 63, 103).

133. Crane had spent most of the summer working on *The Red Badge of Courage* at his brother Edmund's home in Lake View, N.J.

134. See Carroll (No. 29).

135. Another reference to Crane's lack of a jacket and pants is in Beer's biography (1923, 96), the only source for the assertion that John Northern Hilliard lent Crane a suit to attend a dinner party given by Howells. Whether Greene's statement that he, not Hilliard, lent Crane clothing is a silent correction of Beer's text or a reference to another incident is uncertain.

136. It is unclear whether Beer influenced Greene's memory concerning Crane's political affiliation. In his biography Beer quotes Crane as supposedly saying that he "was a Socialist for two weeks but when a couple of Socialists assured me I had no right to think differently from any other Socialist and then quarrelled with each other about what Socialism meant, I ran away" (1923, 205–6). Crane was ambivalent about politics. Although he asked Wickham W. Young on 21 October 1895 to vote for his brother William Howe Crane in an upcoming election, two days later he wrote, "I hate to monkey about politics." Within a few months, however, he was in Washington, D.C., thinking about writing a political novel (Wertheim and Sorrentino, *Correspondence* 125–26; Wertheim and Sorrentino, *Crane Log* 177).

Although none of Crane's other friends mentions his interest in politics, Greene recalled in the first reminiscence (Wertheim 1976, 52) that he and Crane were "the 'radicals'" during political discussions. Greene's assertion that Crane was a Socialist is not that surprising, given the attitude toward socialism in nineteenth-century America. Although the term *socialism* has historically been applied to various reforms, socialists in the nineteenth century, initially responding to the social and economic dislocation caused by the industrial revolution, criticized an acquisitive society fueled by capitalism. In 1871 the Socialist Labor Party was founded in the United States and became a national organization soon after journalist Daniel De Leon joined in 1890. Crane's depiction of poverty in the Bowery is certainly in line with the socialist thinking of his literary fathers, Hamlin Garland and William Dean Howells, as well as a number of other writers and journalists of the time, including Mark Twain. It is thus conceivable that Crane would have explored socialism; however, his distrust of institutions and easy solutions—as well as the growing intolerance of De Leon, who, unable to compromise with other union leaders, established his own organization, the Socialist Trade and Labor Alliance, in 1895—would have made Crane ironically aware that socialist reformers could be as intolerant as the leaders they were criticizing.

137. Crane's knowledge of French and Russian writers has long been a subject of critical debate and has unfortunately involved information found only in Beer's unreliable biography. Beer is the only source for the statement that a Canadian lady gave Crane a copy of Tolstoy's *Sevastopol*, that he considered him the "world's foremost writer," but that he found *The Kreutzer Sonata* boring and *War and Peace* and *Anna Karenina* too long—the same criticism leveled against Flaubert's *Salammbo* (1923, 54, 55, 111, 143, 157). In writing to Nellie Crouse, however, Crane does speak generally about Tolstoy's "greatness" (Wertheim and Sorrentino, *Correspondence* 203).

Similarly, Beer claims that Crane considered Zola "pretty tiresome" (Wertheim and Sorrentino, *Correspondence* 673) and found *Nana* too long, though Beer's anecdote that *La Débâcle* influenced *The Red Badge of Courage* had been earlier suggested by George Wyndham ("A Remarkable Book") and Ripley Hitchcock (Wertheim and Sorrentino, *Crane Log* 90–91). According to Beer, Crane was tired of being asked "from which French realist I shall steal my next book. For it has been proven to me fully and carefully by authority that all my books are stolen from the French. They stand me against walls with a teacup in my hand and tell me how I have stolen all my things from De Maupassant, Zola, Loti, and the bloke who wrote—I forget the book" (1923, 168). Ford Madox Ford claimed that though Crane denied that "he had . . . read a French book . . . [or] a word of Henry James," he and Crane had discussed the writings of Flaubert, de Maupassant, and James. "But whether either James or the French master had any direct influence on him while he was actually writing I should not care to say. They were, however, so extremely in the air of the New York of that day that he cannot have escaped their indirect influence" (Ford 1927, 1). See also Ford (1937, 35–36; 1966, 110) for similar comments. For a different perspective, see Joseph Conrad's observation that Crane "knew little of literature, either of his own country or of any other" (No. 51).

138. Though color is an important image in *The Black Riders*, Greene may be recall-

ing "Each small gleam was a voice," published elsewhere in the fall (*Philistine* 1 [September 1895], 124), in which Crane describes how "[a] chorus of colors came over the water."

139. Crane's call for originality in American art reappears in *The Third Violet* in Great Grief's satirical comments on American painters' reliance on foreign subject matter: " . . . American subjects are well enough, but hard to find, you know, hard to find. Morocco, Venice, Brittany, Holland—all ablaze with color, you know—quaint form—all that. We are so hideously modern over here. And besides nobody has painted us much. How the devil can I paint America when nobody has done it before me? My dear sir, are you aware that that would be originality?" (Crane, *The Third Violet* 101–2).

140. The incident referring to Eddie Mayhew suggests an alternative reading of an inscription in a copy of *George's Mother:* "To my friend Eddie / in memory of our days / of suffering and trouble / in 27th St. / Stephen Crane / New York City / June 14 [1896]" (Wertheim and Sorrentino, *Correspondence* 236). Although it is plausible to suggest that "Eddie" is Elisha J. Edwards (Wertheim and Sorrentino, *Correspondence* 236 n. 1), the reference may be to Eddie Mayhew. Greene mentions that Mayhew was with a prostitute, and the location that Crane cites in the inscription, 27th Street, was infamous for its brothels. Greene and Crane also allude to "trouble" involving Mayhew.

141. That is, David Ericson (No. 25).

142. See Gordon (No. 26).

143. Edward S. Hamilton.

144. Although Greene misspells Irving Bacheller's last name as "Bachellor" or "Batchellor," I have not silently corrected his mistake because he discusses the matter of spelling this name in his reminiscences.

145. Written for the Bacheller, Johnson, and Bacheller Syndicate, "An Experiment in Misery" was published in the *New York Press,* 22 April 1894. See Carroll (No. 29) for Carroll's account of the experience.

146. Crane's friends disagreed about the extent of his sexual experience. For a sample of opinions, see Levenson (xxi). See also a letter from Crane to Armistead Borland (Wertheim and Sorrentino, *Correspondence* 44) and Harry B. Smith (No. 36).

147. Crane began writing *The Red Badge of Courage* in June 1893 and was working on it and his poetry during autumn 1893–spring 1894.

148. Crane intended *The Red Badge* as a potboiler in order to make money quickly and later confessed that he preferred *The Black Riders* to the war novel because it was a "more ambitious effort. In it I aim to give my ideas of life as a whole, so far as I know it, and [*The Red Badge*] is a mere episode,—an amplification" (Wertheim and Sorrentino, *Crane Log* 91–92, 181).

149. Elsewhere in the letter Greene wrote that June was the month.

150. Unlike the earlier reminiscence (Wertheim 1976, 51), in which Greene cites only Crane's father, here he suggests that the sword might have belonged to Crane's uncle.

151. Florinda is characterized as having a "stunning figure—stunning" in *The Third Violet* (Crane, *The Third Violet* 96).

152. Compare Greene's inference that Crane also thought that "A Grey Sleeve" (nor-

malized to read "A Gray Sleeve" in some newspapers) was good with Crane's ambivalent comments to Nellie Crouse on the story. On the one hand, he wrote her, "It is not in any sense a good story and the intolerable pictures [i.e., newspaper illustrations] make it worse" and called the two main characters "a pair of idiots"; on the other hand, he recognized "there is something charming in their childish faith in each other. That is all I intended to say" (Wertheim and Sorrentino, *Correspondence* 171, 180). Crane's shift in position was part of his attempt to woo Crouse. For a discussion of Crane's relationship with Crouse in the light of "A Grey Sleeve," see Sorrentino ("Stephen Crane's Struggle with Romance in *The Third Violet*").

153. Bacheller syndicated a shortened version of *The Red Badge of Courage* in early December 1894. In early February 1895 Ripley Hitchcock wrote Crane to say that Appleton's wanted to publish the novel, and Crane signed a contract on 17 June, about a month after returning from his western trip.

154. Founded in spring 1895, the Lantern Club (also spelled "Lanthorn" and "Lanthorne") included among its members—besides Crane and Bacheller, who served as president—Richard Watson Gilder, Willis Brooks Hawkins, Edward Marshall, and Post Wheeler. They met weekly to discuss their work and literary issues.

155. Accompanying the 1944 reminiscence, which is in the Newark (N.J.) Public Library is a 1 October 1944 letter to Max Herzberg that contains Greene's sketch of Crane entitled "Steve Crane writing the 'Grey Sleeve' in my studio in New York City 1894." See fig. 4.

156. Pike appeared in the *Century Magazine* in several of Charles Dana Gibson's illustrations dealing with young artists in Paris.

157. For additional information on Crane's relationship with the Pike brothers, see Wertheim and Sorrentino, *Crane Log* 135–36.

158. In one of his two 19 October letters (a three-page letter in Greene, Correspondence) to Schoberlin, Greene drew a floor plan of rooms and studios in the old league building and offered a source for the scene in *The Third Violet* in which Hawker, Hollanden, and three or four "swells"—slang for a fashionably dressed person, one of whom is Grace Fanhall—return to Hawker's studio. The other occupants in the building quietly try to listen to the activity in the studio and plan, as soon as Hawker and his friends leave, to "sneak down the hall to the little unoccupied room at the front of the building and look from the window there. When they go out we can pipe 'em off" (Crane, *The Third Violet* 103). Greene wrote that the

incident . . . I am sure had its origin in some of the "doings" at the "den" as Steve calls it—a rather complimentary name for such an awful dump.

The actual incident was tawdry and sordid but I think you might possibly be interested—with regard to happenings that Steve twisted about and put in his writings.

On page [Crane, *The Third Violet* 102–3], is recounted the coming of Hawker's girl and a friend and another girl to Hawker's studio "across the corridor"—it was "upstairs" in reality. In it he tells how the "gang" in the "den" waited until

Hawker and his party went downstairs and then the gang rushed to "the little unoccupied room at the front of the building" and from there, piped off Hawker's girl as she left the door with the party.

Now an actual incident but not a nice one occurred in which the gang did just that.

It was like this.

The den was one-half of what had been the Chase still life room, where I and other students got a try out on still life before we went into Chase's skylight studio to paint from the model—as I also did.

The "den" was at the extreme east of the building, as per diagram. [Greene drew the floor plan at this point in the letter.]

The actual incident happened in the winter of 1894–1895—cold rainy day— gang was inside on a Sunday morning. The studio marked with a * [a studio next to the den] was leased by a small short stout man, who was seldom there. Gang said he got it for a woman once in a while. He didn't know or speak to gang. One Sunday morning, we heard his door open and heard his voice and a woman's. Of course we were all ears. He evidently had a bed or cot close to our wall and al- though things were pretty quiet we heard the goings on—squeaking of springs etc.

I think I prevented the boys from banging on the wall and making bawdy howls. We heard talk after things quieted down—but nothing I could understand except the woman told the man "you should have worn your rubbers." Then when we heard them thumping down the stairs—with our door open, we ran to the "small unoccupied room"—which had been St Gauden's modeling class room— and rubbered out the window—to little effect as all we could see was the tops of their heads—man and woman—and their backs as they walked to the nearby 3rd Ave and 23rd st L. station.

Pretty sordid but I think it is the father of Steve's incident.

159. Crane incorporates one of the songs, which Wrinkles sings while playing the guitar (Crane, *The Third Violet* 86), into *The Third Violet*.

160. In the novel Sanderson supplements his income by working as a gas fitter and admires a friend who is a plumber.

161. Material in "In a Park Row Restaurant" and "Stories Told by an Artist," which were published in the *New York Press* on 28 October 1894, was revised for inclusion in chapters 19 and 20 of *The Third Violet*. Characters in "The Silver Pageant" also appear in the novel, but the sketch was not published during Crane's lifetime.

162. See Johnson (No. 7), n. 66.

163. That is, 1064 Avenue A (formerly Eastern Boulevard). Crane lived there with a number of medical students, including Frederic M. Lawrence (No. 22); they named the boardinghouse the Pendennis Club.

164. That is, 143.

165. The address of the old Needham Building and the Art Students League, which had recently moved to 57th Street.

166. See Linson (No. 21), n. 59.

167. Crane felt that though he had "never been in a battle . . . [he] got [his] sense of the rage of conflict on the football field" (Wertheim and Sorrentino, *Correspondence* 228, 322).

168. Located on Staten Island, Fort Wadsworth was the oldest continuously manned military installation in America until its closing in 1994. It had been the site of a military installation since the late seventeenth century.

169. In 1893 Crane wrote three stories about an unnamed slum child similar to Tommie, Maggie's little brother who dies as an infant, that were not published till later: "An Ominous Baby" (1894), "A Great Mistake" (1896), and "A Dark-Brown Dog" (1901).

170. Garland (1893).

171. "An Experiment in Misery."

172. W. W. Carroll. See Carroll (No. 29).

173. Though the typescript lacks a salutation, a previously printed version of the letter (Stallman and Gilkes 341–42) makes clear that Ames W. Williams was the recipient. Williams showed the letter to Stallman and Gilkes; however, their printed text contains minor differences in transcription from the text printed here. Because the original letter seems lost, it is uncertain how accurate is the text that Stallman and Gilkes printed. Given a few minor idiosyncrasies in their transcription, I have chosen the typescript as copy-text.

174. Lily Brandon Monroe. Stallman and Gilkes (341 n. 91) claimed that this was an unfinished sketch that was eventually lost.

175. W. W. Carroll. See Carroll (No. 29).

176. Crane and Carroll explored the Bowery in early March 1894.

177. R. G. Vosburgh. See Vosburgh (No. 24).

178. Vosburgh also had the same observation.

179. Given his background as a journalist, Crane knew the importance of producing legible script for a typesetter. The circling of a period was a standard way to identify a period as end punctuation.

180. Possibly an allusion to social gatherings at a restaurant called the Boeuf-a-la-mode. See Linson (No. 21), n. 68.

181. Actually, 1894.

182. "Heard on the Street Election Night." A newspaper clipping in Crane's scrapbook in the Crane collection at Columbia University identifies the newspaper as the *New York Press,* but the edition in which it was published has not been identified. The election alluded to occurred in November 1894.

183. Casa Napoléon was a fictional representation of a hotel near Washington Square frequented by immigrants from Spain, Germany, and France. Thomas Janvier—a journalist, short-story writer, and novelist—wrote a collection of stories, *At the Casa Napoléon* (1914), about the hotel.

184. Gordon is alluding to an apocryphal story about a woman who threw a knife at Crane; Beer fictionalized the rumor in his biography (1923, 134–35). See Sorrentino (2003, 192–95).

185. Stallman and Gilkes (158 n. 140) wrongly attribute to Crane a statement in a

letter from William Dean Howells to Brown quoted in *Contacts:* "I think Tolstoi greater than any other novelist because he is a greater artist. His morality is simply that of Christ" (Brown 249).

186. An untitled manuscript fragment (Crane, *Poems and Literary Remains* 109) in the Crane Collection at Columbia may be the opening paragraph of this New York City sketch. The fragment begins to describe the "dual existence" of Sixth Avenue, a "profoundly busy but profoundly decorous" shopping street by day but a sleazy district by night.

187. See Bacheller (No. 31).

188. The syndicated version of *The Red Badge of Courage* appeared in the *New York Press* on 9 December 1894.

189. See also Travis (No. 11), n. 3 for comments on Crane's reading.

190. Early April 1893.

191. Herford (No. 33) and Harriman (No. 56) also claimed that Crane wrote the poems in three days.

192. Harry Thurston Peck called Crane "the Aubrey Beardsley of poetry" (H. Peck 1895).

193. As did Garland (No. 20) and Oliver (No. 6), Barry believed that Crane was fired as a *Tribune* correspondent because of his satirical article about the Junior Order of the United American Mechanics.

194. The Sullivan County tales and sketches.

195. Stars of the New York Metropolitan Opera.

196. Popular Irish song credited to Maude Nugent after she made it a hit. It was first published in 1896.

197. Crane re-created this experience in *The Third Violet:* "Good Grief had fixed the coffee to boil on the gas stove, but he had to watch it closely, for the rubber tube was short and a chair was balanced on a trunk and two bundles of kindling were balanced on the chair and the gas stove was balanced on the kindling. Coffee-making was here accounted a feat" (Crane, *The Third Violet* 64).

198. Though it is unclear when precisely Crane wrote "Black riders came from the sea," he had written an early version by late September 1894 and revised it the following month.

199. Garland (No. 20) recalled an amount of fifteen dollars.

200. See "An Experiment in Misery."

201. Founded in England in 1869, the Charity Organization Society movement quickly spread to America and attempted to systematically address issues created by poverty.

202. The prototype for "the assassin" in "An Experiment in Misery." American author and illustrator Howard Pyle was especially known for his contributions to children's literature.

203. Carroll is alluding to Conrad's introduction to Beer's biography. See Conrad (No. 51).

204. Elisha J. "Holland" Edwards, "Society Leaders' Suffrage Crusade," *Philadelphia*

Press, 22 April 1894, 5 (LaFrance). A reporter for the *New York Press,* Edwards occasionally provided Crane with a place to sleep in New York in his room on West 27th Street during 1892–93. Edwards describes Crane's disappointment in being unable to sell his work and his considering becoming a cobbler. Although LaFrance dates Crane's disappointment as March–April 1893, Edwards's statement that Howells was about to praise Crane in print seems to refer to Edward Marshall's 1894 interview of Howells in "Greatest Living American Writer [Howells]," *New York Press,* 15 April 1894, 2.

205. The "Publisher's Note" to the 1896 Appleton edition of *Maggie* offered another source for this assertion: "The story was put into type and copyrighted by Mr. Crane three years ago . . . " (vi).

206. The Uncut Leaves Society. See the headnote to Barry (No. 28).

207. Besides the *Philadelphia Press,* the Bacheller, Johnson, and Bacheller syndicate arranged for its publication in at least six other newspapers nationwide.

208. The correct wording is as follows: "Stephen Crane is a new name now and unknown, but everybody will be talking about him if he goes on as he has begun in this staving [*sic*] story" (LaFrance 196).

209. Bacheller had written a shortened version of his reminiscence in 1921 for the Newark Public Library's celebration of the fiftieth anniversary of Crane's birth. See Stallman and Gilkes 322–23.

210. Edward Marshall (No. 44).

211. At the suggestion of Marshall, in mid-October 1894, Crane brought the manuscript of *The Red Badge* to Bacheller, whose newspaper syndicate began service on October 29.

212. Crane gave the manuscript to S. S. McClure for publication either through the McClure newspaper syndicate or in the newly formed *McClure's Magazine.* McClure kept the manuscript for six months and remained noncommittal about its status apparently because of financial concerns. Bacheller later wrote, "At least two magazines had declined it" (Bacheller, *From Stores of Memory* 110).

213. Although Garland (No. 20) had lent Crane fifteen dollars in April to have the second half of his manuscript typed, Bacheller saw a manuscript version. His interest in it prompted Crane to ask his fraternity brother John Henry Dick for fifteen dollars to pay for a typescript of the serialized version of *The Red Badge.* Crane's 29 October 1897 letter to his brother William, in which he recalled his habitual borrowing of money—"I believe the sum I usually borrowed was fifteen dollars, wasnt it? Fifteen dollars—fifteen dollars—fifteen dollars. I can remember an interminable row of fifteen dollar requests"—makes clear that Crane was constantly in debt (Wertheim and Sorrentino, *Correspondence* 80, 302).

214. To Bacheller, "One fact surprised me. Here and there I observed that Crane's sense of diction was, more or less, indifferent to grammatical rules. The slips were not glaring. . . . I have learned that he had been a poor student" (Bacheller, *From Stores of Memory* 110).

215. Around the end of October 1894 Bacheller started a "six day serial service" that supplied newspapers with stories of four thousand to fifteen thousand words and ar-

ranged with the A. N. Kellogg Newspaper Company in Chicago to prepare the actual copy for distribution. Years later Wright A. Patterson, an editor for Kellogg, claimed that when he received the manuscript of *The Red Badge,* it "began with a lower case letter, and continued page after page without a break of any kind; no punctuation; no beginning or end of sentences; no paragraphs; no capital letters. It was just one continuous flow of words, that, at first reading were unintelligible." If his detailed description of the manuscript is correct, he obviously was not referring to *The Red Badge* manuscript at the University of Virginia Library. For the text of Patterson's reminiscence and a questioning of its reliability, see Katz ("An Editor's Recollection"). See also Fredson Bowers's comment in the University Press of Virginia edition of *The Red Badge of Courage* (206 n. 31).

216. The syndicated version of the novel appeared in at least seven newspapers nationally.

217. Williams later became dean of the Columbia University School of Journalism.

218. Before 15 December 1894.

219. While waiting to see Williams, Bacheller was impressed with "Crane's excitement over [Rudyard] Kipling's ballads. His favorite was 'The Young British Soldier.' Two or three times, as we sat together, he repeated four of its lines and talked of their content. In this vivid flash was the spirit of an empire:

When you're wounded and left on Afghanistan's plains,
And the women come out to cut up what remains,
Jest roll to your rifle and blow out your brains
An' go to your Gawd like a soldier." (Bacheller, *From Stores of Memory* 111)

220. Bacheller later wrote to Cora Crane that "the editor of a great magazine invited Steve and me to visit him one morning. I went to introduce the newcomer. They were all sending for him those days—men who would not have wiped their old shoes on him before then—precieuses of literature. 'Why did you not give us a chance at *The Red Badge of Courage?* said the editor. Stephen made some evasive answer but coming away he told me laughing that he had sent it there and got it back 'with thanks'" (Stallman and Gilkes 298–99).

221. This gathering led to the formation of the Lantern Club, a group of journalists who met regularly for lunch and dinner in an old house near the Brooklyn Bridge. For Bacheller's description of a typical gathering, see Wertheim and Sorrentino, *Crane Log* 132–33.

222. Crane joined the Lantern Club in mid-May 1895 after returning from Mexico. Because other members were shrewd poker players, Bacheller "warned him not to play poker with the boys but he had to get his trimming, and he did. What a guileless, gentle, lovable country boy he was! The Lanthornites were all fond of him. He was their hero" (Bacheller, *From Stores of Memory* 111).

223. Between January–May 1895 Crane traveled to the West and Mexico to write feature articles for Bacheller's syndicate, which published more than twenty of them.

224. Crane left New York for Jacksonville on November 27; Amy Traphagen (also known as "Amy Leslie"), accompanied him as far as Washington, D.C.

225. Crane met Cora Taylor in Jacksonville. Contrary to inferences by contemporaries, no evidence supports the assertion that Cora and Stephen married.

226. Sylvester Scovel, head of the *New York World*'s delegation of correspondents in Jacksonville, attempted unsuccessfully to charter the *Commodore* as a newspaper dispatch boat.

227. Scovel did not sail on the *Commodore* but on another boat.

228. Although Bacheller suggests that Crane lost the money in the surf while swimming ashore, elsewhere he says that Crane threw the money into the sea before leaving the sinking *Commodore* (Bacheller, *From Stores of Memory* 112).

229. Despite attempts by Crane's literary agent, Paul Revere Reynolds, to negotiate for more money, the magazine paid three hundred dollars (Allen 51).

230. Davis and Bierce were writing for William Randolph Hearst's *San Francisco Examiner* at the time.

231. Chamberlain, managing editor of the *New York Journal*, hired Stephen and Cora Crane to report the Greco-Turkish War and rehired him in 1898 to report the Puerto Rican campaign of the Spanish-American War.

232. Although Linson (1958, 34) states that Crane "had no liking for the somber moods" of Bierce, his work may have influenced Crane. The Sullivan County tales parody the kinds of horror tales written by Bierce (and Poe), and the epigrammatic style of poems in *The Black Riders* is similar to that in Bierce's poetry.

233. In a fictionalized re-creation of this scene, Beer (1923, 97–98) depicted Crane as being in the studio of artist William Dallgren, who was painting the drama critic Acton Davies. When Davies tossed a copy of Emile Zola's *La Débâcle* at Crane, he threw it aside. Annoyed, Davies said, "I suppose you could have done it better?" To which Crane replied, "Certainly."

Beer's association of Crane with *La Débâcle* is probably the result of his having read George Wyndham's 1896 review of *The Red Badge*, which suggests Zola's novel as an influence (Wyndham), and Ripley Hitchcock's preface to the 1900 reprinting of Crane's war novel, which also suggests the influence of *La Débâcle* and alludes to an unverifiable tale that the "origin [of *The Red Badge*] was the challenge of an artist friend uttered in response to Mr. Crane's criticism of a battle story which he had just read" (Hitchcock vi). Linson (1958, 44), however, recalled that he "never heard Stephen name either Zola or Davies in the matter" of a challenge.

Colvert (98) suggests that Crane could have first read about *La Débâcle* in a review in the 10 July 1892 edition of the *New York Times*, which also printed his sketch "The Broken-Down Van." According to Colvert, Crane would have found in the review a discussion of the "aims, method, and point of view" that would later be used in *The Red Badge*.

234. Because Crane's father died in 1880, he could not have given his son the money, though it is conceivable that one of his brothers did. For an allusion to Crane's continual borrowing of money from William Howe Crane, see Wertheim and Sorrentino, *Correspondence* 302.

235. Though the first American reviewers recognized Crane's originality, reviewers in England—most notably George Wyndham—more clearly articulated it. According to Wyndham, Crane was "a great artist"; *The Red Badge,* "a masterpiece"; and the portrayal of war, "more complete than Tolstoi's, more true than Zola's" (Wyndham). The most astute analysis of *The Red Badge* during Crane's life, Wyndham's review still remains an important contribution to the study of the novel.

For a defense of the view that the war novel was already popular in America before being published in England, see Kauffman (No. 30) and the interview with G. H. Putnam (Weatherford 165–67). When Appleton published *Maggie* in 1896, it appended a "Publisher's Note" to correct "a few inaccuracies of statement in regard to the history of [*The Red Badge,* which] was offered to and accepted by the publishers in December, 1894, and it was published in October, 1895. As it happened, the actual publication in England came some two months later. By that time the American press had appreciated the quality of the book so cordially and unanimously as to dispose of the lingering tradition that only a well-known author, or an author with the hall mark of foreign approval, is recognized by our reviewers" (v).

236. The tenement was at the corner of 33rd Street and 6th Avenue. Crane lived there with Charles Pike and his brother. See Wertheim and Sorrentino, *Correspondence* 234 n. 1.

237. Paul Cadmus (1904–99), whose paintings were frequently controversial and confrontational, was known for his realist style.

238. Novelist and playwright Jesse Lynch Williams (1871–1929) won the first Pulitzer Prize for Drama in 1917 with his comedy *Why Marry?*

239. If McBride's chronology is correct in the next paragraph, in which he says that *The Red Badge* had not been published yet, then the luncheon occurred in 1895 and is not the 7 April 1896 dinner honoring Crane held at the Lantern Club.

240. When Stallman and Gilkes published a version of this letter (324–26), their source was an edited typed copy supplied by Thomas Beer's sister, Alice Beer. I have relied on the text of the original letter.

241. Although no other correspondence between Beer and Hilliard has surfaced, Beer cites him as a source in the appendix. According to Beer, Crane "sat by night on a bench in Union Square with John Northern Hilliard or Acton Davies wondering when a check might drop from somewhere, there was pleasure in that and Hilliard could tell him stories about the West" (1923, 87); Crane borrowed Hilliard's "best suit" to dine with Howells (1923, 96); Crane, after visiting the Alamo and reading the legend on a monument to it—"Thermopylae had its messenger of defeat; the Alamo had none"— wrote to Hilliard saying these words "boomed in his ears like the clashing of war-bronze" (1923, 114); and Crane wrote Hilliard that "a man is born into the world with his own pair of eyes, and he is not at all responsible for his vision—he is merely responsible for

his quality of personal honesty. To keep close to this personal honesty is my supreme ambition" (1923, 233). Beer got part of the anecdote about Crane and Hilliard in Union Square from the 1 February 1922 letter to him; he most likely got the quotation about "personal honesty" from one of Hilliard's articles on Crane, and Crane probably borrowed a suit from Nelson Greene, not Hilliard, when he visited Howells (see Greene [No. 23], n. 135).

242. An allusion to John Millington Synge's drama *Playboy of the Western World.*

243. Hilliard had already alluded in the letter to a forthcoming article on Crane in the *Bookman,* but it did not appear.

244. Ford's "Two Americans: Henry James and Stephen Crane," which appeared in the *New York Evening Post Literary Review* on 19 and 26 March 1921. For Beer's response to Ford's reminiscences of Crane, see Ford (No. 53), n. 47, and Beer (1924).

245. Early October 1895.

246. When Joseph Katz published two of Hawkins's columns about Crane in the *Stephen Crane Newsletter* (Katz, "Stephen Crane's Struggles," "Stephen Crane Flinches"), he used carbon copies of the texts supplied by Hawkins's stepson. The complete typescript of "All in a Lifetime" contains a third column, "The Genius of Stephen Crane."

247. Copeland and Day, which published *The Black Riders and Other Lines* in May 1895.

248. Shortly after completing *The Red Badge* in April 1894, Crane submitted it to S. S. McClure for publication through his newspaper syndicate or in *McClure's Magazine.* When McClure had done neither by October 1894, Crane gave the manuscript to Irving Bacheller (No. 31), who published a shortened newspaper version in December 1894 through the Bacheller, Johnson, and Bacheller syndicate.

249. Crane left for England in 1897.

250. Actually, 1893.

251. Actually, 1894.

252. For the complete text of the letter and another one associated with it, see Letters 122 and 126 in Wertheim and Sorrentino, *Correspondence.*

253. For the complete text of the letter, see letter 127 in Wertheim and Sorrentino, *Correspondence.*

254. Letter 131 in Wertheim and Sorrentino, *Correspondence.*

255. For the complete text of the letter, see Letter 132 in Wertheim and Sorrentino, *Correspondence.*

256. See Noxon (No. 14), n. 39, and Hawkins (No. 37).

257. Bragdon later wrote, "I did not tell who cowed them, but it was I. I should not have had the nerve to attempt such a thing, had I not myself been a little drunk. Hubbard was grateful to me for this saving of the situation by my tongue-lashing, but I did not respond to his friendly overtures because I could not take him at his own valuation— or perhaps I should say the valuation at which he wanted to be taken: something between Ralph Waldo Emerson and William Morris. Crane made a deep impression on me, though I never saw him except that once: a youth sincere and ardent, with an inward fire greater than that of other men—so great, indeed, that it was even then burning him up."

Bragdon also reasserted that although the purpose of the Philistine banquet was to honor Crane and "ostensibly to put him on the literary map," it was "really a bit of shrewd advertising of Hubbard himself" (Bragdon 1938, 246).

258. See Wertheim and Sorrentino, *Crane Log* 155–56.

Part 4

1. I have relied on the text in *Prairie Schooner* because of the unavailability of *Library*. Cather's reminiscence has also been reprinted in Bassan 12–17 and Curtin 771–78. The year in the first sentence of the reminiscence is incorrectly printed as 1894 in Curtin.

2. Actually, February. Cather's confusion regarding the time of year leads her later in the reminiscence to speak of "oppressively warm" weather.

3. Will Owen Jones.

4. According to Cather's friend Edith Lewis, Crane, who arrived "about midnight . . . was fascinated by the sight of [Cather's] standing *fast asleep*. He said it was the only time he had ever seen anyone sleep on their feet like that" (Lewis 37).

5. Details in this paragraph and elsewhere in the reminiscence led Bernice Slote to conclude that Cather is dramatizing the meeting with Crane:

> The narrator "Henry Nicklemann" (or Willa Cather), says he was a junior in the university at the time, doing some work for the newspaper in his leisure hours—"I was just off the range; I knew a little Greek and something about cattle and a good horse when I saw one, and beyond horses and cattle I considered nothing of vital importance except good stories and the people who wrote them." In 1895 Willa Cather was a senior at the university and had not really been "on the range" since she was ten years old. She was interested not in horses and cattle but in theater, books, and music. A much-published newspaper writer and drama critic with more than a local reputation, she was not, as the article describes the narrator, a naive, quiet hero-worshipper who must be initiated in the writer's world (as Jim Burden in *My Ántonia* discovers life and art at a performance of *Camille*), but a young woman intensely independent and opinionated, knowledgeable about literature and the arts. She wrote brilliantly, spoke well, and argued a great deal. Whatever was said in the real conversations between Stephen Crane and Willa Cather, it was not one-sided." (Slote 4)

6. Actually, twenty-three years old.

7. In the most detailed analysis of Crane's grammar and literary style during his lifetime, Rupert Hughes (Chelifer) commented that "[t]he famous *Red Badge of Courage* bristles more with false grammar than with bayonets" (Weatherford 159).

8. Crane was in Lincoln 1–3 February and 9 (or 10)–14 February. In between the two visits, he toured the drought area of Nebraska and experienced a devastating blizzard

recorded in "Nebraska's Bitter Fight for Life," the most graphically moving journalistic sketch of his western trip.

9. "An allusion to Professor Lucius Sherman's critical method" (Curtin 774 n. 25). Sherman, head of the English Department at the University of Nebraska, developed a system of laws for the study of literature that involved the counting of words and phrases. Cather rebelled against the system.

10. Richard Harding Davis. See Davis (No. 46).

11. From Maurice Maeterlinck's *Treasure of the Humble* (New York: Dodd, 1899), 45–46, as cited in Curtin 775 n. 26.

12. That is, 13 February.

13. *The Passport.*

14. Crane later lamented, "Of all human lots for a person of sensibility that of an obscure free lance in literature or journalism is, I think, the most discouraging" (Wertheim and Sorrentino, *Correspondence* 232).

15. The conflict resulting from Crane's "double literary life" is a major theme of *The Third Violet.* See Sorrentino, "Stephen Crane's Struggle with Romance in *The Third Violet.*"

16. As Slote (6) questions, "Is this Cather's report of something Crane did say or a dramatization of [Edward] Garnett's comment, 'What he has not got he has no power of acquiring'?" Cather quotes Garnett directly later in the reminiscence.

17. Actually, twenty-eight.

18. Actually, 1898.

19. See Garnett (No. 54). Cather revised Garnett's wording slightly.

Part 5

1. Paine quoted the concluding paragraphs of the last section of "The Open Boat."

2. Paine had successfully made it to Cuba aboard the *Three Friends* in December 1896. The *Three Friends,* the *Dauntless,* and the *Commodore* defied the American blockade of Cuba by routinely bringing men and munitions to insurgents on the island. Though popularly known as the "Cuban navy," the *Commodore* was a fishing steamer, and the *Three Friends* and *Dauntless* were tugboats later used as dispatch boats for American journalists.

3. Paine quoted the description of the captain in the stoke-room from section four of "Flanagan and His Short Filibustering Adventure."

4. A gambler in Bret Harte's "Outcasts of Poker Flat."

5. Paine is quoting lines from Crane's short story "The Five White Mice."

6. On 6 June Lt. Richmond P. Hobson and a crew of seven men attempted to carry out Admiral Sampson's plan to sink the collier *Merrimac* in the harbor at Santiago in order to prevent the escape of Cervera's fleet. The plan failed, however, when the ship sank in the wrong spot and the men were captured by the Spanish. On 6 July the men were freed in exchange for Spanish prisoners. Crane recalled the incident in "War Memories."

7. Paine published an earlier version of the reminiscence as "Bright Roads of Adventure" in *Popular Magazine,* 7 March 1922, 86–94. In this version, Crane says, "*Please* don't sing that, Harry, old man. The words offend me. Rum is poison. You ought to know better. This is the morning after" (95). The difference between the two is an example of the difficulty in establishing with certainty the accuracy of a reminiscence.

8. On 14 June Crane accompanied Capt. George F. Elliott and his troops on a mission to Cuzco, six miles down the coast from Guantánamo Bay, to destroy a guerilla encampment guarding the only well in the area. Crane reported the battle in "The Red Badge of Courage Was His Wig-Wag Flag," *New York World,* 1 July, and Captain Elliott wrote an official report that cited Crane for "material aid during the action, carrying messages to fire volleys, etc., to the different company commanders" (Wertheim and Sorrentino, *Correspondence* 364 n. 1).

9. Paine quoted two paragraphs from chapter two in *The Red Badge of Courage* describing the dead soldier with shoes "worn to the thinness of writing paper."

10. Paine quoted the second half of the story.

11. A portion of the letter was first published in Stallman and Gilkes 339–40. In a 12 January 1934 letter to Stolper in the collection at Columbia, McCready wrote that "in some respects my impressions of [Crane] are clear, and sharply cut &, as I think, significant. . . . Paine and I knew Crane in a way few could claim—or at least, in some aspects and periods."

12. The book was probably *George's Mother,* not a collection of short stories.

13. Unfortunately, Paine (No. 40) does not discuss Cora Taylor.

14. Crane met Cora Taylor at the Hotel de Dream before December 4, not after the sinking of the *Commodore,* as McCready implies.

15. Because McCready forgot that the *Commodore* had sunk on 2 January 1897, he mistakenly remembered a Christmas Eve dinner following the incident.

16. Robert Louis Stevenson.

17. Observation post.

18. Herald Square, the location of James Gordon Bennett's *New York Herald.*

19. Associated Press.

20. McCready's 12 January 1934 letter to Stolper clarifies the allusion. Just as Sir Henry Newbolt (1862–1938), best known for his patriotic sea poems, had commemorated Sir Francis Drake's defeat of the Spanish Armada in the poem "Drake's Drum," McCready portrayed himself and others during the war against Spain as again helping to "singe his Catholic Majesty's beard"—in the fancy of Newbolt's 'Drake's Drum.'"

21. Joseph Pulitzer's motto.

22. See Paine (No. 40).

23. Although McCready's account could have taken place on May 15, the date the *Three Friends* anchored off Puerto Plata in the Dominican Republic, more likely it occurred in Haiti.

24. Brian Oswald Patrick Donn Byrne (1889–1929), Irish-American author of *The Wind Bloweth* (1922) who died in an auto accident.

25. In a letter to Vincent Starrett, 30 March 1922, Cary characterized Crane as "a

drunken, irresponsible and amusing little cuss. He kept me busy trying to get a little work out of him, but I failed in that respect"; however, Crane sent more than twenty dispatches to the *World*.

Part 6

1. On 29 July 1898.
2. On 30 or 31 July.
3. Before Crane left England for Cuba, Edward Garnett (No. 54) interested him in Brede Place. While Crane was in Cuba, Moreton Frewen rented the house to Cora for forty pounds a year on the stipulation that the Cranes make specific restorations to the house. Unfortunately, they never could fulfill their obligation.
4. Adm. Pascual Cervera y Topete, commander of the Spanish fleet.
5. On 1 August.
6. Charles Dana Gibson, best known for his drawings of the Gibson Girl, modeled her companion after Davis.
7. Nelson Appleton Miles, commanding general of the U.S. Army during the Spanish-American War.
8. For a different version of Crane's "capture" of the town of Juana Diaz, see Davis (No. 46).
9. "One Dash—Horses."
10. In an earlier account Michelson added details to the incident: "Crane did not speak a word on the way to the steamer. Once on board he turned to look back, and there, at the edge of the banana patch, stood his horse, watching him. As long as that white spot against the dark green could be seen from the ship Crane waved his handkerchief'" (Brace).

In the same account Michelson offered additional comments on Crane's personality and behavior in Cuba: "An estimate of Stephen Crane must be an analysis of two people. Crane the writer was everything that Crane the man was not. The artist was sensitive, serious, painstaking, conscientious and industrious, imbued with almost perfect taste. The man was flippant, careless, indolent, selfish and an offense against most of the canons of society."
11. "The Battle Hymn" ("All-feeling God, hear in the war-night"). While in Cuba, Crane put the manuscript of the poem into his saddlebags and gave them to Michelson, who later passed them on to Cora.
12. Kipling's poem "Recessional" was written in 1897 in commemoration of Queen Victoria's Diamond Jubilee.
13. "The Passing Show."
14. In writing this biography, Cecil Carnes had Hare's assistance as well as his letters, diaries, and other documents.
15. Sylvester Scovel, bureau chief of the *New York World*.
16. Although Henry M. Cary, manager of the *New York World* staff, and Don Carlos Seitz (No. 47), manager of the newspaper's staff in Cuba, claimed that Crane was lazy,

the *World* published twenty-four of his dispatches, some of which were among his best reporting.

17. The ambush of the Rough Riders at Las Guásimas on June 24.

18. The battles for El Caney and San Juan Hill on July 1.

19. Crane and McNab were schoolmates at Claverack College.

20. In chapter 1 of his biography, Carnes recounts how Hare, after drinking the water in a soldier's canteen, risked his own life during the Battle of Kettle Hill in order to refill it.

21. The passage quoted by Carnes appears in "War Memories" (Crane, *Tales of War* 247–48). Associated with the passage is an incident in which Crane lent Hare his horse, which "ran away with him and flung him off in the middle of a ford" (Crane, *Tales of War* 246–47). For Hare's version of the incident, see Carnes 77–81.

22. George B. Cortelyou, one of Roosevelt's secretaries.

23. An allusion to the Dora Clark incident.

24. Marshall (1898, 273–76; 1899, 138–43) had earlier recounted this experience in greater detail and cited another example of Crane's selflessness. When Marshall lost his blanket, which he used to protect his photographic equipment, shortly after arriving in Cuba, Crane gave him his (1899, 85). Crane recounted his aid to Marshall in the dispatch "Stephen Crane at the Front for the World" (Crane, *Reports of War* 142–46).

25. Actually, 1894.

26. See Gordon (No. 26), who recalled the first meeting between Crane and Marshall.

27. "When Every One Is Panic Stricken," *New York Press,* 25 November 1894. Crane titled the sketch "The Fire" in an 1897 inventory list of his writings. Stallman's assertion (1973, 125) that Crane's sketch is "all fiction" and that "Marshall never discovered he had been hoaxed" seems an exaggeration. As the subtitle, "A Realistic Pen Picture of a Fire," suggests, the *New York Press* did not print it as a news report of an actual fire. Beer (1923, 82) may be alluding to the sketch when he claims, "The *Herald* fired me last week" because of it. Beer claimed that Crane was working for the *Herald* at the time.

28. Frederic Remington.

29. Henry J. Whigham of the *Chicago Tribune.*

30. Another reporter.

31. Sylvester Scovel.

32. Spanish troops were equipped with the Mauser, considered the best rifle at the time, which used smokeless powder. Although American rifles also relied upon smokeless powder, it was in limited supply for U.S. forces at the beginning of the war.

33. The *St. Louis Republic* reported another incident involving Crane and Whigham that occurred at this time:

> Readers of "The Red Badge of Courage" will remember how [Crane] describes with much elaboration the actions of a man [the tall soldier] wounded to the death in battle, how he dilated on the sound the stricken man made as he lurched to the

ground—a sound that was a scream, a moan, and a cry of surprise, but more than anything else a scream. This bit of description was the source of much argument. Some old soldiers who had seen men die in battle denied the accuracy of Crane's description; others only mildly questioned it; still others said a man who could write with such amazing exactitude about the death of a soldier must have seen many men fall at his side.

Crane could not answer the adverse critics. He had never seen that which he described, but he dreamily said that he knew he was right, that it must be so.

That day at El Caney, while he was watching the fighting from an unwholesome but highly advantageous position, a soldier was struck in the stomach by a bullet. The wound was instantly mortal. The man lurched, as Crane had said men in their death agony did lurch, and uttered that cry which is so wholly beyond description that only Stephen Crane, who never had heard it, had succeeded in describing.

As the wounded soldier fell Crane looked up at Whigham and said: 'There, you heard that? What did I tell you'" (Brace).

34. Jimmie Nolan represented for Crane the regular army enlisted man who simply did his duty. He appears as Michael Nolan in the dispatch "Regulars Get No Glory" (Crane, *Reports of War* 170–73) and in the story "The Price of the Harness" (Crane, *Tales of War* 97–113) in which, unaware that he has been shot and wounded, he bleeds to death on the battlefield.

35. Crane briefly recounts the heroism of Sgt. John H. Quick in the dispatch "The Red Badge of Courage Was His Wig-Wag Flag" (Crane, *Reports of War* 134–42) and more thoroughly in the sketch "Marines Signaling under Fire at Guantanamo" (Crane, *Tales of War* 194–200).

36. See Carnes (No. 43).

37. The incident occurred during the battle for the San Juan Heights on 1 July. Davis described the incident in a later reminiscence: "I knew that to Crane, anything that savored of a pose was hateful, so, as I did not want to see him killed, I called, 'You're not impressing any one by doing that, Crane.' As I hoped he would, he instantly dropped to his knees. When he crawled over to where we lay, I explained, 'I knew that would fetch you,' and he grinned, and said, 'Oh, was that it?'" (Davis 1910, 125).

Three other incidents typify Crane's behavior in battle during the Spanish-American War. Langdon Smith of the *New York Journal* also recalled Crane's calmness under fire: "'Crane was standing under a tree calmly rolling a cigarette . . . some leaves dropped from the trees, cut away by the bullets; two or three men dropped within a few feet. Crane is as thin as a lath. If he had been two or three inches wider or thicker through, he would undoubtedly have been shot. But he calmly finished rolling his cigarette and smoked it without moving away from the spot where the bullets had suddenly become so thick'" (Brisbane 557).

In a brief note printed along with Mrs. George Crane's reminiscence (No. 2), a reporter recalled:

During the fight at Guantanamo Dr. Gibbs, who was killed a few hours later in the engagement, Crane and three other correspondents who had just arrived as the battle began were lying flat on their stomachs on the brow of the hill. The bullets were flying about pretty thick when one of the men who had known Crane in New York said:

"I say, Crane, how does this compare with your 'Red Badge of Courage'?

"Oh, hell!" said Crane. "This isn't half as exciting." ("The Reality Not Exciting")

George Lynch of the *London Chronicle* remembered an incident reminiscent of events Crane had previously described in "A Mystery of Heroism":

A company under fire was badly in need of water, and water was seven miles away, down hill at that. Stephen collected all the tin canteens he could find and trotted off for the refreshment. Coming wearily back, there was a sharp ping against one of the cans, and it began to leak. Stephen turned up the can and tried to stop the leak. An officer in the woods near by shouted to him:

"Come here, quick! You're in the line of fire!"

"If you've got a knife, cut a plug and bring it to me," replied the young man, and, as he spoke, bang went a bullet against another can.

"Come under cover, or you'll lose every can you've got!"

This warning had its effect. The loss of the precious fluid terrified him in a way that the danger to himself had failed to do. He finally brought the water up to the thirsty company, and then fainted through exhaustion. (R. Barr 649)

38. The incident occurred on 3 July. See Davis's second reminiscence.

39. On 16 July 1898 the *New York World* printed an unsigned front-page article probably written by Sylvester Scovel, which accused the officers of the 71st New York Volunteer Regiment of cowardice in a battle on the Santiago road on 1 July, in which four hundred Americans were killed or wounded.

40. For a different version of Crane's "capture" of the town of Juana Diaz, see Michelson (No. 42).

41. John Blair Gibbs was one of the first American casualties during the fighting at Guantánamo Bay. Crane dramatized the horror of his death in "War Memories."

42. Seitz's characterization of the dispatch "The Red Badge of Courage Was His Wig-Wag Flag," which appeared in the *New York World* on July 1, reveals his animosity toward Crane. Rather than being "dull," as Seitz charged, the dispatch is one of Crane's best pieces of war reporting, and it was not his "first word." The newspaper had already published a dozen of his dispatches.

43. Francis H. Nichols's *Through the Hidden Shensi* (New York: Scribner's, 1902).

44. Seitz quoted the dispatch, "Conduct of 71st New York" (*New York World,* 16 July 1898), which accused the officers of the 71st New York Volunteer Regiment of cowardice; however, the author was most likely Sylvester Scovel, Crane's bureau chief. For an excerpt from the dispatch, see Wertheim and Sorrentino, *Crane Log* 329.

45. Seitz is confused about the two dispatches by Crane that the *World* published after he had returned to the United States; neither deals with the death of a marine at Guantánamo.

46. In 1924 Seitz claimed that the *World* fired Crane because he had "sent only one dispatch of any merit and that, accusing the Seventy-first New York regiment of cowardice at Santiago, imperilled the paper" (Seitz 241). Besides erroneously identifying the author of the dispatch (see n. 44 above), Seitz ignored the fact that the *World* had published twenty-four of Crane's dispatches, some of excellent quality. In all likelihood, a major reason for Crane's dismissal was that he had cabled Edward Marshall's dispatch to the rival *New York Journal* (see Marshall [No. 44]). Seitz's libelous comments about Crane have been repeated in accounts of the Spanish-American War, including Walter Millis's *Martial Spirit* (1931), Gregory Mason's *Remember the Maine* (1939), and W. A. Swanberg's *Citizen Hearst* (1961).

47. Parker sent the reminiscence to H. L. Mencken on 2 March 1940.

48. Parker's time frame is incorrect. Santiago surrendered on July 17; the peace protocol was signed on August 12; and the peace treaty was signed on December 10.

49. Around the third week in August, Crane sneaked illegally into Havana, which was still controlled by Spanish authorities who had temporarily imprisoned nine other correspondents on a boat in the harbor.

50. Despite Parker's assertion, Crane published seventeen dispatches in the *New York Journal* between 3 September and 17 November 1898.

51. A *centén* was a five-dollar gold piece.

52. Presumably an allusion to the *Commodore* incident. The Cuban may be "the bartender and ex-filibuster" in Carmichael's reminiscence (No. 49).

53. For an incident involving the pursuit of Cuban rebel Julio Sanguili, see Emerson (No. 50).

54. Parker clarified the vague allusion to "Crane's personal shock" in the cover letter sent to Mencken that accompanied the reminiscence:

> He found a girl, living in Havana, whom he had previously known elsewhere in the world. On her mantel there was a photograph of a handsome Cuban. After some discussion with the girl, Crane left the house and took up his abode with an old woman and lived the life of a complete recluse. He desired to see no one and had no liking for companionship. The old woman took as good care of him as she could. In his place of retirement we never visited him as a group, but now and then would send one of the group to learn how he was making out.
>
> It was in this retirement that he wrote "The Ashes of Love," but would never let us see a copy. I do not know that "The Ashes of Love" was ever published.

55. An allusion to two lines—"Thou art my love / And thou art the ashes of other men's love"—in the first "Intrigue" poem (Crane, *Poems and Literary Remains* 96–97).

56. In the peace treaty, signed in Paris on 10 December 1898, Spain renounced all rights to Cuba and allowed for its independence.

57. The fortress, 260 feet above sea level, overlooked the harbor entrance to Santiago.

58. In "In Havana as It Is To-Day" (*New York Journal,* 12 November 1898), Crane described visits with Parker and another correspondent to insurgent posts near Havana.

59. Valeriano Weyler y Nicolau was governor-general of Cuba from 1896 to 1897. His harsh treatment of insurgents earned him the nickname of "the Butcher" and aroused public opinion in America against Spanish policies in Cuba.

60. Carmichael's reminiscence first appeared in the unsigned "Stories about Stephen Crane," *Omaha Daily Bee,* 17 June 1900, 16, and was reprinted in the *Omaha Weekly Bee,* 20 June 1900, 11.

61. At the end of September, Cora Crane desperately wrote John M. Hay, U.S. ambassador to England and secretary of state, Secretary of War Russell A. Alger, and Paul Revere Reynolds in an attempt to locate Crane. The cablegram sent to Alger did not reach Maj. Gen. J. F. Wade in Havana till October 9 (Wertheim and Sorrentino, *Correspondence* 370–73). Crane communicated regularly with Reynolds throughout the fall, but if he wrote letters to Cora or his family, they never received them. Between mid-August and mid-November, Cora heard nothing from him. Despite his awareness of her apprehensions and economic plight, he was apparently not eager to return to her or to England.

62. José Martí y Perez founded the Cuban Revolutionary Party in 1892 and, along with Máximo Gómez Báez, issued the "Manifesto of Montecristi," calling their followers to fight for Cuban independence. Gómez commanded the Cuban Revolutionary Army; Antonio Maceo, Calixto García Iñiguéz, and Jesús Rabí were generals in the army. Martí was killed in Cuba in 1895; Maceo, in 1896.

63. This may be "Crane's Cuban friend" in Parker's reminiscence (No. 48).

64. For a summary of Crane's own experience in Havana, see Helen Crane (No. 8).

65. See Parker (No. 48) for a brief reference to Julio Sanguili, a Cuban rebel banned from Cuba by the Spanish and prohibited from returning. The incident described occurred on 12 December.

66. Major Mott, U.S.V., attached to General Greene's staff, just arrived in Havana from the conquest of the Philippines. [Emerson's note]

67. An allusion to the St. Bartholomew massacre on the night of 23–24 August 1572 in which thousands of Huguenots were killed in Paris. Almost fifty years after publishing *Pepys's Ghost,* Emerson questioned whether the incident actually involved Crane (Wertheim and Sorrentino, *Crane Log* 355).

Part 7

1. Conrad's introduction to Thomas Beer's biography is an expanded form of this reminiscence.

2. Sidney Southgate Pawling.

3. The other person was most likely Harold Frederic, London correspondent for the *New York Times,* whom Crane had met in New York on 31 March 1897 at a formal luncheon given in Crane's honor by Richard Harding Davis at the Savoy. Frederic had

written of the success of *The Red Badge of Courage* in England in "Stephen Crane's Triumph" in the *New York Times* on 26 January 1896. A close friend of William Heinemann, Frederic was probably instrumental in recommending Crane's work to him.

4. Conrad is incorrect; the individual is named "Henry Fleming."

5. Crane had been reading *The Nigger of the "Narcissus"* in the *New Review*, house journal of the publishing firm William Heinemann, which ran it serially from August to December 1897. Shortly after Crane and Conrad met for lunch, Conrad sent him page proofs of the novel. Crane wrote him to express his admiration of it (Wertheim and Sorrentino, *Correspondence* 310) and praised it publicly ("Concerning the English 'Academy,'" *Bookman* 7 [March 1898]).

6. That is, 15 October 1897.

7. In a letter to Conrad, Crane summed up his enjoyment of their first meeting: "Did not we have a good pow-wow in London?" (Wertheim and Sorrentino, *Correspondence* 310).

8. W. E. Henley was editor of the *New Review*.

9. *Blackwood's Edinburgh Magazine*.

10. Crane was plagued by a constant flow of visitors to Brede Place that he contemptuously called "Indians"; Ford Madox Ford (No. 53) derided them as "Crane's parasites." See also Jessie Conrad (No. 52).

11. Borys.

12. That is, 23 May 1900.

13. "One Dash—Horses."

14. The meeting occurred later in the month on November 28.

15. Borys was born on 15 January 1898.

16. Starting on February 19, the Conrads and Mrs. Conrad's younger sister, Dorothy (Dolly) George, visited the Cranes at Ravensbrook for ten days.

17. Two Greek servants, Adoni Ptolemy and his twin brother, accompanied Crane on his trip to England after he reported the Greco-Turkish War. Adoni's brother became a servant in the household of Edward and Margery Pease, friends of Crane.

18. Gilkes (150–51) and Stallman (1973, 419) date this visit in August; but if Cora did not discover that Crane had left the Hotel Pasaje and was "missing" until September 22 (Gilkes 151) and was concerned about his whereabouts when she visited the Conrads, the visit probably did not occur until early or mid-October, shortly before the Conrads moved to Pent Farm.

19. While Crane was in Cuba, Moreton Frewen rented Brede Place to Cora for a token rent of forty pounds a year on the condition that the Cranes make certain repairs to the home. Though Cora planted a large rose garden in front of the home, their constant financial problems prevented them from fulfilling their obligation to Frewen. According to Mark Barr, though Frewen wanted to lend Brede Place to the Cranes, Stephen "insisted upon paying rent" (M. Barr, letter to the editor).

20. See Conrad (No. 51), n. 10.

21. Pent Farm in Postling.

22. The Conrads arrived at Brede Place on 3 June 1899 for another extended visit.

23. Richard Heather, the butler. As part of the rental agreement of Brede Place, Moreton Frewen required that the Cranes retain the three servants employed there, a financial burden that contributed to the Cranes' money problems.

24. In April 1900 Crane was fined thirty-five shillings for not having dog licenses.

25. Conrad's response is probably letter 710 in Wertheim and Sorrentino, *Correspondence* (645).

26. According to legend, Brede Place was haunted by the spirit of its early sixteenth-century owner, Sir Goddard Oxenbridge, a warlock and an ogre who purportedly ate a child for dinner each night.

27. The four servants—William MacVitte (Mack), the valet-groom, coach-gardener, and head of staff; Vernall, the housekeeper and cook; Richard Heather, the butler; and a serving man—drank constantly. MacVitte eventually resigned because the Cranes kept their liquor locked up.

28. At another time Mack accidentally started a fire in Crane's study. The fear of a fire in the house prompted the Cranes to keep liquor away from the servants.

29. At Pent Farm.

30. Captain G. F. W. Hope sold them the boat in the summer of 1899.

31. Crane paid fifteen pounds toward his share.

32. Scholars relying on the 1932 American reprinting of *Return to Yesterday: Reminiscences, 1894–1914* would have not seen Ford's statement; it appeared only in the English edition. Tipped into the copy of the English edition in Special Collections, Newman Library at Virginia Tech, is an undated newspaper clipping that gives further evidence of Ford's looseness with facts: "Ford Madox Ford's biography, which Liveright will bring out here December 14, has been withdrawn in England by the Lord Chamberlain. In one place Ford quotes King George as threatening to abdicate the throne, and upon the appearance of the book in England this was immediately branded as false by a palace official. Subsequently the publishers were asked to take the speech out of the book, and then the Lord Chamberlain took steps to have it withdrawn altogether. 'Return to Yesterday' is the book's title." For a statement on Ford's method of biographical writing, see his reminiscence of Joseph Conrad (*Joseph Conrad* ii–iii).

33. Late June 1897.

34. Close friends and relatives (Edmund B. Crane [No. 1], Wilbur F. Crane [No. 3], Lawrence [No. 22], Oliver [No. 6], Sidbury [No. 9], Wells [No. 55], and Wheeler [No. 5]) reminiscing about a younger Crane often called him "Stevie"; however, to those who first knew him after he became famous, only Ford and Pugh (No. 60) called him "Stevie" or "Steevie," and it is unlikely that Ford actually used it in his presence. In the reminiscence from *Portraits from Life* (34), Ford acknowledged that Crane always called him "Mr. Hueffer" (he did not change his last name to Ford until 1919), and the only surviving letter from Ford to Crane is addressed "Dear Mr. Crane" (Wertheim and Sorrentino, *Correspondence* 432). Unlike Joseph and Jessie Conrad, Ford and his wife were apparently not close friends of the Cranes. Ford claimed that he avoided Brede Place because he found "the sunlight there . . . ghastly" (*Portraits* 30), but on one visit in late

1899–early 1900 with William Hyde, the illustrator of Ford's book *The Cinque Ports*, Ford wrote his wife, "The Cs were very cordial & invited me to stop . . . " (Lindberg-Seyersted 23). The absence of Mrs. Hueffer's address in Cora Crane's address book (Stephen Crane Papers, Rare Book and Manuscript Library, Columbia University), which contains addresses for others like Mrs. Conrad and Mrs. H. G. Wells, suggests that the two families were not in constant touch.

35. "I saw him . . . first at a lecture he was delivering up on the Chart at Limpsfield and I had not been much attracted to him. He was then enormously belauded and, on account of the harshness of his voice and his precision of language as a lecturer, I had taken him to be arrogant. The subject of his discourse was flag-wagging, as he called it—Morse signalling by flags. . . . I remember his standing on an improvised platform in a Fabian drawing-room and looking young, pained, and dictatorial. I avoided being introduced to him" (Ford, *Return* 49–50). This incident seems unlikely. Crane disliked public speaking, and he did not learn about Morse signaling with flags until his combat experiences with the Marines in Cuba.

The American book version of the quotation begins differently: "I saw him . . . first at a lecture he was delivering up on the Chart at Limpsfield, and I was much attracted to him then. He was enormously belauded . . . " (*Return* 55).

36. Ford was temporarily living in Gracie's cottage near Garnett's home, the Cearne, at High Chart. When the Cranes arrived in England in June 1897, they spent a few days "in furnished rooms on Limpsfield Chart, a breezy, uplifting hilltop completely surrounded by Fabians" (Ford, *Portraits* 27), before moving to the nearby village of Oxted. Among their friends were Edward and Margery Pease. Edward was secretary of the local branch of the Fabian Society, and Margery was active in Labour party politics. According to Ford (*Return* 38), Crane gave the lecture on "flag-wagging" at their house.

37. "He came around the corner of the house in the company of Mr. Edward Garnett. . . . He approached, as it were, with caution, like some one coming near to a cave dweller and said, in the most Bowery accent that I have ever heard: 'What a bully old baronial hall' . . . " (Ford, "Stevie" 881–82). " . . . [H]e had really taken it to be a relic of baronial splendour. . . . [Ford's ellipsis] He considered that writers should not take refuge amongst relics of medieval splendour—or in what it is for the moment the fashion to call Ivory Towers. He thought they ought to face life . . . " (Ford, *Portraits* 25).

38. For W. F. Johnson's criticism of Ford's reminiscence, see Johnson (No. 7).

39. Mrs. Margery Pease. The Peases lived in Limpsfield.

40. In one of Ford's reminiscences, Crane arrived home at 11 P.M. ("Stevie" 882); in another, at 12:30 A.M. (*Return* 57).

41. An allusion to Edward John Trelawny's *Recollections of the Last Days of Shelley and Byron* (1858), a lively, but inaccurate, account of Trelawny's friendship with Shelley and Byron. Ford later elaborated upon the comparison between Crane and Shelley: Crane "was honourable, physically brave, infinitely hopeful, generous, charitable to excess, observant beyond belief, morally courageous, of unswerving loyalty, a beautiful poet—and of untiring industry. With his physical frailty, his idealism, his love of freedom and of

truth he seemed to me to be like Shelley. His eyes with their long fringes of lashes were almost incredibly beautiful—and as if vengeful. Of his infinite industry he had need" (Ford, *Return* 29).

42. Later Ford stated that the amount was £10 for a thousand words (Ford, "Stevie" 882), then changed it back to £20: "Pinker had guaranteed him £20 per thousand words. For everything that he wrote! £20 per thousand is £2 per hundred, is nearly 5*d*. per word" (Ford, *Return* 62). See also Ford, *Portraits* 25.

43. Because James B. Pinker did not become Crane's English literary agent until August 1898, this incident could not have occurred until Crane returned to England from Cuba. See Wertheim and Sorrentino, *Crane Log* 273.

44. According to Ford, the Cranes were "seriously into debt" and "were at the moment almost short of food"; in addition, "[t]he local tradesmen had cut off supplies" (Ford, *Return* 62). Nevertheless, Crane celebrated by using the advance to buy "hampers of *foie gras* and caviar and champagne" (Ford, *Portraits* 25) as well as a new collar for his dog Flannel (Ford, *Return* 63).

45. "We sat drinking till seven o'clock next morning, the available liquor in the house being one bottle of claret, which Crane surrendered to me, and two bottles of beer, which he drank himself" (Ford, "Stevie" 882).

> . . . I went to bed in the drawing-room, with the dog on top of me at four in the morning and began again arguing with Crane about writing at a seven o'clock breakfast. Our views on life and letters were not really divergent but Crane would ascribe to me sets of theories and then demolish them with the manner and voice of a Bowery tough hammering an Irish scavenger. He was immensely happy.
>
> Mrs. Crane's alleged reason for making me stay till after midnight had been that Crane, coming down from a momentous interview, would need to talk. Presumably he would want to talk in such Gargantuan gusts that she and Mrs. Rudy [Mrs. Charlotte Ruedy] would be insufficient to sustain his assaults of language. . . .
>
> It had been a crucial moment in his career and I imagine that Mrs. Crane had been anxious that I should stay with her and her friend simply because they could not bear themselves in the suspense. (Ford, *Return* 63, 66)

46. "He was small, frail, energetic, at times virulent. He was full of phantasies and fantasticisms. He would fly at and deny every statement before it was out of your mouth" (Ford, *Return* 35).

47. According to Ford, Crane's habit of role-playing—whether he was pretending to be "the son of an uptown New York bishop," "a Bowery tough," or "a mangy, sheep-stealing coyote" (Ford, *Return* 28)—was the result of a "protean quality in Crane which accounts for the more unfortunate passages [dealing with gossip] in Mr. Beer's lately published book" ("Stevie" 881–82). Annoyed by Ford's 1924 reminiscence in the *New York Evening Post Literary Review,* Beer responded in a letter to the editor pointing out what he considered to be Ford's inaccuracies (Beer 1924).

48. Ford, the grandson of the pre-Raphaelite painter Ford Madox Brown, who raised him after his father's death, grew up surrounded by a number of the more notable pre-Raphaelites. In the 1890s the labels pre-Raphaelitism and aestheticism were interchangeable for many writers and critics.

49. Richard Le Gallienne.

50. "The son of a divine, he had very strongly the Oxford voice and manner, he had read quite a number of French books, and he discussed literary-technical matters impassionately. That was why we had missed our beds. In the same cause, he hammered me over the head. I, as you might say, trying to insert a stiletto between his ribs. He persisted in telling me that the only way to write was to achieve a language as near the vernacular as possible, and I telling him that the only way to write was to achieve a language as near the vernacular as possible. But as we neither of us listened to the other dawn found us without our having arrived at any conclusions" (Ford, "Stevie" 882).

51. Strictly speaking, this is true, although two-thirds of the poems in *War Is Kind* are in free verse as well.

52. Ford had published a volume of undistinguished poetry, *The Questions at the Well* (1893), under the pseudonym "Fenil Haig." E. R. Jones (No. 57) recalled Ford's reading his poetry aloud at Brede Place.

Ford later recast several of the details of his reminiscence:

> So, till breakfast next morning, he went on passionately telling me that he didn't give whatever it was the then fashionable slang not to give for corner lots and battle-fields; that I ruined, ruined, ruined my verse by going out of my way, in the pre-Raphaelite manner, to drag in rhymes which made *longueurs* and diluted the sense. He told me that he was the son of an Episcopalian bishop and had been born indifferently in the Bowery or in Wyoming or on Pike's Peak. There were thus no flies on him, whereas I was simply crawling with them. . . . [Ford's ellipsis]. And he produced from the hip pocket of the riding-breeches into which he had changed from his town clothes, a Colt revolver, with the foresight of which he proceeded to kill flies. . . . [Ford's ellipsis]. He had spilt a little champagne over a lump of sugar on the table and flies had come in companies. He really did succeed in killing one, flicking the gun backhanded with his remarkably strong wrists. Then he looked at me avengingly and said: "That's what you want to do instead of interring yourself amongst purple pre-Raphaelite pleonasms. . . . That's what you learn out in the West . . . " [Ford's ellipses] (Ford, *Portraits* 26).

53. Jones (No. 57), however, recalled that James and the Cranes frequently visited each other.

54. Queen consort of Charles I of England.

55. "In the middle ages they built in bottoms to be near the water and Brede, though mostly an Elizabethan building, in the form of an E out of compliment to Great Eliza, was twelfth-century in site. The sunlight penetrated, pale, like a blight into that damp depression" (Ford, *Return* 29).

In response to Ford's statement that Brede Place was an "ill-fated mansion . . . in a damp hollow . . . full of evil influences" (*Portraits* 27), E. R. Jones (No. 57) replied, "Rubbish! It stood high, looking down over a little valley where flocks of sheep cropped the good grass. And the house radiated with the happiness of the Cranes."

56. More likely, Edward Garnett (No. 54) interested the Cranes in Brede Place.

57. Crane "found himself occupying a real baronial manor-house on the site of the battle of Hastings, with his wife in medieval dress and with, on the floors of the banqueting-hall, rushes amongst which the innumerable dogs fought for the bones which the guests cast them" (Ford, *Portraits* 26).

58. "Crane never forgot a friend, even if it were merely a fellow who had passed a wet night with him under an arch. His wife was minded to be a mediaeval chatelaine. A barrel of beer and a baron of beef stood waiting in the rear hall for every hobo that might pass that way. The house was a nightmare of misplaced hospitality, of lugubrious dissipation in which Crane himself had no part. Grub Street and Greenwich Village did" (Ford, *Return* 29).

59. Toward the end of his career at Brede Place, Crane was constantly writing stories and asking Pinker for advances in order to ward off creditors and lawsuits. When Ford "suggested that [Crane] might end most of his worries by declaring himself bankrupt, he absolutely refused to adopt this expedient, because he owed large sums to small tradesmen in Brede and Winchelsea and Rye, and, English law forbidding preferential payment of debts, he would not have been able if he did become bankrupt to pay his poorer creditors in full" (Ford, "Stevie" 882).

60. The legend surrounding Crane's supposed dislike of Robert Louis Stevenson exemplifies the unreliability of Ford's reminiscences and the confusion surrounding them. Elsewhere in *Thus to Revisit* (75) Ford wrote: "Stephen Crane said the most illuminating thing I ever heard as to the English prose of to-day. He was talking about the author of *Travels in the Cevennes,* and he said: 'By God! when Stevenson wrote: "With interjected finger he delayed the action of the time piece," meaning "he put the clock back," Stevenson put back the clock of English fiction 150 years.'" In 1911, however, Ford offered a different version of Crane's statement: " 'With interjected finger he delayed the motion of the timepiece.' 'By God, poor dear!' Crane exclaimed. 'That man put back the clock of English fiction fifty years' " (*Memories and Impressions* 58). Beer (1923, 55, 63, 159–60, 181, 231) perpetuated the legend of Crane's antipathy toward Stevenson and, as is the case with Ford, supplied details and anecdotes for which he is the only source. Later Beer complicated the details of the legend by saying that Harold Frederic, not Crane, made the remark about Stevenson's prose, then added that Crane "probably quoted it" to Ford (Beer 1924, iv). Beer's conjecture on how Ford heard the statement is presented as fact in Stallman's biography: "Crane repeated it to Ford" (Stallman 1973, 601 n. 3).

61. For another reminiscence that records Crane's playful desire to shock James, see Harriman (No. 56), who also recalls that Crane would dress in riding breeches.

62. Naturalist W. H. Hudson.

63. Elsewhere Ford added that "while Crane was on his deathbed at Brede James's

condition was really pitiable. He would drive over two and three times a day to consult as to what he could *do* for the dying boy" (Ford, "Stevie" 882).

64. William Carlos Williams was so impressed with the reminiscence about Crane that he wrote to Ford to thank him for it (MacShane 249). A fellow New Jerseyan, Williams would have been attracted to Crane as an impressionist and as a forerunner of imagism.

65. Crane told Ford that he had visited "the Painted Desert of Arizona" and unsuccessfully tried to enlist in the army while visiting "the Alamo and Fort Sam Houston" (Ford, *Portraits* 33).

66. Saunders comments on Ford's statement about Crane's desire for privacy: "What he writes of Stephen Crane . . . can be read as an oblique allegory for his own autobiographical fabulation. . . . In Ford's own writing, and in the kind of literature that most appealed to him, the literary personality is best expressed by the fictions which are evolved to spin veils around the self. It is an argument which dissolves the boundaries between autobiography, fiction, and criticism. Conventionally, biographical subjects are seen as the external causes of their writing. Ford places the writer within literature; sees his personality as literary" (460).

67. Strictly speaking, Ford is off by one day: Crane was born on 1 November 1871; Ford, on 17 December 1873.

68. It is unclear whether Crane made this statement to Ford, or whether Ford got it from Beer's biography, which he reread just before writing his reminiscence in *Portraits,* or from another source. See Wertheim and Sorrentino, *Crane Log* 90–91.

69. Garnett's account expands upon his earlier "Mr. Stephen Crane: An Appreciation," *Academy* 55 (17 December 1898): 483–84, which he reprints in the book. For the complete text of Garnett's critical appreciation, which remains one of the most astute analyses in Crane scholarship, see Gullason (1972, 137–45).

In his critical bibliography, Stallman (1972) attributes several unsigned items in the *Academy* to Garnett; however, as Monteiro points out, "the *Academy* printed more than twenty items on the subject of Stephen Crane and his works. Although [Stallman] has suggested that Garnett was the author of at least five of those pieces in *The Academy,* it is simply not known which of these, if any, beyond the one signed piece in 1898 and the obituary on August 11, 1900, should be attributed to Garnett" (1978, 465).

70. *The Open Boat and Other Stories* (London: Heinemann, 1898), published simultaneously in America in April 1898 as *The Open Boat and Other Tales of Adventure* (New York: Doubleday and McClure, 1898). Garnett is referring to the British edition, which contains nine New York City stories not included in the American edition.

71. *Active Service* was published in 1899.

72. For Conrad's discomfort in collaborating with Crane on a play, see Wertheim and Sorrentino, *Correspondence* 325. See also Conrad (1923).

73. H. G. and Amy Catherine Wells lived near the Cranes in Sandgate.

74. In "Stephen Crane from an English Standpoint," one of the most important early critical estimates of Crane, Wells spoke of his "enormous repudiations" of literary tradi-

tion. Wells, like Garnett, believed that America had seriously underrated Crane as a writer. In his parodic novel *Boon,* Wells wrote, "'America,' said Boon, 'can produce such a supreme writer as Stephen Crane—the best writer of English for the last half-century—or Mary Austin, who used to write—What other woman could touch her? But America won't own such children. It's amazing. It's a case of concealment of birth. She exposes them. Whether it's Shame—or a Chinese trick. . . . [Wells's ellipsis] She'll sit never knowing she's had a Stephen Crane, adoring the European reputation, the florid mental gestures of a Conrad" (Wells, *Boon* 144–45).

75. Wells's name for his wife, Amy Catherine.

76. Mason (No. 59) recalled that he had a private room.

77. For the origin of "The Ghost," see Jones (No. 57), n. 126.

78. For reviews of "The Ghost," see Wertheim and Sorrentino, *Crane Log* 418–20, 421, and Crisler (1973, app. I; 1995).

79. Crane's condition would have reminded Wells of his own earlier health problems. He too had contracted tuberculosis when young and had moved to Sandgate for his health.

80. Wells cycled seven miles to Rye and returned with the local physician, Ernest B. Skinner. Wells's visit to Brede Place for the play is documented in Cora's visitor's book with a drawing of a man on a bicycle (Stephen Crane Papers, Rare Book and Manuscript Library, Columbia University).

81. Crane began writing "The Monster" in the summer of 1897 and finished it in Ireland in late August–early September of that year.

82. See Linson (No. 21), n. 59.

83. The Krag-Jorgensen rifle relied on smokeless powder and was used during the Spanish-American War; the Maxim machine gun was used during World War I.

84. See Garland (No. 20), n. 39.

85. Barry (No. 28) and Herford (No. 33) also state that Crane wrote the poems in three days, but they were not immediately printed. Most, if not all, the poems in *The Black Riders and Other Lines* were written between January and March 1894 and were published in May 1895.

86. Crane's impressionistic sketch "An Old Man Goes Wooing," the fifth and last of the "Irish Notes."

87. That is, 4 July 1899. See E. R. Jones (No. 57).

88. Begun in 1839, the Henley Regatta was initially a public fair but quickly began to focus on amateur rowing as its main attraction.

89. The Cranes rented Brede Place, built in the fifteenth century, for forty pounds a year from Moreton Frewen.

90. Robert Barr wrote the last eight chapters of *The O'Ruddy.*

91. When Appleton sold the British and empire rights for *The Red Badge* to Heinemann for thirty-five pounds in October 1895, Crane's contract with Appleton did not stipulate that he would receive any money from the transaction. By 1899 Crane had become dissatisfied with the arrangement with his American publisher and tried unsuccessfully to get "an increased royalty on any of his books" (Katz, *"The Red Badge"* 9 n. 1).

If Harriman is correct, Heinemann must have decided to give Crane twenty pounds as a goodwill gesture.

92. Listed as "The Last Days of Stephen Crane" on the cover of the *New Hope*. The reminiscence was to appear in three parts. Shortly after publication of the first part, however, the *New Hope* ceased publication. Melvin H. Schoberlin obtained from Harriman's widow copies of the second and third parts, which remained unpublished.

93. Héloïse and Barry, two of Harold Frederic's three children by Kate Lyon.

94. The group at the train station that Crane had come to meet consisted of his brother William's daughter Helen and A. H. Peck and his family, Port Jervis neighbors of William. Crane's brother Wilbur was not part of the group.

95. For Crane's playful desire to shock James, see also Ford (No. 53).

96. Harriman's recollection concerning Frederic's relationship with Kate Lyon and their children is confusing. In 1891 Frederic moved his wife, Grace, and their four children to a home outside London and began a second household in the city with the American-born Kate, with whom he had three children—Helen, Héloïse, and Barry. In 1893 Frederic moved his second family to Homefield, in Kenley, Surrey, where Kate was known as Mrs. Frederic. When the Cranes moved to nearby Oxted in spring 1897, they and the Frederics became close friends. When Frederic suffered a stroke in August 1898, Kate, a Christian Scientist, summoned a Christian Science practitioner rather than a doctor. (At Cora's insistence, physicians were also called in.) After Frederic's death on 19 October 1898, Kate was arrested for manslaughter, and though she was eventually found innocent, she was widely attacked in the press. For a few months following Frederic's death, Kate and her three children lived with the Cranes at Oxted; and when the Cranes moved to Brede Place, the two younger children, Héloïse and Barry, continued to live with them. Although the Cranes considered adopting Barry, Kate eventually reunited all her children and returned to America.

97. Given that Frederic was born in 1856, he would have been more like one of Crane's older surviving brothers, who were born in 1850 (George), 1853 (Townley), 1854 (William), 1857 (Edmund), and 1859 (Wilbur).

98. See Wertheim and Sorrentino, *Crane Log* 352 for Cora's testimony.

99. Counter to this view about Cora's feelings toward Kate, Mabel Barr, Kate's niece and Mark Barr's wife, wrote that Cora's support of Kate during a time of crisis was "so splendid" (Gilkes 165).

100. Cora and John Scott-Stokes set up a committee to raise funds to support Kate Lyon's children. Most contributions were small. Henry James and George Bernard Shaw, for example, donated five pounds; Robert Barr, two pounds. Conrad expressed regret that he could do nothing, and others were hostile toward Cora's efforts.

101. Scottish novelist and dramatist James M. Barrie.

102. Robert Barr, a close friend of the Cranes.

103. Cofounder, along with Robert Barr, of the popular illustrated magazine the *Idler.*

104. Editor of the *Illustrated London News.*

105. Hall Caine. Harriman's depiction of him as a miser who refused to donate

money for Kate Lyon's children is incorrect and has led to confusion in Crane biography. See Sorrentino (2003, 198–200).

106. Caine did not write this letter. For his actual response to Cora, in which he did express his willingness to donate to the fund to help the children, see Sorrentino (2003, 199).

107. Contemptuous of current fiction that relied on stereotypical plots, Norwegian novelist Knut Hamsun wrote *Hunger* (1890) as an internal monologue that depicts the anguish of a writer struggling to exist in an indifferent world. In 1920 he won the Nobel Prize in Literature.

108. Harriman is the only contemporary who recorded Crane's contempt for English novelist Mary Augusta Ward, aka Mrs. Humphrey Ward. Crane's other references to her exist only in Beer's biography (1923, 104, 172, 218) and in a typescript of a letter to (Arnold) Henry Sanford Bennett (Wertheim and Sorrentino, *Correspondence* 507–8) in the Beer papers at Yale.

109. James contributed five pounds. For the confusion in Crane biography that Harriman's error has caused, see Sorrentino (2003, 210 n. 53).

110. Beer 1934. For the confusion about the allusion to a Mr. Z in this paragraph, see Sorrentino (2003, 198–99).

111. See Conrad (1923, 18–19).

112. *The Courtship of Morrice Buckler* (1896) is a historical tale of the life and adventures of a seventeenth-century English gentleman.

113. According to Starrett (1923, 10), Crane wrote "Siege," a short story about Brede Place during the time of Oliver Cromwell but destroyed the manuscript.

114. A town near Henley and former site of a Cistercian monastery.

115. William Howe Crane served for one year as an Orange County judge in Port Jervis.

116. For another reminiscence about the regatta, see Harriman (No. 56).

117. Compare with Ford's observation (No. 53) that he rarely saw Crane and James together.

118. Jones is describing the basis for the short story "Manacled."

119. See Gilkes (207) for what is probably the photograph, as well as one of Jones dressed as a gypsy fortune teller, a costume she alludes to later in her reminiscence.

120. Unlike Jones, Conrad (No. 51) and Ford (No. 53) commented on the Cranes' constant money woes and stream of uninivited guests.

121. Although Jones suggests that one purpose of the trip was to gather information for *The O'Ruddy*, only the first two paragraphs are set in Ireland.

122. Cora told the Crane family that "she was the 'Angel Child' of the Whilomville Stories" (E. Crane).

123. Several of these biographical details need clarification. Cora was born in Boston in 1865; her great-grandfather, a local art dealer who became wealthy after inventing a way to restore oil paintings, died in 1864. Her father died when she was six, and her mother remarried, though it is unclear how long she lived. Gilkes (36) suggests that

the biographical account recorded by Jones may be Cora's "version—with omissions unexplained" of her childhood.

124. In January 1889 Cora married an English aristocrat, Capt. Donald William Stewart, in London.

125. Rather than an example of faulty memory, this statement may reflect the Cranes's desire to keep secret the details about Cora and the Hotel de Dream in Jacksonville.

126. Crane asked nine of his literary friends to participate in the creation of the farce by contributing a scene, a sentence, a phrase, or even just a word and decided to center the play on the ghost of Sir Goddard Oxenbridge and his encounter with tourists at Brede. Ultimately Crane did most of the writing.

127. George Gissing, not Pugh, contributed the sentence "He died of an indignity caught in running after his hat down Piccadilly" (Wertheim and Sorrentino, *Correspondence* 554).

128. One of the outstanding figures in English theater, Sir Herbert Beerbohm Tree (1853–1917) was the leading actor-manager of his time.

129. In her Brede Place scrapbook Cora wrote the following notation next to her copy of the program for "The Ghost": "Mr. Beerbohm Tree asked Mr. A. E. W. Mason if 'The Ghost' couldn't follow 'Midsummer Night's Dream' at Her Majestys Theatre. 1900. Mason said no" (Stephen Crane Collection, Clifton Waller Barrett Library, University of Virginia Library).

130. Another character in "The Ghost," Miranda, is based on Mason's novel *Miranda of the Balcony* (or H. B. Marriott-Watson's *Heart of Miranda*).

131. First published in Wertheim 1976. The text for this edition is the typescript.

132. "'Hengist' is old German for a male horse, and 'Horsa' figures in the Anglo-Saxon Chronicle. These horsey names reappear in Scott Fitzgerald's *Tender Is the Night* in the characters of 'Major Hengist and Mr. Horsa'" (Stallman 1973, 615 n. 15).

133. Not a literal quotation. See Beer (1923, 213, 232, 234).

134. French neurologist Jean-Martin Charcot, one of the founders of clinical neurology in the nineteenth century.

135. Compare with Beer's statement: "[Crane] had come under scientific eyes and Mark Barr caught his passion for red. The walls of the study must be made soothing by paint of a shade between vermillion and claret, the colour of fresh sumach on the hills around Port Jervis. This red meant comfort, thrilling excitement or desire according to the mood" (1923, 213).

136. Stephen and Cora also told this anecdote to Curtis Brown (Brown 224–25).

137. Barr later recalled James's admiration for Crane: "Henry James once said to me in Lamb House . . . : 'We love Stephen Crane for what he is; we admire him for what he is going to be.' He meant that while Crane's writings in his early twenties showed talent, he would later become one of the great writers of America" (M. Barr, letter to the editor).

138. Crane was typically friendly toward other newspapermen. One New York reporter recalled that "he was quite an habitue of Jack's Restaurant which as an all night

place was a sort of resort for newspaper people. Time and time again I have seen him sitting there for a long time, being there when I came in, and still there when I left, all by himself at a table, smoking incessantly, drinking a little, and watching everything people did. He was not in the slightest sense unpopular. If one sat down with him, one would be welcomed pleasantly, and the conversation would always be genial and interesting, but so far as I could observe he never made the first step toward inviting such association" (Willis J. Abbott to B. J. R. Stolper, 20 February 1933.)

139. Barr's source would seem to be Beer, who describes an incident in Delmonico's in which Davis defended Crane's reputation by fighting Thomas McCumber, who had spread gossip that "Crane was dying of nameless and disgusting diseases and everybody knew it" (1923, 202). Nonetheless, when Barr retold the incident, shifting the action from the Hoffman Bar to Delmonico's, he claimed to have "irrefutable evidence" supporting the confrontation between Davis and Huneker (M. Barr, letter to the editor).

140. Actually, twenty-eight.

141. Mason later told his biographer that "The Ghost" was "[a]n absurd kind of charade at a mad house-party in Sussex. . . . We all had to write a bit of it—anything we liked—and no one knew their parts" (Green 82).

142. In a 14 February 1946 letter to the noted Crane collector and scholar Ames W. Williams, Mason wrote, "The name of the Solicitor . . . is, I am almost certain, Russell" (Alumni Folder, Special Collections Research Center, Syracuse University Library).

143. According to Mason, Crane "was a very curious, interesting contradiction, a confirmed pacifist, yet intensely interested in the subject of war" (letter to Ames W. Williams, 14 February 1946).

144. Crane published one story in the *Cornhill Magazine* in 1898; three, in 1899. *Lippincott's Magazine* published eight battle articles in 1900, for which he received thirty to fifty pounds each (Wertheim and Sorrentino, *Correspondence* 584).

145. Mason recalled in a letter to Ames W. Williams that Crane had "told me that he had begun *The O'Ruddy* rather as a joke on my book *The Courtship of Morrice Buckler,* and then slid into taking it seriously. I believe that was true from the conversations I had with him" (14 February 1946). Later in a letter to Melvin H. Schoberlin, Mason reiterated his assertion that Crane was initially planning "a parody or satire" on *The Courtship of Morrice Buckler* but added that "[i]t seemed to me—and seems to me now—that it must have been begun rather as a skit on Thackeray's *Barry Lyndon*" (21 January 1948).

146. Robert Barr read the manuscript of *The O'Ruddy* in May 1900 and reluctantly agreed to finish it (Wertheim and Sorrentino, *Crane Log* 439–40). After Crane's death, however, he reconsidered his decision and suggested that Stewart Edward White or Cora herself complete it. Cora was unsuccessful in convincing H. B. Marriott-Watson, Rudyard Kipling, or Mason to finish the manuscript. Mason kept the manuscript for two years but returned it to Cora without having worked on it. Barr then rethought his decision once again and completed it, writing the last eight chapters. The book appeared in 1903.

147. "It has always surprised me how Stephen Crane, who came over to England perhaps a little contemptuous of English ways (although that may have been a mere

façade as self-defense) was taken by ancient England" (Mason to Ames W. Williams, 14 February 1946).

148. The last in Mason's extremely popular series of detective stories featuring the sleuth M. Hanaud.

149. Pugh's reminiscence is part of a review of Thomas Beer's biography.

150. Stallman (1972, 457) states that the garden was at Ravensbrook, but there is no evidence that Pugh knew Crane before 1899.

151. The correct chronology is that Crane went to Greece before going to Cuba.

152. Despite this statement, Crane saw action in Epirus and Velestino during the Greco-Turkish War.

153. To Stallman (1973, 288), Pugh's description of this anecdote reflects a tendency in Crane: "He characteristically either belittled himself or—just the opposite—he boasted."

154. The *Academy* published insightful reviews of *The Little Regiment, The Third Violet,* and *Active Service,* as well as Edward Garnett's essay "Mr. Stephen Crane: An Appreciation" (see Garnett [No. 54], n. 69).

155. See Crane, *Tales of War* 222–23.

156. Hind later characterized it as "an awful play" (Hind 121–22).

157. A day during which artists opened their studios to the public.

Works Cited

Abbott, Willis J. Letter to B. J. R. Stolper, 20 February 1933. Stephen Crane Papers, Rare Book and Manuscript Library, Columbia University.

Åhnebrink, Lars. *The Beginnings of Naturalism in American Fiction.* Uppsala: Almqvist, 1950. Rpt. Nendeln/Liechtenstein, 1973.

Allen, Frederick Lewis. *Paul Revere Reynolds.* New York: privately printed, 1944.

"An Artist in His Hilltop Aerie." *Asbury Park Sunday Press,* 27 March 1932, feature sec., 1 and 14.

"Authors' Associations." *Manuscript* 1 [1901]: 32–34.

Bacheller, Irving. *Coming up the Road.* Indianapolis: Bobbs-Merrill, 1928, 276–79, 292–93.

———. *From Stores of Memory.* New York: Farrar and Rinehart, 1933, 110–12.

Barr, Mark. "The Haunted House of Brede." Typescript, 5 pp. Berg Collection of English and American Literature, New York Public Library. In Wertheim, "Stephen Crane Remembered," 57–59.

———. Letter to the Editor. *New York Herald Tribune,* 7 January 1940, sec. 2, 9.

Barr, Robert. "American Brains in London: The Men Who Have Succeeded." *Saturday Evening Post* 171 (8 April 1899): 648–49.

Barry, John D. "A Note on Stephen Crane." *Bookman* 13 (April 1901): 148.

Bassan, Maurice, ed. *Stephen Crane: A Collection of Critical Essays.* Englewood Cliffs, N.J.: Prentice-Hall, 1967.

Bates, H. E. *Edward Garnett.* London: Max Parrish, 1950.

Beer, Thomas. Letter to Edmund Crane, 30 October 1922. Thomas Beer Papers, Beer Family Papers, Yale University Archives.

———. "Mrs. Stephen Crane." *American Mercury* 31 (March 1934): 289–95.

———. *Stephen Crane: A Study in American Letters.* New York: Knopf, 1923.

———. "Stephen Crane [Letter]." *New York Evening Post Literary Review,* 19 July 1924, 910.

Benfey, Christopher. "Stephen Crane's Father and the Holiness Movement." *Courier* 25 (1990): 27–36.

Bierce, Ambrose. "Prattle: A Transient Record of Individual Opinion." *New York Journal,* 20 September 1896, 6.

Brace, Edson. "Stories and Studies of Stephen Crane." *St. Louis Republic,* 17 June 1900, pt. 2, 6.

Bragdon, Claude. *Merely Players.* New York: Knopf, 1905, 61–70. Rpt. as "The Purple Cow Period." *Bookman* 69 (1929): 475–78.

———. *More Lives Than One.* New York: Knopf, 1938.

[Brisbane, Arthur]. "Some Men Who Have Reported This War." *Cosmopolitan* 25 (September 1898): 556–57.

Brown, Curtis. *Contacts.* London: Cassell, 1935, 222–27.

Bruccoli, Matthew J. "Stephen Crane as a Collector's Item." In *Stephen Crane in Transition: Centenary Essays,* ed. Joseph Katz, 153–73. Dekalb: U of Northern Illinois P, 1972.

Cady, Edwin H. *Stephen Crane.* Rev. ed. New York: Twayne, 1980.

Carmichael, Otto. "Stephen Crane in Havana." *Omaha Weekly Bee,* 17 June 1900, 16. Rpt. in *Prairie Schooner* 43 (1969): 200–204.

Carnes, Cecil. *Jimmy Hare, News Photographer: Half a Century with a Camera.* New York: Macmillan, 1940. 60–63, 70–78, 128–29.

Carroll, William Waring. Untitled reminiscence, with cover letter to Thomas Beer, 20 March 1924. Thomas Beer Papers, Beer Family Papers, Yale University Archives.

Cary, Henry R. Letter to Vincent Starrett, 30 March 1922. R. W. Stallman Collection, University of Connecticut, Storrs, Conn.

Cather, Willa [as Henry Nicklemann]. "When I Knew Stephen Crane." *Library* [Pittsburgh] 1 (23 June 1900): 17–18. Rpt. in *Prairie Schooner* 23 (1949): 231–36.

Cazemajou, Jean. "Pennington Seminary: Étape d'une éducation Méthodiste." *Études Anglaises* 20 (1967): 140–48.

Chandler, George F. "I Knew Stephen Crane at Syracuse." *Courier* 3, no. 1 (1963): 12–13.

Clendenning, John. "Stephen Crane and His Biographers: Beer, Berryman, Schoberlin, and Stallman." *American Literary Realism, 1870–1910* 28 (1995): 23–57.

———. "Thomas Beer's *Stephen Crane:* The Eye of His Imagination." *Prose Studies* 14 (1991): 68–80.

Colvert, James B. "*The Red Badge of Courage* and a Review of Zola's *La Débâcle.*" *Modern Language Notes* 71 (1956): 98–100.

Conrad, Jessie. *Joseph Conrad and His Circle.* New York: E. P. Dutton, 1935, 56–58, 72–75.

———. "Recollections of Stephen Crane." *Bookman* 63 (April 1926): 134–37.

Conrad, Joseph. Introduction to *Stephen Crane: A Study in American Letters,* by Thomas Beer. New York: Knopf, 1923, 1–33.

———. *Notes on Life and Letters.* London: J. M. Dent and Sons, 1921.

———. *A Personal Record.* 1912. Rpt. New York: Doubleday, 1940.

———. "Stephen Crane: A Note without Dates." *London Mercury* 1 (December 1919): 192–93. In Conrad, *Notes on Life and Letters,* 49–52.

Crane, Cora. Address Book. Stephen Crane Papers, Rare Book and Manuscript Library, Columbia University.

————. Brede Place Scrapbook. Stephen Crane Collection, Clifton Waller Barrett Library, University of Virginia Library.

Crane, Edith F. Letter to Thomas Beer, 14 January 1934. Thomas Beer Papers, Beer Family Papers, Yale University Archives.

Crane, Edmund B. "Notes on the Life of Stephen Crane by His Brother, Edmund B. Crane." Typescript, 6 pp. Thomas Beer Papers, Beer Family Papers, Yale University Archives.

Crane, [Elizabeth] Mrs. George. "Stephen Crane's Boyhood." *New York World,* 10 June 1900, sec E, 3.

Crane (Coughlan), Florence. Letter to Edith F. Crane, 5 January 1934. Typed copy. Stephen Crane Collection, Clifton Waller Barrett Library, University of Virginia Library.

Crane, Helen R. "My Uncle, Stephen Crane." *American Mercury* 31 (January 1934): 24–29.

Crane, Robert Kellogg. "Stephen Crane's Family Heritage." *Stephen Crane Studies* 4 (spring 1995): 1–47.

Crane, Stephen. Collection. Clifton Waller Barrett Library, University of Virginia Library.

————. Collection. Special Collections Research Center, Syracuse University Library.

————. *Maggie: A Girl of the Streets.* New York: Appleton, 1896.

————. Papers. Rare Book and Manuscript Library, Columbia University.

————. *Poems and Literary Remains.* Ed. Fredson Bowers. Vol. 10 of *The Works of Stephen Crane.* Charlottesville: UP of Virginia, 1975.

————. *The Red Badge of Courage: An Episode of the American Civil War.* Ed. Fredson Bowers. Vol. 2 of *The Works of Stephen Crane.* Charlottesville: UP of Virginia, 1975.

————. *Reports of War.* Ed. Fredson Bowers. Vol. 9 of *The Works of Stephen Crane.* Charlottesville: UP of Virginia, 1971.

————. *Tales of War.* Ed. Fredson Bowers. Vol. 6 of *The Works of Stephen Crane.* Charlottesville: UP of Virginia, 1970.

————. *Tales, Sketches, and Reports.* Ed. Fredson Bowers. Vol. 8 of *The Works of Stephen Crane.* Charlottesville: UP of Virginia, 1973.

————. *The Third Violet.* Ed. Fredson Bowers. In *The Third Violet* and *Active Service.* Vol. 3 of *The Works of Stephen Crane.* Charlottesville: UP of Virginia, 1976.

Crane, Wilbur F. "Reminiscences of Stephen Crane." *Binghamton Chronicle,* 15 December 1900, 3. Typed copy in Box 20 (Folder "Gen. Bio."), Melvin H. Schoberlin Research Files, Stephen Crane Collection, Special Collections Research Center, Syracuse University Library.

Crisler, Jesse S. "'Christmas Must Be Gay': Stephen Crane's *The Ghost*—A Play by Divers Hands." *Proof* 3 (1973): 69–120.

————. "Crane's *The Ghost* in the *Manchester Guardian*." *Stephen Crane Studies* 4 (fall 1995): 50–52.

Curtin, William M, ed. *The World and the Parish: Willa Cather's Articles and Reviews, 1893–1902.* Vol. 2. Lincoln: U of Nebraska P, 1970.

Davis, Richard Harding. "How Stephen Crane Took Juana Dias." In *In Many Wars by Many War-Correspondents,* ed. George Lynch and Frederick Palmer, 43–45. Tokyo: Tokyo Printing, 1904. Rpt. La Crosse, Wisc.: Sumac Press, 1976.

———. *Notes of a War Correspondent.* New York: Scribner's, 1910, 125–28.

———. "Our War Correspondents in Cuba and Puerto Rico." *Harper's New Monthly Magazine* 98 (1898–99): 938–48.

Davis, Robert H. Introduction to *Tales of Two Wars* (1925), ix–xxiv. Vol. 2 of *The Work of Stephen Crane,* ed. Wilson Follett. 12 vols. New York: Knopf, 1925–27.

Dimock, E. J. "Stephen Crane and the Minisink Valley." Address to the Minisink Valley Historical Society, 23 February 1953. Copies in the Stephen Crane Collection, Special Collections Research Center, Syracuse University Library, and at the Minisink Valley Historical Society, Port Jervis, New York.

Emerson, Edwin. *Pepys's Ghost.* Boston: Richard G. Badger, 1900, 149–51.

Ericson, (Axel) David. Letter to Ames W. Williams, 4 November 1942. Tweed Museum of Art, University of Minnesota, Duluth.

Follett, Wilson. Correspondence to E. R. Hagemann, 12 April 1962. Stephen Crane Collection, Clifton Waller Barrett Library, University of Virginia Library.

———, ed. *The Work of Stephen Crane.* 12 vols. New York: Knopf, 1925–27.

Ford, Ford Madox. *Joseph Conrad: A Personal Remembrance.* 1924. Rpt. New York: Ecco, 1989.

———. *Memories and Impressions: A Study in Atmospheres,* by Ford Madox Hueffer. 1911. Rpt. New York: Ecco, 1985, 58–59. Published in England as *Ancient Lights and Certain New Reflections: Being the Memories of a Young Man.* London: Chapman and Hall, 1911.

———. *Portraits from Life.* Boston, New York: Houghton Mifflin, 1937.

———. *Return to Yesterday: Reminiscences, 1894–1914.* London: Victor Gollancz, 1931. Rpt. as *Return to Yesterday* (with additional silent variants and no subtitle) New York: Liveright, 1932.

———. "Stephen Crane." *American Mercury* 37 (January 1936): 36–45. Rpt. in *Portraits from Life: Memories and Criticisms.* Boston: Houghton Mifflin, 1937, 21–37. Published in England as *Mightier Than the Sword.* London: Allen and Unwin, 1938, 38–58.

———. "Stevie." *New York Evening Post Literary Review,* 12 July 1924, 881–82. Rpt. (with silent variants) in Ford, *Return to Yesterday.*

———. "Stevie and Company." *New York Herald Tribune,* 2 January 1927, sec. 7, 1 and 6. Rpt. in *New York Essays.* New York: William Edwin Rudge, 1927, 21–32.

———. "Techniques." *Southern Review* 1 (July 1935): 20–35.

———. "Three Americans and a Pole." *Scribner's Magazine* 90 (October 1931): 379–86.

———. *Thus to Revisit: Some Reminiscences.* London: Chapman and Hall, 1921. Rpt. New York: Octagon Books, 1966.

———. "Two Americans: Henry James and Stephen Crane." *New York Evening Post Literary Review.* 19 March 1921, 1–2; 26 March 1921, 1–2. Rpt. in Ford, *Thus to Revisit: Some Reminiscences.* London: Chapman and Hall, 1921. Rpt. New York: Octagon Books, 1966.

French, Mansfield J. Letter to Melvin H. Schoberlin. 14 October 1947. Box 11, Stephen Crane Collection, Special Collections Research Center, Syracuse University Library.
———. Note accompanying a baseball used by Crane. 20 February 1934. Box 6, Stephen Crane Collection, Special Collections Research Center, Syracuse University Library.
———. "Stephen Crane, Ball Player." *Syracuse University Alumni News* 15 (January 1934): 3–4.
[Gaines, Charles K.] "Rise to Fame of Stephen Crane." *Philadelphia Press,* 15 March 1896, 34.
Garland, Hamlin. "An Ambitious French Novel and a Modest American Story." *Arena* 8 (June 1893): xi–xii.
———. *Hamlin Garland's Diaries.* Ed. Donald Pizer. San Marino, Calif.: Huntington Library, 1968.
———. Letter to Thomas Beer. 19 December [1923 or 1924]. Thomas Beer Papers, Beer Family Papers, Yale University Archives.
———. "Mr. Stephen Crane: An Appreciation." *Academy* 55 (17 December 1898): 483–84.
———. "A Recollection of Stephen Crane." MS, 2 pp., inserted loosely into Franklin Garland's presentation copy of *Maggie* (1893). Berg Collection of English and American Literature, New York Public Library. In *Studies in* Maggie *and* George's Mother, ed. Stanley Wertheim, 4–5. Columbus, Ohio: Merrill, 1970.
———. *Roadside Meetings.* New York: Macmillan, 1930, 189–206.
———. "Roadside Meetings of a Literary Nomad." *Bookman* 70 (January 1930): 523–28.
———. *A Son of the Middle Border.* New York: Macmillan, 1938.
———. "Stephen Crane: A Soldier of Fortune." *Saturday Evening Post* 173 (28 July 1900): 16–17. In Stallman and Gilkes 299–305.
———. "Stephen Crane as I Knew Him." *Yale Review* n.s. 3 (April 1914): 494–506.
Garnett, David. *The Golden Echo.* New York: Harcourt, 1954.
Garnett, Edward. *Friday Nights: Literary Criticisms and Appreciations.* London: Jonathan Cape, 1922, 201–17.
———. *Letters from Joseph Conrad.* Indianapolis: Bobbs-Merrill, 1928, 11–12.
———. Review of Thomas Beer's *Stephen Crane. Nation and the Athenaeum* (11 October 1924): 58.
———. "Stephen Crane." *Littell's Living Age* 226 (4 August 1900): 320–21. Rpt. in *Academy* 59 (11 August 1900): 116.
Gilkes, Lillian. *Cora Crane: A Biography of Mrs. Stephen Crane.* Bloomington: Indiana UP, 1960.
Goodwin, Clarence N. Letter to Max J. Herzberg. 3 November 1921. Newark Public Library.
Gordon, Ambrose, Jr. *The Invisible Text: The War Novels of Ford Madox Ford.* Austin: U of Texas P, 1964.
Gordon, Frederick C. Letter to Thomas Beer, 25 May 1923. Thomas Beer Papers, Beer Family Papers, Yale University Archives.
Green, Roger Lancelyn. *A. E. W. Mason.* London: Max Parrish, 1952.

Greene, Nelson. Correspondence. Box 14, Melvin H. Schoberlin Research Files, Stephen Crane Collection, Special Collections Research Center, Syracuse University Library.

———. "I Knew Stephen Crane." Typescript, 8 pp. Newark Public Library. In Wertheim, "Stephen Crane Remembered," 50–53.

———. Untitled reminiscence, with cover letter to Melvin H. Schoberlin, 4 September 1947. MS, 24 pp. Box 14, Melvin H. Schoberlin Research Files, Stephen Crane Collection, Special Collections Research Center, Syracuse University Library.

———. Untitled reminiscence, with cover letter to Melvin H. Schoberlin, 3 October 1947. MS, 11 pp. Box 14, Melvin H. Schoberlin Research Files, Stephen Crane Collection, Special Collections Research Center, Syracuse University Library.

Gullason, Thomas A. "The Cranes at Pennington Seminary." *American Literature* 39 (1968): 530–41.

———. "The First Known Review of Stephen Crane's 1893 *Maggie.*" *English Language Notes* 5 (1968): 300–302.

———. *A Garland of Writings: Stephen Crane's Literary Family.* Syracuse: Syracuse UP, 2002.

———. "The 'Lost' Newspaper Writings of Stephen Crane." *Courier* 21, no. 1 (1986): 57–87.

———. "Stephen Crane: Anti-Imperialist." *American Literature* 30 (1958): 237–41.

———. "Stephen Crane at Claverack College: A New Reading." *Courier* 27, no. 2 (1992): 33–46.

———. "Stephen Crane at Lafayette College: New Perspectives." *Stephen Crane Studies* 3 (fall 1994): 2–12.

———. *Stephen Crane's Career: Perspectives and Evaluations.* New York: NYU P, 1972.

Harriman, Karl Edwin. "The Last Days of Stephen Crane." *New Hope* 2 (October 1934).

———. "The Last Days of Stephen Crane." Pt 2. Typescript, 8 pp. Box 20 (Folder "Crane 1899"), Melvin H. Schoberlin Research Files, Stephen Crane Collection, Special Collections Research Center, Syracuse University Library.

———. "The Last Days of Stephen Crane." Pt. 3. Typescript, 8 pp. Box 20 (Folder "Crane 1899"), Melvin H. Schoberlin Research Files, Stephen Crane Collection, Special Collections Research Center, Syracuse University Library.

———. "A Romantic Idealist—Mr. Stephen Crane." *Literary Review* 4 (April 1900): 85–87.

———. [Untitled commentary in "The Lounger"]. *Critic* 37 (July 1900): 14–16.

Hawkins, Willis Brooks. "All in a Lifetime." Typescript. Article 10, "The Genius of Stephen Crane" (3 pp.); article 30, "Stephen Crane Struggles" (3 pp.); article 31, "Stephen Crane Flinches" (3 pp.) Willis Brooks Hawkins Collection, Clifton Waller Barrett Library, University of Virginia Library.

Herford, Kenneth. "Young Blood—Stephen Crane." *Saturday Evening Post* 172 (18 November 1899): 413.

Herzberg, Max. Introduction to *The Red Badge of Courage.* 1925. Rpt. New York: Washington Square, 1959.

Hilliard, John Northern. Letter to Thomas Beer, 1 February 1922. Thomas Beer Papers, Beer Family Papers, Yale University Library.

Hilt, Kathryn, and Stanley Wertheim. "Stephen Crane and Amy Leslie: A Rereading of the Evidence." *American Literary Realism* 32 (spring 2000): 256–69.

Hind, C. Lewis. *Authors and I.* New York: John Lane, 1921, 71–73.

———. *Naphtali: Being Influences and Adventures While Earning a Living by Writing.* London: John Lane, 1926.

Hitchcock, Ripley. Preface to *The Red Badge of Courage.* New York: Appleton, 1900.

Hoffman, Daniel. *The Poetry of Stephen Crane.* New York: Columbia UP, 1956.

"Holland" [Elisha J. Edwards]. "Society Leaders' Suffrage Crusade." *Philadelphia Press,* 22 April 1894, 5.

Holloway, Jean. *Hamlin Garland: A Biography.* Austin: U of Texas P, 1960.

Hubbard, Elbert. "As to Stephen Crane." *Lotos* 9 (1896): 676.

Hueffer, Ford Madox. See Ford, Ford Madox.

Johnson, Willis Fletcher. "The Launching of Stephen Crane." *Literary Digest International Book Review* 4 (1926): 288–90.

———. Letter to the Editor. *New York Evening Post Literary Review* 14 (2 April 1921): 14.

Jones, Claude. "Stephen Crane at Syracuse." *American Literature* 7 (1935): 82–84.

Jones, Edith Richie. "Stephen Crane at Brede." *Atlantic Monthly* 194 (July 1954): 57–61.

Karl, Frederick R., and Laurence Davies. *The Collected Letters of Joseph Conrad.* Vol. 1, *1861–1897.* Cambridge: Cambridge UP, 1983.

Katz, Joseph. "An Editor's Recollection of 'The Red Badge of Courage.'" *Stephen Crane Newsletter* 2 (spring 1968): 3–6.

———. "*The Red Badge of Courage* Contract." *Stephen Crane Newsletter* 2 (summer 1968): 5–10.

———. "Solving Stephen Crane's *Pike County Puzzle.*" *American Literature* 55 (1983): 171–82.

———. "Stephen Crane at Claverack College and Hudson River Institute." *Stephen Crane Newsletter* 2 (summer 1968): 1–5.

———. "Stephen Crane Flinches." *Stephen Crane Newsletter* 3 (fall 1968): 6–7.

———. *Stephen Crane in the West and Mexico.* Kent, Ohio: Kent State UP, 1970.

———. "Stephen Crane: Muckraker." *Columbia Library Columns* 17 (February 1968): 3–7.

———. "Stephen Crane's Struggles." *Stephen Crane Newsletter* 1 (spring [for summer] 1967): 3–5.

Kauffman, Reginald Wright. "The True Story of Stephen Crane." *Modern Culture* 12 (October 1900): 143–45.

Kearns, Doris. "Angles of Vision." In *Telling Lives: The Biographer's Art,* ed. Marc Pachter, 90–103. Philadelphia: U of Pennsylvania P, 1985.

Kindilien, Carlin T. "Stephen Crane and the 'Savage Philosophy' of Olive Schreiner." *Boston University Studies in English* 3 (1957): 97–107.

LaFrance, Marston. "A Few Facts about Stephen Crane and 'Holland.'" *American Literature* 37 (1965): 195–202.

Lawrence, Frederic M. Letter to Lester G. Wells, 5 February 1953. Stephen Crane Collection, Special Collections Research Center, Syracuse University Library.

———. "The Real Stephen Crane." Typescript, 25 pp. Newark Public Library, Newark, N.J.

———. *The Real Stephen Crane.* Ed. Joseph Katz. Newark, N.J.: Newark Public Library, 1980.

Levenson, J. C. Introduction to *The Third Violet* and *Active Service*. Vol. 3 of *The Works of Stephen Crane*. Ed. Fredson Bowers. Charlottesville: UP of Virginia, 1976.

Lewis, Edith. *Willa Cather: A Personal Record.* New York: Knopf, 1953.

"Library Exhibit to Honor Novelist Trained on Hill." *Syracuse Herald,* 3 October 1926, 20–21.

Lindberg-Seyersted, Brita. *Ford Madox Ford and His Relationship to Stephen Crane and Henry James.* Atlantic Highlands, N.J.: Humanities Press, and Oslo, Norway: Solum Forlag A.S, 1987.

Linson, Corwin Knapp. "Little Stories of 'Steve' Crane." *Saturday Evening Post* 177 (11 April 1903): 19–20.

———. *My Stephen Crane.* Ed. Edwin H. Cady. Syracuse: Syracuse UP, 1958.

MacShane, Frank. *The Life and Work of Ford Madox Ford.* New York: Horizon Press, 1965.

Mane, Robert. "Une recontre littéraire: Hamlin Garland et Stephen Crane." *Études Anglaises* 17 (1964): 30–46.

Marshall, Edward. "Greatest Living American Writer [Howells]." *New York Press,* 15 April 1894, 2.

———. "Loss of Stephen Crane—A Real Misfortune to All of Us." *New York Herald,* 10 June 1900, sec. 6, 8. Rpt. with minor changes as "Stories of Stephen Crane" in the *San Francisco Call* and in *Literary Life* n.s., no. 24 (December 1900): 71–72.

———. *The Story of the Rough Riders, 1st U.S. Volunteer Cavalry: The Regiment in Camp and on the Battle Field.* New York: G. W. Dillingham, 1899.

———. "A Wounded Correspondent's Recollections of Guasimas." *Scribner's Magazine.* 24 (September 1898): 273–76.

Mason, A. E. W. Letter to Ames W. Williams, 14 February 1946. Alumni Folder, Special Collections Research Center, Syracuse University Library.

———. Letter to Melvin H. Schoberlin, 21 January 1948. Box 16 (Folder "Chapter XI, Forests and Symbols"), Stephen Crane Collection, Special Collections Research Center, Syracuse University Library.

———. Letter to Vincent Starrett, 4 October 1945. Stephen Crane Papers, Rare Book and Manuscript Library, Columbia University. In Stallman and Gilkes 342–45.

McBride, Henry. "Stephen Crane's Artist Friends." *Artnews* 49 (October 1950): 46.

McCready, Ernest W. Letter to Benjamin R. Stolper, 12 January 1934. Stephen Crane Papers, Rare Book and Manuscript Library, Columbia University.

———. Letter to Benjamin R. Stolper, 22 January 1934. Stephen Crane Papers, Rare Book and Manuscript Library, Columbia University.

———. Letter to Benjamin R. Stolper, 31 January 1934. Stephen Crane Papers, Rare Book and Manuscript Library, Columbia University.

———. Letter to Benjamin R. Stolper, 3 March 1938. Stephen Crane Papers, Rare Book and Manuscript Library, Columbia University.

McIntosh, Burr. *The Little I Saw of Cuba.* London: F. Tennyson Neely, 1899, 124–27, 132–33.

McMahon, William. "Syracuse in the Gay '90s: Steve Crane Told to 'Stick to Poems' after 'Bangup' Piano Recital at Party." *Syracuse Post-Standard,* 20 February 1955, 13.

Michelson, Charles. Introduction to *"The Open Boat" and Other Tales.* (1927), ix–xxiv. Vol. 12 of *The Work of Stephen Crane,* ed. Wilson Follett. 12 vols. New York: Knopf, 1925–27.

Monteiro, George. "Addenda to Stallman and Hagemann: Parodies of Stephen Crane's Work." *PBSA* 74 (1980): 402–3.

———. "A Capsule Assessment of Stephen Crane by Hamlin Garland." *Stephen Crane Newsletter* 3 (fall 1968): 2.

———. "Stephen Crane: A New Appreciation by Edward Garnett." *American Literature* 50 (1978): 465–71.

Noxon, Frank. Letter to Corwin Knapp Linson. 14 April 1930. Box 11, Stephen Crane Collection, Special Collections Research Center, Syracuse University Library.

———. Letter to Mansfield J. French. 29 June 1934. Box 11, Stephen Crane Collection, Special Collections Research Center, Syracuse University Library.

———. "The Real Stephen Crane." *Step-Ladder* [Chicago] 14 (January 1928): 4–9.

O'Donnell, Thomas F. "DeForest, Van Petten, and Stephen Crane." *American Literature* 27 (1956): 578–80.

———. "John B. Van Petten: Stephen Crane's History Teacher." *American Literature* 27 (1955): 196–202.

Oliver, Arthur. "Jersey Memories—Stephen Crane." *Proceedings of the New Jersey Historical Society* 16 (1931): 454–63.

Paine, Ralph D. *Roads of Adventure.* Boston: Houghton Mifflin, 1922, 162–71, 214–17.

Parker, Walter. "Memorandum by Walter Parker, Re: Stephen Crane, New Orleans, March, 1940." Typescript, 8 pp. H. L. Mencken Papers, Manuscripts and Archives Division, New York Public Library. In Wertheim, "Stephen Crane Remembered," 53–56.

Peaslee, Clarence Loomis. "Stephen Crane's College Days." *Monthly Illustrator and Home and Country* 13 (August 1896): 27–30.

Peck, George. *Wyoming: Its History, Stirring Incidents, and Romantic Adventures.* New York: Harper, 1858.

Peck, Harry Thurston. Book review of *The Black Riders and Other Lines. Bookman* 1 (May 1895): 254.

Petry, Alice Hall. "Stephen Crane's Elephant Man." *Journal of Modern Literature* 10 (1983): 346–52.

Phillips, Henry. Letter to the Editor. *Syracuse Post-Standard,* 26 December 1947, 6.

Pizer, Donald. "The Garland-Crane Relationship." *Huntington Library Quarterly* 24 (November 1960): 75–82. Rpt. in *Realism and Naturalism in Nineteenth-Century American Literature.* New York: Russell and Russell, 1966. [The article is deleted from the 2nd edition of the book.]

———, ed. *Hamlin Garland's Diaries.* San Marino, Calif.: Huntington Library, 1968.

"Playlot to Rise at Birthplace of Stephen Crane." *New York Herald Tribune,* 1 January 1940, 20.

Pound, Ezra. *Pavannes and Divagations.* Norfolk, Conn.: New Directions, 1958.

Pratt, Lyndon Upson. "The Formal Education of Stephen Crane." *American Literature* 10 (1939): 460–71.

Price, Carl F. "Stephen Crane: A Genius Born in a Methodist Parsonage." *Christian Advocate* (New York) 98 (13 July 1922): 866–67.

Pugh, Edwin. "Stephen Crane." *Bookman* (London) 67 (December 1924): 162–64.

"The Rambler: Comments on Stephen Crane and His Work." *Book Buyer* 13 (April 1896): 140–41.

"The Reality Not Exciting." *New York World,* 10 June 1900, sec. E, 3.

Richter, Heddy A. "The Long Foreground of Corwin Knapp Linson's *My Stephen Crane.*" *Studies in the Novel* 10 (spring 1978): 161–67.

Ridge, W. Pett. *I Like to Remember.* London: Hodder and Stoughton, 1925, 210–11.

Robertson, Michael. *Stephen Crane at Lafayette.* Easton, Pa.: Friends of Skillman Library, 1990.

Saunders, Max. *Ford Madox Ford: A Dual Life.* Vol. 2, *The After-War World.* New York: Oxford UP, 1996.

Schoberlin, Melvin H. Melvin H. Schoberlin Research Files, Special Collections Research Center, Syracuse University Library.

Seitz, Don Carlos. *Joseph Pulitzer: His Life and Letters.* New York: Simon and Schuster, 1924.

Sheridan, Clare. *Naked Truth.* New York: Harper, 1928.

Sidbury, Edna Crane. "My Uncle, Stephen Crane, as I Knew Him." *Literary Digest International Book Review* 4 (1926): 248–50.

Sloane, David. E. E. "Stephen Crane at Lafayette." *Resources for American Literary Study* 2 (1972): 102–5.

Slote, Bernice. "Stephen Crane and Willa Cather." *Serif* 6 (December 1969): 3–15.

Smith, Ernest G. "Comments and Queries." *Lafayette Alumnus* 2 (February 1932): 6.

Smith, Harry B. *First Nights and First Editions.* Boston: Little, Brown, 1931, 177–78.

Sorrentino, Paul. "The Legacy of Thomas Beer in the Study of Stephen Crane and American Literary History." *American Literary Realism* 35 (2003): 187–211.

———. "Nelson Greene's Reminiscences of Stephen Crane." *Resources for American Literary Study* 24 (1998): 49–83.

———. "New Evidence on Stephen Crane at Syracuse." *Resources for American Literary Study* 15 (1985): 179–85.

———. "Newly Discovered Writings of Mary Helen Peck Crane and Agnes Elizabeth Crane." *Courier* 21 (spring 1986): 103–34.

———. "The Philistine Society's Banquet for Stephen Crane." *American Literary Realism 1870–1910* 15 (1982): 232–38.

———. "Stephen Crane's Struggle with Romance in *The Third Violet.*" *American Literature* 70 (June 1998): 265–91.

Stallman, R. W. *Stephen Crane: A Biography.* Rev. ed. New York: Braziller, 1973.

———. *Stephen Crane: A Critical Bibliography.* Ames: Iowa State UP, 1972.

Stallman, R. W., and Lillian Gilkes, eds. *Stephen Crane: Letters.* New York: NYU P, 1960.

Stallman, R. W., and E. R. Hagemann, eds. *The War Dispatches of Stephen Crane.* New York: NYU P, 1964.

Starrett, Vincent. *Stephen Crane: A Bibliography.* Philadelphia: Centaur, 1923.

———. "Stephen Crane at Claverack." *Stephen Crane Newsletter* 2 (summer 1968): 4.

"Three Poems by Stephen Crane." *Bookman* 69 (April 1929): 120–22.

Travis, Abram Lincoln. "Recollections of Steven [*sic*] Crane." With cover letter from Travis to Mansfield French, 20 March 1930. MS, 4 pp. Alumni Folder, Special Collections Research Center, Syracuse University Library.

Van Doren, Mark. Review of Thomas Beer, *Stephen Crane. Nation* (16 January 1924): 66.

"A 'Varsity Boy." *Syracuse Standard,* 26 January 1896, 6.

Vosburgh, R. G. "The Darkest Hour in the Life of Stephen Crane." *Criterion* n.s. 1 (February 1901): 26–27. Rpt. in *Book Lover* 2 (1901): 338–39.

Weatherford, Richard M, ed. *Stephen Crane: The Critical Heritage.* London: Routledge, 1973.

Webster, H. T. "Wilbur F. Hinman's *Corporal Si Klegg* and Stephen Crane's *The Red Badge of Courage.*" *American Literature* 11 (1939): 285–93.

Wells, Anna E. "Reminiscences of Stephen Crane." Typescript, 6 pp. R. W. Stallman Collection, University of Connecticut Library, Storrs, Conn.

Wells, H. G. "Another View of *Maggie.*" *Saturday Review,* 19 December 1896, 655.

———. *Boon, the Mind of the Race, the Wild Asses of the Devil, and the Last Trump.* London: Unwin, 1915.

——— *Experiment in Autobiography: Discoveries and Conclusions of a Very Ordinary Brain since 1866.* New York: Macmillan, 1934, 522–25.

———. "The New American Novelists." *Saturday Review,* 5 September 1896, 262–63.

———. "Stephen Crane from an English Standpoint." *North American Review* 171 (August 1900): 233–42.

Wells, Lester G. Letter to Rees Frescoln. 3 June 1941. Typed copy [p. 2 missing]. Alumni File, Special Collections Research Center, Syracuse University Library.

Wertheim, Stanley. "Crane and Garland: The Education of an Impressionist." *North Dakota Quarterly* 35 (winter 1967): 23–28.

———. "Frank Norris's 'The Green Stone of Unrest.'" *Frank Norris Studies* 15 (spring 1993): 5–8.

———. "The Saga of March 23rd: Garland, Gilder, and Crane." *Stephen Crane Newsletter* 3 (winter 1968): 1–3. [For typographical corrections to the article, see the preface in *Stephen Crane Newsletter* (spring 1969): 1.]

———. *A Stephen Crane Encyclopedia.* Westport, Conn.: Greenwood, 1997.

———. "Stephen Crane in Galveston: A New Letter." *Stephen Crane Studies* 5 (spring 1996): 2–4.

———. "Stephen Crane Remembered." *Studies in American Fiction* 4 (1976): 45–64.

———. "Stephen Crane to Clarence Loomis Peaslee: Some New Letters." *Resources for American Literary Study* 22 (1996): 30–36.

———. "Why Stephen Crane Left Claverack." *Stephen Crane Newsletter* 2 (summer 1968): 5.

———, ed. *Studies in* Maggie *and* George's Mother. Columbus, Ohio.: Merrill, 1970.

Wertheim, Stanley, and Paul Sorrentino. *The Crane Log: A Documentary Life of Stephen Crane, 1871–1900.* New York: Macmillan, 1993.

———. "Thomas Beer: The Clay Feet of Stephen Crane Biography." *American Literary Realism* 22, no. 3 (1990): 2–16.

———, eds. *The Correspondence of Stephen Crane.* 2 vols. New York: Columbia UP, 1988.

Wheeler, Post, and Hallie E. Rives. *Dome of Many-Coloured Glass.* Garden City, N.Y.: Doubleday, 1955, 20–22, 98–101, 106–7.

Wickham, Harvey. "Stephen Crane at College." *American Mercury* 7 (March 1926): 291–97.

Winterich, John T. "Romantic Stories of Books: *The Red Badge of Courage.*" *Publisher's Weekly* 118 (20 September 1930): 1303–7.

Wyndham, George. "A Remarkable Book." *New Review* 14 (January 1896): 30–40. Re-titled "An Appreciation" and rpt. as the introduction to *Pictures of War.* London: Heinemann, 1898. Also in Weatherford 106–14.

Index

DATE DUE
